UNDELIVERED

Also by Jeff Nussbaum

Had Enough? A Handbook for Fighting Back (with James Carville)

Intelligence Matters: The CIA, the FBI, Saudi Arabia, and the Failure of America's War on Terror (with Bob Graham)

UNDELIVERED

THE NEVER-HEARD

SPEECHES THAT WOULD

HAVE REWRITTEN HISTORY

JEFF NUSSBAUM

FLATIRON
BOOKS
NEW YORK

www.flatironbooks.com

Designed by Donna Sinisgalli Noetzel

Library of Congress Cataloging-in-Publication Data

Names: Nussbaum, Jeff, 1975– author.
Title: Undelivered : the unseen speeches that would have rewritten
  history / Jeff Nussbaum.
Description: First edition. | New York : Flatiron Books, 2022. | Includes
  bibliographical references.
Identifiers: LCCN 2021054249 | ISBN 9781250240705 (hardcover) |
  ISBN 9781250240712 (ebook)
Subjects: LCSH: Speeches, addresses, etc., American—20th century. |
  Speeches, addresses, etc., American—21st century.
Classification: LCC PS668 .N87 2022 | DDC 815.008—dc23/
  eng/20220113
LC record available at https://lccn.loc.gov/2021054249

Our books may be purchased in bulk for promotional, educational,
or business use. Please contact your local bookseller or the Macmillan
Corporate and Premium Sales Department at 1-800-221-7945, extension
5442, or by email at MacmillanSpecialMarkets@macmillan.com.

First Edition: 2022

10 9 8 7 6 5 4 3 2 1

To Ada and Sophia

my greatest joy is watching you write your own stories

Contents

Introduction

My obsession with undelivered speeches began late in the evening on November 7, 2000, Election Night.

Working for Vice President Al Gore in the White House was my first job out of college, and it was heady stuff for a twenty-two-year-old. When Gore's campaign for president moved from Washington, D.C., to Nashville, Tennessee, I moved along with it. Even for my idealistic young self, the Gore 2000 campaign was an affair strangely disconnected from its candidate and unloved even in its home state. (On my drive to the campaign headquarters each morning, I could count on somebody to spot my GORE 2000 bumper sticker and give me the finger.)*

Like all campaigns, there was plenty of camaraderie and carousing, but when each day's tracking polls would come in, either showing Gore up or down by a couple of points, a fatigued, beleaguered staffer would inevitably mutter under his or her breath, "And that's just at headquarters."

---

* That said, I was driving a Saab.

Even the most relentless enthusiasm can succumb to the numbing grind of a relentless campaign. We will bring prosperity and progress! Or was it progress and prosperity? Was it change that works? Or change that works for working families? Nobody could quite remember.

But as Election Night approached, you could begin to feel an actual change; the pallor from sleeplessness and fast food was replaced with the flush of hope. There was hope for the nation, certainly—America would be moving into a new century and a new millennium as the sole superpower on earth, led by someone who understood the challenges of climate change and the potential of technology.

But there were also more granular, grounded, and, let's just admit it, self-involved hopes for those of us who had toiled on the campaign. *I might get to work in the White House! I might get to work at the State Department! I might be a* presidential *speechwriter!*

And so on Election Night, as the last get-out-the-vote phone calls were dialed, we headed to the outdoor plaza in downtown Nashville.

Vice President Gore prepared to head there as well. In keeping with political superstition, he had both a victory and a concession speech prepared. Because of what the campaign had seen in its polling, he also had a third version of the speech prepared: in case he had won the electoral vote but lost the popular vote.*

As polls closed, it appeared Gore would be giving the victory speech: just before 8:00 p.m., the Associated Press, followed by CNN and the other networks, declared that Al Gore had won Florida's twenty-five electoral votes. Within the hour, they also called Michigan, Illinois, and Pennsylvania for Gore. We were euphoric. Al Gore was going to be the next president.

And yet the people crunching the numbers inside both campaigns were seeing something less definitive than what was being reported. I had received a call earlier in the afternoon from a college acquaintance who told me that his grandmother and some of her friends in Palm Beach, Florida, were having trouble figuring out the ballot. At the time, I reported the call to the campaign "boiler room"—where the Gore campaign's high command was handling Election Day operations, but didn't

---

* When all was said and done, the exact opposite had occurred.

think much of it. On Election Days, all sorts of rumors run rampant, and it becomes hard to separate the signal from the noise. Partly that's because people who were previously working eighteen-hour days now must sit and wait for results like everyone else, so they trade every bit of information they come across. *What are you hearing about turnout? What is exit polling saying?* And sometimes they traffic in rumor and paranoia.

But it turned out that call about Florida was prophetic, because Palm Beach's ballot was designed in such a visually challenging way that an estimated 2,800 Gore voters actually voted for third-party candidate Pat Buchanan, one of many problems with Florida's voting system that would soon be revealed.

Back in Nashville, we didn't know any of that yet. What we knew was that Gore had lost Ohio and his own home state of Tennessee. It was all going to come down to Florida, and Bush was claiming that he was actually going to win Florida. Something seemed to be changing, and just before 10:00 p.m., it did: in an unprecedented and embarrassing move, the networks took Florida out of Gore's column and declared it "too close to call." Over the next couple of hours, Bush's lead in Florida grew, and shortly after 2:00 a.m., the networks declared Bush the winner in Florida and the winner of the presidency. Gore called Bush to concede. But as Gore was en route from his hotel to address the crowd in Nashville, Bush's lead in Florida began to drop again, as numbers from several of the late-reporting counties came in.

At this point, I was with a number of campaign staffers in a bar near the plaza, taking shelter from the persistent drizzle. All our pagers (not everyone had cell phones at the time) began going off. We were being asked to return to campaign headquarters. In a tense phone call, Gore had called Bush to retract his concession. Back at headquarters, staffers who had law degrees or a connection to Florida were being told to pack overnight bags and head to the airport, where the campaign plane would take them to Florida to begin working on the automatic recount the closeness of the election had triggered. At the same time, other groups were dispatched to the other states where the race was too close to call: Wisconsin, Iowa, New Mexico, and Oregon. I ended up in Madison, Wisconsin, in desperate need of a new winter coat, helping prepare for a recount that never happened.

That night, Vice President Gore gave no speech at all. Just after

4:00 a.m., Gore's campaign chairman, William Daley, stepped to the lectern and said,

> I've been in politics for a long time. But there's never been a night like this one . . . As everyone in America knows, this race has come down to the State of Florida. And without being certain of the results in Florida, we simply cannot be certain of the results of this national election. . . . Until the recount is concluded and the results in Florida become official, our campaign continues.

Far from being a statement for posterity, posterity was put on pause. I've been through stacks of files trying to find my printed copy of the speeches Al Gore was prepared to give that evening, or the floppy disk they were stored on, to no avail. Whatever it was that Al Gore had planned on saying to the cold, wet assembled crowd may be lost to history.*

Since that night, I've nursed an obsession with finding and bringing to light the undelivered.

Growing up, we all learned about Martin Luther King Jr.'s dream. But what if the March on Washington had taken on a different tone and tenor? What if John Lewis, the fieriest speaker of the day, had preceded King by declaring that he could not support Kennedy's civil rights bill, "for it is too little and too late"? What if King had kept his dream to himself and taken the stage on the steps of the Lincoln Memorial to declare that there would be "normalcy never again"? Both of them went to bed the night before the 1963 March on Washington with prepared speeches that did just that.

Today, we don't have to consider what would have happened if the D-day invasion failed, with bad weather leaving tens of thousands of Allied troops to be massacred on the beaches of Normandy. But Dwight Eisenhower did, and he prepared an apology for it.

---

* Joe Lieberman, Al Gore's running mate, had also planned on speaking that night. He had worked with my colleague Paul Orzulak on those remarks, and Lieberman's hand-edited copy currently hangs in Paul's office.

And what if, on the other side of the world, Emperor Hirohito had been the one to apologize? Instead of becoming Japan's longest-reigning emperor and the man who oversaw Japan's full transition from an aggressor nation to a modern democracy, would he have exited the stage as part of a cabal of warmongers who led the nation to ruin?

In the following pages, I'll share speeches of historic import that were never given because events intervened, or a leader had a change of heart, or history took a sudden turn. Several of these speeches have never before appeared in public. Others were known to small groups of history buffs, but they weren't easily accessible. For each, I've tried to add new context and new understanding, both about the moment in which they were written and about the process that went into writing them.

Even when, with hindsight, we know the precariousness of a historical situation, what we didn't know is often chilling. For example, this book will share the speech in which John F. Kennedy announces an aerial bombardment and ground invasion of Cuba. In the draft, there is a harrowing blank, noted only as "*Follows a description of first reports of action.*" And only later did we realize that the "first action" could have been already-operational Soviet tactical nuclear weapons vaporizing our base at Guantánamo Bay and an entire American invasion force.

Sometimes speeches go undelivered because of the choices leaders make, and sometimes they go undelivered because of whom the people choose to be their leaders. Such was the case on November 8, 2016, when America elected Donald Trump to be president. Hillary Clinton had expected to win. Her victory speech had been written, and wrestled over, and edited. But it was never delivered. Her speech lays out a very different future from the one America is still living through. It, along with the story behind its creation, is published here for the first time.

Each of these speeches provides a window into the fraught moments in which it was penned. In the aggregate, they provide an alternative history of key twentieth- and twenty-first-century events. But these are not simply historical novelties, moments encased in amber. They show that history is in constant conversation with itself. Indeed, you'll find in these undelivered speeches an almost eerie relevance to our world today.

Progressive Illinois governor John Altgeld's undelivered 1897 farewell address was a clarion warning about partisan passions overwhelming the need to govern, and it resonates powerfully. Emma Goldman's undelivered speech at her trial for inciting a riot has something to say about how words of outrage, righteous or otherwise, can lead to action in the streets. Helen Keller's undelivered speech on giving the women the right to vote reminds us of how intimidation can keep the disenfranchised voiceless. Richard Nixon's undelivered speech in which he refuses to resign the presidency presaged President Trump's actions in 2020 by showing the arguments that could be made by a leader who refuses to accept accountability.

In these historic undelivered speeches, we find the beginnings of an answer. These words not only tell us something about their moments in time—they tell us something about ours.

For more than twenty years, I've been a speechwriter to those who hold positions of influence in the White House, in Congress, in sports and culture, and in the corporate world. My job has been to help leaders articulate their visions for the future and to put to paper the words and ideas to respond to events that nobody foresaw.

Sometimes the act of writing a speech is the act of envisioning the many paths history can take and arguing forcefully for—or against—one of them. Sometimes it's the act of responding to the moments beyond our control where history takes a sudden turn. In those moments, schedules and plans get thrown out the window; there's a rush to gather information and figure out how to respond. The speaker and the speechwriter know that people will be listening, needing to be informed, inspired, comforted, and led. And as the world enters a new reality, the words written for the old reality get left behind.

Anyone who writes speeches for a living has files littered with drafts and statements that were never delivered for a variety of reasons. There's even a joke among our small family of scribes in which a speechwriter dies and is offered a choice between heaven and hell. Being a good researcher (as all speechwriters must be), he asks to see both, starting with hell. Saint Peter shows him a crowded room in which row upon row of stressed-out looking speechwriters are hammering away on computers, facing a looming deadline. "That's my worst nightmare," says the speechwriter. "Please show me heaven."

And Saint Peter shows him an identical room in which row upon row of speechwriters type away, trying to meet a deadline.

"But this is the same as hell," protests the speechwriter.

"Not at all," answers Saint Peter. "Up here, we *use* their stuff."

As the late William Safire noted in the introduction to his classic compendium *Lend Me Your Ears,* words on a page are no more a speech than a screenplay is a movie: "What makes a draft speech a real speech is the speaking of it."

Most words that go unspoken are not particularly illuminating, because the dirty secret is that most of what is said by political, business, and cultural leaders is mundane, fulfilling a less-exalted goal of saying little if anything at all.

There are times when it isn't a snowstorm or a scheduling change that causes a speech to go undelivered, however, but occasions when History—with a capital *H*—intervenes, when leaders are forced to choose, and the words they didn't use tell us as much as the ones they did.

What happens to those undelivered words? Are they simply relegated to a parallel rhetorical universe in which the victor is the vanquished?*

Or can they tell us something about the fateful moments in which they were crafted—the thoughts of leaders in times of choosing and consequence, victory and defeat, joy and pain, triumph and catastrophe? Can they clarify our understanding of what might have been had events allowed for or necessitated their delivery?

The only way to know is to salvage some of those speeches from the dustbin of history, to re-create the tense moments in which the words were set to paper, to understand the context or conflict in which very different outcomes were possible and, indeed, envisioned, and then to deliver the undelivered.

A Note on Organization

I've organized this book into six parts, with each section representing a category of speech that might go undelivered. In almost every chapter,

---

* A wonderful 2000 article by Cullen Murphy in *The Atlantic Monthly* calls this "reality that never quite became real" or "provisional history."

I have tried to not only tell the story of that speech but to provide some insight on the writing process, techniques, and uses of language that are related to it; everything from passive voice and the language of leadership, to the five elements found in every persuasive speech, to the rituals of concession and apology. My goal isn't just to revisit and uncover lost history, it's to look under the hood at process and technique and reveal a bit about why some words make history in the first place.

I should also add that the quotations you see on the title page of each chapter aren't technically quotations at all, given that they feature unspoken words from never-delivered speeches. *The Chicago Manual of Style* doesn't have a guide for that, so I've put them in quotation marks.

Part 1 is "Words That Are Too Hot"; examples of how rhetoric gets tempered (or not) based on the expectations and demands of event organizers. This includes the original versions of what Martin Luther King Jr. and John Lewis wanted to say at the 1963 March on Washington. It also includes a lesser-known speech that a Native American leader, Wamsutta Frank James, was prohibited from giving at the 350th anniversary of the Pilgrims landing in Massachusetts.

Part 2 is "A Change of Mind, a Change of Heart." These are the times where someone sees two choices before them and, at the eleventh hour, chooses one, leaving behind a draft speech as evidence of their thinking about how they would argue for the other. In this section, we see the speech Emma Goldman would have given at her sentencing for inciting a riot in 1893 had she chosen to further gin up her supporters and the speech Helen Keller would have given in 1913 at a suffrage parade had she not feared for her safety. It also includes the speech President Nixon was prepared to make *refusing* to resign in 1974 as well as the speech Boston mayor Kevin White was prepared to make later that same year defying a judge's order to use busing to integrate Boston's segregated schools.

Part 3 is "Crisis / Crisis Averted," those moments when speakers were prepared for (or pushing toward) a crisis that did not come to pass. Here we have Edward VIII's refusal to abdicate the British throne in 1936, instead asking the British people to choose his fate and the fate of his relationship with Wallis Simpson. We also have the fraught moment in 1975, when New York teetered on the verge of bankruptcy, and Mayor Abe Beame was minutes away from having to announce that bankruptcy to the world.

Part 4 is titled "The Fog of War, the Path to Peace," and it includes General Dwight Eisenhower's prepared apology had the D-day invasion failed, Emperor Hirohito's shame-ridden apology for his role in starting World War II, and President Kennedy's harrowing announcement of the military operation to destroy the nuclear missile sites in Cuba in 1962.

Part 5 is "The People Choose," and shares two speeches that didn't get delivered because of electoral outcomes: Governor John Peter Altgeld's prophetic farewell address in 1897, and Hillary Clinton's emotional victory remarks had she been elected president in 2016.

Part 6 is "Events Intervene," the moments when some external factor prevents a speech from being delivered. The gravity of those events varies widely; from the speech that George W. Bush's national security advisor Condoleezza Rice was slated to give on the world-changing day of September 11, 2001, to the speech that director Barry Jenkins had intended to give when his film, *Moonlight,* won the Academy Award for Best Picture had the presenters not read the wrong name. The book concludes with a chapter on the four speeches that four leaders had yet to deliver at the times of their deaths: Pope Pius XI, Franklin Delano Roosevelt, John F. Kennedy, and Albert Einstein. These speeches, across nations and generations, all share the theme of peace.

This list is by no means exhaustive. In every conversation I've had about this book over the years, someone will wonder aloud about whether there was a never-delivered speech written for this or that event. For example, as I write this book, our world is in the grip of the COVID-19 pandemic. A friend wondered if there had been any undelivered speeches about previous pandemics. Was there an unheeded warning about the 1918 influenza epidemic? Did President Reagan have an earlier speech about the AIDS epidemic that he scrapped? Perhaps. But just as this book is the culmination of one twenty-year search, those speeches will have to be the subject of my next search. After all, as every speechwriter knows, at a certain point you have to put down the pen, hit Print, and get the thing delivered.

A Note on Sources

Over the years, I've developed a bit of an instinct about where to uncover a never-given speech. For example, in the case of the undelivered speech in which Mayor Beame declared New York City bankrupt, I saw a *New York Times* story by the incomparable chronicler of New York history Sam Roberts, which indicated bankruptcy was so close at hand that Beame actually had prepared a speech. I first found Beame's communications consigliere from that time, Howard Rubenstein. In the intervening years, Rubenstein had become a well-known New York publicist, so the challenge wasn't finding him, it was getting a meeting. Rubenstein remembered writing a speech, but he didn't have a copy, and he recalled that there were only two other people who had seen a copy. One was Sid Frigand, the mayor's then press secretary. I was able to interview Frigand, who said he'd look for the speech. Within months, however, he'd passed away, and no speech could be found in his archives. The other person who might have had the speech was the lawyer who had prepared the bankruptcy filings, Ira Millstein. Millstein was in poor health and unable to see me, but he had the original bankruptcy filing on his wall and told me I was welcome to go to his office and photograph it. When I did, I chatted with his longtime executive assistant, Sally Sasso (always chat up the gatekeepers). She opened a filing cabinet and said, "I think I might have what you're looking for." And she did.

In other cases, the bread crumbs are publicly available, one just needs to follow them. Whenever I hear a story about "how close" America came to some event or another, odds are there's a speech there. Such is the case involving the terrifying prospect of nuclear war with Cuba or Mayor White of Boston fighting a court order to desegregate the city's schools.

Sometimes, however, the bread crumbs lead to a brick wall. One speech that defied my attempts to find it was the speech that Bill Quandt prepared for President Carter in 1978 had the Camp David discussions broken down. At that time, President Carter had spent over a week sequestered at Camp David alongside Egypt's Anwar Sadat, Israel's Menachem Begin, and their respective delegations. But a deal proved elusive. At one point, Sadat and the Egyptian delegation went so far as to pack their bags. In a tense meeting, Carter told Sadat his departure would mean the end of the United States' relationship with Egypt, their personal relationship, and probably Carter's presidency. Yet it was Begin who ultimately proved the most intransigent. Quandt prepared a speech, which would have been delivered to a joint session of Congress, laying the blame largely at the feet of Begin and perhaps foreshadowing Carter's later pro-Palestinian stance. President Carter reviewed and marked up the draft, but the speed of events, particularly as the negotiations accelerated in the final days, meant that papers and drafts routinely got discarded and misfiled. For example, everything that was on President Carter's desk on the last day of the Camp David meetings was simply tossed into one box. Unfortunately, the draft isn't in there, nor was I able to find it anywhere else. Perhaps the publication of this book will trigger its re-emergence.

Just the knowledge that a "failure speech" was created in this situation is a reminder that the agreement—one that showed the world that peace between Israel and its Arab neighbors was possible, that has (mostly) lasted to this day, and that earned both of its counterparties the Nobel Peace Prize—was one conversation away from ending in stinging failure.

I have also tried to include only speeches for which there is some evidence that the speaker wrote and/or edited it, or at least saw and considered it. That is why this book doesn't include speeches like an address drafted for President Truman by State Department director of policy planning George Kennan, announcing that the United States would *not* develop the hydrogen bomb.

> The American people view with abhorrence all weapons of mass destruction. It is a source of profound regret to us that failure to reach international agreement on atomic energy control has made it necessary for us to proceed with the production of atomic bombs. I hope that we will never lose our balance by entering on a race for the development of weapons of pure mass destruction unless it is clear that our security will be materially served thereby, on balance. In the present instance [development of the hydrogen bomb], I do not find that to be the case.

Though the words are tremendously powerful, and would have changed the course of the arms race, there is no evidence Truman ever saw them or seriously considered the idea. In the fateful meeting, Truman had one question: "Can the Russians do it?" And when the answer came back in the affirmative, the president replied, "In that case we have no choice. We'll go ahead."*

I should also note that I am not a historian. While, for the speeches themselves, I went to or unearthed primary sources wherever possible, in the course of writing this book I relied heavily on secondary sources to re-create the drama of the moment. Occasionally, those sources conflicted, and I either took what I found to be the most reliable given the other information I had, or I explained the conflict. Given this reliance on sec-ondary sources, and the fact that speechwriters choose to be (somewhat) anonymous while historians don't, I have tried wherever possible to give the original works due credit, either in the text or with an explanation in the bibliography.

And while I've focused this book on *speeches* that went undelivered, I want to close this introduction with a poem that, at least initially, went undelivered. For his inauguration in 1961, President Kennedy had re-quested that the poet Robert Frost either read from his poem "The Gift Outright" or compose a poem for the occasion.

Frost composed an original poem he titled "Dedication" and, with no time to memorize it, planned to read from a printed text at the inaugu-ration. But Frost was in his late eighties, and the wind, cold, and glare of the sun made it impossible for him to see the page. So, after stumbling through the first few lines of the new poem, he instead recited "The Gift Outright" from memory, modifying the last line from "Such as she [the land] would become" to the more active and affirmative "Such as she will become."

"Dedication" went undelivered. Later, Frost renamed it "For John F. Kennedy His Inauguration," and released it in a compendium of his poems. It's a poem that's almost overly specific to its moment, but in it, there's a quatrain that describes how I feel about all the speeches in this book.

---

* For more about this chapter in history, I highly recommend Nicholas Thompson's Cold War history, *The Hawk and the Dove*. Nic, by the way, was the editor of newyorker.com in 2015, and his willingness to publish my first sample chapter of this book, the undelivered speech Mayor Abe Beame was to give declaring New York City bankrupt in 1975, gave me hope there might be an audience for other stories of this type. An updated and expanded version of that story appears in chapter 7.

"New order of the ages" did we say?
If it looks none too orderly today,
'Tis a confusion it was ours to start
So in it have to take courageous part.

The words and people featured in these pages were sometimes on the winning side and sometimes on the losing side. History has borne out their wisdom—and occasionally their folly. But in a world of confusion, they have taken courageous part. And that part deserves to be more fully heard.

PART 1

Words That Are Too Hot

The goal of a speech, in almost all cases, is to persuade. Persuading someone to take an action requires shaking them from their complacency or encouraging them to act on an already-held belief. Persuading someone to see a different point of view often requires challenging their previously held assumptions. But there are times when an audience can be shaken too hard or challenged too much. What happens when someone other than the speaker decides that a speech goes too far?

John Lewis prepares to speak at the 1963 March on Washington for Jobs and Freedom. (© Bob Adelman)

1

John Lewis on the March on Washington, August 1963

Ensuring That Multiple Speeches
Fit the Moment

"Patience is a dirty and nasty word."

The organizers of the 1963 March on Washington for Jobs and Freedom had promised a peaceful march, and it was this promise that allowed many faith leaders and white liberal organizations to join. President Kennedy, in endorsing the march, also emphasized peace, describing the gathering as a "peaceful assembly for the redress of grievances."

Twenty-three-year-old John Lewis, just months into his job as the head of the Student Nonviolent Coordinating Committee (SNCC, pronounced *snick*), the student wing of the civil rights movement, saw the endorsement of the event by the president as co-opting the urgent, insistent, and antiestablishment nature of the movement. Lewis had been active in the civil rights movement since he was turned away from his local library in Alabama at the age of sixteen, when he showed up to get a library card and check out some books. While in college in Tennessee, he became a leading figure in the Nashville sit-in movement and had endured being spat on and burned with lit cigarettes during sit-ins. He had been one of the original thirteen freedom riders, who boarded a Greyhound bus in Washington, D.C., and attempted to ride to New Orleans, Louisiana, in 1961 to test the recent Supreme Court decision that found segregation in interstate travel unconstitutional. At a stop in Rock Hill, South Carolina, Lewis and his seatmate were attacked and beaten by an angry mob of white supremacists. By the time he assumed the SNCC chairmanship, he had been arrested more than thirty times (over the course of his life, he would be arrested forty-five times).

SNCC was on the front lines of the civil rights movement, leading boycotts and demonstrating for desegregation, and Lewis was at the front of the front. Having seen both injustice and inaction, Lewis "felt defiance in every direction: against the entrenched segregation of the South; against the neglect of the federal government; and also against the conservative concerns of the established factions."

And now the March on Washington, a pivotal moment for civil rights, was being neutered and defanged by the other organizers, the president, and faith leaders. Courtland Cox, the SNCC representative on the march committee, recognized that Lewis, speaking on behalf of SNCC, would bring a "different energy" to the march—after all, they were the ones living with volunteers, witnessing extreme poverty and unchecked violence, and quite literally risking their lives every day for the cause of civil rights.

SNCC members didn't want a march *in* Washington, they wanted a march *on* Washington, and there was some debate as to whether SNCC should just pull out of the event entirely. But John Lewis felt that "we needed to be there, to have our voice heard, in our own words, with our own tone."

A week before the event, with these concerns front of mind, Lewis began drafting his remarks.

He described his thinking succinctly: "I didn't want to be part of a parade. I wanted to see discipline and organization on this day, but I wanted it to have an air of militancy as well, even some disruption if necessary—*disciplined* disruption . . . I have always believed in aggressive nonviolence.

I've always believed in putting some *sting* into it. I wanted this march to have some sting, and if the only place for that sting would be in my speech, then I needed to make sure my words were especially strong."

James Forman, the executive secretary of SNCC, a decade older than most of its members and more confrontational, stressed the importance of Lewis's speech having concrete details. Forman advocated for the mention of Marion King, who, six months pregnant, was walking with her children to the jail in Albany, Georgia, to bring food to imprisoned civil rights protesters when she was knocked to the ground and kicked in the midsection by two policemen. She lost consciousness, and she lost the baby.

The Friday before the march, Lewis went to New York to attend a fundraising concert for the march at the Apollo Theater. It featured stars Quincy Jones, Tony Bennett, Thelonious Monk, and many others. While at the march headquarters, he shared the draft of his speech with some trusted friends. Courtland Cox suggested adding the observation that both political parties had abandoned the cause of civil rights. After all, an avowed racist like James Eastland of Mississippi was a Democrat just like Kennedy, and a progressive Republican like Jacob Javits sat in the Republican caucus with Barry Goldwater, a fierce opponent of civil rights. "Where," the question was asked, "is *our* party?" That went into the speech. As did a discussion of how weak the pending civil rights bill that Kennedy had sent to Congress was. That weekend, Lewis was struck by a photo in *The New York Times* showing a group of women in what is now Zimbabwe holding a sign reading, ONE MAN, ONE VOTE. It seemed a perfect summation of everything they were fighting for, and into the speech it went. And as a coup de grâce, Lewis added to the draft a stern rebuke to those who counseled patience: "To those who have said, 'Be patient and wait,' we must say that 'patience' is a dirty and nasty word."

Ultimately, Lewis wanted to remind people that this wasn't just freedom rides, or sit-ins, or marches; it was a revolution, one that was sweeping across America. He wove the concept of revolution throughout the draft, but wanted to somehow sharpen it. An idea came from Tom Kahn, an aide to Bayard Rustin (another one of the march organizers): "Tom came up with the notion of using General William Sherman's 'March to the Sea' during the Civil War. Like Sherman, we were an army—a nonviolent army—bent on nothing less than destruction—the destruction of segregation." This became the line, "We will march through the South, through the heart of Dixie, the way Sherman did. We shall pursue our own 'scorched earth' policy and burn Jim Crow to the ground—nonviolently."

Lewis was happy with the draft, and the next day, he headed to D.C.

While John Lewis wanted his words at the march amped up, most Americans wanted the march itself toned down. Analysis done by the Pew Research Center found that most Americans were wary of the March on Washington. By that August, 69 percent had heard about the march, and 63 percent of them had an unfavorable opinion of it. Even with more than half of Americans outside the South favoring equal rights legislation, a large majority thought mass demonstrations by African Americans would be detrimental to the cause.

Despite the promises of peace, Washington, D.C., prepared for war. On the evening of Tuesday, August 27, as marchers began arriving, the city was on high alert.

Leaves for every police unit in the district had been canceled so that all were on duty, with backup units from the surrounding suburbs on standby. At the request of the Washington police, which would be facing "a severe strain," the Washington Senators did not play their scheduled game against the Minnesota Twins that Tuesday, nor would they the next day. Instead, they played a doubleheader the day before, and they'd play another doubleheader on the twenty-ninth. Two thousand members of the National Guard had been deployed, a force that included Washington Redskins quarterback Norm Snead and four of his teammates. Seeing Snead surrounded by guardsmen, one writer quipped, "That's the most protection Norm has had this year." Four thousand army troops stood ready in the D.C. suburbs and 15,000 paratroopers had been put on standby in North Carolina. Thirty army helicopters patrolled the skies, swooping low over the city. The city ordered 350 firefighters to switch roles and take on police duty on the day of the march. Hospitals canceled elective surgeries. And that night at midnight, for the first time since Prohibition, a ban on liquor sales went into effect for all of D.C.'s 1,900 licensed liquor outlets.

While D.C. was nervous, the march planners were remarkably calm. Everything was in good shape, and the day before the march was a quiet and orderly one. As the SNCC contingent arrived at the Hilton on

Sixteenth Street, Courtland Cox saw that advance copies of Whitney Young's speech were being made available for the press. From the beginning of John Lewis's time as SNCC chairman, Cox and others had been urging him to step forward, to demand more attention. Lewis, who was less attracted to the spotlight, did so only reluctantly. Cox saw an opportunity to get some attention for Lewis and SNCC. Bayard Rustin, seeing Cox distribute copies of Lewis's speech, asked, "What are you doing that for? No one is seeing King's speech."

(In point of fact, Martin Luther King Jr.'s speech wasn't nearly complete at that hour, and even the version he delivered at the march diverged significantly from the text he brought to the lectern.)

That evening, Archbishop Patrick O'Boyle of Washington, D.C., was hosting a reception at the Mayflower Hotel for a few of the bishops who had come to Washington for the march. The Catholic community in general and Archbishop O'Boyle in particular had been early and strong proponents of the march. O'Boyle may not have fit the picture of a champion of racial justice, but at a time when Washington, D.C., was living under Jim Crow segregation, he worked to desegregate Washington's Catholic schools, starting with colleges and universities and working his way down to elementary schools, often facing stiff resistance. He developed programs to aid Black people of all faiths in the city. Although nervous about the march, O'Boyle had encouraged parishioners to attend, and readily agreed to deliver the opening invocation.

While O'Boyle was at the reception, an aide brought him a copy of John Lewis's speech. What he saw caused him to rethink his position. He couldn't deliver an invocation at the march if this was the type of language he was blessing. He called an aide to Walter Reuther, the head of the AFL-CIO and another march organizer. His message was clear: if Lewis insisted on giving his speech as written, O'Boyle wouldn't deliver the invocation.

And if O'Boyle dropped out of the march, it would put President Kennedy and his brother, the attorney general, in a bind. As Drew Hansen wrote in his masterful history of Dr. King's speech, *The Dream: Martin Luther King, Jr., and the Speech That Inspired a Nation,* "If the Catholic Church's most prominent representative withdrew from the march at the last minute, it would mar the image of the event as a peaceful, multiracial, and multireligious demonstration for civil rights . . . The Kennedys hoped the presence of priests in clerical collars and nuns wearing habits would reassure an anxious Washington public."

The politics of multispeaker events are particularly fraught. I have had the opportunity, honor, and trauma of helping lead the speechwriting operation for the six Democratic national conventions from 2000 through 2020. The job involved soliciting drafts of, scheduling, rehearsing, fact-checking, and message-checking the roughly 150–250 speeches that make up a national political convention. In 2016, after Melania Trump's speech included entire passages lifted from a previous speech by Michelle Obama, we added plagiarism-checking via software to the list as well. On top of this, it was also our job to ensure that each of the speeches was at or under its assigned time limit.

Much like John Lewis at the March on Washington, all those speakers were *nominally* on the same page and generally aligned on goals. But each one represents his or her own constituency and, naturally, has his or her own ego.

The Democratic National Convention in 1996 was to be the first convention where all speakers had to speak from a teleprompter—nobody was to bring paper onstage. The teleprompter serves two goals. The first is that conventions are now made-for-television events, and holding papers just doesn't look good on television. The second is that forcing the speeches through the teleprompting system allows the organizers to make sure that somebody gets eyes on every speech before it is delivered into millions of homes.

Not having any paper at all, naturally, makes speakers uncomfortable. At the conventions on which I worked, we told speakers that we would have a production assistant following along with a hard copy of their speech in a binder so that they could be handed the binder, at the correct page, should the prompter go down. For many speakers, that wasn't comfort enough. In 2004, I remember in particular that Rev. Al Sharpton, who had run for the Democratic nomination for president that year, didn't want to rehearse his speech, and he didn't want to submit it for the teleprompter.

One of the (few) powers convention organizers have is the ability to shift time slots if speakers don't play ball. As a last resort, you can shrug and say, "Fine, give the speech you want, but you can give it at 4:30 p.m.

to an empty arena." Under such threats, we ultimately coerced Sharpton into the rehearsal room, where he couldn't have been more agreeable. He submitted his speech, we put it in the prompter, and he rehearsed it flawlessly.

When he was announced onto the stage, Sharpton soaked up the applause, waved to his supporters, reached into his breast pocket, pulled out a stack of papers, and proceeded to deliver a set of remarks that bore no resemblance to the speech he had rehearsed.

Afterward, people told me the remarks had been really good. All I knew was that they were twenty minutes long, far exceeding the allotted time slot.

At the 2012 Democratic National Convention, nothing broke my heart more than my experience with Barney Frank, a political hero of mine and a congressman who represented the district in Massachusetts near where I grew up. Frank had announced his retirement, and we wanted this to be a powerful valedictory. Famously ornery, Frank had no interest in working with the convention staff. All he was willing to tell us was that he wanted to do a riff about the difference between "Mitt Romney" and "Myth Romney." The problem, as we had to delicately convey to Congressman Frank, was that with his speech impediment, both Mitt Romney and Myth Romney sounded, coming from Frank, like "Miff Romney."

I don't remember how we decided who would tell Frank this, but he took the message well, and when he got up on stage, he actually said, "Here is the problem, and this is a hard one for me because of my diction"—and he delivered a completely understandable and hilarious takedown of the myths of Mitt. Unfortunately, because he had refused to work with us, we were forced to recommend his time slot be moved earlier. And so Frank's last convention speech as a member of Congress was delivered at 5:42 p.m. To add a further indignity, Frank went well over his allotted time, and as he approached minute nine of a five-minute time slot, convention CEO Steve Kerrigan began signaling to Frank that they'd lower the lectern as he was talking. So Frank finished up, mid-thought, and left the stage. He seemed pretty unconcerned about the whole affair and was unsentimental about it being his final convention in the remarks he ultimately did give. I, however, was devastated.

Ultimately, someone has to be responsible for the event itself, for making sure the entirety of the experience is on time and on message.

And someone has to make sure that the speeches don't contradict each other. On the second day of the 2012 Republican National Convention, Ann Romney, the wife of Republican nominee Mitt Romney, gave the second-to-last speech of the night. She stated the theme of her speech at the outset: "Tonight, I want to talk to you about love."

Her speech was followed by the convention's keynote, delivered by New Jersey governor Chris Christie. The theme of his speech? The importance of respect over love. "The greatest lesson Mom ever taught me, though, was this one: she told me there would be times in your life when you have to choose between being loved and being respected. She said to always pick being respected, that love without respect was always fleeting—but that respect could grow into real, lasting love."

For the audience, it was rhetorical whiplash. For me and my colleagues, it was another lesson on why speakers at large events need to be aligned. It's not enough for a speech to work as a standalone performance—it has to also work in concert with the other speeches at the event.

In the case of the March on Washington, the person responsible for the entirety of the event was A. Philip Randolph, and Lewis's speech was causing him a major problem.

Lewis returned to his hotel room the night before the march to find a note slipped under the door from one of the organizers: "John. Come downstairs. Must see you at once. Bayard [Rustin]."

On a personal level, Rustin agreed with much of Lewis's speech. He had no issue with the word *revolution* or calling elected officials "cheap political leaders" or even the reference to Sherman. But that night, his one job was to keep the Catholic leaders on board, and that meant focusing on the rebuke of "patience."

Rustin pointed out that "Catholics believe in the word 'patience.'" Lewis, assuming that this was a theological issue, said he would have no problem taking out the line about patience being a "dirty and nasty word," and prepared to head upstairs to go to bed.

Rustin thought that was a good idea, given that it was late, but as he warned Lewis, there would be more edits coming in the morning as others looked at the speech.

As he headed upstairs, Lewis became increasingly incensed that one mis-worded phrase meant that his entire speech was up for inspection. "The more I thought about it as I fell asleep that night . . . the less inclined I was to change one word."

The next morning, Lewis, along with the other leaders of the march, met for breakfast and then headed up to Capitol Hill for a meeting with congressional leaders. In that meeting, what did Lewis feel knowing that he was prepared to deliver a speech, hours later, in front of hundreds of thousands of people and millions more watching at home, saying, "Both the Democrats and the Republicans have betrayed the basic principles of the Declaration of Independence?"

By the time the meeting was over, the march had started, and the leaders struggled to catch up. At the Lincoln Memorial, the rally began with music from Odetta, Joan Baez, Bob Dylan, Mahalia Jackson, and Peter, Paul and Mary, as the crowd kept growing. Backstage, however, there was discord, and its focal point was John Lewis's speech.

By now, Walter Reuther, the head of the United Automobile Workers, was upset that Lewis intended to say, "In good conscience, we cannot support wholeheartedly the administration's civil rights bill, for it is too little and too late," a statement that was followed by an extended enumeration of the bill's shortcomings.

Roy Wilkins, who led the NAACP, got in Lewis's face, accusing him of "double-crossing" the supporters of the bill, shaking a finger at him, asking why the SNCC people always had to be different. Lewis shook his finger right back, saying that Wilkins hadn't been on the front lines and hadn't seen what Lewis had seen.

Rustin separated everyone and designated a smaller group that included Martin Luther King Jr. and A. Philip Randolph to hash things out with Lewis. In the meantime, Archbishop O'Boyle had received enough assurances that the speech would be changed that he went out to deliver the invocation. But backstage, the drama continued. Courtland Cox and Jim Forman had heard about what was happening and hustled backstage as well.

King, who had been a mentor and idol to Lewis, and affectionately referred to him as "the boy from Troy," was relatively silent, observing only that the Sherman line "doesn't sound like you."

Lewis agreed, but pointed out that it sounded like *us,* the young people of the SNCC.

Perhaps King's reticence had something to do with the fact that in the previous days, he, too, had wrestled with a similar challenge. While he didn't face the pressure of responding to the more activist and aggressive SNCC wing of the movement, he and his advisors felt a sense of urgency and frustration, and King had been working to calibrate that frustration and anger in his initial drafts.

King's advisors had heard him give many speeches that ended with versions of what we now know as the "I have a dream" lines. They had suggested new language for the speech at the march; language that was stronger and more combative.

Some of that language made it into his remarks. For example, there was a new passage about America giving its Black citizens a "bad check." Stories of its genesis differ, but one of the most convincing is that when King's lawyer and advisor Clarence Jones went to the main branch of the Chase Manhattan bank to borrow the bail money King needed to be released from the Birmingham jail, he had to sign a document stamped with the words *Demand Promissory Note.*

Over the course of several drafts, that image ultimately became the passage, "When the architects of our republic wrote the magnificent words of the Constitution and the Declaration of Independence, they were signing a promissory note to which every American was to fall heir. This note was a promise that all men," and King then added at the podium, "yes, black men as well as white men," and continued,

> would be guaranteed the unalienable rights of life, liberty, and the pursuit of happiness. It is obvious today that America has defaulted on this promissory note insofar as her citizens of color are concerned. Instead of honoring this sacred obligation, America has given the Negro people a bad check, a check which has come back marked "insufficient funds." But we refuse to believe that the bank of justice is bankrupt. We refuse to believe that there are insufficient funds in the great vaults of opportunity of this nation. So we have come to cash this check—a check that will give us upon demand the riches of freedom and the security of justice.

The initial draft, a version that was written but not delivered, also pushed back against any expectation that things could return to what they were before: normalcy.

I read a newspaper editorial recently which speculated upon when the leaders of this civil rights movement would become "satisfied" so that America could return to normalcy . . . we do not want to return to normalcy.

It was normalcy in Alabama which made a racist Governor defy the Supreme Court and the President of the United States. It was normalcy in Jackson, Mississippi, which enervated a mad killer and gave him the brutal urge to erase the meaningful life of Medgar Evers. It was normalcy on a lonely Alabama road which triggered the gun which took the life of a white postman who sought to deliver a message from freedom. It was normalcy in the state of Mississippi which made it possible for authorities to say that a Negro must starve if he wanted to vote. It is normalcy with keeps the filibuster alive—that legislative incinerator in which every smoldering hope for racial justice has been converted into ashes. It is normalcy which has been the betrayal of all that we mean when we recite the Oath of Allegiance. It is normalcy which makes eleven o'clock on Sunday morning the most segregated hour in America and many Sunday schools the most segregated schools in our country. Every inspired genius who has given something to the world; every people who have ever struck for freedom has rejected the normal and embraced the abnormal.

In fact, it was the normalcy language from which King's speech took its official title: "Normalcy, Never Again." But while "normalcy" remained in the speech's title, by the time of the march, almost all of that language had fallen out.

Interestingly, King's draft at that point did still contain a similar military metaphor to the one Lewis wanted to use. King's read, "This offense we share mounted to storm the battlements of injustice must be carried forth by a biracial army." Perhaps in reaction to the edits he was seeing and recommending Lewis make, King decided to cut it.

Of course, before King could get to his own speech, there was still the subject of Lewis's, and Lewis, now flanked and buttressed by Cox and Forman, wasn't in a mood to make further edits.

King's advisor Clarence Jones recalled, "As dug in as Lewis was, even

Martin didn't have the leverage to get him to soften his point of view. It seemed that, once again, the only one among us who could stand a chance of persuading Lewis to change the text of his prepared remarks was the pioneer of the enterprise, A. Philip Randolph."

And when Randolph returned, that's what happened. In spite of the massive turnout and success of the march to that point, he looked beaten down and tired. He addressed the SNCC trio: "I have waited twenty-two years for this. I've waited all my life for this opportunity. Please don't ruin it."

Lewis describes what happened next:

Then he turned to me. "John," he said. He looked as if he might cry. "We've come this far together. Let us *stay* together." This was as close to a plea as a man as dignified as he could come. How could I say no? It would be like saying no to Mother Teresa. I said I would fix it.

Forman, Cox, and Lewis retreated to the back of the Lincoln Memorial and began to go through every phrase. (While both Lewis and Cox remember Forman sitting at a portable typewriter, a photo capturing that moment shows them hand-editing the draft.) As had been decided

In the back of the Lincoln Memorial, John Lewis (right) makes changes to his speech as Jim Forman (center, right) and Courtland Cox (center, left) take notes and Mildred Forman, who coordinated the freedom singers, looks on. (Johnson Publishing Company Archive, courtesy Ford Foundation, J. Paul Getty Trust, John D. and Catherine T. MacArthur Foundation, Andrew W. Mellon Foundation, and Smithsonian Institution)

the night before, the claim that "'patience' is a dirty and nasty word" had been cut. And now they made other changes.

In the section on the civil rights bill that so outraged Walter Reuther, Lewis initially wanted to say, "In good conscience, we cannot support wholeheartedly the administration's civil rights bill, for it is too little and too late."

He changed that to, "We come here today with a great sense of misgiving. It is true we support the administration's Civil Rights Bill. We support it with great reservation, however."

The speech also included a dramatic list of the abuses the bill would *not* protect against: from the use of dogs and fire hoses on protesters, to arrests made on trumped-up charges.

Speakers who call for change often want to give themselves and their targets a little wiggle room, and that's what Lewis did by adding the words "In its present form." So the passage now began, "In its present form, this bill will not protect the citizens of Danville, Virginia, who must live in constant fear of a police state. It will not protect the hundreds of thousands of people who have been arrested on trumped up charges."

And even "of" a police state was a change from the original "in" a police state—a two-letter change that historian Angus Johnston notes is fascinating and significant: "'In a police state' is an emphatic statement about lived conditions, explicitly naming what it meant, what it was, to be Black in the Jim Crow South. 'Of,' on the other hand, is both tempered and ambiguous—the fear of a police state is a fear of something external, and maybe even hypothetical."

Gone was the true but potentially compromise-thwarting claim that both major political parties "have betrayed the basic principles of the Declaration of Independence."

Gone was the acknowledgment of the size and diversity of the crowd. With words that would have been just as relevant in 2020 as they were in 1963, Lewis wanted to say, "This nation is being awakened to the fact that segregation is evil and that it must be destroyed in all forms. Your presence today proves that you have been aroused to the point of action."

Gone were the charges of a "conspiracy on the part of the federal

Selections From John Lewis's Draft Speech

(Notable deletions in italics)

We march today for jobs and freedom, but we have nothing to be proud of, for hundreds and thousands of our brothers are not here. *They have no money for their transportation,* for they are receiving starvation wages, or no wages at all.

In good conscience, we cannot support wholeheartedly the administration's civil rights bill, for it is too little and too late. There's not one thing in the bill that will protect our people from police brutality.

This bill will not protect young children and old women from police dogs and fire hoses, for engaging in peaceful demonstrations: This bill will not protect the citizens in Danville, Virginia, who must live in constant fear *in a police state....*

For the first time in one hundred years this nation is being awakened to the fact that segregation is evil and that it must be destroyed in all forms. Your presence today proves that you have been aroused to the point of action.

We are now involved in a serious revolution. *This nation is still a place of cheap political leaders* who build their careers on immoral compromises and ally themselves with open forms of political, economic and social exploitation. What political leader here can stand up and say, "My party is the party of principles?" The party of Kennedy is also the party of Eastland. The party of Javits is also the party of Goldwater. Where is our party?...

I want to know, which side is the federal government on?

The revolution is at hand, and we must free ourselves of the chains of political and economic slavery. The nonviolent revolution is

Selections From John Lewis's Delivered Speech

(Notable additions in bold)

We march today for jobs and freedom, but we have nothing to be proud of, for hundreds and thousands of our brothers are not here, for they are receiving starvation wages or no wages at all. **While we stand here, there are sharecroppers in the Delta of Mississippi who are out in the fields working for less than three dollars per day, 12 hours a day. While we stand here, there are students in jail on trumped-up charges. Our brother James Farmer, along with many others, is also in jail.**

We come here today with a great sense of misgiving. **It is true that we support the administration's Civil Rights Bill. We support it with great reservation, however. Unless title three is put in this bill,** there's nothing to protect the young children and old women who must face police dogs and fire hoses in the South while they engage in peaceful demonstration.

In its present form this bill will not protect the citizens of Danville, Virginia, who must live in constant fear **of a police state....**

We must have legislation that will protect the Mississippi sharecroppers, who have been forced to leave their homes because they dared to exercise their right to register to vote. We need a bill that will provide for the homeless and starving people of this nation. We need a bill that will ensure the equality of a maid who earns five dollars a week in the home of a family whose total income is 100,000 dollars a year. We must have a good FEPC bill.

My friends let us not forget that we are involved in a serious **social** revolution. **By and large,** politicians who build their career on immoral compromise and allow saying, "We will not wait for the courts to act, for we have been waiting for hundreds of years. We will not wait for the President, the Justice Department, nor Congress, but we will take matters into our own hands and create a source of power, outside of any national structure, that could and would assure us a victory."

To those who have said, "Be patient and wait," *we must say that "patience" is a dirty and nasty word*. We cannot be patient, we do not want to be free gradually. We want our freedom, and we want it now. *We cannot depend on any political party, for both the Democrats and the Republicans have betrayed the basic principles of the Declaration of Independence.*

We all recognize the fact that if any radical social, political and economic changes are to take place in our society, the people, the masses, must bring them about. In the struggle, we must seek more than civil rights; we must work for the community of love, peace and true brotherhood. Our minds, souls and hearts cannot rest until freedom and justice exist for all people.

The revolution is a serious one. Mr. Kennedy is trying to take the revolution out of the streets and put it into the courts. Listen, Mr. Kennedy. Listen, Mr. Congressman. Listen, fellow citizens. The black masses are on the march for jobs and freedom, and we must say to the politicians that there won't be a "cooling-off" period.

All of us must get in the revolution. Get in and stay in the streets of every city, every village and every hamlet of this nation until true freedom comes, until the revolution is complete. In the Delta of Mississippi, in southwest Georgia, in Alabama, Harlem, Chicago, Detroit, Philadelphia and all over this nation, the black masses are on the march!

We won't stop now. All of the forces of Eastland, Barnett, Wallace and Thur-

themselves an open forum of political, economic and social exploitation dominate American politics.

There are exceptions, of course. We salute those. But what political leader can stand up and say, "My party is a party of principles"? For the party of Kennedy is also the party of Eastland. The party of Javits is also the party of Goldwater. Where is our party? **Where is the political party that will make it unnecessary to march on Washington? Where is the political party that will make it unnecessary to march in the streets of Birmingham? Where is the political party that will protect the citizens of Albany, Georgia?...**

To those who have said, "Be patient and wait," we must say that we cannot be patient. We do not want our freedom gradually but we want to be free now.

We are tired. We are tired of being beat by policemen. We are tired of seeing our people locked up in jail over and over again, and then you holler "Be patient." How long can we be patient? We want our freedom and we want it now.

We do not want to go to jail, but we will go to jail if this is the price we must pay for love, brotherhood and true peace. I appeal to all of you to get into this great revolution **that is sweeping this nation.** Get in and stay in the streets of every city, every village and hamlet of this nation until true freedom comes, until a revolution is complete. We must get in this revolution and complete the revolution. In the Delta of Mississippi, in Southwest Georgia, in the Black Belt of Alabama, in Harlem, in Chicago, Detroit, Philadelphia and all over this nation the black masses are on a march for jobs and freedom.

They're talking about slow down and stop. We will not stop. All of the forces mond won't stop this revolution. The time will come when we will not confine our marching to Washington. *We will march through the South, through the heart of Dixie, the way Sherman did. We shall pursue our own scorched earth policy and burn Jim Crow to the ground — nonviolently.* We shall fragment the South into a thousand pieces and put them back together in the image of democracy. *We will make the action of the past few months look petty.* And I say to you, wake up America.

of Eastland, Barnett, Wallace, and Thurmond will not stop this revolution. **If we do not get meaningful legislation out of this Congress,** the time will come when we will not confine our march into Washington. **We will march through the South, through the streets of Jackson, through the streets of Danville, through the streets of Cambridge, through the streets of Birmingham. But we will march with the spirit of love and with the spirit of dignity that we have shown here today.**

By the forces of our demands, our determination and our numbers, we shall send a desegregated South into a thousand pieces, put them together in the image **of God and** Democracy. We must say wake up America, wake up! **For we cannot stop, and we will not and cannot be patient.**

government and local politicians in the interest of expediency," and the question, "I want to know, which side is the federal government on?"

And gone was the statement that "the black masses are on the march for jobs and freedom, and we must say to the politicians that there won't be a 'cooling-off' period."

Gone was the threat that

> the time will come when we will not confine our marching to Washington. We will march through the South, through the heart of Dixie, the way Sherman did. We shall pursue our own scorched earth policy and burn Jim Crow to the ground—nonviolently. We shall fragment the South into a thousand pieces and put them back together in the image of democracy.

"Fragment" became the gentler "send" as the entire passage morphed into the following:

By the forces of our demands, our determination and our numbers, we shall send a desegregated South into a thousand pieces, put them together in the image of God and Democracy.

By the time the edits were completed, Lewis was angry. Even though he hadn't compromised his message, he felt he had watered down his speech.

The frustration Lewis was feeling is something that often happens with speakers who amend their remarks at the last minute. Because they know what they had *wanted* to say, they forget that the audience never saw or heard the initial draft. I often tell speakers that the audience doesn't see your first draft or your favorite draft. They don't get to hear what you might have said given your druthers. The audience only listens for how you say what you ultimately do say.

The experience that brought this into sharpest relief for me was then mayor of San Antonio Julián Castro's keynote speech to the 2012 Democratic National Convention. In it, Castro wanted to develop the idea of America's "infrastructure of opportunity," a concept he and his congressman brother, Joaquin, had been talking about a lot. Castro drafted this language:

> America didn't become the land of opportunity by accident. My grandmother's generation and generations before gifted us with many things that make opportunity possible. As Joaquin has articulated so well, they created an Infrastructure of Opportunity. You see, just as Americans built out a physical infrastructure—our roads, our highways, our railroads—to get people and goods to their destination on a map, they also built out the Infrastructure of Opportunity—strong public schools, great universities, student aid, Medicare and Social Security—that, matched with hard work and the freedoms enshrined in our Constitution, make the American Dream possible.

We thought it was a lovely, powerful, fresh articulation, in keeping with Castro's role as an exciting new voice on the Democratic stage.

However, when Obama's chief strategist, David Axelrod, saw the draft, he was almost incredulous, saying, "We don't even use the word *infrastructure* to describe infrastructure!"*

It had to go. Castro was frustrated. He was approaching what would be his first moment in the national spotlight, and he had just been told he couldn't give the speech he wanted to give.

But he regrouped, sitting down with his advisors and speechwriter Sarada Peri, who would later go on to write speeches with President Obama. Maybe they couldn't say "infrastructure of opportunity," but they could find ways to convey the idea that today's opportunity becomes tomorrow's prosperity.

There's a story that one of my clients once told me about expense reporting. An employee broke his umbrella on a business trip. So he bought a new one and added its cost to his expense report. That seemed reasonable; if he hadn't been on the trip, the umbrella wouldn't have broken. Besides, looking presentable was part of the job, and given the pouring rain, the umbrella would allow him to do that. The expense was denied, to the employee's frustration. So the next time the employee filed an expense report, he submitted his hotel and meal and travel expenses. And then added the words: "*Now* find the umbrella."

Castro's team followed a similar strategy in revising his speech:

America didn't become the land of opportunity by accident. My grandmother's generation and generations before always saw beyond the horizons of their own lives and their own circumstances. They believed that opportunity created today would lead to prosperity tomorrow. That's the country they envisioned, and that's the country they helped build. The roads and bridges they built, the schools and universities they created, the rights they fought for and won—these opened the doors to a decent job, a secure retirement, the chance for your children to do better than you did.

Now find the "infrastructure of opportunity."

---

* That has since changed, with subsequent administrations focusing on "infrastructure week" and "infrastructure bills."

Castro wasn't entirely happy with the new construction. But he knew he had a good speech, one that contained some powerful moments. And the audience didn't know Castro had an earlier version he would have preferred to give, because they responded to the one he did give. As he reached his concluding crescendo (the technical term for this part of a speech is *peroration*), he said:

> In the end, the American dream is not a sprint, or even a marathon, but a relay. Our families don't always cross the finish line in the span of one generation. But each generation passes on to the next the fruits of their labor. My grandmother never owned a house. She cleaned other people's houses so she could afford to rent her own. But she saw her daughter become the first in her family to graduate from college. And my mother fought hard for civil rights so that instead of a mop, I could hold this microphone.

The New York Times would report, "The applause in the arena was reminiscent of the party's convention eight years ago in Boston when an Illinois state senator named Barack Obama brought delegates to their feet."*

Lewis wasn't entirely happy with his draft after making what felt like the mandatory edits, but he was committed to it. When it came time for him to speak, A. Philip Randolph introduced "Young John Lewis, National Chairman, Student Nonviolent Coordinating Committee." Perhaps the "young" was an attempt to inoculate against whatever Lewis was about to say.

Meanwhile, Lewis remembered Bayard Rustin standing behind him, "close enough, it felt, to yank me away if I got out of line."

Lewis's words, delivered with a tone of righteous indignation, walked right up to the invisible line of passion and propriety without stepping over it. As Lewis hit his stride, the audience, not hearing what was missing from the page, responded to what was on it—affirming his roll call of civil rights hot spots and roaring in response to Lewis's demand that "we do not want our freedom gradually, but we want to be free now." It was,

---

* I was in the arena for both, and I would say that it was louder for Castro.

according to *The New York Times,* the "harshest" of the speeches given that day. But it did not cause the archbishop to flee or the crowd to riot. The only injuries that day were heat related. Rather, it roused a wilting crowd and reminded them that they weren't at a march *in* Washington, they were at a march *on* Washington.

Fifty years later, in discussing that day with the journalist Bill Moyers, Lewis was asked again about his edits. With the perspective that only comes from hindsight, Lewis said, "I think it was the right thing to do."*

The last speaker that day was Martin Luther King. If Lewis's speech had been the stick, King's was the carrot, although not by design.

King's speech, too, had been tougher in its earlier iterations. But by the final draft, the "normalcy" language had fallen out of his speech entirely. Instead, it had morphed into a phrase King is not believed to have previously used, "the fierce urgency of now," a powerful summary of King's impassioned impatience:

> This is no time to engage in the luxury of cooling off or to take the tranquilizing drug of gradualism. Now is the time to make real the promises of democracy.

And though the word *normalcy* doesn't appear once in the speech he delivered, King did make a version of the normalcy argument and why the nation couldn't return to "business as usual."

> This sweltering summer of the Negro's legitimate discontent will not pass until there is an invigorating autumn of freedom and equality. Nineteen sixty-three is not an end, but a beginning. Those who hope that the Negro needed to blow off steam and will now be content will have a rude awakening if the nation returns to business as usual. There will be neither rest nor tranquility in America until the Negro is granted his citizenship rights. The

---

* Courtland Cox recalls being called a "sellout" by several SNCC members because of the changes.

whirlwinds of revolt will continue to shake the foundations of our nation until the bright day of justice emerges.

The audience was responding to King, too. So much so that about ten minutes into his prepared remarks, King realized he had violated what he had described to his friend, chief of staff and fellow pastor Wyatt Tee Walker, as his first priority in constructing sermons: know where you want to end. "First I find my landing strip. It's a terrible thing to be circling around up there without a place to land."

And yet, that's where he was, speaking to his largest audience, carrying them forward on a wave of emotion, but moving toward a conclusion that no longer seemed to fit the moment.

In King's telling, using his "I have a dream" set piece, which he had used many times before, came to him "just all of a sudden."

Had he heard Mahalia Jackson, standing behind King, beseeching him to "tell them about the dream, Martin"? He never acknowledged that he heard her. But in a speech full of set pieces—effectively a rhetorical greatest hits album—the dream became the perfect final track.

That said, some in King's inner circle, like Walker, thought, *Here we go again,* upon hearing King launch into "the dream." Some from the SNCC thought it was too saccharine, a missed opportunity to do what Lewis had done, to reveal the horrors inflicted upon those who would dare stand up to the legal and moral outrages of the segregated South.

What they failed to recognize was the power King's words held for the hundreds of thousands of people hearing them for the first time. Those doubters didn't account for the yearning people had not just to be confronted with outrage but to be lifted by hope.

In retrospect, the two most influential speeches of that most influential day worked in perfect tandem; a yin and a yang balanced together to fit the needs of the moment. Lewis's words tapped into outrage without going so far as to alienate any audiences, and then King balanced out the horror with hope. It was not what either of them had intended, nor was it what either of them had drafted—but it worked to powerful, lasting effect.

Wamsutta Frank James speaks in front of the statue of Massasoit in Plymouth, Massachusetts, in 1970. (Photo courtesy of UAINE)

2

Wamsutta Frank James on the 350th
Anniversary of the Pilgrims Landing at
Plymouth Rock, September 1970

The Five Elements Found in
Every Persuasive Speech

"It is with a heavy heart that I look back on what
happened to my people."

Cole's Hill, in Plymouth, Massachusetts, rises sharply from Plymouth
Harbor, as if the inlet that houses Plymouth Rock was dug out of the
coastline and lumped upon the land.

Standing just north of where the Pilgrims built their first struc-
tures, it became the burial ground for the *Mayflower* settlers who died
in the winter of 1620, a winter that took the lives of 52 of the original
102.

On the hill you'll find a sarcophagus, built by the General Society of

Mayflower Descendants, to house the remains of those original arrivals that had been unearthed by floods and construction. The sarcophagus is inscribed with the names of the settlers who died that first winter, and the words *History records no nobler venture for faith and freedom than this Pilgrim band.*

Today, there is another monument there, a large stone. Unlike the Plymouth Rock of legend, which is just down the hill, this rock has a plaque embedded in it.

The plaque carries a different message:

Since 1970, Native Americans have gathered at noon on Cole's Hill in Plymouth to commemorate a National Day of Mourning on the U.S. Thanksgiving holiday. Many Native Americans do not celebrate the arrival of the Pilgrims and other European settlers. To them, Thanksgiving Day is a reminder of the genocide of millions of their people, the theft of their lands, and the relentless assault on their culture. Participants in National Day of Mourning honor Native ancestors and the struggles of Native peoples to survive today. It is a day of remembrance and spiritual connection as well as a protest of the racism and oppression which Native Americans continue to experience.

Those words, of course, run counter to Plymouth's well-curated image as "America's Hometown," as well as to our nation's founding narrative of partnership and friendship. That sunnier narrative is advanced by a different monument on Cole's Hill: a statue of the Wampanoag leader Massasoit, who is described at the statue's base as "protector and preserver of the pilgrims." And while it is true that Massasoit signed a treaty with the new settlers, and provided (or accepted the thievery of) provisions such as corn, wheat, and beans, Native Americans have long understood that the story of brotherhood is not nearly the full story.

When he was invited to address the 350th anniversary celebration of the landing of the Pilgrims in 1970, Wamsutta Frank James, the president of the Federated Eastern Indian League, wanted to tell the full story. But event organizers prevented him from delivering that speech. This led directly to the creation of the National Day of Mourning, believed to be the longest continuing protest in America, and gave James's undelivered words more power than he had imagined.

On September 11, 1970, Frank's son, Roland Moonanum James, was aboard the USS *Independence,* which was at sea as part of a seven-month deployment in the Mediterranean. Moonanum, who played clarinet, saxophone, and flute, was part of a navy band aboard the ship. Although the band members practiced daily, and stood watches like the other sailors, they had ample time for other tasks. One of Moonanum's was to keep up with the AP and UPI newswires, bringing the captain the news, including stories that might have been of particular interest to him. The captain, Gerald O'Rourke, was from New England, so James was on the lookout for local New England news when he was stunned to see his father's name come across the wire for an act of defiance that was now being discussed statewide in Massachusetts.

Beyond seeing his father's name crop up from half a world away, the surprise also stemmed from the fact that the younger James knew that his father, while proud of his Native American heritage, was no radical. He was the first Native American graduate of the New England Conservatory of Music and a music teacher at Nauset High School on Cape Cod. His wife, Priscilla, was white. He described his activities with the Federated Eastern Indian League this way: "We're not a militant group. We do things like sponsoring scholarships for Indians."

And so, when the Massachusetts Department of Commerce and Development was looking for a Native American to speak at the 350th Pilgrim anniversary kickoff dinner, they reached out to the leaders of the Wampanoag tribe, and those leaders suggested James.

The dinner would kick off fifteen months of events: parades, tours, speeches, concerts, and visits of dignitaries from neighboring states, England, and Holland. It was also to include a reenactment of the Pilgrims' landing followed by a speech by evangelist Billy Graham as a "symbolic rededication of our faith in the God of our Fathers."

James accepted the invitation and got to work on his speech. He wanted, in the words of his wife, to take "ten minutes out of 350 years . . . to hear the other side of the story."

(Courtesy of Moonanum James. The full text of the speech appears in the appendix.)

James consulted a Civil War–era copy he had of *Mourt's Relation,* a contemporaneous journal written largely by Pilgrims Edward Winslow and William Bradford in which they detail digging up Native American graves and stealing corn and cookware.

He wanted to recount the history of how before the Pilgrims ever landed, European explorers had already captured some thirty-five Native Americans and sold them into slavery. He wanted to reclaim an understanding of Native American culture, not as "savage, illiterate, uncivilized," but "just as human as the white man," noting, "The Indian feels pain, gets hurt, and becomes defensive, has dreams, bears tragedy and failure, suffers from loneliness, needs to cry as well as laugh. He, too, is often misunderstood."

He wanted to call his audience to help create a "more humane America, a more Indian America, where men and nature once again are important, and where the Indian values of honor, truth, and brotherhood prevail."

And he wanted to celebrate not one but two beginnings. "You the white man are celebrating an anniversary. We the Wampanoags will help you celebrate in the concept of a beginning. It was a beginning of a new life for the Pilgrims. Now, 350 years later it is a beginning of a new determination for the original American."

With his wife editing and iterating, Frank tapped out his speech and, satisfied that his speech would provide an important, missing perspective, submitted it to the event organizers.

Speechwriting techniques are like religions, in that everyone believes they are in possession of the one true path.

For my money, the best book on the topic of speechwriting is *The Political Speechwriter's Companion,* by Bob Lehrman and Eric Schnure, for whom I interned at the White House when I was twenty years old. At the time, Bob was Al Gore's chief speechwriter, and he was working on the first edition of the book. When I was assigned to his office, he handed me the beginnings of that book, assembled in a three-ring binder.

The section that became my one true path was called "Monroe's Motivated Sequence."

I'll give you the abridged version.* Monroe's motivated sequence is named for a Purdue University professor named Alan H. Monroe, who, in the mid-1930s, used the (early) psychology of persuasion to outline the components of speech that deliver results. He codified this into five steps in sequence: attention, need, satisfaction, visualization, action.

To begin, Monroe argued that no matter how compelling your ideas, they wouldn't persuade people who weren't paying attention. Audiences are fickle. You need to get them absorbed as close to the first sentence as possible. Statistics and studies vary, but it's generally accepted that speakers have seconds—not minutes—to capture an audience's attention. And yet, most speakers spend the first minutes of their talks doing the one thing that is guaranteed to cause audiences to tune out: thanking people.

---

* If you want the unabridged version, I again recommend *The Political Speechwriter's Companion*, by Bob Lehrman and Eric Schnure. You can also go directly to the source, and find a copy of *Monroe's Principles of Speech,* which was printed in the 1930s.

Ironically, Gore was perhaps the greatest violator of this rule, painstakingly thanking person after person as the energy drained out of the room. Extended acknowledgments are terrible strategy for two additional reasons. First, you will inevitably forget somebody. Second, most of these acknowledgments are meaningless. If you are truly feeling gratitude for something somebody in the room has done, that's worth discussing in a substantive way: in the middle of the speech. If someday on my tombstone it is written, "He got people to move the acknowledgments into the body of the speech," I will be happy.

One of the reasons TED Talks are so viral and addictive is that they master step one: whether it's the speaker making a joke or telling a story or offering a prediction or a bold or counterintuitive claim, they open by capturing your attention.

The second step is to articulate the need, or problem. Most persuasive speeches want to convince audiences that something is true, a good idea, or something to value. But why is that important? Only if the idea solves a problem important and compelling to the audience. One mistake speakers often make is that they're so excited to tell you about their idea, insight, or solution, they fail to connect that idea to a problem important to the audience. Before presenting your good idea, you need to convince the audience they need it by outlining the problem it solves.

This prepares the audience for the third step, satisfaction, or solution. If you've articulated the problem, now you can describe your solution—your policy, plan, or agenda.

The oft-forgotten fourth step is vision, or visualization. It's not enough to show how you can solve a problem; that's an academic exercise. To truly motivate an audience, Monroe advocated showing them what the future would be like once your idea was adopted. Think: I have a dream.

Fifth and finally, Monroe argued that if you've gotten your audience's attention, if you've identified a problem in a way that they find compelling, and shared a solution that is similarly compelling, and painted a clear picture of the world once this solution is in place, then get them to do something about it. Thus he recommended concluding with a call to action.

In the world of speechwriting, this is the "roughage" section, because there's a lot of "lettuce": "Let us do this . . . ," "Let us do that . . ." Action can be donating time or money, marching or voting, or any number of other things. But since the goal of most speeches is to inspire audiences to action or allegiance, it's important to suggest some actions.

From a process standpoint, using the five steps of Monroe's motivated sequence as the key to a five-part outline has been my cure for writer's block. If I just write a sentence for each of those things, I feel like I'm beginning to have a speech.

In the case of Wamsutta James, he instinctively hit on each of the five steps of Monroe's motivated sequence. For starters, he chose to capture the audience's attention right off the bat with his statement that a time of celebration for the audience is essentially a time of mourning for him, one that brings him a "heavy heart."

He then outlines the problem; the fact that the Wampanoag's welcome of the white man has led to a complete loss of freedom, that history records "that the Indian was a savage, illiterate, uncivilized animal," and that both the native culture and language were being driven to extinction.

After detailing the brutal history suffered by Native Americans, he moves toward a solution. His solution is for Native Americans to stand together, to declare who they are, to begin the process of righting the many wrongs that had been committed, and that this anniversary be celebrated as a "beginning of a new determination for the original American."

While these words may have been perceived as radical, it's worth noting again that Frank James was not a radical, and he makes that clear in his vision: "What has happened cannot be changed, but today we must work towards a more humane America, a more Indian America."

And in service of this vision, he offers a call to action, for his people to take 350 years of hard history and hard-won understanding about white culture, and to compete for top jobs, to not hide or attempt to disappear through assimilation. He calls on his people to "regain the position in this country that is rightfully ours."

On September 9, two days before the event, a representative from the Massachusetts division of tourism came to James's home with an edited copy of the speech, which had been cut down to three minutes from its original ten.

Harry Hartog, who was with the state's Department of Commerce and was helping organize the event, claimed the draft delivered to James was simply an attempt to "consolidate his thoughts," although he did admit that "the theme of the anniversary celebration is brotherhood and anything inflammatory would have been out of place."

Particularly inflammatory to another member of the Commerce Department, Ernest Lucci, was a reference to the Pilgrims stealing from the Wampanoag, both food and the remains of a member of the tribe. "You can't go around calling people grave robbers," he told James.

James replied, "But that's what happened."

Similarly, Lucci reacted negatively to the section of the speech in which James was to say, "We are uniting. We're not standing in our wigwams but in your concrete tent. We stand tall and proud, and before too many moons pass we'll right the wrongs we have allowed to happen to us." To Lucci, that sounded like a threat, and he pleaded, "What is the world coming to, in these days of discord, when we can't even have a speech calling for unity at a function such as this?"

James answered the question with a question, "Why is my son serving on an aircraft carrier . . . when back home you can't say the things you want to say?"

Like many Native Americans, James had been walking a fine line in his life between celebrating and educating people about his culture and playing into stereotypes. A month earlier, James had joined a plane flight that retraced the *Mayflower*'s journey, a flight on which the governor was also aboard. James did so shirtless, wearing only a leather loincloth and moccasins, with a feather in his hair.

But that night, James looked at his original draft and the draft that had been handed to him, one that seems to have been lost to history but that James indicated painted a lovely picture of Pilgrim and Indian harmony, and grew increasingly frustrated. He felt that to deliver such a speech would make him look like a kindergartener.

At 2:00 a.m., he went to bed, his mind made up.

The next morning, he sent a telegram to Governor Francis Sargent in which he stated that he would be boycotting the event. It concluded with the words, "I must tell the truth."

The organizers found another Native American to appear at the event instead—Lorenzo Jeffers, the sachem of the Wampanoags who, incongruously, wore a Lakota Sioux war bonnet, the type of decorative costume most Americans at the time thought of as quintessentially Indian.

Jeffers, too, faced the same tension between celebration and caricature. A day after giving the state-sanctioned speech* at the dinner, he made a different speech as part of the ceremonies in which he argued that "Chief Massasoit who met the Pilgrims when they came here, though he could not read or write, had more human principles, more human decency, than any person who landed on these shores. I ask only one thing. That you help my people now."

His words may have also been a reaction to what he saw when he opened *The Boston Globe* the morning after the dinner. There, on the front page, was a photo of Governor Francis Sargent wearing the war bonnet as Jeffers stood by, smiling. The caption read, "Chief Sarge."

At that point, James's wife, Priscilla, in the indelicate and outdated phrasing of the *Cape Cod Standard-Times,* "went on the warpath," firing off a blistering letter to the governor and other state leaders.

> That your committee chose to stop Mr. James from delivering his speech was their right . . . To my way of thinking that erases all of their [the organizers] altruistic words of brotherhood and that their "hearts were in the right place." Your committee's actions do indeed speak louder than their words.

Mrs. James received a conciliatory letter from Governor Sargent, in which he wrote that he regretted that the speech hadn't been delivered and that he was sending a copy of it to all the dinner attendees.

Mr. James, however, wasn't satisfied. In response to the governor's letter, he said that a true apology would be accompanied by the State of Massachusetts paying for 227 acres of land the state had taken from the Watuppa Indian reservation in order to create a reservoir, something the state has never seriously considered doing.

More immediately, James decided that if the Native American story wasn't going to be told in ceremonial dinners, it would have to be told

---

* Despite searching the state archives, I was unable to find the speech that was delivered that night.

in protest. James, along with Tall Oak, Shirley Mills, and other leaders of the United American Indians of New England, called for a national day of mourning.

Word of James's censorship and the day of mourning spread throughout Native American communities by the "moccasin telegraph," the informal word-of-mouth network that shared tribal news.

On November 26, 1970, Thanksgiving Day, more than one hundred Native Americans, representing tribes from across North America (and including both Lorenzo Jeffers and Frank James) arrived in Plymouth. Some of the protesters who showed up were part of a nascent Indian rights movement that had occupied Alcatraz Island in 1969.

Russell Means, the prominent American Indian Movement (AIM) activist, led a group to Plymouth Rock itself, and, noting that "Plymouth Rock is covered with Indian blood," they buried Plymouth Rock in sand.

From there, another group ran to the *Mayflower II*, a beam-by-beam replica of the original ship, and threw a mannequin representing Christopher Jones, the *Mayflower*'s original captain, overboard.

When asked to leave, the group did so. No arrests were made.

This became the National Day of Mourning.

In subsequent years, the crowd would grow. There would be other attempts to bury Plymouth Rock or to cover it in blood. The event has been largely peaceful, with the exception of 1997, in which the Day of Mourning event threatened to intersect with the Town of Plymouth's traditional Thanksgiving Day Parade. The ensuing scuffle resulted in several arrests on the Native American side for offenses ranging from loud and tumultuous rioting to illegal use of a sound system—but all the charges were eventually found to be without merit and were dropped.

As part of the settlement for those unnecessary arrests, the Town of Plymouth agreed to fund and place the National Day of Mourning monument on Cole's Hill.

Today, the National Day of Mourning is believed to be the longest-running protest in the United States. Moonanum James finds it ironic that "had my father been allowed to give his speech, we wouldn't be marking the 50th national day of mourning next year [2020]."

Instead, the day of mourning now serves as a loud and continuing echo from a speech that included all the necessary steps of persuasion, but became even more persuasive by the fact that it was never given.

PART 2

A Change of Mind, a Change of Heart

A speech is an act by which an idea is introduced to the world; the moment at which a person, through public utterance, embraces a plan. Sometimes a speaker, seeing a speech in hand, realizes that they don't want to own those words and the consequences of those words, at least not at that moment. Such were the cases of the anarchist Emma Goldman, who feared inciting a riot at her own trial, and Helen Keller, who was so shaken from the violence that engulfed the suffrage march in which she was participating that she didn't feel able to speak. Richard Nixon had prepared a draft announcing his intention to fight impeachment. Similarly, mayor Kevin White of Boston, who, in the midst of his city's busing crisis, considered defying a judge's order. Each chose an alternate path, but in their speeches, we see what it would have looked like had they decided differently.

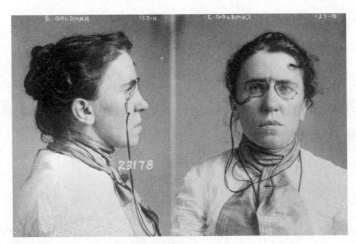

Emma Goldman's 1901 mug shot.

A mob breaks up the 1913 suffrage parade in Washington, D.C., after which Helen Keller was slated to speak.

3

Emma Goldman at Her Sentencing, October 1893, and Helen Keller at the Suffrage Parade, March 1913

The Power of Speech to Move People to Action

"The wealth, the luxury, the pomp and glory of power are bought at the price of murdered and disfigured mankind."

—Emma Goldman

"I am blind; but I see the dawning light of a new day when there shall be no woman enslaved."

—Helen Keller

They called her "Red Emma," "the Queen of the Anarchists," "the most dangerous woman in America," and the inspiration for President William McKinley's assassin in 1901. Political cartoons pictured her towering above the crowd, wearing bloomers, hoisting a red flag, urging her followers on to rebellion. In truth, Emma Goldman was barely five feet tall, and in 1893, the year she was arrested for using a speech to incite a riot, she was all of twenty-five years old.

By the early 1900s, Helen Keller was world famous for learning to communicate despite her deafness and blindness, and beloved for her inspirational message of overcoming adversity. But when her story evolved from finding her voice to using her voice to speak out for women's rights, workers' rights, and civil rights, the perception changed, and on one dramatic afternoon in 1913, an unruly crowd at a historic march for women's suffrage prevented her from speaking at all.

Why were the words of these women considered so threatening, so disturbing to the established order? Because we know that some words have the power to move people to action, and when those words come from women, they are viewed through another lens as well.

Emma Goldman was born in 1869 in a poor Jewish family in what is now Lithuania, then under the control of imperial Russia. She was educated in Germany, and then came to the United States at age sixteen, hoping to avoid an arranged marriage. In Russia, her family was living in St. Petersburg when Tsar Alexander II was assassinated by bomb-wielding socialist terrorists, setting off a violent crackdown on protests. The ensuing upheaval began to shape Emma's revolutionary outlook.

In the United States, she settled in Rochester, New York, where she found the condition of America's factory workers just as inhumane and unequal as in Russia. In 1887, when four of the labor activists implicated in throwing a bomb during the Haymarket riot in Chicago were hanged,* she felt she couldn't stand idly by. She moved to New York City and joined the cause of the so-called anarchists who advocated for a society free of organized government.

She quickly fell in with Johann "Hans" Most, who became a mentor (and perhaps a lover). In Goldman, Most found an eager student for his concept of *Attentat,* or propaganda of the deed, which he described this

---

* For more, see chapter 11.

way: "The existing system will be quickest and most radically overthrown by the annihilation of its exponents. Therefore, massacres of the enemies of the people must be set in motion."

He also saw in Goldman an uncommonly powerful spokesperson: young, idealistic, passionate, able to speak several of the languages of the working classes. He set about arranging a speaking tour for her, which was a huge success. Goldman would often start her speeches in English and then switch to Russian and Yiddish, a fluency that further inspired her crowds—and confused the police standing by, who couldn't understand her. And thus Emma Goldman became the face of anarchism in America.

She rocketed to further fame and infamy when her new romantic partner (in her words to the police, "I am his wife, but in the anarchistic way"), Alexander Berkman, attempted to assassinate the industrialist Henry Clay Frick, the chairman of the Carnegie Steel Company. Goldman, who had been involved in the plot, escaped prosecution, but was unapologetic about the effort: "The bullets did not kill [Frick]," she told one crowd in early 1893, "but others are being molded and they will fly with surer aim."

Berkman was sentenced to twenty-one years in prison, ultimately serving fourteen before his release. Goldman was now a bona fide celebrity.

All of this took place against the general backdrop of the Gilded Age, summed up aptly by Andrew Carnegie, one of the world's richest men, when he told a reporter in 1892, "It isn't the man who does the work that makes the money. It's the man who gets other men to do it." And it took place against the more immediate backdrop of the so-called Panic of 1893, the start of a four-year economic depression in the United States that shuttered fifteen thousand businesses and put tens of thousands out of work. On the night of August 21, 1893, there was a parade and rally in Manhattan's Union Square Park, a longtime favorite spot for political activists. The crowd marched behind a red banner, symbolic of socialists and laborers around the world. They spoke immigrant languages— German, Russian, Polish, Yiddish, and Italian. Goldman described the Union Square marchers as thousands of people "charged with bitterness and indignation." She was the eighth and final speaker on the program that night. When she got up, the notes she had prepared seemed insufficient to the moment, and so she didn't use them.

Instead, she launched into the address that would get her arrested. She began speaking in English, and nearly every sentence was interrupted by cheers and applause. At some point, she switched to German.

Men and women, do you not realize that the State is the worst enemy you have? It is a machine that crushes you in order to sustain the ruling class, your masters. Like naïve children you put your trust in your political leaders. You make it possible for them to creep into your confidence, only to have them betray you to the first bidder.

But even where there is no direct betrayal, the labour politicians make common cause with your enemies to keep you in leash, to prevent your direct action. The state is the pillar of capitalism, and it is ridiculous to expect any redress from it. Do you not see the stupidity of asking relief from Albany with immense wealth within a stone's throw from here? Fifth Avenue is laid in gold, every mansion is a citadel of money and power. Yet there you stand, a giant, starved and fettered, shorn of his strength.

Cardinal Manning long ago proclaimed that "necessity knows no law" and that "the starving man has a right to a share of his neighbour's bread." Cardinal Manning was an ecclesiastic steeped in the traditions of the Church, which has always been on the side of the rich against the poor. But he had some humanity, and he knew that hunger is a compelling force. You, too, will have to learn that you have a right to share your neighbour's bread. Your neighbours—they have not only stolen your bread, but they are sapping your blood. They will go on robbing you, your children, and your children's children, unless you wake up, unless you become daring enough to demand your rights.

Well, then, demonstrate before the palaces of the rich; demand work. If they do not give you work, demand bread. If they deny you both, take bread. It is your sacred right.

The above is Goldman's own account of her words. Other accounts vary slightly in content and translation. The star witness at her eventual trial, Detective Charles Jacobs, had been undercover at the rally and spoke some German. He testified that there was nothing particularly inflammatory about what she said in English, "but when she began speaking in German, she made statements which I considered were unlawful, including the call to 'take everything . . . by force.'" Her lawyer would argue the confusion lay in the translation.

Another account had her saying,

> Most of you left Russia, where you had a Czar who acted in as brutal a way as any man on earth. Here in America we have capitalistic czars . . . We have Gould and Astor and Sage and Rockefeller and Vanderbilt. . . . You built the palaces and others are living in them. The politicians are misleading you . . . We are told God will feed the starving, but that is humbug in the nineteenth century. I will speak, they can arrest me if they please, but they cannot shut my mouth.

Update the names of those "capitalistic czars" and instead call them "billionaires" or "the 1 percent," and you can hear similar words being spoken today by activists on both ends of the political spectrum, as wealth and income inequality in America rivals that of the late nineteenth century.

Even though Goldman's words didn't cause a riot that night, the police certainly thought they could have. And New York's power structure knew what they had heard. Ten days after her Union Square speech, Goldman was arrested as she prepared to speak in Philadelphia. The charge was "Incitement to Riot" even though no riot had taken place. When she was brought from her cell in New York's infamous "Tombs" prison to the courtroom, the city was prepared to enforce martial law. Newspapers had run stories about "preparations for a forcible rescue of Emma Goldman" and "anarchists planning to storm the court-room." The police had put known radicals under surveillance, and now there were police on every corner and buildings cordoned off. Nobody other than Goldman, a few friends, the lawyers, and the press was allowed in the court building, whose halls were lined with even more police officers.

Prior to her sentencing, Goldman was to be given the opportunity to speak. Goldman's lawyer, Abraham Oakey Hall, had previously served as mayor of New York, and had mounted a strong, thoughtful defense. Now he was advising his client not to speak, fearing that another incendiary address could rile up her supporters inside and outside the courtroom, providing the police with the opportunity to arrest even more anarchists.

When Goldman insisted on speaking, Hall withdrew from the case.

As Goldman stood to make her remarks, she hesitated. She seemed conflicted. She had told her lawyer she was going to speak, and he had stepped down because of it. And she knew the power of her own words to galvanize people's rage and frustration.

So when she stood to make her statement, nobody quite knew what to expect. But very few expected her to do what she did, which was to reverse course and take her lawyer's advice. So when she stood, she said only, "In view of the fact that the police have done everything they could to incite my friends, the Anarchists, to some demonstration, so that they could put them in jail also, I shall refrain from delivering any speech here."

In a case where she was pleading "not guilty" to inciting a riot, she declined to speak for fear of inciting a riot.

The judge proceeded to read the sentence: guilty, sentenced to one year at Blackwell's Island Penitentiary.* Goldman, in a final act of defiance, paid no attention, smiling and making gestures at several of her friends.

As she was put on the barge that would deliver her to the prison, she remarked to the pack of reporters who followed her, "I travel in queenly state, just look at my satraps [subordinates]." And when she got off the boat, she bade the journalists goodbye by jauntily saying that she would see them in a year and, in the meantime, they shouldn't write any more lies than they could help.

This combination of youth, danger, and sauciness made Goldman an irresistible subject, and guaranteed an audience for her message.

So, had she chosen to speak, what would her message have been in court that day?

---

* Blackwell's Island is, today, Roosevelt Island in Manhattan's East River.

Thanks to *The New York World,* which obtained a copy of Goldman's prepared remarks, we know the answer:

I speak not to defend myself, but to defend my right of free speech, trampled upon by those who have caused the curtailing of my liberty.

I know that the right of free speech was once guaranteed to every man and woman in this land.

What do those who have brought me here understand by the right of free speech? Does it give a right to all to say what appears to the individual good or bad, or has it been granted to permit the expression of only that which to a certain class of the citizens appears right?

Is free speech solely for the purpose and use of the Government and its officers, are individuals prohibited from say[ing] that which is true, even though hardly to the taste of a certain class or portion of the public? Can I only say that in which I do not concur, and must I say it?

I am positive that the men who shed their blood for the independence of this land, and who offered up their lives to secure the liberty and rights of the American people, must have had a very different understanding of the right of free speech than those who to-day represent the Government, and who so interpret the right as to permit the expression only of that which is conducive to their benefit.

According to such an interpretation of the right of free speech I must call them despots, and as such, without the right to commemorate in celebrations the memory of those who fell in the fight for Independence, for the former deliberately trample underfoot the principles of those heroes, and when decorating their graves commit blasphemy.

Why don't the representatives of the State drop the so-called mantle of free speech, discard the mask of falsehood and admit that absolutism reigns here?

Under such a condition of things the American citizen has no shadow of right in pointing the finger of contempt at European institutions and in speaking of the downtrodden hungry of the Old World.

The sorrowful condition of the workingmen of the Old as well as the New World increases from day to day, and it reached a high point in its horizon this very year.

Devoid of all means of sustenance, the workingmen assemble to consult, to devise means to remedy their need. Those who throughout the year utilize the people and gather riches at their cost perhaps feel that it would not go well with them should the workingmen become half conscious of their exigencies, and in their terror the latter seek the aid of government. Innumerable policemen and spies are sent into the meetings of the unemployed, to control all their deliberations, to control the speakers.

I belonged to that class of speakers who endeavored to show the workingmen the real reason of their misfortune.

The speeches made by me must have contained much that was unpleasant for the rich of the City of New York, because they set in motion whole bands of spies to cause my apprehension and confinement, for the reason, as the indictment reads, that I had offended against the law and exhorted those present at my speeches to acts of violence.

If what I said at Golden Rule Hall and at Union Square was a violation of the laws, then all those who were present at those meetings, and who by protracted and loud applause evinced their approval of what I said, were equally guilty with me. Why, then, did the city authorities proceed against me alone? Why? Because the authorities know that no danger lies in the workingman's ignorance of the true cause of his privations.

From the moment that I, as an Anarchist, showed them that the workingman could never expect relief from his despoilers, from that moment I made the ruling masses uncomfortable, and had to be put out of the way.

I do not acknowledge laws made to protect the rich and oppress the poor. Who are the law makers? Senators, the great of the land? Capitalists. Capitalists who torture thousands to slow death in their factories, they are people who live in affluence, robbing the workingman of his strength to deprive him of the results of his labor; they are men whose fortunes have been built upon a foundation formed by pyramids of children's corpses.

The wealth, the luxury, the pomp and glory of power are bought at the price of murdered and disfigured mankind.

Ever rises the voice of the disinherited people, a voice growing in volume, and to which the overbearing classes will not listen, and to still which they devise new laws intended to silence the masses. Bands of priests are sent out to teach subjection, to propagate superstition and keep the people in ignorance.

The demands of the workingmen are met with the Winchester rifle and the Gatling gun, and I must confess that my brethren and myself will ever oppose such a state of "order"; an "order" in which we do not believe, and whose representatives we will never be compelled to meet in the struggle for advancement.

Here, she goes on for several hundred words describing how anarchy will lead to the "happiness and contentment of man" before reaching her conclusion:

I tell you, the day of reckoning is not far—a time when no concessions will be granted to the tyrants and despots.

Such is my belief, spread by me among the workingmen, and this belief will cease only with my life.

You have convicted me, you may pass sentence of imprisonment upon me, but I tell you that I hate your laws; that I hate your "order," for I know but one "order"—it is the highest potency of order—Anarchy.

Goldman said none of these words that day. When asked if she had anything to say about why the sentence should not be passed, she said only that the court could do its worst, but it wouldn't change her views. Had she given the speech she intended to give, is there a chance she would have faced an even harsher sentence? After all, the opposing counsel had argued that if Goldman went free, property would be destroyed, the children of the rich would be murdered, and the streets would run with blood. A speech that spoke of gallows and Winchester rifles and Gatling guns (regardless of her point that they were all used against workingmen and -women, and not the wealthy) may have tipped the scales further against her and elicited an even longer sentence.

Instead, Goldman's restraint allowed her to emerge into the public eye more quickly and afforded her even more influence when she did. She launched into an even more aggressively public phase of her life, speaking boldly and defiantly not just on free speech but on women's emancipation, free love, birth control, and socialism.

Ultimately, Goldman's words helped give rise to one of America's greatest defenders of free speech, the American Civil Liberties Union (ACLU). In 1908, Roger Baldwin heard Emma Goldman speak in St. Louis. He was so moved that he decided to dedicate his life to the cause of freedom, founding the ACLU in 1920. As he wrote to Goldman in a letter, "You always remain one of the chief inspirations of my life, for you aroused in me a sense of what freedom really means." In his old age, Baldwin said, "Emma Goldman opened up not only an entirely new literature to me, but new people as well, some who called themselves anarchists, some libertarians, some freedom lovers . . . bound together by one principle—freedom from coercion."

Emma Goldman not only helped inspire the creation of the ACLU, she also helped inspire the dawning political consciousness of Helen Keller.

In 1886, when Keller was six years old, her parents took her from their home in Alabama to Baltimore, to see an oculist, who they thought could help restore Keller's vision. The oculist encouraged them to visit the world-famous inventor Alexander Graham Bell, who was deeply interested in the study of speech, hearing, and voice, and was working with deaf children in Washington, D.C. It was Bell who encouraged the Kellers to visit the Perkins School for the Blind in Boston, which led to the fateful meeting with Anne Sullivan, the teacher who would change Helen Keller's life.

When Keller was fourteen, she met Mark Twain at a luncheon. Twain, like Bell, was world famous, and he was charmed by Keller,* who followed Twain's hand gestures with her fingertips. After the lunch, Twain wrote a letter encouraging his wealthy friends to fund Helen's college education, becoming her second world-famous friend and champion.

---

* Twain would later say, "The two most interesting characters of the 19th century are Napoleon and Helen Keller."

While enrolled at Radcliffe College, Keller began to write *The Story of My Life*, which was published in installments in *The Ladies' Home Journal.* The book and subsequent speaking engagements made her famous in her own right.

But as Keller entered adulthood, she grew frustrated; everyone wanted to hear her inspirational childhood story of being rescued from the isolation of her disabilities. They were happy to hear her call for charity for the deaf and blind. But fewer wanted to hear her characterize those disabilities as civil rights issues. And fewer still wanted her to talk about her personal politics. She realized that when she spoke about her disabilities, she was referred to as brilliant, but when she talked about her political beliefs, the newspapers infantilized her, reporting that she was being "used" and didn't fully understand what she was advocating.

In November 1912, Keller published an essay titled "How I Became a Socialist." And a few months after publishing the essay, she decided to speak for herself. She agreed to join a major suffragette rally in Washington, D.C., which was planned "to bring before the country in the most public manner possible the 'nation-wide demand for an amendment to the Constitution of the United States enfranchising women.'"

The rally was to be held on March 3, 1913, the day before the inauguration of President Woodrow Wilson, to ensure that plenty of reporters would be in attendance. The hope was that Wilson would recommend equal suffrage in his inaugural address and support a constitutional amendment throughout his term,* and the march organizers delivered Wilson a letter to that effect.

The rally began with a parade at 3:00 p.m. in front of the U.S. Capitol and marched down Pennsylvania Avenue. It was a spectacle, with all-women bands, women on horses, floats representing everything from women in the Bible to women in sweatshops, delegations from every state, and different organizations and professions in color-coordinated outfits marching behind banners.

While the afternoon timing allowed for significant press coverage, it also allowed time for a large, rowdy, drunken crowd to assemble. The

---

* Wilson didn't speak out in favor of women's suffrage in a full-throated way until his second term in office.

five thousand marchers were soon outnumbered a hundred to one by the half-million spectators.

Almost immediately, the crowd surged in on the parade route. Marching suffragettes were reduced from one procession to small groups, where they were jeered, taunted, and physically harassed. Men tried to grab the flowers off the women's coats or pull them down off the floats. The women had lighted cigarettes thrown at them. When one marcher had tobacco spat on her, she appealed to a nearby police officer, who responded, "There would be nothing like this if you women would stay at home."

While the police did nothing to protect the women, the only groups to step up were a contingent of Boy Scouts and students from the Maryland Agricultural College; a small collection of boys and young men trying to protect women from a rampaging mob of grown men. Ultimately, cavalry troops from nearby Fort Myer were called in, terrifying both the crowd and the marchers as soldiers and horses started charging up and down the parade route.

The planned speeches that were to be given following the march in Continental Hall, near the White House, ultimately became an "indignation meeting." A resolution was adopted calling on President-Elect Wilson to demand a full congressional investigation.

The Baltimore Sun reported that "Miss Helen Keller, the noted deaf and blind girl, was so exhausted and unnerved by the experience in attempting to reach a grandstand where she was to have been a guest of honor that she was unable to speak later at Continental Hall."

And what was Keller to have said?

The speech opens with some of Keller's most powerful lines:

I am proud to share in your brave work for the emancipation of women. From my victorious fight against the dark I bring you good cheer in your world-wide battle for light, for freedom. I am deaf; but I hear the glad tidings of woman's liberation which shall soon be flung abroad through the land. I am blind; but I see the dawning light of a new day when there shall be no woman enslaved, no child robbed of the sweet joy of childhood in the war of daily bread. All earthly opposition cannot stay our onward march.

I am proud to share in your brave work for the emancipation of
woman. From my victorious fight against the dark I bring you
good cheer in your world-wide battle for light, for freedom. I
am deaf; but I hear the glad tidings of woman's liberation which
shall soon be flung abroad through the land. I am blind; but I
see the dawning light of a new day when there shall be no woman
enslaved, no child robbed of the sweet joy of childhood in the
war of daily bread. All earthly opposition cannot stay our onward march. For we bear the life of the world. We are strong
with the uplifting sense of woman's true destiny. We are strong
with mother-love and the unconquerable mind, and such power is
irresistible!

I ask nothing for myself. I am not among the victims of un-
just laws. But with my whole heart I cry aloud for freedom that
shall right the wrongs of all my sisters who are oppressed. I
call for freedom that shall save wives and mothers from being
broken in ill-requited, daylong toil. I have clasped the hands
of young girls who suffer in the dismal haunts of poverty, and I
demand freedom that shall save them from overwork, misery and
shame. Every child has a right to be well-born, well-nurtured
and well-taught, and only the freedom of woman can guarantee him
this right.

I would not belittle the value of political power, of legislation for woman. But our effort to enfranchise woman is only part
of the mighty work which shall free all mankind. We are striving
to win a freedom which shall quicken and ennoble the whole life
of the race. That means freedom for every man and every woman to
earn the sweet bread of life and eat it in content; freedom for

every man to work, to achieve all the splendor of manly power;
freedom for every woman to use all her gifts of body, mind and
soul and be the glad mother of lovely children; freedom for every
child to play, to learn, to laugh, to be merry; freedom for all
human beings to live decently and enjoy the beauty, the comforts,
the luxuries which their hands have wrought. Let us unite with
all who follow this ideal. Let us unite, men and women, and free
men and women together, and our bondage shall be broken asunder
forever.

*(Reprinted with permission from the American
Foundation for the Blind)*

The rhetorical device used here, which employs a similar sentence structure with the words *not* or *but* to show contrast, is called *antithesis*, and it provides a cadence and a contrast that is appealing for the listener.

Keller's well-constructed words, powerful in their own right, might have gained more power from her distinctive delivery. Keller explained that her greatest disappointment in life was that she couldn't "speak normally." Listening to audio of Keller, you can hear that she spoke in the distinctive diction and modulation found in those who have learned to talk without being able to hear. But an accent or unusual inflection can sometimes cause an audience to lean forward and listen more intently.

Still, in the case of the suffragette rally, the speeches not given may have had more influence than any that were given. According to an exhaustive analysis of media coverage of the event conducted by University of Arizona journalism professor Linda Lumsden, the aftermath and the ensuing Senate hearings found that "the riot forced even anti-suffrage newspapers to acknowledge women were citizens who possessed the right to assemble peacefully. That acknowledgment moved the media a big step closer to the inexorable conclusion women also possessed the right to vote."

Keller may not have spoken that day, but she didn't remain silent for long. As historian Kim Nielsen of the University of Toledo documented, Keller continued to put forward a social and political agenda, encouraging public health officials to get over their "false modesty" and educate women about venereal diseases, which, when passed from mother to baby, were one of the leading causes of blindness in the United States. She spoke on behalf of workers' rights and spoke out against World War I and those who profited from it. She corresponded frequently with and about Emma Goldman. In 1916, Keller wrote to the editor of *The New York Call* defending Goldman against imprisonment for educating women about birth control, saying, "She has consecrated her life to the salvation of the oppressed. She is now engaged in a contest with authorities of oppression. If we stand aside and allow her to be imprisoned, you and I will be imprisoned likewise." Goldman, for her part, described hearing Keller speak at Carnegie Hall in 1916 as "one of the most stirring events in my life."

Keller also continued to develop arguments for women's suffrage. Seven months after her undelivered speech, she published an article in which she wrote that men need women's suffrage, which includes the cheeky observation: "When women vote men will no longer be compelled to guess at their desires—and guess wrong."

She then followed this with the more serious point: "Women will be able to protect themselves from man-made laws that are antagonistic to their interests. Some persons like to imagine that man's chivalrous nature will constrain him to act humanely toward woman and protect her rights. Some men do protect some women. We demand that all women have the right to protect themselves and relieve man of this feudal responsibility."

To be relieved of responsibility is also to be relieved of some measure of power and control. And perhaps that is why these—and so many other—speeches by women throughout history have been feared, stopped, and shouted down.

Women have also been stopped from speaking not because those in power couldn't tolerate hearing their words, but because we have always understood that words can lead to actions.

The hope (or fear) that one person's words could move another person's limbs is baked into the idea of rhetoric from the beginning. In his book *Lend Me Your Ears,* William Safire cites the saying supposedly made by Pericles, comparing his speeches with those of his countryman Demosthenes: "When Pericles speaks, the people say 'how well he speaks.' But when Demosthenes speaks, the people say, 'Let us march!'"

It's a great quote, and it contains two valuable lessons for speechwriters. The first is that the goal of a speech is to inspire some sort of action, from writing a check to storming the ramparts.

The second lesson is to always check your quotes. Pericles died in 429 B.C. Demosthenes was born in 384 B.C., forty-five years later. Pericles never heard Demosthenes speak.

But the understanding that speech could motivate acts has been a cause of concern throughout history. After all, if words could entrance people into acting out, wouldn't that make rhetoric a form of hypnosis or black magic? And what have we historically called practitioners of black magic? Witches.

This is where gender comes into play, and why Emma Goldman—who didn't actually throw bombs or fire weapons—was seen as more dangerous than many of her male peers who did. It's why so many were intent on interrupting the march and rally of the suffragettes; so intent that three hundred marchers were injured. Throughout history, we have branded women who put us under spells, literal or figurative, as witches. Society has resisted giving women the power to make their voices heard.

As author Madeline Miller points out, when Joan of Arc was captured by the British, she was tried for witchcraft, "citing as partial proof . . . her ability to outwit her examiners in debate." When women lead countries or movements, the result is often the same, whether it's Cleopatra or Anne Boleyn. We fear and punish women who hold or seek power.

In his seminal treatise on speech, *Rhetoric,* Aristotle expressed concern that rhetoric, like any tool, can be misused—no matter the gender or sex of the speaker. But he argued that the benefits that could be derived from rhetoric—convincing people that policies or people were good (or bad)—outweighed the risks. And he felt that perhaps the best defense against the misuse of rhetoric would be to help listeners identify which lever in their minds was being pulled. This is where we get the ideas of logos, or logic; ethos, or character; and pathos, or emotion,* which are essentially a description of which mental "strings" are being pulled by the speaker.

To this day, we wrestle with the knowledge that speeches can pervert truth, and inspire action, for good and for ill. And we worry about who has that power. As Ralph Waldo Emerson said in one of his Table Talk lectures, "Speech is power—speech is to persuade, to convert, to compel."

During her time in prison, Emma Goldman would become a devotee of Emerson's writing. After all, she and Helen Keller and many other women—along with many of their detractors—recognized that the ability to persuade, convert, and compel is a tremendous tool and that it can also be, in the wrong hands, a tremendous threat.

If we have hesitated to put women forward as leaders because we feel that elevating women necessitates a loss of agency for men, it's important to remember that the real loss of responsibility and agency comes not when we assign power to any speaker, man or woman. The real danger is when we, as listeners, behave as if we have no power at all.

---

* For more, see chapter 14.

President Richard Nixon, flanked by aide Alvin Snyder, prepares to give his resignation speech. (Oliver Atkins)

4

President Richard Nixon's
Refusal to Resign, August 1974

The Precarious Position
of the Speechwriter

"Far more damaging than even the conviction and
removal of a President, would be the descent toward
chaos if Presidents could be removed short of
impeachment and trial."

On July 27, 29, and 30, 1974, the United States House of Representatives approved three articles of impeachment against President Richard Nixon. Nixon's allies in the House estimated that there would be more than enough votes to impeach him. His allies in the Senate felt that with the recently obtained audio recording proving that Nixon had ordered a coverup of the break-in and attempted bugging of the Democratic National Committee headquarters, he was trending downward. Soon there would be the necessary two-thirds agreement in the Senate to remove him from office. The writing may not have been fully legible, but it was on the wall.

Nixon knew it. As he would later tell his speechwriter Ray Price, "I had to think about what a Senate trial would mean." He had to think about resigning. And, though he informed only a select few close advisors, that is the decision he had made by August 1.

The plan was for the president of the United States to announce his resignation on Monday, August 5, effective at noon the next day.

Price got to work on the resignation speech in secret. As he recounted in his book *With Nixon,* "The need for total secrecy stemmed partly from the need to make preparations in an orderly way, without letting things fall apart in the meantime." What Price didn't know was that one of his new young aides couldn't stop telling everyone that he "could not talk" about the top-secret project he was working on, thus succeeding in giving several people a pretty good idea of what Price was working on!

But beyond the need to keep up appearances, Price's secrecy in writing the resignation draft was also due to the nature of Nixon's decision-making. No decision was "final" until it was announced*—"and on this most final, most personal decision of his presidency, Nixon obviously was going to keep reassessing, keep re-examining, possibly reverse himself."

On Saturday, August 3, that's what happened. Price was called into the office of Chief of Staff Al Haig. Nixon had changed his mind. He would still speak on Monday, and he would release the transcripts of the tapes the court had ordered him to hand over, but he would not resign.

Presidents have always had people who helped them with their speeches; this was one of the jobs Alexander Hamilton performed for George Washington. But the first person hired expressly to be a speechwriter was Judson Welliver, during the Warren G. Harding administration in the 1920s. Welliver's actual title was *literary clerk.* That accurate

---

* To this day, I tell my staff to never call a speech "final" until it has been delivered. And at that point, I want them to call it "as delivered." To me, a speech almost never exists as "final."

but slightly misleading designation gets at one of the innate tensions of the job: the word *speechwriter* itself betrays a confidence. For a long time, the thinking was that speechwriters should be heard, but not heard *from* and certainly not heard *about*.

When asked about my job, I often tell people it's a bit of a Faustian bargain, as you have to give up ego and voice in exchange for the opportunity to witness (and help narrate) history. But the speech ultimately belongs to the speaker. It's considered gauche at best and disloyal at worst to take or seek credit for a novel argument or memorable line. The experience of speechwriter David Frum provides a cautionary (if not entirely accurate) tale in this regard. According to the story, after President George W. Bush used the phrase "Axis of Evil" in his 2002 State of the Union address, Frum's wife emailed several friends to share with "wifely pride" that her husband wrote the line. The email became public, and Frum left the White House shortly thereafter. Although Frum argued that he had given a month's notice while the speech was being written, the story became the professional equivalent of using a dead crow to ward off other crows: don't take credit.

That dictate has softened as speechwriters have become minor celebrities in the political firmament. In the United States, we now know the names of many of the speechwriters for our presidents. But the rise in the visibility of the job has, ironically, occurred alongside a diminishment of the role.

In the days of Ted Sorensen and Arthur Schlesinger Jr., who wrote speeches for President John F. Kennedy, speechwriters tended to be policymakers first, poets second; thought partners, rather than ghostwriters (or "scribes," as my old boss Al Gore once bellowed from his office to summon my colleagues and me). But more recently, speechwriting offices have come to fit the description that the journalist D. T. Max used during the George W. Bush administration: "Policy and prose work their way on separate tracks at the White House, only meeting at higher levels."

Just as the existence of speechwriters is a surprise to many, it was a huge surprise to me upon reading Peggy Noonan's masterful *What I Saw at the Revolution* to realize that the woman wielding the pen behind some of Reagan's most powerful rhetoric had almost no relationship with Reagan at all.

This creates a situation where speechwriters are sometimes asked to prepare arguments for policies or actions they don't understand or don't agree with.

Nixon felt that if he could make his case for why the evidence against him wasn't as damning as it appeared, perhaps he could hang on to the presidency. And he had reason to believe it, and to believe in his own powers of persuasion.

Twenty-two years earlier, amid accusations of fundraising improprieties, then senator Nixon gave what would come to be known as the "Checkers speech." He was facing allegations about a political slush fund, and though those allegations were thin at best, they were endangering his quest to become Dwight Eisenhower's vice president.

Nixon decided to bypass a hostile media, buy thirty minutes of airtime following the popular *Texaco Star Theater* (which later became *The Milton Berle Show*), and take his case directly to the American people. It would be the first nationally televised political address in American history. Nixon arranged to speak from a set that looked like a living room. His wife, Pat, was on the set—and made an appearance on camera—during the remarks.

If the medium was new, so, too, were the tone and substance of the rhetoric. The speech was personal, confessional, and powerful.

In the speech, Nixon describes the fund and what it was used for, pointing out that unlike many of his colleagues, he didn't have personal wealth, nor could he continue his law practice and still be a senator, nor did he feel comfortable putting his wife on the government payroll (as many elected officials did at the time).

He describes his family's modest circumstances and, in what today we'd consider a humblebrag, mentions his military service: "Let me say that my service record was not a particularly unusual one. I went to the South Pacific. I guess I'm entitled to a couple of battle stars. I got a couple of letters of commendation."

And then he delivered a section worth reading again today, because of how much it presaged our current obsession with the power of a humble personal narrative to demonstrate the everyman qualities of a politician:

When we came out of the war—Pat and I—Pat during the war had worked as a stenographer, and in a bank, and as an economist for a Government agency—and when we came out, the total of our savings, from both my law practice, her teaching and all the time that I was in the war, the total for that entire period was just a little less than 10,000 dollars. Every cent of that, incidentally, was in Government bonds. Well that's where we start, when I go into politics.

Now, what have I earned since I went into politics? Well, here it is. I've jotted it down. Let me read the notes. First of all, I've had my salary as a Congressman and as a Senator. Second, I have received a total in this past six years of 1600 dollars from estates which were in my law firm at the time that I severed my connection with it. And, incidentally, as I said before, I have not engaged in any legal practice and have not accepted any fees from business that came into the firm after I went into politics. I have made an average of approximately 1500 dollars a year from nonpolitical speaking engagements and lectures.

In excruciating detail, Nixon goes on to describe their home, their rent, his Oldsmobile, and then he continues:

Well, that's about it. That's what we have. And that's what we owe. It isn't very much. But Pat and I have the satisfaction that every dime that we've got is honestly ours. I should say this, that Pat doesn't have a mink coat. But she does have a respectable Republican cloth coat, and I always tell her she'd look good in anything.

One other thing I probably should tell you, because if I don't they'll probably be saying this about me, too. We did get something, a gift, after the election. A man down in Texas heard Pat on the radio mention the fact that our two youngsters would like to have a dog. And believe it or not, the day before we left on this campaign trip we got a message from Union Station in Baltimore, saying they had a package for us. We went down to get it. You know what it was? It was a little cocker spaniel dog in a crate that he'd sent all the way from Texas, black and white, spotted. And our little girl Tricia, the six-year-old, named it "Checkers." And you know, the kids, like all kids, love the dog, and I just want to say this, right now, that regardless of what they say about it, we're gonna keep it.

Pundits hated it. The legendary journalist and commentator Walter Lippmann felt it was overpopularizing the political process. Robert Ruark, who was a columnist for the Scripps-Howard news service, wrote, "Dick Nixon stripped himself naked for all the world to see, and he brought the missus and kids and the dog and his war record into the act." (To be fair, Ruark also evinced some sympathy for Nixon, pointing out that it was the speech of a "little man struggling" to save his career.) Tom Wicker, a Nixon biographer, wrote that the speech was "a sort of comic and demeaning public striptease that cast Nixon forever as a vulgar political trickster . . . exploiting his wife and his children's dog to grub votes." And this was before Nixon made an appearance a couple of years later on NBC's *Tonight Show,* which author Jeffrey Frank described in his book *Ike and Dick* as providing "a glimpse of a low-rent future in which solemn politicians unashamedly went on comedy shows." (Again, to be fair, Nixon's "performance" on *The Tonight Show* was hardly undignified; he played a piano concerto he had written himself.)

Nixon was disappointed with his performance as well, not because of his message but because he mistimed his closing. His goal was to get people to write to the Republican National Committee, and tell them whether he should stay on the ticket (thus defying Eisenhower's request for him to step down and taking the decision out of Eisenhower's hands); but he had forgotten to mention the address. Upon leaving the stage, he threw his notes to the floor, saying, "I loused it up."

But the audience loved it and responded in huge numbers. By one account, some four million responses were sent. Three hundred thousand of them made it to the Republican National Committee, and they ran 350–1 in Nixon's favor.

Eisenhower ultimately re-embraced Nixon, at least publicly, and the Eisenhower-Nixon ticket marched on to victory.

While the major facts of the Checkers speech were true, most of the details about the dog weren't. Checkers wasn't a surprise, the dog didn't show up in Baltimore, and Nixon had barely met the pooch when he gave the speech.

Still, the dog, the references to his family, the transparency about his home and financial life, these things, according to Lee Huebner, who wrote speeches in the Nixon White House and later went on to be the publisher of the *International Herald Tribune,* "foreshadowed the emergence of a new conservative populism in America, emphasizing appeals to social and cultural 'identity' rather than economic interest."

Journalist Murray Kempton summed it up, uncharitably but accurately, "The Fifties were not the Eisenhower years but the Nixon years. That was the decade when the American lower middle class in the person of this man moved to engrave into the history of the United States, as the voice of America, its own faltering spirit, its self-pity and its envy."

There was indeed a silent majority, they heard Nixon loud and clear, and they rallied to his defense.

Twenty-two years later, here was Nixon again, dealing with another scandal. And Nixon again wanted to make his case directly to the people. When he changed his mind on resigning, most of his inner circle did, too. This worried Price. He felt that Nixon's closest advisors were simply echoing the president, not advising him. Price was concerned that there was no path to political survival for Nixon and that the only way for him to leave with dignity was to leave directly. He registered his dissent with Haig, the chief of staff, and then "went back to my office upset, distraught, shifting gears to write the speech I thought would be a disastrous mistake."

One of the questions I'm often asked is whether I've ever had to write a speech for someone I disagreed with. While I've had the luxury of choosing to write for those whom I agree with and admire, there have been moments where people whom I admire wanted to make statements with which I disagreed.

When the attacks of September 11, 2001, occurred, I was working for Senate majority leader Tom Daschle. Legislative ideas were coming at us fast and furious; everything from an (overly expansive) use-of-force resolution authorizing the president to deploy the military against those responsible for the attacks, to an (again, overly expansive) Patriot Act, which sought to enable unlimited surveillance of Americans in the name of national security. In every instance, Senator Daschle diligently tried to limit and temper any overreach; not an easy task at a time of great national pain and passion. But a reality of politics is that it's incredibly hard to fight every fight, especially with so much incoming.

One of the ideas that came up was to allow airline pilots to carry guns in the cockpit. I remember asking Senator Daschle where we stood on it. Daschle was a licensed pilot and had served in the Air National Guard. He told me that when you're trained as a pilot and something is going on in your plane, your only job is to get the plane safely to the ground. The last thing you want to do is be a cowboy, and here he made a finger pistol and mimicked firing backward as he continued to face forward. Also, he added, imagine what a misfired gun could do on a pressurized aircraft. "So we're against it?" I asked. He sighed and said, "No, we're for it."

I remember once asking one of my mentors, the famed political strategist James Carville, how I could write a speech arguing for something that I personally thought was wrongheaded. "Here's how," he replied with characteristic brusqueness. "You can write a speech you don't love for someone you agree with 90 percent of the time who can get 51 percent of the vote . . . or you can find someone you agree with 100 percent of the time and write nothing for them, because they can't hire you, because they only got 49 percent of the vote."

I wrote the speech, though Daschle thankfully didn't give it. Instead, he worked to ensure that pilots would have to undergo specialized training if they wanted to carry guns, and to add a rule that pilots had to lock the cockpit door when flying, and made a host of other changes that would limit the chance that a gun would actually be fired on a commercial aircraft. In retrospect, it was masterful legislating. Then, along with eighty-six of his colleagues, he voted for the bill.

Our political climate doesn't allow for much nuance in our debate. Was this a "pro-gun" vote? To me, it still was. But when it came time to put words to paper on behalf of the person who actually had to vote on the issue, I was able to convince myself that it wasn't. That was my job, and I'm grateful that it has only been infrequently that I've had to write with my mind and not with my heart.*

---

* That's not been the case for everyone. I have always admired the courage of former Robert Kennedy aide Peter Edelman and Mary Jo Bane, who both resigned from the Department of Health and Human Services in 1996 over what they saw as the cruelty of welfare reform legislation Bill Clinton agreed to sign.

Ray Price had now been handed an assignment he felt was ill advised. And President Nixon wanted to see him at Camp David the next day. So Price wrote a non-resignation draft.

He also wrote what he called "Option B"—a resignation draft that he thought could help persuade Nixon to resign by guessing at some language that he hoped "was somewhere close to the truth of the matter."

This is something speechwriters are often forced to do. The job requires you to channel your boss, becoming a Method actor who inhabits that person. I almost always hear the voice of whomever I'm writing for in my head as I write. But hearing their voice in *your* head doesn't mean you know exactly what's in *theirs*. That's why, as part of the speechwriting process, my colleagues and I insist on interviewing the principal. When that's not possible, you have to make a best guess. That's what Ray Price did here, hoping he would tap into a truth that Nixon, upon seeing, would be forced to acknowledge.

Knowing the best version of Nixon was the most plainspoken one, Price wrote,

> I thought the break in itself was stupid, as well as wrong. But once it had taken place, I knew that I had inherited the consequences— and that with the presidency at issue, those potential consequences reached out also to the nation and the world.
>
> In retrospect, it would have been better to have explained this fully and frankly when Watergate and the cover-up again became a national issue early last year—at a time when the cover-up had reached dimensions that I did not fully comprehend. Instead, I felt trapped by events and chose a different way of attempting to defend what I believe to be in the interests of the presidency, and to preserve my capacity to function in what I believed to be in the interests of the nation.
>
> I say this not in defense, but in explanation.

The draft also attempts to remind listeners of Nixon's accomplishments. In particular, he argues that the real abuse of power were the protests and riots that convulsed the nation in the early 1970s.

> We have heard much about what was called the abuse of power— and in particular about the measures I took in 1969, 1970, 1971

to deal with what I considered serious threats to the nation's security and well-being. From the relative calm of today's conditions, it is easy to look back and to condemn the remedy without regard for the ill it was meant to cure. It is easy to forget the burning cities, the ravaged campuses, the college deans barricaded in their office, the orgy of riots and mass, violent demonstrations that were designed to and did strike terror across the nation. These were not democracy in action. These were brutal and dangerous assaults against the Democratic System.

The Option B speech concludes with the words,

There is a time to fight, and a time to leave. At each step of the way, I have tried to serve what I believed to be the best interests of the country. When I believed that those interests would best be served by fighting to retain office, I fought to retain it. Now I believe they would best be served by my leaving office—and so I shall leave.

The Option B speech is not structured at all like Nixon's ultimate resignation; it begins with a resignation, and then offers a long explanation as to why that resignation shouldn't have been necessary. Nixon's ultimate resignation speech spends very little time justifying or even discussing the Watergate scandal.

At the same time, Price did have a job to do, and so he also penned the requested speech in which Nixon refused to resign. Like the Checkers speech, it, too, presents a sort of striptease, putting both assets and liabilities into the open. For example, the text doesn't shy away from what would have been the most incriminating piece of information. Price's draft has Nixon saying, "I also want to tell you about one new piece of evidence I have discovered, which I recognize will not be helpful to my case."

And while, or perhaps because, Nixon's personal defense sounds so insufficient, Price makes his impeachment about something larger; he makes it about governmental stability, arguing that an assassination (JFK) followed by a president so hounded that he chose not to seek re-election (LBJ) followed by a resignation (Nixon) would be an abdication of our responsibility to the world.

It's not a great argument, but it was the best Price had, and so he went with it.

Good Evening.

With the deliberations of the House Judiciary Committee completed and its recommendations awaiting action by the full House of Representatives, questions have been raised about my own plans for dealing with the impeachment issue.*

I have requested this time in order to tell you how I intend to proceed.

Debate on the committee's impeachment recommendations is scheduled to begin on the House floor two weeks from today—on Aug. 19.

In the wake of the Judiciary Committee's action, there has been a very substantial erosion of the political base that I would need in order to sustain my position in the House of Representatives. Therefore, at this time it appears almost a foregone conclusion that one or more articles of impeachment will be voted by the House, and that the matter will go to a trial in the Senate. . . .

It is not my purpose tonight to argue my case. There will be time for that later. Rather, I want to explain how I intend to proceed.

I also want to tell you about one new piece of evidence I have discovered, which I recognize will not be helpful to my case—but which I have instructed my attorneys to make available immediately to the Judiciary Committee. . . .

In the past several days, I have been engaged in an intensive review of the 64 taped conversations covered by the Special Prosecutor's subpoena and the Supreme Court's recent order that they be turned over to Judge Sirica. With one exception, I have found that they bear out what I said on April 29 when I announced my decision to make public the original transcripts: that the evidence I have turned over to the Judiciary Committee tells the full story

---

* "Questions have been raised" is a prime example of the passive voice, which is discussed in chapter 8.

of Watergate, insofar as the President's knowledge or involvement is concerned. These 64 additional tapes are being turned over to Judge Sirica. . . . As they become public, which they undoubtedly will, the truth of this will be evident.

The one exception is a conversation I held with H. R. Haldeman on June 23, 1972, which concerns my instructions with regard to coordination between the F.B.I. and the C.I.A. In reviewing the tape it is now clear to me that Mr. Haldeman and I did discuss the political aspects of the situation, and that we were fully aware of the advantages this course of action would have with respect to limiting the possible public exposure of involvement by persons connected with the re-election committee. Because this conversation took place just a few days after the break-in, I know it will be widely interpreted as evidence that I was involved from the outset in efforts at cover-up.

Let me take a moment to explain why I did not make this public sooner, although I should have. In May of this year I began a review of the 64 tapes subpoenaed by the Special Prosecutor, but then postponed completing it pending the decision that was finally handed down 12 days ago by the Supreme Court. In the course of that earlier partial review I listened to this tape, but did not focus on it thoroughly. I did not at the time consider it inconsistent with my past statements, nor did I have transcripts made or advise my staff or counsel about any possible concern with it.

I now recognize this as having been a serious mistake, because as a result of it my counsel, my staff, and others, including members of the Judiciary Committee, who defended my position did so on the basis of facts that were incomplete. . . .

Let me turn now to the future.

There has been a great deal of speculation that I would resign, rather than face trial by the Senate. Some cite the erosion of my political base, and say that this either dims or dooms my chances in the Senate. Some cite the costs to the nation of more months of distraction and uncertainty. Some say I should not see the Constitutional process through, because even if vindicated by the Senate I would be so weakened politically that I could not govern effectively for the remainder of my term.

Some suggest that if I persevere, I am not only ignoring what they consider the inevitable outcome, but doing so at considerable political risk.

Indeed, when I reviewed the June 23 tape, and realized the interpretations that will probably be placed on it, I seriously considered resigning.

I have thought long and hard about all of these questions. . . . I have explored the questions thoroughly with my family. They share in my belief that the Constitutional process must not be aborted or short-circuited—that having begun, it must be carried through to its conclusion, that is, through a fair trial in the Senate. . . .

If I were to resign, it would spare the country additional months consumed with the ordeal of a Presidential impeachment and trial.

But it would leave unresolved the questions that have already cost the country so much in anguish, division and uncertainty. More important, it would leave a permanent crack in our Constitutional structure: it would establish the principle that under pressure, a President could be removed from office by means short of those provided by the Constitution. By establishing that principle, it would invite such pressures on every future President who might, for whatever reason, fall into a period of unpopularity. . . .

Whatever the mistakes that have been made—and they are many—and whatever the measure of my own responsibility for those mistakes, I firmly believe that I have not committed any act of commission or omission that justifies removing a duly elected President from office. If I did believe that I had committed such an act, I would have resigned long ago. . . .

For me to see this through will have costs for the country in the short run. The months ahead will not be easy for any of us. But in the long run—whatever the outcome—the results will be a more stable form of government. Far more damaging than the ordeal of a Senate trial, far more damaging that even the conviction and removal of a President, would be the descent toward chaos if Presidents could be removed short of impeachment and trial.

Throughout the Western world, governmental instability has

reached almost epidemic proportions. . . . In the United States, within the last dozen years one President was assassinated; the next was in effect driven from office when he did not even seek re-election; and now the third stands on the verge of impeachment by the House of Representatives, confronted with calls for his resignation in order to make the process of removal easy.

This country bears enormous responsibilities to itself and to the world. If we are to meet those responsibilities in this and future Presidencies, we must not let this office be destroyed—or let it fall such easy prey to those who would exult in the breaking of the President that the game becomes a national habit.

Therefore, I shall see the Constitutional process through—whatever its outcome.

I shall appear before the Senate, and answer under oath before the Senate any and all questions put to me there.

At the same time, having developed the draft, Price then developed his two main arguments against it, arguments he hoped to make to Al Haig and to Nixon himself. Why give a prime-time national address to state that he would fight on, even in light of new evidence that looked bad for him? Wouldn't a prime-time address be better used to temper the reaction to that new evidence after it was released? Also, didn't a pledge to see the fight through a Senate trial unnecessarily limit Nixon's options?

Still, it was the best draft he could write. When Nixon's advisors arrived at Camp David, Nixon summoned his chief of staff, Al Haig, for a private meeting, leaving Price and the others to cool their heels in a cabin nearby. When Haig returned, Nixon's strategy had changed. No resignation, yet. But also, no speech.

Price's draft wouldn't be seen for another twenty-two years.

On August 6, 1974, two high-wire acts were in motion. In New York, Philippe Petit was finalizing his preparations to pull off the "artistic crime of the century," surreptitiously stringing a wire between New York's Twin Towers that he would walk the next morning. And in Washington, Nixon was assuring his cabinet that he would fight on and that resigning would be "outside the Constitution."

But by that point, Nixon knew his act was ending. Even as *The Washington Post* was going to press with a banner headline, NIXON SAYS HE WON'T RESIGN, Nixon had already made his decision. Shortly after 4:00 p.m., Price was summoned to Al Haig's office. As he recounted in his memoir, Haig's request was simple:

"We'll need a thousand words."

"He's finally decided?"

"Yes."

Price wrote a draft that evening, so the president could have it the next morning. It was far different from the original Option B speech he had drafted just four days earlier. It is less defensive and more reflective, recognizing that "the interest of the nation must always come before any personal considerations." It celebrates accomplishments like opening diplomatic relations with China and reminds Americans that his life "as a Congressman, a Senator, a Vice President, and President" has been a life of service.

Price attached to the draft a cover memo addressed to Nixon personally, dated August 7, 1974.

"A first draft is attached. I'll be working on additional thoughts for it. As I believe you know, I think this has become a sad but necessary decision in the circumstance. But I do hope you'll leave office as proud of your accomplishments here as I am proud to have been associated with them, and to have been and remain a friend. God bless you; and He will."

Boston, September 14, 1974. (AP photo)

5

Mayor Kevin White on School Busing,
December 1974

The Rhetorical Technique of Litany

"There is no odor, save death, worse than that of a
public official too frightened and fearful to say, above
a whisper, what he honestly believes."

Driving his Ford Mustang, unaccompanied by his standard detail of
police protection, Boston mayor Kevin White pulled up to the home of
state senator Billy Bulger. It was 1:30 in the morning on Monday, September 16, 1974. White's chief of staff, Ira Jackson, stayed in the car as
White went inside. Already inside were city councilwoman Louise Day
Hicks and state representative Michael Flaherty. The mayor wanted to
talk about a threat he and his staff had caught wind of.

The city of Boston had experienced its first two days of court-
mandated busing to integrate the city's schools the week prior. In the
initial phase of busing, ordered by district court judge Arthur Garrity,
white students would be bused from South Boston to integrate predominantly Black Roxbury, and Black students would make the opposite

trip to integrate predominantly white South Boston. The first two days had not gone well; chaos ruled, several buses had been damaged, and six students and one police officer had been injured. Now the word on the street was that on Monday of the first full week of school (later that very morning), Boston's notorious Irish American Mullen Gang intended to co-opt a planned anti-busing march and get violent, potentially even trying to shoot and kill Black students.

The mayor had reason to believe the threat was real. Earlier that summer, a fire was set at an elementary school about half a mile from Judge Garrity's home in the affluent suburb of Wellesley. Earlier that week, a Molotov cocktail had been thrown through the back window of the John F. Kennedy National Historic Site, the late president's childhood home, and the words *Bus Teddy*—in reference to Senator Ted Kennedy's support of integration—had been scrawled on the sidewalk. Whitey Bulger, an organized crime boss who, along with the Mullen Gang, ruled over South Boston, was rumored to be behind both attacks.

Billy Bulger, Whitey's state senator brother, was no fan of busing himself, but had a slightly more intellectual argument against busing. Like many, he leaned on one conclusion from the influential and controversial 1964 federal report led by sociologist James Coleman, known as the Coleman Report, which found that socioeconomic standing—class—was the key determinant of student success. Therefore, he argued, it did no good to bus lower-income white kids to swap places with lower-income Black kids.

Regardless, the mayor hadn't shown up at the Bulger home to debate policy; he was there to stop a riot. The meeting's other two attendees proved expectedly unhelpful. City councilwoman Louise Day Hicks and state representative Michael Flaherty said they had nothing to do with the march. No matter, Mayor White was there to get word to the senator's older brother that the FBI was being mobilized, and if, later that morning or that week, any gang member took it upon himself to get violent or interfere with busing, the FBI would come down on them with the full force of the federal government.

While the threat of FBI involvement may have been effective, White wasn't exactly sure if he was bluffing. When rumor of the threat made it to his office, Mayor White first called Speaker of the United States House of Representatives Tip O'Neill, asking O'Neill to get in touch with President Gerald Ford to ask him to put the Eighty-Second Airborne—the same army unit that had helped quell the 1967 riots in Detroit—on standby. The answer from Ford, whose disagreement with Judge Garrity's order became a rallying point for the antibusing movement, was no.

White asked Ira Jackson to call Judge Garrity at his home, to request that federal marshals get involved. That way, if Black children's rights were violated in any way, it would be a violation of federal civil rights law, punishable as a federal felony, and not a twenty-five-dollar misdemeanor fine in the South Boston district court. Garrity's wife picked up the phone, and Jackson relayed the message. In a demonstration of how truly toxic relations between the mayor's office and the judge had become, Mrs. Garrity returned to the phone to tell Jackson, "My husband told me to tell you that if you ever call him at home again, he will hold you in contempt of court."

White fumed: "That stupid son of a bitch, he issues his damn order then retires to his suburban estate and refuses to talk with the only guy who can make it work."

Bob Kiley, the former CIA operative who had become White's deputy mayor, called Clarence Kelley, the FBI director, to ask his help as well. It wasn't clear how responsive the FBI was going to be.

And so, at 2:30 a.m., White left Billy Bulger's house with no choice but to stop the rally himself. The next few days would have a lot to say about the future of the city of Boston and Mayor White's prospects for reelection. And in a matter of months, Mayor White would have to face the city council and deliver his report on the state of the city.

For nearly a decade, the racial imbalance in Boston's schools, described in legal terminology as de facto (segregation by preference, prejudice, and social norms) rather than de jure segregation (segregation by law), had been declared illegal under the Massachusetts legislature's 1965 Racial Imbalance Act. Ever since that law's passage, the Boston School Committee had disobeyed orders from the state board of education to develop and then implement a busing plan. One of the reasons the school committee was able to do this was that Boston had a five-member school committee, and rather than representing districts, every member was "at large," representing the entire city. Historically, that had meant five white, mostly Irish, members.

In 1972, the NAACP filed a lawsuit on behalf of fourteen Black parents and forty-four Black students against James Hennigan, the chairman of the school board. The plaintiffs, headed by Tallulah Morgan, a Black mother of three, argued that "the city and state had consistently denied black children equal opportunities to a public education by intentionally creating and maintaining a segregated educational system."

On June 21, 1974, Garrity issued his decision. He found that the Boston School Committee had "knowingly carried out a systematic program of segregation affecting all of the city's students, teachers, and school facilities and have intentionally brought about and maintained a dual school system. Therefore, the entire school system of Boston is unconstitutionally segregated."

But the fifteen months Garrity had spent writing his decision left only three months before the start of school to actually enact it.

That task fell to Charles Glenn, the state director of the Bureau of Equal Educational Opportunities. In his description, recounted in J. Anthony Lukas's Pulitzer Prize–winning history, *Common Ground,* "We simply took a large map and started moving across the city in a big arc from northwest to southeast, dividing it into districts so that each school would include the right proportions of Black and white kids. When we got to the end of the arc, we were left with South Boston and Roxbury. We didn't have any choice but to mix those two neighborhoods."

The effect would be to bus students from one of Boston's most cloistered white enclaves to the heart of its Black community, and vice versa. Although eighty schools and eighteen thousand students were affected by the overall redistricting, the pairing of South Boston and Roxbury was destined to be a flash point, forcing together two of the communities that were most isolated, both racially and geographically, from one another. To many, it seemed both a plan and a punishment; a slap in the face to the bigots on the Boston School Committee who had been so hostile to busing. Ira Jackson saw Garrity as a latter-day Cotton Mather, vengeful, self-righteous, and determined "to exact his pound of flesh, almost like the pillory stocks on Boston Common."

Or perhaps it was, in the colorful analogy of Dr. William Reid, South Boston High School's headmaster, "like the hostage system of the Middle Ages, whereby the princes of opposing crowns were kept in rival kings' courts as a preventive against war."

Rather than preventing a war, the plan further inflamed one. That summer, Judge Garrity gave the school committee a chance to offer a modified plan, but the committee refused to submit any plan that required busing. Meanwhile, Garrity refused to comment on, or even admit reviewing with any depth, the plan his decision was about to put into effect.

The mayor and his team got to work as best they could to prepare the city for what was about to happen. And to make matters worse, 1974 opening day was only phase 1 of the court-ordered plan. Phase 2 would go into effect the following year and touch the even more homogenous ethnic enclaves of Charlestown and East Boston, which White described as "heavily Irish and Italian communities with powerful neighborhood identities and deep-seated xenophobia." *The New York Times* described Charlestown as "an isolated, mile-square neighborhood that makes 'Southie' look almost cosmopolitan by comparison."

All summer, the city had tried to lay the groundwork for busing, with the mayor hosting over one hundred community coffees and sunset teas in living rooms and community centers throughout the city, meeting with over two thousand parents. The city had hired hundreds of extra crossing guards to guide and protect students. And three days before the start of school, the mayor had given a televised address, pleading with all Bostonians to recognize that "the city has exhausted all avenues of appeal . . . the judge's finding stands. It cannot be refuted; it can no longer be appealed . . . and it must and will be carried out." White enumerated what he saw as the problems with the ruling, but then, referencing Nixon's resignation a month earlier, continued, "But it is now the law. And as the traumatic events of the past several months in Washington have shown all of us, we are a government of laws, and not of men. No man, not even the president, stands above that law. And no city or group within it, can stand in defiance of that law." He reminded his listeners that "compliance with the law does not mean acceptance of it, and that tolerance does not mean endorsement." He beseeched the city not to be "polarized by race or paralyzed by fear" and to "not forget for even a moment our responsibilities to the children who stand to lose the most from disruption and violence."

It was a powerful statement.

At the same time, and even on that same day, the mayor's work and his statements were actively being countered by anti-busing groups like Restore Our Alienated Rights (ROAR), local elected officials like Ray

Flynn, a hometown basketball hero who had been elected to represent South Boston in the state house (and who would later go on to be elected mayor of Boston), and the school board itself. They referred to Mayor White as "Mayor Black," and at every turn, they sought to undercut his efforts to prepare for busing by arguing, even at the last minute, that it could be stopped with legislation from Washington, or rallies, or boycotts, or a combination of the three.

September 12, opening day for the Boston's public schools, dawned mild and clear. Children put on new outfits and headed for their buses. In Roxbury, Black parents gathered to welcome and greet white children as they got off the buses at their new schools.

Those buses were nearly empty: in response to calls to boycott, nearly half of the city's white students stayed home.

It was a different scene in South Boston. The plan was for the buses to pick up the children on their routes in Roxbury and then drive to a vacant shopping mall where they would line up and then head to South Boston together, as a single motorcade.

Helicopters buzzed overhead as the buses approached South Boston, where crowds had already gathered, holding signs and bananas, and chanting "Niggers go home" and, as if it were a sporting event, "Here we go, Southie, here we go." When the buses approached the schools, the crowd surged into the street, blocking the buses and throwing bricks. Children screamed as bus windows shattered and glass rained down on them, and protesters tried to get into the back door of one of the buses.

Some buses were forced to divert to Andrew Station, the MBTA train stop, where medics assembled to attend to any students who had been cut by flying glass and where police assembled to escort the buses on a second attempt to get to the school.

Ultimately, the buses were able to approach the front door of South Boston High, where the students filed inside, both observed and protected by a gauntlet of news cameras and police officers. Many in the crowd outside the school were high schoolers who should have been in school themselves. The headmaster, William Reid, urged them to go home or get into school.

Ira Jackson was on-site that day as Mayor White's eyes and ears. As this all unfolded, he radioed to let the mayor know the good news: nobody had been killed.

The ride home would be even uglier. Crowds again gathered in front of South Boston schools, angrier, louder, and, in many cases, drunk. They pelted the buses with rocks and cans. Some of the Black students, who had been terrified earlier in the day, now felt emboldened, giving the crowd the finger and yelling back, "We're in your school now!"

The crowd cursed, surged at, and eventually overran the police who were assigned to protect the students. Many of the police officers were their friends and neighbors. When people in the crowd identified police officers they knew, they screamed at them to quit.

By the end of the school day, six students and one police officer had been injured, and six buses were damaged.

That evening, the mayor announced that anyone disrupting students, buses, or traffic would be arrested. Groups of more than three people would be forbidden to gather near public schools, and police would escort all buses in and out of South Boston.

He then went to a gathering of Black parents in the Grove Hall neighborhood, between Roxbury and Dorchester. The violence had been beyond what any of them had expected. They blamed the mayor and the police for failing to protect their children. Now they were threatening a boycott. The mayor asked for them to give him one more day, one more chance to get things right.

Despite all of this, the next day's headline in *The Boston Globe* was BOSTON SCHOOLS DESEGREGATED, OPENING DAY GENERALLY PEACEFUL.

Citywide, that was true. But inside and outside the schools in South Boston, it certainly was not the case.

The violence of day one resulted in a second day of school that saw fewer than four hundred students out of an enrollment of four thousand show up. There were more people in the streets of Southie than in the schools. And now, after these initial two days of school, the mayor faced the fear that rather than settling things down, the upcoming weekend was giving the most violent anti-busing forces time to gather and organize a march for the Monday of school's first full week. While church leaders were using Sunday services to tell people not to march, the Mullen Gang and others were telling people to show up. Sound trucks were driving around South Boston echoing the call. Rumors about guns and gangs and vans full of Molotov cocktails were swirling. This was the toxic situation that had brought Mayor White to Senator Bulger's house. And upon leaving in those early-morning hours, it's what forced his decision to do everything in his power to shut down the march. As White said to police superintendent Joe Jordan: "Tomorrow's test is not whether Southie gets over its temper tantrum, but whether we're gonna have a long-term problem like Belfast." Ira Jackson called it D-day.

White made his decision: the bars would be closed on Monday.* The police would move in on the neighborhood with force. Helicopters looked for gathering crowds, and then police, sometimes with dogs, would come in and break them up. Bricks and rocks were thrown, arrests were made, skirmishes raged all day. At the end of the day, twenty-two people had been arrested, nine people, including three police officers, had been injured, and one police officer suffered a heart attack and would die a few weeks later.

But there had been no shooting, no Molotov cocktails, no children killed. And that was enough to call the day a success.

As the city settled into its new busing routine, South Boston continued its battle. Teachers were breaking up ten to fifteen fights a day. Airport-style metal detectors had been installed in school.

And then on December 11, one of the in-school fights resulted in a white student named Michael Faith being stabbed. As the ambulance arrived, rumors flew through the neighborhood that he had died (he didn't). Immediately, a crowd gathered outside the school, angry and violent.

By coincidence, the state police unit that would have normally been posted at the school had reported to a prison uprising in Walpole that morning, and the sixty policemen on duty were soon outnumbered ten to one. White students were ordered out of the school, which had the effect of swelling the crowd further.

One police cruiser was smashed and another flipped over, and the police ordered the school not to evacuate the Black students until reinforcements arrived. Police on horses and motorcycles tried to break up the crowd, and fights broke out. Meanwhile, the more than 130 Black students would remain trapped inside for nearly four hours.

---

* Some defied the order.

Two additional ambulances arrived for people who had been injured in the skirmishes. *The New York Times* described what happened next: "Suddenly, the young driver of the lead ambulance pitched over, struck in the head by a rock. The police bundled him into the back of his own ambulance and someone else drove it off. 'Niggers, niggers,' people in the crowd shrieked at the police. 'You protect the nigger children and look what you do to the whites.'"

Ultimately, in order to evacuate the Black students, decoy buses were sent to the front of the school to attract the crowd's attention. Students were instead evacuated out of a side door to board a separate group of buses around the back.

Superintendent William Leary ordered the school closed for the remainder of the week. That closure would last through Christmas and into the new year.

That news overshadowed another event that occurred on the same day: Roslindale High School, in a part of town that had once been part of Roxbury, was closed when six hundred students attempted to walk out.

Two weeks later, three members of the Boston School Committee formed a majority in blocking approval of a citywide school desegregation plan, a stand that risked them being held in contempt of court.

Ira Jackson called it "our Selma." White again invoked Belfast, reportedly telling an aide, "Sometimes when I look out this window, I see Belfast out there."

Whatever your geographic or historical analogy, this was the situation in Boston's schools as Mayor White began preparing his eighth annual State of the City address, to be delivered three weeks later, on January 6.

In approaching the speech, Mayor White faced two realities. The first was that he was dealing with a court order, one that was final, irrevocable, and had to be enforced by the city. The second, as he would later tell a reporter from *U.S. News & World Report,* was that "eighty percent of the people in Boston are against busing. If Boston were a sovereign state, busing would be cause for revolution."

In fact, that September, Judge Garrity had named White himself as a codefendant in the busing case; a response to White speaking publicly about how hard it would be to implement the busing plan. The judge seemed to see language like that as encouraging school boycotts.

In reality, however, White was a true progressive, and to be lumped into the suit alongside an intransigent school committee was a stinging insult. For a time in 1972, he had been George McGovern's preferred choice as his vice presidential running mate. In addition to being a progressive idealist, White was a savvy political operator. In the summer leading up to the first phase of busing, he had been trying to notify the judge that the plan needed changes and to bring disaffected whites into some sort of brokered deal.

Though White admitted that he had been against busing in the past, he was doing his damnedest to enforce the judge's order—and he saw himself as the one guy who could make it work.

But as he sat down to write his State of the City address, he was no longer sure. He was beleaguered, taking heat and verbal abuse from all sides. It had now been nearly half a year of late nights, tense community meetings, and angry parents. During an interview with *The Boston Globe* that September, yawning from yet another late-night meeting, White admitted, "I didn't think that it would be this tough on me physically. I didn't think the political leadership in South Boston would lose control as rapidly, nor did I expect South Boston to resist as long as it did."

The mayor had never seen the schools as his primary responsibility; that's what the school board was for. And when proposals were put before the voters that year to abolish or reform the school board and give the mayor greater control, they had chosen to keep the board as it was. Beyond that, White had other problems to deal with. The economy was struggling, and crime was on the rise. He had always seen public safety as his primary responsibility, and the last few months had shown that it was becoming increasingly difficult to keep students, citizens, the media, and even his own police safe.

What message should he deliver? And how would he handle the divisive issue of busing?

Cullen Murphy, the former editor of *The Atlantic,* observed that first drafts are often acts of catharsis, not meant to see the light of day. President Lincoln's letter to General George Meade after Meade failed to pursue Robert E. Lee's army following the Battle of Gettysburg is one famous example. Lincoln wrote, in what would be considered a scorching hot take today, "I do not believe you appreciate the magnitude of Lee's escape. He was within your easy grasp, and to have closed upon him would, in connection with our other late successes, have ended the war . . . Your golden opportunity is gone, and I am distressed immeasurably because of it." Lincoln never signed or sent the letter. President Truman, too, was famous for writing missives that were never launched at their targets. Historian David McCullough writes, "He called them his longhand spasms, and there appears to have been something sudden and involuntary about them. They seemed to serve some deep psychological need, as a vent for his anger, and were seldom intended for anyone to see."

White, too, seemed be seeking catharsis as he wrote the first draft of his State of the City address. But in this case, he appeared to also have been prepared to follow through, with staff having done at least some of the groundwork that would be required to implement his policies.

As he prepared the draft, the first thing he decided to do was to make the audience wait for his thoughts on busing. He wanted to use the anticipation to get them to listen to his plans on crime prevention (crime in Boston had spiked the previous year and was the subject of nearly as much attention and concern as busing), his ideas to "relieve the hardships imposed by the national economic crisis," and his plans to keep taxes low. Then he planned to turn to the question of busing, and intended to announce several steps that could have changed Boston history forever.

To set the tone, he began by decrying "suburban liberals . . . who view busing as the solution to racial balance—as long as it stays inside the city."

From there, he wanted to announce that he had hired legal counsel to represent the segregationist Boston School Committee, and he was prepared to name the distinguished constitutional scholar Philip Kurland to appeal Judge Garrity's ruling to the Supreme Court, and to request a stay of the busing order until the Supreme Court rendered a decision.

He further wanted to announce that he was directing the city to fund the Home and School Association, an organization of parents that had traditionally taken a conservative approach to the schools, in helping that organization limit busing dramatically. In the words of the mayor's draft, "to ensure that court-imposed remedies be limited to areas where intentional constitutional violations occurred." Hiding behind this legal language was a seismic change. De jure segregation (segregation by law)

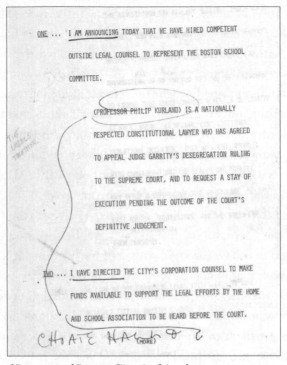

ONE ... I AM ANNOUNCING TODAY THAT WE HAVE HIRED COMPETENT

OUTSIDE LEGAL COUNSEL TO REPRESENT THE BOSTON SCHOOL

COMMITTEE.

(PROFESSOR PHILIP KURLAND) IS A NATIONALLY

RESPECTED CONSTITUTIONAL LAWYER WHO HAS AGREED

TO APPEAL JUDGE GARRITY'S DESEGREGATION RULING

TO THE SUPREME COURT, AND TO REQUEST A STAY OF

EXECUTION PENDING THE OUTCOME OF THE COURT'S

DEFINITIVE JUDGEMENT.

TWO ... I HAVE DIRECTED THE CITY'S CORPORATION COUNSEL TO MAKE

FUNDS AVAILABLE TO SUPPORT THE LEGAL EFFORTS BY THE HOME

AND SCHOOL ASSOCIATION TO BE HEARD BEFORE THE COURT.

(MORE)

(Courtesy of Boston City Archives)

had been declared illegal under the Massachusetts legislature's 1965 Racial Imbalance Act. The entire court case had been decided on the idea that there was de facto segregation, segregation by custom rather than intent. The mayor was arguing that the court could only act in areas where there was de jure segregation, which was nowhere. The distinction was a key one. As former secretary of defense and CIA director Leon Panetta, who early in his career served as the director of the Office of Civil Rights under President Nixon, said, "The old bugaboo of keeping federal hands off Northern school systems because they are only de facto segregated, instead of de jure segregation as the result of some official act, is a fraud. . . . There are few if any pure de facto situations. Lift the rock of de facto, and something ugly and discriminatory crawls out from under it."

White seemed to be capitulating to the forces that were streaming out from under the rock. Because his next sentence made clear what he hoped would be a solution: "That argument, coupled with considerations for health and safety, may offer a compelling case to exclude East Boston, Charlestown, and the North End from inclusion in phase II." Essentially,

White wanted to get the neighborhoods that were most opposed to busing, and most likely to be violent, out of the busing equation.

Further, he wanted to propose that Judge Garrity assemble a "citizens
committee" to offer remedies and provide a "mechanism for community
input." White intended to continue, "The state board made an arrogant
mistake when it failed to change the South Boston district upon the
recommendations of its own hearing officer. For the judge to fail now to
reach out for broad-based citizen involvement, would be a serious mistake that could fatally flaw any of his efforts."

Essentially, White was laying the blame for the South Boston violence
at the feet of the judge and threatening that there could be more if Garrity
didn't listen to parents. To White, one must assume, this idea, if enacted,
would have the further benefit of making a judge whom he saw as detached
and aloof take some of the same political heat the mayor was feeling.

Most dramatically, Mayor White was prepared to announce that he
was ordering the permanent closure of South Boston High School, moving most of the students into a different downtown area. Essentially,
this would mean taking South Boston High out of South Boston, in the
hopes that a neighborhood school could be separated from the toxicity of
its neighborhood—a neighborhood that had become all the more toxic
as the police and the community, despite many of the police being from
the community, turned on each other.

White demonstrated the internal conflict he was wrestling with,
writing down a series of "unrecognized truths" that he felt must be acknowledged, including "the truth that rigidity and insensitivity in the
courtroom never justifies intolerance and violence in the classroom" and
"the truth that all too often vehement resistance to court orders leads to
the violent tyranny of mob rule."

A look at the "truths" section of his draft demonstrates an important
trick of speechcraft, called *litany*. Litany is a term that describes a series
of repetitive sentences. The repetition can be at the beginning of the sentence, where it is called *anaphora,* and which we see in our Declaration
of Independence, where King George III's offenses are enumerated in
thirteen sentences that each begin with the words "He has."

The repetition can take place at the end of a sentence, where it is called
epistrophe, and is well exemplified by Barack Obama's 2008 victory speech,
in which he ends five consecutive sentences with the words "Yes, we can."

The human brain is tremendously good at recognizing patterns, and therefore speeches with patterns of language become more engaging and satisfying to listen to. Beyond that, a litany demonstrates to the audience that the speaker has a lot of evidence to marshal to their cause, and allows them to do so clearly.

White is also demonstrating another speechwriting trick, called *bucketing*. He's created a rhetorical bucket—a list of truths—into which he can toss a lot of information without making the speech sound and feel unnecessarily dense.

Over a series of pages and notes, no fewer than eleven "truths" are listed. They range from "the truth that some community leaders, both white and black, are more concerned about headlines than heartaches" to "the truth that this city is no different from any other . . . that bigotry and racial intolerance are wrong."

In listing these "truths," White is trying to achieve a delicate political balance, providing all his various constituencies a "truth" that would feel relevant to them. He's also trying to use a little political sleight of hand, employing the truths to tell everyone that he agrees with them without necessarily taking the actions that would follow from that agreement.

Regardless of the truths enumerated, the truth is that these remarks, if delivered, would have represented a seismic shift in the mayor's attitude toward busing. They would have aligned him with an anti-busing school board, appealed to an anti-busing Supreme Court (a step he ultimately did endorse, in a more measured form), tried to exempt the city's most anti-busing neighborhoods, and, wherever possible, and for good measure, thrown Judge Garrity, for lack of a better term, under the bus.

And yet, when Mayor White stepped into the packed City Council chamber, he delivered a very different message. Gone were the outside counsel, the effort to close South Boston High, the support for the Home and School Association. They were replaced with the softer and more generic promise to "take whatever action necessary to provide education and safety for our children and any action that is in the public interest."

In the final draft, the list of "truths" has been modified and distilled down to seven. Gone are the truths that "phase I is failing because people (we) are excluded from the process of planning, politicians are evasive, and the judge remains rigid and insensitive to community concerns."

Added is the truth that "blacks should be allowed to walk the streets in any section of this city and so shall whites."

Gone is the truth that "phase II is doomed to failure if parents remain outside the process of formulation." Included is the truth that "the law must be obeyed unless and until it is changed."

Gone is the truth that "all too often vehement resistance to court orders, leads to the violent tyranny of mob rule." Added is "the greatest truth of all is that we have the skills, the resources, and the people to honorably resolve . . . this problem."

The shift in tone is dramatic.

Interestingly, the entire discussion of busing had also been moved to the beginning of the speech, instead of the conclusion, where it had been in the earlier draft. This is frequently a debate when crafting speeches, as it clearly was here: Do you lead with the piece that everyone is listening for, or do you end with it? The benefit of ending with the "news" is that the audience is forced to listen to everything else you want to say. The benefit of leading with it is that you "lance the boil" up front, as is said in speechwriting circles. The drawback, as Ira Jackson put it, "is that we wouldn't be able to sustain interest afterwards."

The toughest language from White's first draft that remained in the final cut was the criticism he leveled at other elected officials, who "were so scared of this issue that they'd attend a rally for their own execution if it were big enough."

And in a line in which White may have illuminated his own thinking and steeled his own spine: "There is no odor, save death, worse than that of a public official too frightened and fearful to say, above a whisper, what he honestly believes."

So what changed Kevin White's mind?

In short, smart politics. This might seem counterintuitive, given that the city was 80 percent against busing, but White knew there was something more politically damaging than supporting busing, and that was opposing it in word and being unable to stop it in deed.

As White had said to advisors at the very beginning of Southie's resistance, "I don't like to make threats. If you say it, you have to deliver on it."

In Ira Jackson's words, "We had no credible role or standing with Garrity and felt that we had no leverage to affect his decision making.

So we didn't want to look even less competent or more impotent than we were."

Ultimately, White and his team decided not to call for an exemption they couldn't deliver. "The last thing we wanted to do was raise expectations and look even less capable of delivering public safety and order and tranquility . . . than we already had."

And then, of course, they wanted to continue to walk a fine—though fraying—line. The mayor wanted to give voice to parents and their legitimate concerns, without fanning the flames and suggesting that unconstitutional segregation should continue.

This approach toward busing presaged the approach President Clinton would take toward affirmative action twenty years later: "Mend it, don't end it."

Had White delivered his original draft of his remarks, he would have aligned himself firmly with the loudest, most violent, and most regressive elements in the city. Rather than leaving a progressive legacy, he might have been remembered as a Northern George Wallace, metaphorically standing in the schoolhouse door in defense of segregation.

White's actual remarks didn't make many waves. The next morning's *Boston Globe* led with White's unspecific promise to "take whatever action is necessary to provide education and safety for our children" and his equally nonspecific vow "to hold this city together and to effect a peaceful resolution of our differences."

White was able to do that, but change came slowly. He was elected to another four-year term that November. It was a narrow victory, but one that vindicated White. In 1977, John O'Bryant was elected to the Boston School Board, replacing the anti-busing Pixie Palladino. In 1981, after Boston opted to expand the school board to thirteen members, Jean McGuire was elected. Both were African American. Robert Schwartz, a former education advisor to White, jokes that one of the great unknowns is how many people in South Boston unwittingly voted for those candidates because of their Irish-sounding names.

Those new school board members, combined with a series of new and progressive superintendents from outside the system, began to enact change. In 1982, with the creation of what was called the Boston Compact, business and civic leaders began investing in the city's schools, and all the stakeholders began working to help the schools recover from a truly lost decade.

In 1989, busing ended. Ray Flynn, the anti-busing councilman who was now mayor, teamed up with Boston's first Black superintendent, and switched the city to a "parental choice" pupil-assignment plan.

The legacy of busing is a complicated one and is still being discussed in today's political debates. White flight to suburban and parochial schools accelerated. In 1972, 60 percent of the students in Boston schools were white, 33 percent Black, 5 percent Hispanic, and 2 percent Asian. By 1993, 48 percent of Boston's students were Black, 23 percent were Hispanic, 19 percent white, and 9 percent were Asian. Put another way, Boston schools had gone from 60 percent white to 80 percent minority, ironically making schools more technically "segregated."

Still, by 1981, the headmaster of South Boston High School was able to report that desegregation was no longer a problem. And throughout the city, students of all races were benefiting from greater and more equal investment. Less tangibly, busing opened up the city, exposing different communities to each other and creating more of a unified city and less a cluster of enclaves. One local real estate agent recalls helping an African American member of the Boston Police Department find an apartment. He had joined the force in 1979, so when she suggested South Boston as a possible neighborhood, he was skeptical. But, in 2012, looking at how the neighborhood had changed, he decided Southie was the right place for him. As he signed the lease, he commented, "My parents would not have believed this."

Ira Jackson describes it simply as a story of redemption, a city that, as late as 1980, was predicted to have a future along the lines of Detroit, Michigan, or Camden, New Jersey, or Gary, Indiana. When Mayor White said that Boston would become a world-class city, he was mocked. But today, Boston is just that, in part because a mayor, facing internal doubts and external pressure, had the courage to say, above a whisper, what he honestly believed.

PART 3

Crisis / Crisis Averted

When we look back at historic events, we do so with a sense of certainty: Events happened because they had to happen that way. In retrospect, the outcome seems preordained. What we fail to realize is that there could just have easily been a very different path, and the following speeches give us a peek down that alternate path.

The Duke of Windsor and Wallis Simpson meet Adolf Hitler in a 1937 visit to Germany. (PA Images / Alamy Stock Photo)

6

Edward VIII's Refusal to Abdicate
the Throne, December 1936

Writing for Public Figures
About Their Private Lives

"I am firmly resolved to marry the woman I love, when
she is free to marry me."

In October 1937, Edward, the Duke of Windsor* and his new wife,
Wallis Simpson, against the wishes of British officials, made a trip to
Germany that was treated as a state visit by the Nazi regime. In Berlin,
Edward reviewed military cadets training to serve in the SS. He visited
factories that were helping Germany arm for the coming war, and toured
the Mercedes-Benz factory, delivering the Nazi salute upon his departure

---

* Christened Edward Albert Christian George Andrew Patrick David, he held several titles
over the course of his life: Prince Edward, the Prince of Wales, King Edward VIII, Prince
Edward again, and later the Duke of Windsor. His family and friends called him David. For
simplicity, I refer to him mainly as Edward throughout this chapter.

and calling the Nazi economic model "a miracle." He dined with top Nazi brass, including Joseph Goebbels, Hitler's minister of propaganda, who found Edward sympathetic to the Reich and described him as a "tender seedling of reason." He also spent time with Hitler at the führer's residence in the Bavarian Alps. Although some of the meetings were conducted with translators, Edward spoke German fluently, and felt a deep kinship with the German people and the German cause.*

Had Edward made this visit a year prior, he would have been making it as the King of England. With the deadliest war in human history looming, the king of the nation that was the last bulwark against Hitler in Europe would have been fully on the side of fascism.

It would have been a vastly different war and a vastly different world had Edward not, one year earlier, made the difficult decision to abdicate the throne, leaving his brother, George VI, at the helm of the British Empire when the world descended into war. The decision was so difficult that Edward had prepared a draft of a speech appealing directly to the British people to decide his fate as their monarch. Edward never delivered that speech, and instead became the first English monarch to voluntarily relinquish the throne. Why did he do it? Love.

Edward, to the consternation of his family, had been a serial bachelor, carrying on several affairs with married women. One paramour was Thelma Furness, who, in the words of Conservative politician and author Henry "Chips" Channon, "Americanised him [Edward], making him over-democratic, casual and a little common."

Furness also did something else: she introduced Edward to a friend of hers, Wallis Simpson, the American daughter of a wealthy flour merchant, who was living in England with her second husband, Ernest Aldrich Simpson.

Edward became obsessed with Simpson, "struck by the grace of her carriage and the dignity of her movements," and began bringing her on holidays and gifting her money and jewels. Edward would later write, "I looked upon her as the most independent woman I had ever met, and presently the hope formed that one day I might be able to share my life with her."

---

* As late as the 1960s, Edward claimed, "I never thought Hitler was such a bad chap."

But Simpson was an unacceptable choice for a wife. At the time, the Church of England didn't allow marriage to divorcees with living former spouses, and Wallis had two. George V and Queen Mary referred to her derisively as "that woman" and hoped the romance was an infatuation that would pass. But now Edward had chosen "that woman" over the throne.

On December 10, 1936, Edward and his brothers signed the instrument of abdication.* That afternoon, he had lunch with one of his staunchest allies, Winston Churchill. Churchill was out of power, but just one week earlier had seen, in Edward's refusal to abdicate, a potential path back. It would prove to be a dead end. Churchill's full-throated support of Edward in Parliament resulted in him getting heckled and walking out of Parliament in shame. Now a chastened Churchill, whose role in drafting the King's never-delivered speech refusing to abdicate remains unclear, offered modest suggestions on the abdication remarks Edward was to deliver the next day. As they dined, the Abdication Bill was read and passed in the House of Commons, and was shuttled over to the House of Lords, where it was passed in minutes. Edward was no longer king; all that was left was for him to explain to his subjects why.

Shortly after 9:30 p.m. on December 11, the former king arrived at Windsor Castle, where he was greeted by Sir John Reith, director-general of the British Broadcasting Corporation (BBC). Edward, who had seen his father make the first ever royal broadcast on the radio and recognized its power, now wanted to use that power to explain to the British people why he had made this choice. Technicians had set up two matching microphones and a "cue lamp" in a small suite of rooms in the castle that was frequently used by Edward. Reith felt that the best course of action was to interrupt regular programming, and for Reith himself to introduce Edward. Reith had received word that Edward was to be referred to

---

* It read: "I, Edward the Eighth, of Great Britain, Ireland and the British Dominions beyond the Seas, King, Emperor of India, do hereby declare my irrevocable determination to renounce the Throne for Myself and My descendants, and My desire that effect should be given to this Instrument of Abdication immediately. In token whereof I have hereunto set My hand this tenth day of December, nineteen hundred and thirty-six, in the presence of the witnesses whose signatures are subscribed."

as His Royal Highness Prince Edward, since he was no longer king and had not yet been given a new title by his brother.*

A half hour before the broadcast, Reith suggested "a trial for voice" and gave Edward an evening paper to read aloud, carefully folding it so that he would see the racing news and not any headlines about himself.

The King then went to the bathroom, leaving the door open as he told those assembled he didn't know when he'd be using that place again. He then went to make some final edits to his draft. Lord Clive Wigram, who had served as George V's private secretary, confided in Reith that he thought Edward wasn't sane; he would come to regret what he'd done.

And then it was time to speak. Reith had Edward stand to the right of the chair in which he'd sit to do the broadcast. Reith spoke into the microphone: "This is Windsor Castle. His Royal Highness Prince Edward."

Reith then got up to leave the room. As Edward sat, he kicked the table leg, a thump that was audible on the radio. Some reports would later speculate, incorrectly, that the sound was Reith slamming the door in disgust.

Perhaps flustered by the kick, or because the weight of his abdication was settling in on him, Edward sounded hesitant as he began his remarks. But he soon picked up confidence, speed, and volume. He began by stating that he always wanted to share his heart and mind with the British people, "but until now it has not been constitutionally possible for me to speak."

He then declared his allegiance to his brother, before getting to the crux of it:

> You must believe me when I tell you that I have found it impossible to carry the heavy burden of responsibility and to discharge my duties as King as I would wish to do without the help and support of the woman I love.

---

* His brother, known colloquially as Bertie, was also undergoing a title transformation. Just days before, he had been the Duke of York, and now, in an attempt to show continuity with his father (and to mark his brother's short reign as an aberration), he would be known as King George VI.

He then spoke to the issue of continuity, punctuated with a Churchillian flourish and a dig at those who forced him to choose between the monarchy and the love of his life.

This decision has been made less difficult to me by the sure knowledge that my brother, with his long training in the public affairs of this country and with his fine qualities, will be able to take my place forthwith without interruption or injury to the life and progress of the empire. And he has one matchless blessing, enjoyed by so many of you, and not bestowed on me—a happy home with his wife and children.

Having brought the country to the brink of a constitutional crisis, Edward continued with a declaration that being "bred in the constitutional tradition" (another Churchillian flourish), he never would have allowed the situation to become a full-blown showdown between the king and Parliament.

During these hard days I have been comforted by Her Majesty my mother and by my family. The ministers of the crown, and in particular, Mr. Baldwin, the Prime Minister, have always treated me with full consideration. There has never been any constitutional difference between me and them, and between me and Parliament. Bred in the constitutional tradition by my father, I should never have allowed any such issue to arise.

With that, he "quit altogether public affairs," offered his service to the new king, his brother, "in a private station," and, voice rising with emotion, wished the British people "happiness and prosperity with all my heart."

Upon delivering his final declaration, "God save the King," Edward sat silent for a moment, and then stood up and put an arm on the shoulder of Sir Walter Monckton, who had been serving as his abdication advisor and confidant throughout the ordeal, and said, "Walter, it is a far better thing I go to."

Days earlier, Edward had held a different view. He felt he had a chance of a different outcome, one that would have had dramatic implications for both the monarchy and a world on the verge of war, had he had the opportunity to deliver an alternate speech.

From an early stage, political leaders and members of the royal community were concerned that Edward was unfit to become king. He was a drinking, womanizing, indiscreet playboy—charming at times but childish and temperamental at others. As an officer during the First World War, he had maintained an extended liaison with a Parisian prostitute, writing her love letters, which she kept. When she shot her husband in London, it was suspected that handing over those letters bought her an acquittal. Before Edward ever ascended to the throne, Alan "Tommy" Lascelles, his private secretary, admitted that his charge wasn't fit to be king, and "the best thing that could happen to him, and to the country, would be for him to break his neck." While perhaps not wishing him bodily harm, others shared the same sentiment.

Stanley Baldwin, who would serve as prime minister during Edward's brief reign, described him as "an abnormal being, half child, half genius . . . it is as though two or three cells in his brain had remained entirely undeveloped."

Even Edward's father, King George V, is reported to have admitted, upon the prince's fortieth birthday, "After I am dead, the boy will ruin himself within twelve months."

Shortly before his death, King George went further: "I pray to God that my eldest son [Edward] will never marry and have children, and that nothing will come between Bertie [Albert] and Lilibet [Elizabeth] and the throne."

The concern stemmed from Edward's personal behavior, as well as his willingness to get involved directly in politics, a breach of precedent and protocol for the members of the royal family. And it was not just his involvement in politics that was problematic, it was also his political leanings. In 1935, when speaking to the British Legion, he advocated sending a delegation of members to Germany "to stretch forth the hand of friendship." Over time, Edward's pro-German sympathies would evolve into full Nazi support.

On January 20, 1936, George V died, and Edward became king. To allow time for planning and travel for the representatives of the dominions (the countries where Edward was also king, which included Canada, Australia, South Africa, and New Zealand), the date for his official coronation was set for May 12, 1937.

Throughout 1936, the King's relationship with Simpson gained steam. In July, Ernest Simpson, who had been conducting an affair of his own, moved out of the couple's home. In August, Wallis Simpson joined the King on a Mediterranean cruise, where they were photographed together, leading the American and European press to speculate about their relationship, with *Time* magazine writing about the fun "that Edward of Wales [was] having at Cannes last week with beautiful Mrs. Wallis Simpson." The British press adhered to a "gentleman's agreement" not to publish anything about the affair, leading to a disconnect that wouldn't be possible today—the world knew of the King's paramour, whereas many Brits did not.

In October, Simpson moved into a house in London's Regent's Park rented for her by the King. It was becoming clear that this wasn't a passing infatuation, and on October 20, Prime Minister Baldwin felt compelled to address the affair in a meeting with the King. Reports of the meeting suggest it was tragicomic: "Tired from the drive in his unpleasant little car, and in considerable pain from arthritis, the prime minister asked for a whisky and soda. Having got it, he raised his glass and said: 'Well, Sir, whatever happens, my Mrs. and I wish you every happiness from the depths of our souls.' At this, the king burst into tears, and Baldwin began to cry too."

Upon composing themselves, the two got to the point. The prime minister noted that he was getting increasing heat about the King's affair and asked if he could be more discreet. The King is said to have responded, "The lady is my friend and I do not wish to let her in by the back door." He also parried the prime minister's questions about delaying Mrs. Simpson's divorce ("That is the lady's private business") and a request for her to leave the country so the rumors could die down (no response).

When Simpson's divorce case was heard and her divorce granted at the end of October, the courtroom was crowded with media—but while the American reports were lurid, the British reports were almost entirely defanged, going only so far as to say that Mrs. Simpson "had been well known in social circles in London for several years."

If, in October, the prime minister had given the King his thoughts on the relationship, the King now wanted to return the favor. In mid-November, he called for Baldwin and informed him that he wished to marry Wallis Simpson.

When Baldwin pointed out that whomever the King married would become queen, and argued that the British public wouldn't accept Simpson in that role, the King replied that he was prepared to abdicate if he was opposed by the government.

Up until that point, Baldwin had hoped that the King would give up Mrs. Simpson. But now the stakes were clear: Move on from Mrs. Simpson and remain king, or marry and abdicate.

Perhaps realizing that he had painted himself into a corner, the King began to warm to an idea that he felt would allow him to keep his crown and still marry Simpson. On November 25, he met with Baldwin again, proposing a "morganatic" marriage to Wallis Simpson.

A morganatic marriage—sometimes called a *left-handed marriage*—is a marriage between people of unequal social rank. In a royal context, the spouse and any children have no claim to a royal title, rank, or hereditary property. This would make Simpson not Britain's queen, but Edward's consort.

It's not entirely clear where this plan came from. Some historians claim it was Churchill, back-channeling ideas to the King. Historian Michael Bloch writes that Churchill's role in the morganatic marriage idea was "shadowy . . . [one] of which he did not afterwards wish to tell the world."

By that point, Churchill's relationship with Baldwin was a fraught one. Although Churchill didn't have much respect for Baldwin ("a countrified businessman who seemed to have reached the Cabinet by accident," he called him), and though they were not closely aligned politically, Churchill did serve under Baldwin as chancellor of the Exchequer for nearly five years at the end of the 1920s. When Baldwin became prime minister again in 1935, there was no offer of another role for Churchill, nor would Churchill have wanted one. By that point, he had fallen out with Baldwin over the subject of India's status, and now found deeper and more urgent differences with him on Britain's posture in the face of an increasingly aggressive Germany. Churchill's words toward Baldwin also became more derisive and acerbic, describing him as "no better than an epileptic corpse."

For Baldwin, rumors of Churchill's role became the breaking point. Until then, he had hoped the King would change his mind. But with his political enemy potentially putting forward an idea that would enable the King to marry and stay, Baldwin began to believe abdication was the only option.

A morganatic marriage was not as clean a solution as it sounded. First, it would effectively require the King to admit that he was marrying a woman who was unsuitable. Because it would affect the line of succession, it would require new legislation in Britain and its dominions. Baldwin told the King that this was unacceptable, but the King pushed him to raise the issue with the cabinet, which he did on November 27. The cabinet rejected it outright. Over the next several days, so, too, did the governments of the dominions.

On December 1, the press silence started to crack. A Church of England bishop named Alfred Blunt, gave a speech suggesting the King would need God's grace to do his duty faithfully and added, "We hope that he is aware of his need. Some of us wish that he gave more positive signs of such awareness." The media read this as a reference to the King being unaware of what his relationship with Wallis Simpson would do to the country and used it as an opening to begin writing the story of the King's relationship. In actuality, Blunt had barely heard of Simpson. He was simply expressing his hope that the King would become more serious about his duties as the leader of the Church of England.

The crisis was now coming to a head. On December 2, Baldwin informed the King that none of his governments were willing to agree to a morganatic marriage. The King now had three choices: end his relationship with Simpson; abdicate and marry her; or marry against the advice of his ministers, who would then resign.

The third of these options would have set off a constitutional crisis, pitting the crown against the prime minister and his cabinet. In England, where history echoes daily, the "immediate" precedent for such an act was the Civil War of 1642, the last time the crown had been pitted against Parliament. The fear was that Edward might just be selfish and petulant enough to follow that precedent, and that he might have an ally in Winston Churchill should he choose to do so.

Adding urgency to the decision, the next day (December 3), the British press finally broke the story, and the affair and hoped-for marriage came flooding into the public light. The British public, which knew little, if anything, about the affair was now treated to blazing headlines simultaneously introducing them to the affair and to the crisis it was causing.

The name Simpson was on everybody's lips, and the King's future was at stake.

In a tense meeting with the prime minister, the King asked to be allowed to speak via the BBC directly to his subjects, the British people. In making this request in the face of an ultimatum, Edward did have some leverage. He was charming and popular, and felt that if he could just address his subjects directly, he could bring them around to his way of thinking.

Out of both affection and obligation, Walter Monckton helped the King draft an address appealing to the British people.

Public figures make deeply personal declarations all the time—about their health, their reasons for seeking (or not seeking) office, about their lives and loves (and sometimes their less-than-discreet lusts); and about the lessons they wish to share. The more personal the declaration, the odder it seems to have someone other than the speaker involved in the writing. Yet the job of the speechwriter is not to assemble some platonic ideal of a speech; it's to help the speaker be their best self, and often that best self is most needed when the words become the most personal.

In my work, I have been asked by clients to help prepare wedding toasts and eulogies for loved ones. In one instance, I was asked to help script a video message that would be shown to a client's family after his death. One of my colleagues joked, "well, that's the first time you'll literally be a ghostwriter."

Requests like this always strike me as strange, and I often decline them. After all, these are the moments that call for raw truth more than professional polish. At the same time, it's an honor to be brought into people's lives at their most emotional and vulnerable moments and to help them find a way to share their most personal thoughts and reflections.

Writing these statements is no easy task—it requires the writer be willing to ask deeply personal questions, dig for truths that the speaker often hasn't fully admitted to themselves, and achieve a mind meld that often goes beyond the bounds of any professional relationship save that of a therapist. In fact, I often begin these conversations with an almost therapeutic disclaimer. I tell clients, "I'm going to ask you a lot of questions, and I want you to remember that I'm not a journalist and you're not giving up control of the story. Sometimes when you see the things you say on paper, it can be jarring and feel too open, and you'll want to dial them back—that's fine. The speech ultimately belongs to you."

One of the best and most successful examples of this personal and professional mind meld is the one that formed between Senator John McCain and his longtime chief of staff Mark Salter. McCain initially hired Salter, who was working for former UN ambassador Jeane Kirkpatrick, to work with him on policy issues in Central America and Southeast Asia, but added, "I want you to do a lot of the writing around here." And when it came to writing, the two clicked from the jump. They had tastes in literature that, if not fully shared, were overlapping—including W. Somerset Maugham, F. Scott Fitzgerald, and Irish writers like William Trevor. For Salter, the breakthrough from the political to the personal occurred as Senator McCain prepared to address the U.S. Naval Academy graduating class of 1993. Senator McCain's father, Admiral Jack McCain, had addressed the academy in 1970 while his son was being tortured as a prisoner of war in Vietnam. Senator McCain's invitation to speak there seemed to surface some of the challenges McCain had in the relationship with his father.

In the speech, McCain quoted his father's words, but noted wryly, "I would have greatly enjoyed attending that graduation had I not been otherwise engaged at the time." And while the references to his father in that speech didn't open the Freudian floodgates, they cemented a relationship in which Salter felt free to ask McCain anything (although McCain never felt obligated to answer), and which led to the cowriting of five books, including the deeply personal family memoir *Faith of My Fathers*.

Reflecting on his time with McCain, Salter said, "I'm never going to have that kind of connection again. I don't think it's possible." Their last piece of writing together, McCain's farewell to the American people, concludes with the words, "Americans never quit. We never surrender. We never hide from history. We make history."

As Monckton and the King worked on his speech to the British people, the King didn't want to quit, either. His plan was to say that he wished to marry Mrs. Simpson, but neither of them would insist that she be queen. He would then go away to a foreign country while people made up their minds. If he were called back, he would resume his reign with Mrs. Simpson as his consort. If he wasn't, he would abdicate.

He now shared this plan and the draft speech with Baldwin. Baldwin remembered the King being "frantically keen" to speak to the British people. But Baldwin also felt that such a speech would be constitutionally improper and said as much. The King challenged him, "You want me to go, don't you."

Baldwin took the speech to the cabinet, who shared his view that not only would such a speech be improper, but it was, in the words of cabinet member and former prime minister Ramsay MacDonald, "a plausible and blatant attempt to get the country and Empire to throw over his ministers." The original document has a handwritten note on the bottom, presumably by one of the cabinet members who viewed it. "No word about abdication."

At this point, several cabinet ministers feared the King would go directly to the BBC, demand airtime, and make a speech in which he did not abdicate but rather put the question of whether he could marry Simpson and still be king directly to the British people. Sources are divided on whether one of Baldwin's aides reached out to Sir John Reith to secure a commitment that no broadcast from the King be made without prior approval or whether they simply trusted Sir John to understand the situation.

In a special cabinet meeting on December 4, the King's last possible avenue of escape—that direct appeal to the British people—appeared to be cut off. The prime minister shared the opinion of his constitutional advisors:

"The sovereign can make no public statement on any matter of public interest except on the advice of his ministers.

"The king's ministers must take responsibility for every public act of the king. This is the basis of the constitutional monarchy.

"If the king disregarded it, *constitutional monarchy would cease to exist.* The king is bound to accept and act upon the advice of his ministers . . . for the king to broadcast in disregard of that advice would be appealing over the heads of his constitutional advisers."

There was no speech, no morganatic marriage, only a narrowed ultimatum: find a more suitable partner, or, if you are determined to marry Simpson, abdicate.

But would the King assent? At this point, he was boxed in, agitated, and with Simpson having escaped to southern France to avoid the media crush, isolated.

The King had a request: could he meet with his old friend Winston Churchill?

Baldwin agreed, although he later admitted that doing so was "my first blunder."

Churchill had known the King socially since childhood, and the pair had corresponded throughout their lives.* In fact, it was Edward, then Prince of Wales, who, in a series of letters with Churchill in the early 1900s, told him that "parliamentary and literary life" rather than "the monotony of military life" would suit him well.

That's the life Churchill had entered, and he had done so as a staunch royalist. Churchill's wife, Clementine, joked that he was the last believer in the Divine Right of Kings. He saw the monarchy as a stabilizing force in a rapidly changing world. Of course, he also saw in the King's quandary a chance to humiliate the government in power, and potentially make a comeback himself. It would prove to be a bad miscalculation.

The full extent of Churchill's role in Edward's final weeks as king isn't entirely clear. Was he simply being loyal to a friend? Or was he seeking to

---

* Churchill, no slouch with a pen and no stranger to the persuasive powers of sycophancy, wrote to the King upon his ascension to the throne, "in the long swing of events, Your Majesty's name will shine in history as the bravest and best beloved of the sovereigns who have worn the island crown."

become prime minister by dividing Britain into a "King's Party" (which he would lead) and an "anti-King's party"?

We don't know, because his detractors saw his fingerprints everywhere (even where they weren't), and Churchill later sought to minimize his role in the crisis and wipe away any fingerprints he had actually left.

Certainly, Churchill had been all over the map on Edward's relationship with Simpson. At times, he felt it was Edward's duty to move on from the relationship; that he was putting the country in "great danger, and just as men have given their arms and legs and indeed their lives for the sake of the country, so the king must be prepared to give up a woman." (He had even endured four months of silence from Edward for suggesting as much.) And yet, he was also a royalist and a romantic and someone whose own father had married an American woman.

We also know that Churchill felt for the King on a personal level, writing at one point that when the King was with Simpson, "many little tricks and fidgetings of nervousness fell away from him. He was a completed instead of a sick and harassed soul." And we know that Churchill had been spoiling for a fight, "completely on the rampage, saying that he was for the King and was not going to have him strangled in the dark by ministers and bumped off without a chance of saying a word to parliament or the country in his own defence." We know, too, that Churchill did help the King with speechwriting and speech-making from time to time.*

It is not known how much of a hand Churchill had in the Moncktonwritten non-abdication draft. Churchill, in his private diary, wrote that he had no contact with the King prior to December 4. Did he have contact with Monckton? On that point, his diary is silent.

But now, with a chance to advise Edward directly, Churchill recommended that the King should resist the ultimatum and instead ask for time. As Churchill recounted in his papers, "Your majesty need not have the slightest fear about time. If you require time there is no force in this country which would or should deny it to you. . . . Mr. Baldwin

---

* In an interview released by the BBC shortly after Edward's death, Edward describes how Churchill taught him to assemble a makeshift lectern using a finger bowl, a dinner plate, and a water glass, to help deliver toasts and after-dinner remarks.

is a fatherly man and nothing would induce him to treat you harshly in such a matter. Ministers could not possibly resign on such an issue as your request for time."

Churchill could not say whether the King would win if he stood and fought, but that he ought to take time in order to see what measure of support he received.

Just three days later, in the House of Commons, Churchill would learn in embarrassing fashion how little support there was for the King and for his defenders. After a statement by Stanley Baldwin, Churchill rose to ask a question about just that issue of whether the King would be given time: "May I ask my right honorable Friend whether he could give us an assurance that no irrevocable step . . ." Immediately, Churchill was shouted down from all sides with cries of "Sit down" and "You're making a speech." Churchill tried again, but was again shouted down, "completely staggered by the unanimous hostility of the House."

Did Churchill give up the fight at that point? Letters to his friend and Conservative member of the Parliament Robert Boothby suggest not. They describe a "formula which we had all helped to devise," though the exact nature of that scheme is unclear.

Regardless, Churchill's desire for the King to fight on was greater than the King's own desire to do so. The King had already begun conversations about what royal rank he could keep and where he could live if he abdicated. Monckton was dispatched to draft an abdication statement and coordinate with the prime minister on the particulars of the abdication.

On December 10, 1936, the King's abdication statement was read to the House of Commons. Prime Minister Baldwin then rose and spoke plainly and movingly of the difficult previous months and the King's graciousness in abdication.

However, there was one thing Baldwin didn't include: a reference the King wanted him to assert—that Mrs. Simpson had done all she could to dissuade him from abdicating. The King, now as a private citizen, wanted to speak to the nation himself, justify his actions, throw his support behind his brother, and say farewell.

In addition, he wanted to remedy what he saw as Baldwin's omitted defense of Mrs. Simpson, which he did with the words, "I want you to know that the decision I have made has been mine and mine alone. This was a thing I had to judge entirely for myself. The other person most nearly concerned has tried up to the last to persuade me to take a different course."

The case he had wanted to make for taking Simpson as his wife, and for letting the British people have a say as to whether he stayed on—the one he had made in the speech shared with Baldwin and the cabinet—was filed away, not to be seen for nearly seventy years. Edward's words, rediscovered in a series of documents released by the British Public Record Office in 2003, reveal a man who felt that the British people would rally to him if they could only hear his reasoning, in his own voice, and call him back to the throne.

By ancient custom, the King addresses his public utterances to his people. Tonight, I am going to talk to you as my friends—British men and women wherever you may reside, within or without the Empire. The last time I broadcast to you all, on Saint David's Day, I told you that you had known me better as The Prince of Wales. I am still the same man whose motto was 'Ich Dien', I serve. And I have tried to serve this country and the Empire for the last twenty years. And tonight, I am not forgetting the great Dominions and Dependencies beyond the seas, who have always shown me such open-hearted kindness.

Now I realize that the newspapers of other countries have given you full cause for speculation as to what I am going to do—as to what is going to happen. And I want here to express my gratitude to the newspapers of Great Britain for the courtesy and consideration they have shown.

It was never my intention to hide anything from you. Hitherto it has not been possible for me to speak, but now I must. I could not go on bearing the heavy burdens that constantly rest on me as king unless I could be strengthened in the task by a happy married life; and so I am firmly resolved to marry the woman I love, when she is free to marry me.

You know well enough to understand that I never could have contemplated a marriage of convenience. It has taken me a long time to find the woman I want to make my wife. Without her, I have been a very lonely man. With her I shall have a home and all the companionship and mutual sympathy and understanding which married life can bring. I know that many of you have had the good fortune to be blessed with such a life, and I am sure that in your hearts you would wish the same for me.

Neither Mrs Simpson nor I have ever sought to insist that she should be Queen. All we desired was that our married happiness should carry with it a proper title and dignity for her befitting my wife.

Now that I have at last been able to take you so fully into my confidence, I feel it is best to go away for a while, so that you may reflect calmly and quietly but without undue delay on what I have said.

Nothing is nearer to my heart than that I should return; but whatever may befall, I shall always have a deep affection for my country, for the Empire and for you all.

The effect of the speech, if delivered, would have been explosive and far-reaching. By downplaying the King's desire to have Simpson as his queen, it aimed to appeal to the British people as a reasonable compromise. In fact, an early draft of the non-abdication speech, found in Lord Monckton's archives, shows how carefully worded this key point was. In the draft, the reference to Simpson reads, "Mrs. Simpson has had no wish to become Queen, and she would assume such status as would be fitting." It was changed to read, "Neither Mrs. Simpson nor I have ever sought to insist that she should be Queen." In other words, it's not that Mrs. Simpson didn't want to become queen, it's just that Edward didn't intend to make it a precondition.*

Had this speech been delivered, perhaps the British people would have rallied behind Edward's request to retain his position. But by going against the wishes of and operating without the approval of his ministers, Edward would have triggered the constitutional crisis that, in his delivered abdication speech, he claimed he would never risk.

If he had won the battle to stay on the throne, what would it have done to the monarchy when news broke that Simpson was carrying on

---

* The images of this draft speech remain under Crown copyright, and therefore cannot be reproduced here.

an additional affair (with a dashing car salesman named Guy Marcus Trundle) even as she was with the King?

Of greater consequence, what impact would King Edward have had on the course of the Second World War? Two years after his 1937 visit to Germany, Edward reopened the lines of communication with Adolf Hitler, telegramming him to "appeal for your utmost influence towards a peaceful solution to the present problems." A captured telegram sent by a Nazi operative in 1940 claimed that Edward was "convinced that had he remained on throne war would have been avoided and describes himself as firm supporter of a peaceful compromise with Germany" and, more shockingly, "Duke believes with certainty that continued heavy bombing will make England ready for peace." If Edward had indeed suggested this, it would be a callous betrayal of his former subjects in their darkest hour. Rumors circulated that Hitler was considering reinstalling Edward as a puppet king following a successful invasion of Britain.

Former politician and political biographer Roy Jenkins notes what would have faced Edward's most loyal political supporter, had Churchill succeeded in keeping Edward on the throne in 1936: "He might well have found it necessary in 1940–1 to depose and/or lock up his sovereign as the dangerous potential head of a Vichy-style state." As it was, Britain's wartime prime minister forced his friend to take up the post of governor of the Bahamas to keep Edward safely out of Europe for the duration of the hostilities.

This alternate history could have been set in motion by one speech, drafted but never delivered, by a king who wished to retain his crown.

In 1940, as the Battle of Britain raged, Churchill delivered an address on the BBC in which he described the heroics of the "unknown warriors" who would turn the outcome of the war: "There are vast numbers, not only in this Island but in every land, who will render faithful service in this war, but whose names will never be known, whose deeds will never be recorded. This is a War of the Unknown Warriors; but let all strive without failing in faith or in duty, and the dark curse of Hitler will be lifted from our age."

Seen this way, the much-maligned Stanley Baldwin, in forcing Edward's abdication, deserves credit as one of Churchill's "Unknown Warriors" who set in motion the events that allowed "the dark curse of Hitler" to be "lifted from our age."

New York City mayor Abe Beame holds up the New York Daily News *headline that encapsulated the federal government's response to the city's financial crisis. (Bill Stahl Jr. / NY Daily News, via Getty Images)*

7

New York City Mayor Abe Beame Declares
Bankruptcy, October 1975

*The Risks and Rewards of
Sherman Statements*

"Now we must take immediate steps to protect the
essential life support systems of our city."

On October 16, 1975, New York City was deep in crisis. At 4:00 p.m. the next day, $453 million of the city's debts would come due, but there was only $34 million on hand. If New York couldn't pay the debts, the city would officially be bankrupt.

At Gracie Mansion, the mayor's official residence, Mayor Abe Beame had already signed the formal bankruptcy filing.

In a few minutes, he would head some forty blocks downtown to join 1,700 of New York's financial and political elite, who were gathering at the Waldorf-Astoria for the white-tie Alfred E. Smith Memorial Foundation Dinner, a fundraiser for the Catholic charities named in honor of former governor Al Smith, the first Catholic candidate on a major-party presidential ticket. In the room would be the only people who could help the city escape bankruptcy.

And the chances of that happening looked slim. The prospect of federal help had already been slapped down by President Gerald Ford and his advisors. Banks were refusing to market the city's debt, which left New York unable to borrow. Earlier that year, to get the city through its ongoing fiscal crisis, Governor Hugh Carey and the state legislature created the Municipal Assistance Corporation (MAC), commonly referred to as Big Mac for its power to overrule city spending decisions. The MAC also created bonds that were backed by the city's sales tax and stock-transfer tax. The first round of MAC bonds had sold well. But now demand for the second round of bonds was much lower, and Governor Carey had just learned that the Teachers' Retirement System was unlikely to make another significant purchase of city bonds (it had already invested $138 million in such bonds). That had been the city's last remaining lifeline, and now it was severed. Default was all but inevitable.

Abraham Beame, who was in his second year as the mayor of New York, was no stranger to the city's budget and its challenges. During his two separate terms as comptroller, he had seen the drop in manufacturing jobs, the wave of middle-class families moving to the suburbs, and the massive growth of the city's municipal labor force. He was aware of, and at times condoned, the gimmicks that were used to mask widening budget gaps.

Yet while Beame was described by allies and adversaries alike as kind and honorable, he also seemed paralyzed by the intensifying challenges of his office. Ed Koch, who was serving in Congress at the time and would go on to succeed Beame as mayor, later said of Beame's ability to manage the numbers, "Abe Beame is an accountant, you know, but it's hard to understand that he has that title."

Under Beame's watch, the financial picture continued to deteriorate. Koch remembered hearing testimony before Congress about the city's fiscal situation and thinking that "it was like somebody escaping from the Warsaw ghetto and saying they're killing people there. Nobody believed it."

At the Al Smith dinner, diners were working their way through a "bicentennial menu," featuring Maryland terrapin soup and baskets of colonial sweets. The night's featured speakers were New York's preeminent builder and power broker, Robert Moses, and Connecticut's first woman governor, Ella Grasso. Typically speeches at the Al Smith dinner practice a unique brand of political comedy, but speeches that had been loaded with humor in past years now sounded notes of gloom.

Mayor Beame used his turn on the five-tier dais to excoriate Washington for refusing to bail out New York: "The problems were simpler and less complex in [former governor] Smith's day, and there even seemed to be a greater sense of responsibility on Washington's part." He then left the dinner to see if there was any way to stave off the impending fiscal calamity.

Referring to Smith, Governor Carey said, "We could use the Happy Warrior today." Robert Moses, who had previously referred to the city's leaders as "third-rate men," simply paid tribute to Governor Smith. Only Governor Grasso tried to infuse some humor, joking that she must have been chosen to speak to the dinner because she was Italian and that the cardinal and all the bishops "have been working for my people for many, many years."*

By ten o'clock, Felix Rohatyn, the financier who served as chairman of the MAC, and others had learned that the Teachers' Retirement System wouldn't invest in more MAC bonds. Teachers' trustee Reuben Mitchell said, "We must watch that investments are properly diversified, that all our eggs aren't put in one basket." Governor Carey left the dinner

---

* In a joke ahead of its time, Grasso playfully noted that there was no reason a woman governor should play second fiddle to the men when it came to national aspirations: "I appreciate the kind words of the various presidential candidates who, when they come-a-courtin' say I would make a good running mate. In response, I tell them I would like to return the compliment."

and phoned state and federal leaders with a simple message: default was imminent.

The governor placed another call that night, summoning to his office a developer named Richard Ravitch, who had been serving as a minister without portfolio for Carey. When Ravitch arrived at the governor's office, Carey was still in white tie and showing the effects of a couple of drinks. Carey told Ravitch to find Al Shanker, the powerful head of the teachers' union, and convince him to buy the bonds that would save the city. A car and driver were waiting outside.

In his memoir, Ravitch would later write that when he got to Shanker's apartment, Shanker "was genuinely distressed by his decision not to buy MAC bonds. He knew the risks to the city, but he believed his primary obligation was his fiduciary responsibility to his teachers. As city employees, they had already been put at risk by the city's fiscal crisis. It was no small thing to make their pension money subject to the same risk." They talked until five o'clock that morning, but reached no agreement.

At the same time, Mayor Beame, convinced that there would be no stay of financial execution, had assembled a small team in the basement of Gracie Mansion. Ira Millstein, then a young lawyer at Weil, Gotshal & Manges, which was representing the city, prepared the legal filing.

Sid Frigand, the mayor's press secretary, recalled the point at which the conversation turned from *if* the city would go under to *how.* "We needed to figure out which services were essential, and which weren't," he said. "It was an interesting exercise because when you think of what is essential and what is not essential that there are functions of public service that we don't know about that are very essential. Bridge tenders who raise and lower bridges were essential. Teachers weren't life-or-death. Hospital services and keeping the highways open were essential."

As the mayor's team was making the list, Frigand remembers looking over and seeing Howard Rubenstein writing on a pad of paper. Rubenstein was a sort of unpaid booster for New York City who was making his living doing public relations work for many of the city's real estate developers and unions. *The New Yorker* would later describe him as "ubiquitous, trusted, a kind of gentle fixer for those who run New York."

Rubenstein and Beame were friends. At one point in the late sixties and early seventies, Rubenstein had lived across the street from Beame in Belle Harbor, Queens. One of Rubenstein's more vivid memories was seeing Beame on the beach, tucking a series of folded papers into his bathing suit. Rubenstein asked what they were, and Beame showed him that each was covered with tiny handwriting: he was writing a platform for his mayoral run. "Here's my program," Beame said. Rubenstein's response: "What happens if you go in the water?"

In 1974, Beame was elected mayor. And now, less than two years later, he was about to announce the bankruptcy of America's richest and largest city.

As October 16 became October 17, the mayor's Contingency Planning Committee was summoned to Gracie Mansion to make final determinations as to how, exactly, a bankruptcy would play out. But what would the mayor say in his official declaration speech, and how would he say it?

Rubenstein was working on the mayor's statement. It was to be a clear, concise description of what had happened, what would happen next, and how the mayor was working to protect average New Yorkers. But even within that context, the mayor wanted to do some score settling. Beame had no love for the comptroller, Harrison Jay Goldin, and wanted him implicated in the bankruptcy. The first words of the statement read: "I have been advised by the Comptroller that the City of New York has insufficient cash on hand to meet debt obligations due today." (Frigand began an early draft of the press release that would accompany the statement with the words "City Comptroller Harrison Jay Goldin announced today . . ." It was unclear whether Frigand was making a serious suggestion or a joke.)

Similarly, Beame seemed to want to place some of the blame on the teachers' union, continuing, "The financing which was to be made available by the Municipal Assistance Corporation will not be forthcoming because the Teachers' Retirement Fund failed to approve its participation in the State Financing Plan."

With fingers of blame now firmly pointed in two directions, the mayor's remarks got to the point: "This constitutes the default we have struggled to avoid."

The draft goes on to explain that the mayor is now engaged in legal action to protect the city's essential services, and prioritize those above the repayment demands of the banks and bondholders.

After several hours of work, Rubenstein handed Beame the statement. The mayor looked at it, said nothing, and nodded. Rubenstein had it typed up. At 12:25 a.m., Beame attempted to call President Ford to advise him that the city would be defaulting. Ford was asleep.

Al Shanker's meeting with Dick Ravitch wrapped up at 5:00 that morning, and Ravitch called the governor with the readout: Shanker wouldn't budge.

On the morning of October 17, New Yorkers woke to a series of grim headlines: BALK BY UFT PUSHING CITY TO DEFAULT in the *Staten Island Advance*, TEACHERS REJECT 150-MILLION LOAN CITY NEEDS TODAY in *The New York Times*. United Press International reported that economists in London were warning that New York's default would hurt the dollar abroad. The Dow dropped ten points at the opening bell (a significant drop at a time when the Dow was below 1,000), the price of gold began to rise, and "trading of bonds of other cities and states slowed to a near standstill, and even the prices of most credit-worthy bonds fell."

The city ordered the sanitation department to stop issuing payroll checks, and one bank said it would not cash city payroll checks unless they were drawn on an account held by the bank itself. New York City's bonds, issued by the MAC, plunged to between twenty dollars and forty dollars per thousand-dollar face value, and city note-holders began to line up at the Municipal Building in an attempt to redeem whatever they could.

That morning, Rohatyn told the press that everything hinged on the teachers' union: "The future of the city is in their hands."

It was more than just the future of one city. New York's bonds were held by banks throughout the United States and around the world. By some estimates, New York's default would bring down at least a hundred banks.

One newspaper in North Carolina ran a cartoon of a homeless man lying on trash under the Brooklyn Bridge, with the caption, "We're going down, America, and we're taking you with us."

President Ford began hearing from leaders around the world about the dangers of a New York default. His press secretary, Ron Nessen, said that Ford would monitor the situation throughout the day, but wouldn't change his mind about granting assistance to the city. In Nessen's words, "This is not a natural disaster or an act of God. It is a self-inflicted act by the people who have been running New York City."

Shortly after 9:00 a.m., Ravitch was in the governor's office when he got a call from Shanker, who asked for another meeting. Since Governor Carey's office was swarmed with reporters, Shanker requested that they meet somewhere private. Ravitch's apartment, at Park Avenue and Eighty-fifth Street, was between Gracie Mansion and the governor's office.

Ravitch remembered how unprepared he was to host such a high-level meeting. There was so little food at his apartment that Harry Van Arsdale, the head of the New York City Central Labor Council, began eating matzo he had found in the cabinet.

The teachers' union was in a bind. Shanker later called it blackmail. If the city went bankrupt, a judge could order thousands of teacher dismissals, undo the raises the teachers had recently negotiated, and override any pension laws, stripping retirees of their pension checks.

Three hours into the meeting, Shanker had made up his mind. He left to meet with the Teachers' Retirement System. Ravitch remembers that the only evidence of the momentous decision that had just taken place in his apartment was a trail of matzo crumbs.

At 2:07 p.m., the teachers' union announced that it would reverse course and would make up the city's $150 million shortfall with their pension funds. "No one else was coming forward to save the city," Shanker said.

The mayor's statement, prepared by Rubenstein, was never read. Most of the statement speaks in a workmanlike way to how grim a bankruptcy could have been. Only at the end is there a rhetorical flourish, in which the mayor pledges to continue his work, "to restore this city to fiscal stability and to permit us to fulfill our great and continuing promise to our citizens and to the entire world."

The immediate crisis averted, New York's leaders continued to petition for federal help. Twelve days later, President Ford stepped to the podium at the National Press Club and delivered a stinging rebuke: "What I cannot understand—and what nobody should condone—is the blatant attempt in some quarters to frighten the American people and their representatives in Congress into panicky support of patently bad policy. The people of this country will not be stampeded; they will not panic when a few desperate New York City officials and bankers try to scare New York's mortgage payments out of them."

Later in the speech, he added, "I can tell you, and tell you now, that I am prepared to veto any bill that has as its purpose a federal bailout of New York City to prevent a default."

October 17, 1975

STATEMENT BY MAYOR ABRAHAM D. BEAME

I have been advised by the Comptroller that the City of New York has insufficient cash on hand to meet debt obligations due today.

The financing which was to be made available by the Municipal Assistance Corporation will not be forthcoming because the Teachers Retirement Fund failed to approve its participation in the State Financing Plan.

This constitutes the default that we have struggled to avoid.

Now we must take immediate steps to protect the essential life support systems of our City--and to preserve the well-being of all our citizens.

At my direction Corporation Counsel W. Bernard Richland and Co-counsel Weil, Gotshal and Manges this morning applied to and received from Supreme Court Justice Irving Sapol and order to preserve the City's assets under the Special Emergency legislation adopted at the recent Special Session. This step is necessary to ensure that the City will remain capable of providing its citizens with necessary services.

(more)

-2-

Were I to take no legal action at this moment, I have been advised that such funds as the City as would first be used to pay debt service rather than life support and other essential services. These priorities to financial institutions and bondholders, under State law, would be binding on the recently created Emergency Financial Control Board unless legal steps are taken to forestall it.

To accomplish the primary use of the City's funds for life support and other necessary services, I am, under State law, required to file a petition in State court seeking the protection of the court from the City's creditors--and this I am doing.

Last night my Contigency Committee, headed by Robert Rivel, President of Union Dime Savings Bank, recommended a rational and humane set of priorities. Shortly thereafter, these priorities were adopted by the Board of Estimate and endorsed by the City Council leadership.

- Police protection, fire protection, sanitation, public health and all realted life support services.
- Food and shelter, for those who are dependent on City support.
- Hospital and emergency medical care for those who have no other resources for these.
- Payment to vendors who provide essential goods and services necessary for the ongoing delivery of all of the above.
- Maintenance of primary public schools and secondary schools.
- Interest on the City debt.
- Payments due to the retired and aged, payable by separate pension trust funds will of course be paid as heretofore.

-3-

Many of these priorities are obviously interrelated. And other needs and services, so essential to the life of our City--now and in the future--must be addressed. The extent of ancillary costs, related to the mentioned priorities, will be studied and met to the extent possible.

During the period of stay granted by the court, a sound reorganization plan will be developed and an orderly procedure for dealing with the problems will be announced.

I will, of course, continue to press for immediate assistance in Washington to permit us to restore this City to fiscal stability and to permit us to fulfill our great and continuing promise to our citizens and to the entire world.

# # #

Ford's speech may actually have been harsher than many of his advisors intended. According to David Gergen, who was, at the time, an assistant to Treasury Secretary William Simon, Ford was certainly offended by the city's profligate spending, but was generally a moderate Republican who liked New York. (He had chosen a New Yorker, Nelson Rockefeller, as his vice president.)

The first five drafts of the speech, while strongly worded, contained no veto threat at all. The papers of Robert Hartmann, a speechwriter for Ford, show that, in drafts up until two days before the delivery of the speech, Ford is content to simply say, "I am fundamentally opposed to this [bailout] solution." In several of the earlier drafts, Ford treats default as a foregone conclusion, welcoming its prospect and promising that if that happened, "the federal government will work with the court to assure that police, fire, and other essential services for the protection of life and property are maintained."

Only as the draft neared final do we see handwritten changes that make the veto threat:

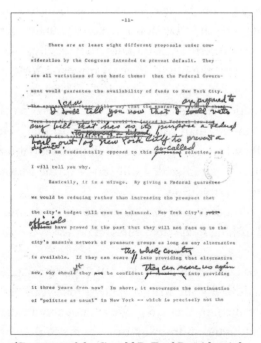

(Courtesy of the Gerald R. Ford Presidential Library)

While the handwriting isn't Ford's, the harshness of the speech that Ford ultimately delivered led to a headline that ran in the following morning's *New York Daily News* and will forever be associated with Ford, although he never said it: FORD TO CITY: DROP DEAD.

Ford's definitive statement can trace its rhetorical lineage back to the summer of 1884. As that year's political conventions approached, Republican party leaders felt that their best hope for victory lay in nominating the Civil War hero William Tecumseh Sherman. Sherman, however, had no interest, writing to Congressman (and eventual nominee) James Blaine, "I would account myself a fool, a madman, an ass to embark anew at 65 years of age" on a political career.

When that letter failed to dissuade the hopeful Republicans, he sent an even more strongly worded telegram. "I will not accept if nominated, and will not serve if elected."

This became known as a "Sherman statement," a statement of intent so clear that its meaning could not be missed. Since that time, countless politicians have used similar statements to disclaim their own ambition (or lack thereof). President Lyndon Johnson made his intentions about running for a second term in 1968 known by saying, "I shall not seek, and I will not accept, the nomination of my party for another term as your president."

The construction of these statements became so recognizable that when Arizona congressman Mo Udall wanted to make clear he would not challenge President Carter for the 1980 presidential nomination, he did so by saying, "If nominated, I will run—for the Mexican border. If elected, I will fight extradition."

Today, the term *Sherman statement* doesn't apply only to political ambitions, and making such statements can be a risky—and rewarding—strategy.

In the case of Lyndon Johnson, his 1968 Sherman statement was set in motion by a different Sherman statement four years earlier regarding America's involvement in Vietnam: "We are not about to send American boys 9- or 10-thousand miles away from home to do what Asian boys ought to be doing for themselves." Even though that statement was, itself, taken out of context, it served as a clear and useful summation of a promise that Johnson had broken, and it made a run for reelection nearly impossible.

There's a beautiful clarity in statements like this; they make for wonderful rhetoric. But people do not look kindly on clear promises or definitive statements about the future that fail to materialize.

George H. W. Bush made waves at the 1988 Republican National Convention when he declared, "Read my lips: no new taxes." Bush's view at the time was that he would raise taxes only as a last resort. Of course, "Read my lips: tax increases only as a last resort" is not a galvanizing message. But that statement also served as a political time bomb that Bush had strapped to himself. When budget deficits and spending needs forced Bush to increase fees and levies, David Letterman summed up the outrage best, suggesting Bush should update his famous statement to, "Read my lips: I was lying."

There are countless examples of statements like this that come back to haunt those who made them. President Reagan in a televised address in 1986 declared, "We did not—repeat—did not trade weapons or anything else for hostages—nor will we." Months later, he had to backtrack and publicly accept responsibility for the Iran-Contra affair. President Obama faced a similar rhetorical reckoning in 2013 when he spoke about Syrian president Bashar Assad's use of chemical weapons as "a red line for us . . . that would change my calculus." When Assad then launched a massive chemical weapons attack against his own people, President Obama backed down from his own threat, at significant cost to his credibility. And in 2020, voters punished President Trump, in part, for his statement regarding COVID-19 that "one day—like a miracle—it will disappear."

Even on less weighty matters, overly definitive predictions can undercut even the most successful outcomes. Consider that when basketball star LeBron James "took his talents" to the Miami Heat in 2010, he pledged, in front of an arena full of screaming fans, "Not one, not two, not three, not four, not five, not six. . . . I came here to win seven titles. And when I say that, I really believe it."

By any standard, James's four seasons in Miami were spectacularly successful, winning two NBA Championships. Had LeBron simply said at that rally, "I intend to bring this team a championship," he would have exceeded expectations. But measured against the standard of his statement, he failed to live up to his own pledge.

So is there anything to be gained from making statements that replace uncertainty with certainty? Indeed. After all, definitive language rallies people to a cause.

When President Kennedy told Congress in 1961, "This nation should commit itself to achieving the goal, before this decade is out, of landing a man on the moon and returning him safely to the earth," he set America on a far more ambitious and aggressive course than our nation would have taken had he simply said, "This nation should commit itself to achieving the goal, at some point in the future, of landing a man on the moon and returning him safely to the earth."

Perhaps most famously, in June 1940, Winston Churchill declared before the House of Commons,

> Even though large tracts of Europe and many old and famous States have fallen or may fall into the grip of the Gestapo and all the odious apparatus of Nazi rule, we shall not flag or fail. We shall go on to the end, we shall fight in France, we shall fight on the seas and oceans, we shall fight with growing confidence and growing strength in the air, we shall defend our Island, whatever the cost may be, we shall fight on the beaches, we shall fight on the landing grounds, we shall fight in the fields and in the streets, we shall fight in the hills; we shall never surrender.

His words became a self-fulfilling prophecy.

In a way, President Ford's words became a self-fulfilling prophecy as well, but they prophesied his own doom, because while Ford's tough words, and the even tougher headline they engendered, may have served to save New York, they also served to sink Ford. For New York, Ford's statement convinced the key players that no federal help would be forthcoming. It galvanized the city to cut spending and increase fees. And these changes allowed Ford to backtrack and approve federal loans for the city, which then made it easier to sell additional MAC bonds.

Rubenstein, Koch, and others would later say that by refusing to save the city, Ford did the city a service. For better or worse, it may also have enshrined brinksmanship as a bankruptcy negotiating tactic, something America has seen play out on the federal level during a series of debt ceiling negotiations.

Although Ford would later approve federal support for New York, New Yorkers wouldn't forget the headline. The following year, Jimmy Carter received the third-highest vote share a Democratic presidential candidate ever garnered in New York City and narrowly won New York state and with it the forty-one electoral votes that gave him the presidency—a history-moving impact from one speech that wasn't given, and one that was.

Presidents Kennedy and Eisenhower discuss the Bay of Pigs invasion at Camp David in 1961. (AP photo / Paul Vathis, file)

PART 4

The Fog of War, the Path to Peace

Important undelivered speeches derive from the times and places where outcomes are in doubt, the stakes are high, and the wheel of history is turning. We see all those factors at play in times of war and conflict.

Supreme Allied Commander Dwight Eisenhower's undelivered apology for the failure of the D-day landings provides a lesson in the language of leadership; Emperor Hirohito's undelivered apology reveals the crushing burden of responsibility and the hidden meanings in the words we choose and those we don't; and President John F. Kennedy's speech announcing airstrikes on Cuba during the Cuban missile crisis demonstrates how outcomes that seem certain in hindsight were precarious at the time, while also raising the complicated question of speech authorship.

Dwight Eisenhower addresses American paratroopers on June 5, 1944, as they prepared for the first assault of D-day. (U.S. Army photograph)

8

Dwight Eisenhower's Apology for the Failure of the D-Day Invasion, June 1944

The Language of Leadership

"The troops, the air and the Navy did
all that bravery could do."

On June 5, 1944, leading up to the D-day invasion by Allied troops at the beaches of Normandy in Nazi-occupied northern France, Supreme Allied Commander General Dwight Eisenhower described all of southern England as "a tense and coiled spring . . . a great human spring, coiled for the moment when its energy should be released and it would vault the English Channel in the greatest amphibious assault ever attempted."

That "human spring" included some 156,000 troops who would make up the landing force and who were now encamped in southern England. The need for secrecy was so vital that the southernmost barracks were surrounded with barbed wire to prevent any soldier from leaving the camp once briefed on his role in the attack.

The operation had been set for June 5, but the weather report wasn't good: low clouds, high winds, rough seas.

The attack was postponed. The meteorologists predicted that the next day could produce an opening, perhaps only for thirty-six hours. There was a chance the landing would succeed and then the forces would be stranded, "the isolated original attacking forces easy prey to a German counteraction." Eisenhower feared a horrific echo of Dunkirk, where three hundred thousand British, French, Canadian, and Belgian soldiers had been backed up against the English Channel, with thousands falling prey to German artillery and air attack.

By the evening of June 4, it was clear that the initial delay was the right decision. The rain had not stopped, and the wind was still raging. But what about the sixth?

A delay beyond the sixth meant that the next window to attack would be two weeks later when the moon and tides would be more favorable, because the attack required calm-enough seas to cross the channel without boats colliding into one another or too many soldiers getting sick, and a low tide occurring late enough so that the mines, submerged barriers, and iron fences known as "Belgian gates" in the shallows could be seen and destroyed, but early enough that there would be a second low tide before dark for a second wave of landings. The moon had to be full enough so that pilots of the planes carrying the paratroopers could have just enough light to navigate by. And hopefully, there would also be a wind blowing inshore, to carry the smoke and dust of battle toward the enemy.

But that would also be two weeks in which secret plans could leak, two weeks in which those 156,000 American, British, and Canadian service members would have to remain bottled up on ships and in bases, and two weeks of fighting weather squandered with the fighters stuck on the wrong side of the English Channel.

"The question," Eisenhower said, "is just how long can you keep this operation on the end of a limb and let it hang there."

In planning the assault, Eisenhower and his commanders had been meeting twice daily, at 4:30 a.m. and 9:00 p.m., in the library of Southwick House, a Georgian mansion near Portsmouth, where the Allied Expeditionary Force was headquartered.

As rain lashed the windows and the wind rattled the floor-to-ceiling french doors, they had to decide whether to launch on the sixth.

Admiral Sir Bertram Ramsay, who had overseen the evacuation from Dunkirk and was now coordinating the fleet that would bring 156,000 men onto the beaches of Normandy, voted go. Eisenhower's chief of staff, Major General Walter Bedell Smith, said it was a good gamble, but a gamble nonetheless. Eisenhower turned to General Bernard Law Montgomery, who was in command of all Allied ground forces during Operation Overlord (as the invasion was code-named): "Do you see any reason why we should not go on Tuesday?" Monty, usually cautious, was definitive in his answer: *"I would say go."*

At 9:45 p.m. on the fourth, Eisenhower made his preliminary decision; the order to go would be given. Slower ships would be given the order to set sail. He still had a few hours to order them back if necessary.

By the time of the meeting at 4:30 a.m. on the fifth, the wind and rain had not subsided. Eisenhower made the muddy one-mile drive from his camp to Southwick House. As Eisenhower entered, he passed the large drawing room where members of Britain's Women's Royal Naval Service rolled ladders along the floor, marking on a floor-to-ceiling map of the European coastline the progress of the convoy of ships toward Normandy's beaches. (The operation was so secret that the workers who had installed the Normandy section of the map were detained until after the invasion.)

Eisenhower wanted one more meteorological briefing. Despite the weather outside, Group Captain J. M. Stagg was confident it would clear. Eisenhower had to make his decision at that moment. Any longer and the 5,400 craft already at sea wouldn't have enough fuel to return to port and launch the next night.

After the briefing, Ike took a few minutes to consider. By some reports, he needed less than a minute. By others, he paced alone on the library's blue carpet for five minutes.

Reports are also divided on what Eisenhower said next. His words have appeared as everything from "I don't like it, but we have to go," to "Okay, we'll go," to "Okay, let 'er rip," to "All right, we move," to "We will attack tomorrow."

Whatever Eisenhower's exact words, what was clear is that he made the announcement without great fanfare. As Eisenhower's biographer Kenneth S. Davis writes, "There was nothing dramatic in the way he made [the decision]. He didn't think in terms of 'history' or 'destiny,' nor did there arise in him any of that grandiose self-consciousness which characterizes the decisive moments of a Napoleon or Hitler."

In his personal diary, Captain Harry Butcher, who was Eisenhower's naval aide, wrote, "As the big day approaches Ike is bearing his responsibility with remarkable ease. Actually, he is fatalistic about it—someone has to make the decision when the time comes and he simply happens to be the one who bears the responsibility and he will not hesitate to take it."

Getting back into his car, he told his driver, Kay Summersby, "I hope to God I'm right."

But what if he wasn't?

After all, the air commander of the Allied Forces, Sir Trafford Leigh-Mallory of the Royal Air Force, had said that three-quarters of the airmen would become casualties.*

"I am very uneasy about the whole operation," said Field Marshal Sir Alan Brooke, the head of the British Army. "At the best it will fall so very far short of the expectations. At worst, it may well be the most ghastly disaster of the whole war."

After Eisenhower shared the plan with Charles de Gaulle, the leader of the French Resistance in exile in England, de Gaulle lectured him on its shortcomings.

Despite his confidence that only the weather could stop the Allies, Eisenhower felt full responsibility for not only ordering the operation but designing it. And so, as ships headed across the English Channel and paratroopers prepared to drop behind enemy lines, Eisenhower sat down to write.†

As he had before each amphibious operation he ordered, he wrote a short statement taking responsibility for its failure. Upon its successful

---

* After the success of the airborne operation became clear, Leigh-Mallory wrote to Eisenhower that it is sometimes difficult in life to admit that one was wrong, but he never had a greater pleasure than in doing so on this occasion. Ike's aide Harry Butcher noted in his diary, "You simply can't stay mad at people like this."

† The exact timing of Eisenhower writing the draft is unknown, but given the paper and the haste, and the fact that he had written a longer letter to his wife earlier in the day, my best guess is that he wrote it at night.

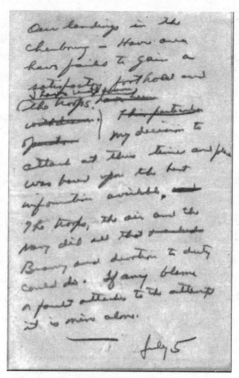

(Courtesy of Dwight D. Eisenhower Presidential Library)

conclusion, he would tear up the draft. The statement he wrote in advance of D-day is the only one that survives.

> Our landings in the Cherbourg-Havre area have failed to gain a satisfactory foothold and I have withdrawn the troops. My decision to attack at this time and place was based on the best information available. The troops, the air and the Navy did all that bravery and devotion to duty could do. If any blame or fault attaches to the attempt it is mine alone.

These remarks were unlike the polished "order of the day"—the statement that Eisenhower had prerecorded days earlier and that was to be broadcast and handed out in printed form to his men as he sent them into battle on the morning of the invasion. He had begun composing that statement four months earlier. It contained the soaring language of purpose—

"The free men of the world are marching together to Victory!"—as well as the rhetorical flourish of epistrophe, or repetition of the same word or phrase at the end of a sentence: "The eyes of the world are upon you. The hopes and prayers of liberty-loving people everywhere march with you."

By contrast, the D-day "failure" remarks had been written in haste, the day before the attack. But even in its brevity, the draft is telling.

We see, in Eisenhower's own hand, his switch from the passive "The troops have been withdrawn" to the active "I have withdrawn the troops." The passive voice, as you may remember from middle school English class, is when you make the object of an action into the subject of a sentence. A common example used to demonstrate the passive voice is the age-old question: "Why was the road crossed by the chicken?" In the more familiar phrasing, the chicken is the one doing something, crossing the road. In the passive phrasing, the focus is on the fact that the road is having something done to it.

Passive voice plays an interesting role in speechwriting. As a general matter, it sounds detached, boring, and bureaucratic. "The program was implemented" is passive. Leaders are action-takers: "I started the program."

Ulysses S. Grant crystallized this reality when he told his doctor, "I am a verb." Verbs are action words, and leaders are action-takers. There's even a joke about this that circulates among investment bankers: "Nobody says, 'It's raining.' They say, 'I made it rain.'"

That's why, when the passive voice is used in admitting an error of failure, it sounds tremendously squirrely. The most famous example of this is the too-often-used phrase *mistakes were made.* William Safire, in *Safire's Political Dictionary,* described it as "a passive-evasive way of acknowledging error while distancing the speaker from responsibility for it."

Safire also identified the first usage of this passive term, and that honor ironically goes to the man who described himself as a verb. In his final report to Congress in 1876, President Grant acknowledges (but doesn't take responsibility for) the scandals of his administration by writing, "Mistakes have been made, as all can see and I admit."

Since then, "mistakes were made" has been uttered by leaders time and again, from President Ronald Reagan discussing the Iran-Contra affair to President Bill Clinton describing a fundraising scandal, to a number of cabinet secretaries and advisors.

However, there are times, especially when used in making a threat or a promise, that the passive voice can have an authority to it. Because it's not clear who is initiating the act, the passive voice can invoke an almost biblical wrath.

This was a favorite approach of both Presidents Bush. In describing (and threatening action against) Iraqi president Saddam Hussein's invasion of Kuwait in 1990, George H. W. Bush famously said, "This will not stand, this aggression against Kuwait."

Eleven years later, President George W. Bush's address to a joint session of Congress following the September 11 terrorist attacks contained one of the most powerful uses of the passive voice I've ever heard:

> Tonight, we are a country awakened to danger and called to defend freedom. Our grief has turned to anger and anger to resolution. Whether we bring our enemies to justice or bring justice to our enemies, justice will be done.

In his undelivered final speech in 1945,* President Franklin Delano Roosevelt uses this technique as well, writing, "The once powerful, malignant Nazi state is crumbling. The Japanese war lords are receiving, in their own homeland, the retribution for which they asked when they attacked Pearl Harbor." But passive voice in an apology doesn't sound biblical, it sounds bumbling, and Eisenhower recognized that.

What else do we see in Eisenhower's statement? He crossed out "This particular operation" and instead substituted "My decision to attack," which is anything but passive. He reinforces the point at the end by thickly underlining "mine alone."

In his haste, Eisenhower dated his document July, rather than June 5.

On the twentieth anniversary of D-day, Eisenhower returned to Normandy and gave an interview with legendary CBS news anchor Walter Cronkite.† Standing in front of the original invasion map, Cronkite asked

---

* Roosevelt's final speech is discussed in depth in chapter 15.
† In the early part of that interview, as in his undelivered speech, he again states the invasion date of "July 5."

about the message Eisenhower intended to deliver had the operation ended in disaster.

Eisenhower knew there were German troops in the area and antiair-craft batteries loaded with lots of flak. He knew there would be loss of life. In his words, "Goodness knows those fellas meant a lot to me. You just have to make decisions when you're in war. I'm going to do some-thing to my country's advantage for the least cost. You can't say no cost, because you know you're going to lose people."

But he also had confidence in his plan. Even when others argued that the route into Europe had to be through the Mediterranean, this was the course of action he wanted to pursue. Being so wedded to the idea seemed to give him greater comfort in accepting the risks that came with it.

Regarding his planned message had the invasion failed, Eisenhower said in the interview,

> From the beginning, I had been partly responsible for this plan. I had been . . . head of the staff that originally outlined this opera-tion way back two years ago. From all those two years I believed in this thing, I believed it would defeat Germany, and consequently I felt not only as a commander but as sort of a fellow who'd be try-ing to convert everybody to the need of this thing, I felt a partic-ular responsibility. So I wrote a little thing that soundly assumed that we were going to be defeated, but I told no one else about it; and it must have been an aide who got this thing out and told people about it. I just said the landing had been a failure and it's no one's fault but mine. I was the one who picked out—I knew I couldn't fail except on weather—I was the one that was respon-sible for the decision to go and all the fault belongs to me, and that's that. If it did fail, you know this—I was going into oblivion anyway so I might as well take full responsibility.

Eisenhower didn't remember how his undelivered remarks became public, and one legend arose that Ike threw the note out and an aide salvaged it. The truth is more prosaic. According to the diary of Captain Harry Butcher, Eisenhower's aide, on the afternoon of July 11, 1944, more than a month after the invasion, "Ike called me into his office and handed me a sheet of note-paper on which he had scribbled a message. He said he had found it in his wallet. After reading it, I told him I wanted it for the diary. He reluctantly assented, saying that he had written one in similar vein for every amphibious operation but had secretly torn up each one. If I put this one in the diary it might be bad luck. I apparently argued him out of an ill omen."

If Butcher's account is to be trusted, and since it's contemporaneous there's no reason why it shouldn't be, it seems Eisenhower simply forgot the whole episode.

Having been salvaged, this note serves two roles.

First, it provides insight into the initial chapter of a dramatic alternative history. On the seventy-fifth anniversary of D-day, the BBC asked several historians and military leaders what would have happened if the D-day invasion had failed. Military historian Dennis Showalter believes that "there would have been an agonising reappraisal among the Americans who had pushed for a cross-channel invasion. Eisenhower would almost certainly have offered his resignation, it would almost certainly have had to be accepted. It's also possible that US President Roosevelt could have lost the November 1944 election, so there could have been a change in administrations."

Military historian Gary Sheffield argued that the Soviets "could have won the war singlehandedly, perhaps by 1946. I think we may well have seen the hammer and sickle flying not simply in Poland and Eastern Germany, but in Western Germany, the Benelux countries, and France."

General Sir Richard Dannatt asked, "Could the Allies still have managed to get an unconditional German surrender, or would there have been a negotiated end to the war? In that case, what would Europe look like today?"

The questions are intriguing, and we are lucky not to have the answers. What we do have is a speech that was thankfully never delivered. So rather than writing the first chapter of an alternate and terrifying reality, it instead serves a second role: to provide an object lesson in the language of leadership and responsibility.

Emperor Hirohito in 1935.

9

Emperor Hirohito Apologizes
for World War II, 1948

Dog Whistles, Chameleons,
and Apologies

"Our heart burns with grief."

When historian and journalist Kyoko Kato finally got around to returning the files she had borrowed from the Tajima family, her biography of Michiji Tajima* had already been in print for seven months. She was frustrated with herself for not having returned the documents earlier, but since her work on a massive two-thousand-page manuscript had required so much sorting and re-sorting of papers, she had a lot of organizing to do before she could return everything.

Michiji Tajima had been one of the most important people in early

---

* For consistency, I have written the Japanese names in this chapter as given name, family name—as names are in the rest of this book.

postwar Japan. He had been a bank president, a cabinet minister, and a board member at Sony. Additionally, he had served as the "Grand Steward" of the Imperial Household office from June 1948 until the end of 1953. In this role, he was essentially the personal aide, chief of staff, and confidant of the emperor. To write the biography, Kato had borrowed his books and personal writings from Tajima's family.

To return those overdue items, she packed up the heavy books in a series of cardboard boxes and sent them along. But when it came to the handwritten papers, she thought it best to deliver those personally. She was handing a stack of papers to Tajima's son, Kyoji, and glanced at two sheets of faded brown paper that stuck out from the pile. She would have simply shuffled them back in, except one distinctive character caught her eye, 朕, or *chin*. This was the first-person pronoun used only by the emperor. And the handwriting was Tajima's.

There are times when a speechwriter makes a best guess as to what a speaker would want to say,* and there are times when the speechwriter serves as a glorified stenographer, not a wellspring from which a speaker's words pour forth but a channel through which they flow. By using the character *chin*, Tajima seemed to be saying, "these really are the emperor's words."

Kyoji looked at the paper, and reached that conclusion immediately, "Those are the emperor's own words, I believe. I did not know there was any such document."

August 15, 1945, marked the first time the Japanese people would hear the voice of their forty-four-year-old sovereign, Emperor Hirohito.

Prior to then, all pronouncements, including the decision to go to war against the United States, were delivered in what was called a *rescript*—a written statement that would then be read and distributed by others.

Hirohito had become emperor of Japan at age twenty-five, upon the death of his father. The process of naming his reign resulted in the title Showa, which translates to "enlightened harmony" or "illustrious peace." And though his reign would ultimately be the longest imperial

---

* Nixon's speechwriter, Ray Price, navigated this in chapter 4.

reign in Japan's history, its first twenty-five years delivered neither peace nor harmony.

Historians are divided on whether Hirohito was an architect of Japan's aggressive wars of expansion or simply powerless to stop them. While the prevailing opinion for a long time held that Hirohito was simply too weak to outmaneuver pro-war ministers and the military, more recent scholarship from Herbert Bix and others shows Hirohito had much more agency than previously believed.

Regardless of his actual role, what is not disputed is that he presided over an increased militarization of the Japanese political leadership and either actively promoted or offered no objection to the 1931 invasion of Manchuria, in China. He also presided over the use of chemical weapons against the Chinese in 1938 and the attack on Pearl Harbor in 1941. And ultimately, he presided over the utter destruction of his country.

Throughout World War II, Hirohito had been advised by a war council of six men: the prime minister, the minister of foreign affairs, the minister of war, the minister of the navy, the army chief of staff, and the navy chief of staff. They met regularly in a bunker built into a hillside on the grounds of the Imperial Palace.

When they met on August 9, 1945, to decide whether Japan could fight on in the Second World War, Nagasaki was burning from the atomic bomb dropped by U.S. forces.

Previously, every decision made about the prosecution of the war had been brought to the emperor unanimously. But on the question of surrender, the war council was evenly divided. Prime Minister Suzuki and Foreign Minister Togo made the decision to do something never previously done: present their emperor anything other than a unified recommendation.

They requested his presence in the bunker. For the emperor, it was a journey of several hundred feet, from a separate shelter built specifically for the imperial couple. Emotionally, the journey must have been much longer than that. He entered through the foot-thick steel blast door just before midnight.

Eyes averted out of respect, Prime Minister Suzuki presented the emperor with the Potsdam Declaration—the document in which the United States, Great Britain, and China laid out the terms of Japan's surrender—and their split decision on whether or not to sign it.

Although what the declaration meant for the emperor was less clear, those in the bunker could see their own doom spelled out in its unequivocal words: "There must be eliminated for all time the authority and influence of those who have deceived and misled the people of Japan into embarking on world conquest, for we insist that a new order of peace, security and justice will be impossible until irresponsible militarism is driven from the world," and "stern justice shall be meted out to all war criminals, including those who have visited cruelties upon our prisoners."

The emperor absorbed it, and responded, "Continuing the war can only result in the annihilation of the Japanese people and a prolongation of the suffering of all humanity. It seems obvious that the nation is no longer able to wage war, and its ability to defend its own shores is doubtful. That is unbearable for me. The time has come for me to bear the unbearable. I give my sanction to the proposal to accept the Allied proclamation."

The toll of the war to that point had been tremendous. Though precise numbers vary, out of a prewar population of seventy-four million, it's believed that nearly two million Japanese soldiers were dead, as were another million Japanese civilians. More than twice that number were wounded or homeless.

More than forty of Japan's cities had been completely obliterated, and in sixty-six of Japan's major cities, more than 40 percent of the urban areas were destroyed. Four-fifths of all Japanese ships had been sunk. A quarter of all vehicles had been demolished. Close to nine million people were homeless. Many of those who survived were starving, with some cities recommending "emergency diets" of "acorns, grain husks, peanut shells, and sawdust."

Hirohito's advisors first communicated that they would accept the Potsdam terms of surrender with the caveat that Hirohito remain emperor, and because of this, the U.S. bombing runs continued. Within a week, Hirohito was prepared to accept the terms of surrender with no caveats.

Still, how could Japan admit defeat when citizens had been told they were engaged in a holy war and that the only choice was to fight to the last man? Would people commit seppuku, ritual suicide, and die with honor rather than surrender in shame? Would military leaders assume that the emperor was under the spell of traitors and rise up to overthrow him? Hirohito wanted to address his subjects—and these concerns—directly.

He ordered that his advisors write a radio script announcing Japan's surrender. In a historic first, his people would hear his words delivered in his own voice. As Hirohito left the bunker, several of his men collapsed to the ground, sobbing. They wept for their nation and feared for the fate of their emperor, whom they believed had put himself at grave risk.

The process of writing and recording the emperor's remarks was conducted in secret. The remarks were not finalized until midnight the night before they were to be broadcast. The emperor recorded his remarks to a phonograph, which was then hidden from his military officers out of concern that those opposed to a surrender would stop its broadcast. Indeed, a last-minute coup attempt had to be thwarted and the recording secreted out of the palace in a laundry basket.

The emperor of Japan spoke a formalized version of Japanese, full of antiquated and ornamental phrases, difficult for most everyday listeners to understand. In this case, the message was made more confusing by the emperor's stilted delivery, and by the fact that the words *surrender* and *defeat* never appeared in the address. Rather, the emperor framed surrender as a magnanimous act, "resolved to pave the way for a grand peace for all the generations to come." And while the emperor spoke of his great pain at the number of dead and the mourning of their families, he took no responsibility for the decision to go to war in the first place.

To make sure the people understood what had just been said, the emperor's remarks were followed by a second reading by a broadcaster, this time in colloquial Japanese. Avoidance of responsibility was a stance Emperor Hirohito maintained after the war as well. Between March and April 1946, expecting to be called before the war crimes tribunal, he dictated to his aides his own version of wartime events and decisions. While the recordings showed that the emperor had detailed knowledge of personalities and procedures, he also used these sessions to lay responsibility at the feet of his subordinates.

The emperor's fate remained an open question.

Among the occupying Americans, there was a distinct fear that absent the emperor, the Japanese people would rise up and fulfill their wartime promise to fight to the last man. Maintaining an intact emperor system would make it easier to reform Japan's political system, put in place a new constitution, and demilitarize the country.

American brigadier general Elliott Thorpe, who was in favor of keeping Emperor Hirohito on the (much diminished) throne, recalled to historian John Dower, "Otherwise, we would have nothing but chaos. The religion was gone, the government was gone, and he was the only symbol of control. Now I know he had his hand in the cookie jar, and he wasn't any innocent little child. But he was of great use to us."

General Douglas MacArthur himself, in a telegram to Dwight Eisenhower, said of the emperor, "Destroy him and the nation will disintegrate," continuing that if the emperor were deposed, "it would be absolutely essential to greatly increase the occupational forces. It is quite possible that a million troops would be required which would have to be maintained for an indefinite number of years."

That view certainly wasn't unanimous. In Tokyo, George Atcheson, the State Department's representative, argued that the emperor was a war criminal and should be treated as such. In the United States, a Gallup poll that was never published found that 77 percent of Americans wanted Hirohito "severely" punished. The U.S. Senate took up a resolution declaring that Hirohito be tried as a war criminal.

And among America's allies, there was near unanimity that there should be proceedings against Hirohito.

Even support for Hirohito in Japan was far from unanimous. As the war crimes tribunal prepared to render judgment on Japan's leadership during the war, a quarter to a half of the Japanese people wanted Hirohito to abdicate.

The Japanese leadership, too, was divided on the question. In February 1946, Prince Naruhiko Higashikuni, the emperor's uncle by marriage, revealed in an interview that the idea of the emperor's abdication had been discussed among those close to the emperor for months. And it appeared that many of the Japanese people, war-weary and resentful, would be happy to see the emperor go.

However, there was still support for the emperor in Japan. Letters received by General MacArthur ran heavily in favor of the emperor staying on, with statements like "The emperor is not a war criminal. The emperor is a parent to us, the people," and "He is like a rudder to a ship.

If something should happen to His Majesty, we the people would lose our direction."

MacArthur needed something from the emperor to help avoid a trial and likely execution for war crimes. And the answer was a statement in which the emperor would renounce his divinity and model himself, in the words of author Victor Sebestyen, as a "peace-loving, European-style figurehead who had been betrayed by the ruthless military men around him." On January 1, 1946, the emperor issued his "humanity declaration" renouncing his divinity. MacArthur cheered this renunciation (which the Americans had mandated and drafted), gratified that Hirohito "undertakes a leading part in the democratization of his people."

No longer was Hirohito a living god but instead a symbol of his much-diminished nation. That new role allowed the Japanese people to relate to him in a new way, especially as, later that year, he started touring his shattered country, making what were termed "blessed visitations."

By all accounts, the initial visits on these tours were awkward, with the emperor not knowing how to interact with commoners and commoners having no idea how to approach their emperor, whom they had previously seen only in carefully curated images, frequently astride a white horse. This was a far cry from what they saw of their emperor in person: a man who offered stilted questions and reacted to the answers the same way over and over; a man who wore ill-fitting suits, carried himself with a stooped posture, wore thick glasses, and shuffled forward in scuffed shoes.

And yet, these traits, along with his habit of tipping his hat to the people, made him a more sympathetic character and increased the public's adoration for him. The tours also, as John Dower put it, "revitalized and refocused this mass psychology of self-criticism and apology. Obviously, the emperor was undertaking these excursions for the people's sake. Just as obviously, this was not a natural or easy thing for him to do. A feeling emerged that one should . . . apologize for embarrassing and inconveniencing his majesty."

Perhaps due to seeing the sorry state of his country and his citizens, the emperor also seemed to feel an increased need to apologize to his people, an unprecedented act that would have far-reaching consequences. And it appears that he tried to offer this apology on at least two separate occasions.

The first occurred as the war crimes tribunal, which was called to hold Japanese leaders to account for their wartime actions, prepared to reach its verdict in November 1948.

By that time, the emperor was no longer a deity, Japan had a new constitution, and the Imperial Household had been downgraded from a ministry to an office, operating under Japan's prime minister.

As part of a wholesale move to make the emperor's court more democratic and less aristocratic, Prime Minister Hitoshi Ashida reached out to Michiji Tajima and asked him to take the role of grand steward.* Tajima was a court outsider, which made him an unprecedented choice. What's more, Tajima was personally in favor of the emperor abdicating.

But the choice was also a strategic one; Tajima was a restructuring expert who had previously reformed Japan's Railway Bureau and, in the wake of a wave of Depression-era bank failures, its banking system. Now it was the institutions of the emperor that needed reform. Tajima reluctantly took the job, but quickly earned the trust of the emperor.

As he began his work, Tajima also began reversing his view on abdication, fearing that rather than stabilizing and moving Japan forward, an abdication could destabilize the one system that was not being disrupted by the occupation.

From the end of April 1946 until early September 1947, the Japanese wartime leaders faced trial in the very war ministry building where many of them had once worked. Modeled after the Nuremberg trials, which had held Nazi leaders to account, special charges were reserved for top leaders who had planned and directed "crimes against peace: namely, planning, preparation, initiation or waging of a war of aggression, or a war in violation of international treaties, agreements or assurances."

After the defense rested, the tribunal took fifteen months to formulate its verdict, which was to be announced on November 12, 1948.

According to Tajima's diaries, as the verdict of the war crimes tribunal approached, the emperor was suffering, wanting to, in some way, express his remorse for the pain people were feeling, and perhaps wanting to ex-

---

* The prime minister also replaced the chamberlain, the second-ranking staffer in the Imperial Household, with a man named Takanobu Mitani, who had previously served as ambassador to France.

press the pain he was feeling at the prospect of many of those who were close to him being imprisoned and perhaps put to death.

The evening before the verdict, seven of the prime minister's and emperor's department heads gathered to draft statements to be released after judgment had been rendered. The meeting, which went until about 9:00 p.m., yielded six different draft statements in which the prime minister would describe the emperor's feelings.

None seemed right. At issue was one particular term, *hansei*. It English, it literally means to acknowledge one's own mistake and pledge improvement. But among the ways to express sorrow or culpability in Japanese, this term is considered neutral. Therefore, it ran the risk of inflaming other countries as being not sufficiently sorry, while the robuster apology could inadvertently admit culpability to a domestic audience. No statement seemed to successfully walk that line, and so none was made.

The emperor continued to look for an opportunity to unburden his soul, especially that December, after General Hideki Tojo and six of his other military leaders were executed for war crimes.

It's natural, in reviewing the notes and journal entries of those closest to the emperor, to think about him as having feelings like any other individual—in this case, feelings of guilt and responsibility. But it's important to recognize that the emperor is not supposed to have individual feelings. In fact, the very idea of private life and private feelings was somewhat alien to the Japanese people during the war. For example, a family couldn't mourn a son lost in war; they could only celebrate his valor on behalf of the empire. And the emperor couldn't have personal feelings because he *was* the empire.

And yet, the emperor clearly felt torn between his position and his feelings as an individual, something that would be difficult to admit to any royal insiders. It seems understandable, then, that he might confide in someone close to him, but who had a bit more of an outsider's perspective: Tajima.

So the emperor ordered Tajima to put together a draft rescript of an apology. The two men discussed what the emperor wanted to say. And Tajima put the words to paper. The draft was believed to be completed sometime in late 1948, as the war crimes tribunal was getting ready to hand down its decisions.

Now, for the first time in English, we can see the Showa emperor's undelivered words.*

We, in the more than twenty years since Our enthronement, have striven day and night to avoid betraying Our imperial ancestors and the people, but unable to alter the current of the times, [Japan] lost the friendship of its near neighbors and fought with the great powers, [which,] ultimately ending in grievous defeat, has led to the devastating extremity [we face] today. Countless corpses lie exposed on the battlefield, countless people lost their lives in their workplaces, and when We think of the dead and their bereaved families, We truly cannot suppress Our heartache. Countless people, too, bear the wounds of battle, or of the devastation of war, or are prisoners in foreign lands or have lost the property they had in the colonies. Moreover, the depression of industry, soaring prices, and straitened [conditions in] basic food, clothing, and shelter have caused sufferings beyond counting that cannot but be understood as an unprecedented calamity for the nation. Quietly thinking of these matters, Our heart is seared with grief. We are deeply ashamed before the realm for Our lack of virtue. Residing within the Imperial Palace though We do, Our heart does not rest easy, and when We think of Our people, We are overcome by the weight of Our [cares].

However, the present time is one of unknown upheaval, and the realm is in a state of tumult. We believe that for Us to hasten to purify [rectify] Ourself† to seek immediate relief from this sorrow of a hundred years would not be self-respecting [an act of dignity] in the true sense of the term. Bearing in mind the present situation inside and outside Japan, We will apologize to Our ancestors and to the people by giving Our life [to the effort], facing all hardship, and practicing virtue and accumulating good

---

* Some of the phrases of this speech have appeared in English before, and translations vary slightly. This translation was completed by Louisa Rubinfien, a veteran translator, researcher, and historian of Japan who has previously translated works on economic history, historical memory, arts and culture, and politics. It was reviewed by Jordan Sand, a professor of Japanese history at Georgetown University.

† This is understood to mean "purify Ourself through the act of abdication."

deeds, and We vow to give Our [fullest] to the reconstruction of the nation's destiny [fortunes] and the happiness of the people. It is Our earnest wish, too, that all the people will conform to Our will, realize the situation all around us [at home and abroad], and, cooperating with each other as with one heart and giving their all in their respective callings, will overcome this extraordinary situation and extend the nation's honor far and wide.

This statement is best understood as two speeches: the first is an apology to the Japanese people, and the second is a statement of the emperor's intent *not* to abdicate.

In the summer of 1948, there was a lot of discussion in the press of abdication. The emperor himself, on the day the verdict was handed down, had a conversation with one of his advisors in which he said that he wanted to step down. At this time, some of the Americans in charge of the occupation feared that Hirohito would not only abdicate but commit suicide.

And yet, in November, the emperor delivered a secret message to MacArthur, reaffirming his commitment to working for the reconstruction of Japan and the promotion of world peace.

This draft describes his reasoning. One idea that stands out here is the idea that staying on, rather than abdicating, is the path of greatest difficulty and therefore the right one: "By giving Our life to the effort, facing all hardship, and practicing virtue and accumulating good deeds."

The apology itself is more complicated. As candid as these remarks seem to be, this isn't an apology for the war itself; it's an apology to the Japanese people for the emperor's "lack of virtue."

To understand the apology, it's important to recognize that part of the imperial tradition in Japan has Confucian roots; and one of those beliefs is that the virtue of the leader keeps order in society and in the natural world, that the emperor is "coeval with heaven and earth." Therefore, if some calamity befalls Japan, it must be a result of the emperor's lack of virtue. There's a cosmological level to this apology—it's not that the emperor makes decisions or policy, it's something elemental inside the emperor that has caused these terrible things.

There are also several interesting word choices. The first thing that would have captured an audience's attention is the use of the word *chin* throughout. When the emperor renounced his divinity, he stopped using the word *chin,* the royal we. But here we find it, one last time, in this "apology" speech. One interpretation is that it was the only way to make the speech weighty enough, to reclaim his cosmological responsibility so that he could fully apologize for falling short of it.

Another interesting choice is the decision not to use the word *hansei,* a neutral term to acknowledge regret. Japanese, Chinese, and Korean share some characters, and with those characters come distinct shades of meaning—and to the Chinese and Koreans, *hansei* is a completely insufficient apology and is, in fact, offensive in its mildness.

In this draft, the Emperor jettisoned that word in favor of the term *hadzu,* which means something approaching "deep shame" and is often used in places where people talk about the idea of conscience or guilt— something that would have been groundbreaking for the emperor to do. In the emperor's speech, we see it in the phrase "Our heart is seared with grief."

Kyoko Kato, who discovered the draft of the speech, noted that not only is the word chosen an intense and raw one, the character chosen to represent the word, 愧, is one that would resonate most intensely.

There's another interesting word choice, involving the description of defeat, and it's the term *haisen.* This translates to: defeat in war. *Shusen* would be a more neutral term to describe simply "the end of the war."

Haisen, as a word choice, would have been alarming to nearly every audience.

For Japanese conservatives, it's the very concept of talking about "defeat"—a term not even used in Japan's surrender. For Japanese liberals, it would have the effect of implying that it was the defeat that was terrible, rather than the war. And similarly for Americans, who took the position that the war was inherently evil, it would have been offensive to have the emperor say that it was the *defeat* that was to be regretted. This ran totally counter to the occupation's narrative that Americans had exorcised the evil and were now in the process of building a new, better Japan.

So, given all that, why did the emperor choose to use *haisen* in this draft? We have to look more deeply into the use of language to hazard a guess.

In Japanese, there's a term for words that contain different shades of meaning, and mean different things to different audiences. These are called *tamamushi,* or chameleon words. Like chameleons, they are intended to blend in and to take the color of their surroundings so as to go essentially unnoticed. Everyone can hear a chameleon word the way they want to hear it.

Chameleon words are not-too-distant cousins of something we have in English: dog whistles. Just as a dog whistle is silent to humans but audible to a dog, dog-whistle language is heard clearly by one group of people and almost not at all by another.

According to Berkeley Law professor Ian Haney López in his book *Dog Whistle Politics,* most dog whistles are intended to trigger a passionate response in one audience, while not going so far as to offend other audiences. He traces this back to George Wallace, who, after losing his 1958 campaign for governor of Alabama, decided that "no other son-of-a-bitch will ever out-nigger me again."

On a promise to uphold segregation (now, tomorrow, and forever), Wallace won the governorship in 1963. But as he sought more of a national profile, he had to figure out how to communicate his message in ways that would be heard by the intended audiences without making a direct appeal to racism. According to Haney López, "The key lay in seemingly non-racial language. At his inauguration, Wallace had defended segregation and extolled the proud Anglo-Saxon Southland, thereby earning national ridicule as an unrepentant redneck. Six months later, talking not about stopping integration but about states' rights and arrogant federal authority," Wallace had found an alternate vocabulary, indeed an entire alternate language, that served as a code that channeled ideas that couldn't be spoken clearly, aloud, in polite company.

Over the years, that vocabulary has expanded dramatically. To argue against gays and women in the military, opponents talk about "unit cohesion" and "military readiness." The term "family values" came to signify alliance with Christian conservatives. "International bankers" became a code word for Jews, as did "cosmopolitan" and, to an extent, "globalists." "Urban" and "inner city" became less directly offensive ways to say Black or Hispanic. Attempts to weaken unions sounded downright positive to workers when called "paycheck protection" and "right to work." And they sounded even better to corporate leaders, who were too politic to say they wanted to "bust" unions, but for whom "right to work" conveyed the exact same thing.

Dog whistles are not limited to politics (or to dogs). In *Safire's Political Dictionary,* William Safire points out that the president of the upscale clothing store Henri Bendel described trafficking in "dog-whistle fashion . . . clothes with a pitch so high and special that only the thinnest and most sophisticated women would hear their call."

And there are times when the effect can be unintentional. Safire also cites pollster Richard Morin's observation that "subtle changes in question-wording sometimes produce remarkably different results . . . researchers call this the 'Dog Whistle Effect': Respondents hear something in the question that researchers do not."

Morin, in this case, was talking about the wording of a question about happiness. A National Opinion Research Center poll asked the question, "Would you say that you are very happy, are pretty happy, or are you not too happy?" A Gallup poll asked, "Are you very happy, are you fairly happy, or are you not too happy?"

The only difference in the questions was the use of the word *pretty* in one poll, and *fairly* in the other. And yet, 15 percent more people were "very happy" when the alternative was being "fairly happy."

As political consultant Frank Luntz, best known as one of the message architects of Newt Gingrich's Contract with America, points out in his book *Words That Work,* the same is true with "welfare" (on which Americans believe we are spending too much) and "assistance to the poor" (on which Americans believe we are spending too little).

"It's not what you say, it's what people hear," Luntz offers, in an important insight for all practitioners of political rhetoric. No matter what words and language you use, "the person on the receiving end will always understand it through the prism of his or her own emotions, preconceptions, prejudices, and preexisting beliefs. It's not enough to be correct or reasonable or even brilliant. The key to successful communication is to take the imaginative leap of stuffing yourself right into your listener's shoes to know what they are thinking and feeling in the deepest recesses of their mind and heart. How that person perceives what you say is even more real, at least in the practical sense, than how you perceive yourself."

In the case of Emperor Hirohito's use of *haisen,* it's likely that this was an unintentional dog whistle. Hirohito wasn't trying to deliver a different message to different audiences; that just happened to be what those audiences would hear.

And this raises the issue of apology itself. There are volumes of study devoted to the subject of apologies in general, and the rhetoric of apology in particular. Professor William Benoit at the University of Alabama posits that most apologies contain some combination of the following elements: denial (which can include blame shifting), evading of responsibility (which can include good intentions), reducing the offensiveness of the event (which can include differentiation from more serious infractions, or an attack on the credibility of the accuser), corrective action (what I, the speaker, am going to do to make up for this), and then mortification (some description of shame).

Of course, not all of these elements square with what makes an apology politically palatable. After all, shifting blame and describing how things could have been worse are the leadership equivalent of the passive voice.*

Apologies are difficult even when it comes to admission of minor transgressions. That's because it's rare that individuals accept full blame. As the writer Joy Clarkson notes, that's because we don't want our faults and our mistakes to become part of our identities. "Accepting full blame is like being able to lick your elbow: lots of people think they can, but in reality, only a few people are able to." For Hirohito in particular, the idea of fault and identity were so closely tied that, had he apologized, his fault and his identity would have been one and the same.

President Ronald Reagan's statement apologizing for the Iran-Contra affair tries to separate fault from identity: "First, let me say I take full responsibility for my own actions and for those of my Administration. As angry as I may be about activities undertaken without my knowledge, I am still accountable for those activities. As disappointed as I may be in some who served me, I'm still the one who must answer to the American people for this behavior. And as personally distasteful as I find secret bank accounts and diverted funds—well, as the Navy would say, this happened on my watch." But even Reagan's speech ultimately regresses to the political apology mean, with this rhetorical and intellectual leap:

---

* Which is discussed in chapter 8.

"A few months ago I told the American people I did not trade arms for hostages. My heart and my best intentions still tell me that's true; but the facts and the evidence tell me it is not."

More recently, we've seen some evidence that in politics, at least, apologizing is actually a risky strategy. Recent studies have shown than an apology can decrease rather than increase overall support for those who said or did things that others considered offensive. According to Harvard Law School professor Cass Sunstein, who conducted the research, "One reason may be that an apology is like a confession. It makes wrongdoing more salient. It can lead people to think: 'We thought he was a jerk; now we know he is. He admits it!'"

For Hirohito, while different audiences may have heard different messages, his undelivered "apology" speech is a stunningly clear and candid statement. Had he delivered it, it almost certainly would have raised the question of war responsibility and perhaps required the emperor to abdicate, despite his pledge to continue the work of rebuilding.

Instead of becoming Japan's longest-reigning emperor and overseeing Japan's full transition from a militarist nation to a modern democracy, would he have exited the stage as part of a cabal of warmongers who led the nation to ruin?

Or would the speech have done the opposite? Would it have brought him even closer to the people? Would it have done through words what the emperor had been doing through his body language on those tours, demonstrating to the people that he felt their pain?

The draft was shelved, and it wouldn't see the light of day until Kyoko Kato discovered it fifty-five years later.

There's another wrinkle to this story, and it comes from Lennox Tierney, who served as a civilian cultural advisor to General MacArthur during the occupation. Tierney claims that Hirohito tried to meet with MacArthur to apologize, and "MacArthur refused to admit him or acknowledge him."

No other reputable records of such an attempted meeting or rebuff exist, and it seems unlikely that Hirohito, who met MacArthur in only ten highly choreographed meetings over the course of the entire occupation, would simply drop by to unburden his soul.

However, the August 2003 issue of *Bungei shunju,* a Japanese literary magazine, includes a debate among several historians, journalists, and others. All of them believe that some attempt along these lines was made by the emperor, either to address MacArthur directly or to get a message of responsibility to him, and that MacArthur refused to hear it.

Either way, it seems clear that the desire to apologize gnawed at Hirohito. The issue arose again in the late summer of 1951, as preparations began for the events marking the restoration of Japan's independence.

Normally for ceremonial events, the organizers would draft the emperor's statement, and the Imperial Household Agency would approve them. However, in this case, the Imperial Household Agency took on the job of drafting, because the emperor wanted to deliver his own message.

In fact, Tajima had been at work on this statement for a year and had met with the emperor in August 1951 to discuss the draft. This statement, as well, was to be heartfelt, personal, and uncharacteristically blunt. It also included elements of the original undelivered apology. In particular, the neutral apology, *hansei,* is again replaced with the deep shame of *hadzu.*

When the draft was previewed for then prime minister Shigeru Yoshida, he felt it was far too candid. It was also clear that the prime minister didn't want a backward-looking statement of regret. Speaking to Tajima, Prime Minister Yoshida pointed out that this was an opportunity to celebrate the country resuming its place in international society. The prime minister felt that an apology at this point would be unbecoming and, if the emperor must apologize, *hansei* was sufficient.

Tajima, who wanted to share the candid thoughts of the emperor, was indignant. In a scene familiar to all speechwriters, he "became sullen and his color changed, and he said, 'In that case, you write it.'"

The emperor, too, wanted to express remorse. In February 1952, he again pushed the idea, saying to Tajima, "I really want to include remorse for the past and self-discipline for the future, with different wording. Please revise again."

Together, the emperor and Tajima came up with a new draft that expressed remorse and seemed to meet the prime minister's approval. But just weeks before the address, the prime minister reversed himself.

The statement delivered on behalf of the emperor to commemorate the restoration of Japan's sovereignty described accepting the Potsdam

Declaration as something to commemorate the restoration of Japan's sovereignty decided to do "for the sake of the world, to bring about peace." Though it expressed condolences and sympathy for the victims of the war and promised to never repeat the past, statements like "Our heart is seared with grief" and "We are deeply ashamed before the realm" are nowhere to be found.

Rather, Hirohito said, "We believe that Japan must renew its devotion to the tenets of democracy and resolve to uphold international principles, join eastern and western cultures, foster the national polity, promote trade and industry, cultivate civic strengths, and thereby secure our nation's security and prosperity and enable world harmony and accord."

As Kato puts it so well: "The people who edited out the harsh portions of the text were surely sincere in their conviction. But their sincerity did not necessarily express the true intent of the emperor."

Absent the ability to express his feelings directly, Hirohito turned to poetry. On the tenth anniversary of his country's surrender, in 1955, the emperor alluded to his feelings about the war in a *waka,* a poem that, in Japanese, consists of thirty-one syllables:

> *Awakened from sleep while on a trip*
> *My heart choked*
> *With memories of things a decade ago.*

The words Hirohito delivered in 1951 may have been heartening to the people of Japan, but they denied the shame that burned in his own heart, shame for whatever failing of virtue had caused such misery— shame that remained a secret until a faded sheet of paper, found in a pile of notes, brought his undelivered words and his unspoken anguish to light.

An October 1962 meeting of the Executive Committee of the National Security Council (EXCOMM)
Clockwise from President Kennedy (who is to the left of the American flag): Secretary of Defense Robert S. McNamara, Deputy Secretary of Defense Roswell Gilpatric, Chairman of the Joint Chiefs of Staff General Maxwell Taylor, Assistant Secretary of Defense Paul Nitze, Deputy USIA Director Donald Wilson, Special Counsel Ted Sorensen, Special Assistant McGeorge Bundy, Secretary of the Treasury Douglas Dillon, Attorney General Robert F. Kennedy, Vice President Lyndon B. Johnson (hidden), Ambassador Llewellyn Thompson, Arms Control and Disarmament Agency Director William C. Foster, CIA Director John McCone (hidden), Under Secretary of State George Ball, Secretary of State Dean Rusk. (Photo by Cecil Stoughton, courtesy of the John F. Kennedy Presidential Library and Museum)

10

President Kennedy on the Military Operation
That Destroyed the Nuclear Weapons
Buildup in Cuba, October 1962

The Mysteries of Speech Authorship

"We could not negotiate with a gun at our heads."

On October 19, 1962, President John F. Kennedy's public schedule included a campaign trip to Cleveland, Ohio, and then two stops in Illinois: Springfield and Chicago. Pictures, video, and reports of the day show Kennedy, smiling and relaxed, riding in open-top convertibles with state officials and joking at an outdoor rally in Cleveland, where he was speaking to "fellow Democrats and whatever Republicans are passing through the square for lunch." From there he went on to Springfield and talked about his administration's efforts to bolster the rural economy.

Only in his final stop of the day, at a fundraiser at McCormick Place in Chicago, did he mention the nation that had so preoccupied him and his closest advisors. "It has been said so often that we are in a period of competition with the Soviet Union. Of course it is true. We can meet that competition in part by making ourselves militarily strong, by being first in space, which this Administration has decided to do, with the country's support, but it is also important to remember what Mr. Khrushchev once said, and that is that the day that the Soviet Union begins to outproduce the United States, the greatest productive power in the world . . . 'The hinge of history would begin to move.'"

In that room, only Kennedy knew that it already had, but not because of production. It had to do with the prospect of nuclear war. On October 16, his national security advisor McGeorge Bundy had shown Kennedy evidence that the Soviets were building nuclear missile sites in Cuba. In Kennedy's run for president, he argued that Republicans were being weak on defense and that America was on the short end of "the satellite missile race with the Soviet Union." Though the numbers didn't bear this out, the myth of a "missile gap" combined with the fact that the Soviets had beaten the United States into space created a sense that United States leadership and security were at risk. And now it appeared they were.

As his advisors deliberated behind the scenes on how the United States should respond, Kennedy kept his public schedule.

On October 19, at 9:45 a.m., before boarding Air Force One for the campaign swing, Kennedy met with the Joint Chiefs of Staff. They had recommended a massive surprise airstrike against Cuba, featuring eight hundred sorties using conventional weapons. They wanted approval immediately, because an attack of that scale and scope would take forty-eight hours to stage and launch.

Though consensus of Kennedy's advisors at that point was moving toward a naval blockade of any military shipments headed to Cuba, the Joint Chiefs dismissed that idea, arguing that a blockade of Cuba followed by some diplomatic action was insufficient, hard to implement, and just as likely to lead to a war with the Soviet Union. General Curtis LeMay, the air force chief of staff, described that plan as "almost as bad as the appeasement at Munich," referring to the agreement by which Nazi Germany had been allowed to annex the Sudetenland parts of Czechoslovakia in the hopes that it would be Hitler's last act of territorial expansion in Europe.

Kennedy immediately saw the risk that things could escalate quickly and catastrophically. He argued that if the United States attacked the missile sites in Cuba, there was bound to be a reprisal from Russia, likely, Russia "just going in and taking Berlin by force at some point. Which leaves me only one alternative, which is to fire nuclear weapons."

With that grim reality out in the open, the conversation went back and forth, ranging from Russia's motivations, to what missiles were already in Cuba, to the state of play when the longer-range missiles already there became operational (they estimated it would be in six to eight weeks), to the political implications for Kennedy. LeMay summarized it thus: "You're in a pretty bad fix at the present time."

"What did you say?" Kennedy snapped.
"You're in a pretty bad fix," LeMay responded.
Kennedy forced a laugh. "You're in there with me."

Kennedy's irascibility in an already-tense situation may have been heightened by an earlier conversation he had that morning. As the president was getting dressed, McGeorge Bundy came to visit him in the residence at the White House and told Kennedy that although consensus had been in favor of a naval blockade, he had changed his mind overnight, and now he, too, was supporting military action.

Accounts differ on whether Bundy's equivocating frustrated Kennedy or was actually encouraged by him. Bundy offered several different rationales and versions of his story over the ensuing years. He would later tell friends that he had been playing devil's advocate, keeping the airstrike option open because he wasn't convinced the blockade was a good one. In his own writing, he described himself as a "straw boss" for airstrikes.

In *The Color of Truth*, Pulitzer Prize–winning author Kai Bird's biography of the brothers McGeorge and William Bundy, we find a series of notes that Bundy wrote for himself in early 1964, in which he said that when he confided that he wasn't as certain about the blockade as he would like to be, Kennedy replied, "I'm having some of those same worries, and you know how my first reaction was the airstrike. Have another look at that and keep it alive."

Attorney General Robert Kennedy, the president's brother and closest advisor, was less charitable, saying that Bundy "did some strange flip-flops." Advisor and speechwriter Ted Sorensen had recalled that the president "didn't like it."

What was clear is that elusive consensus was now moving toward an airstrike, a sudden, violent act that caused RFK to observe: "I now know how Tojo felt when he was planning Pearl Harbor."

So as not to alert the press to the brewing crisis, Kennedy's campaign trip went on. That night, as Kennedy concluded his remarks in Chicago, the sky was illuminated by fireworks. We can only wonder what was going through Kennedy's mind as the guests oohed and aahed at the rockets arcing skyward.

After Kennedy had left his morning meeting with the Joint Chiefs, another group gathered at the State Department, in the conference room of Under Secretary of State George Ball.

This group was the Executive Committee of the National Security Council, referred to as EXCOMM. It included members of the National Security Council, as well as several other senior government officials whose advice Kennedy sought. The meeting began with a surveillance report on the installations in Cuba and then turned to the requirements any blockade or military action would need to meet to be approved by international organizations like the United Nations and the Organization of American States.

Bundy described his morning meeting with President Kennedy and his feeling that a blockade's "effects were uncertain and in any event they would be slow to be felt . . . An air strike would be quick and would take out the bases in a clean surgical operation. He favored decisive action with its advantage of surprise and confronting the world with a fait accompli."

Former secretary of state Dean Acheson, whose advice JFK trusted, argued for "cleaning the missile bases out decisively with an airstrike." After all, "Khrushchev had presented the United States with a direct challenge, we were involved in a test of wills, and the sooner we got to a showdown, the better."

General Maxwell Taylor, the chair of the Joint Chiefs of Staff, who had been at the earlier meeting, pointed out that a blockade would mean abandoning the possibility of an airstrike, because it would let the Soviet Union know what we knew. He argued for a quick decision in favor of an airstrike.

Secretary of Defense Robert McNamara didn't necessarily favor an airstrike, but he agreed to give orders for the preparations to be made.

At that point, the meeting had been going for roughly two hours and was getting tense.

Secretary of State Dean Rusk suggested that two groups form to present the president with two fully thought-out options: a blockade group and an airstrike group.

McGeorge Bundy would lead the airstrike group. Ural Alexis Johnson, the deputy under secretary for political affairs at the State Department, would lead the blockade group. Ray Cline, the director of the CIA, referred to these two groups as the "warhawks" and "Picasso doves."

Those labels were shared with journalist Charles Bartlett (the Pulitzer Prize–winning reporter who had introduced JFK and his wife, Jacqueline) and columnist Stewart Alsop for an article they would later write for *The Saturday Evening Post*, which popularized the expression "hawks and doves."*

Robert Kennedy, in his memoir of the Cuban missile crisis, *Thirteen Days*, wrote that each group's recommendation had to begin "with an outline of the President's speech to the nation." This was one of the reasons that President Kennedy had also asked his trusted advisor and speechwriter Ted Sorensen to join EXCOMM.

The draft that emerged in favor of the airstrike is a haunting document, both for what it says and what it doesn't.

Not only does it announce the airstrike but it also announces that "further military action has been authorized to ensure the threat is fully removed and not restored"—in other words, a land invasion.

The speech then lays out, in detail, the contents of the "rapid, secret, and frequently denied military operation," the number of missile launchers, the nuclear payload they could carry, and the distance they could travel. (A full text of the speech appears in the appendix to this book.)

The sixth page contains what may have been the most consequential parenthetical in history: "(Follows a description of first reports of action.)"

In his book *Living Faith*, President Jimmy Carter recalls a sermon that says that when we die, the marker on our grave has two dates: the day we're born and the day we die, and a little dash in between, representing our whole life on Earth. To God, the tiny dash is everything.

---

* That article also included the first use of the expression "eyeball to eyeball."

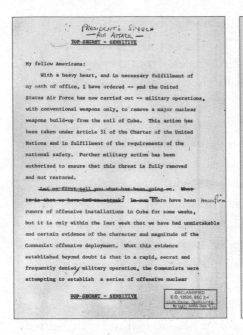

The first and sixth pages of President Kennedy's airstrike speech. Page 6 includes the powerful parenthetical on "first reports of action." The full text of this speech appears in the appendix. (Photos courtesy of the Papers of Robert F. Kennedy/John F. Kennedy Presidential Library and Museum)

To the fate of mankind, this parenthetical could have contained everything.

Often when events are moving quickly, speechwriters will write their equivalent of the journalist's TK, which means that additional material is "to come" later.* Usually, these are meant to be filled with things like statistics that are being finalized, or policy proposals that are undergoing a review, or the names of supporters who are still being recruited.

This parenthetical, however, would be filled with much more than the budget impact of a policy proposal. This parenthetical would be filled with a description of the battle, the scale of the destruction, the response from the USSR, the number of dead, and sympathy for those lost.

Indeed, the draft anticipates this, and continues by saying: "The

---

* Why not TC, then? The legend is that *TK* is an uncommon letter combination, whereas *TC* or the words *to come* themselves could be mistaken for part of the text.

tragedy here—self-evidently—is in the loss of innocent lives on all sides. For the United States Government, I hereby accept responsibility for this action and pledge that all appropriate efforts will be made, on request, to assist the families of these innocent victims. Neither Cubans nor Russians, as individuals, can be held accountable for the extraordinary and irresponsible conspiracy which has required this action."

Of course, the draft assumes that most of the losses will be Cuban and Russian. Kennedy was certainly concerned that the Soviets might retaliate against U.S. missile sites in Turkey and Italy, and he takes pains in the draft to point out that "for many years, both the Soviet Union and the United States have deployed such weapons around the world with great care, never upsetting the precarious status quo which balanced off the use of those weapons in the absence of some vital challenge. These deployments [in Cuba] are not comparable."

What it fails to account for is a fact that remained secret for thirty years following the crisis: the Soviets *already* had nearly one hundred short-range tactical nuclear weapons on the island. What's more, the Soviet commanders on the island did not need permission or launch codes from Moscow to fire these weapons.

As James Lindsay of the Council on Foreign Relations wrote on the fiftieth anniversary of the Cuban missile crisis, if the United States engaged in the airstrikes, the Soviets likely would have retaliated by vaporizing the U.S. military base at Guantánamo Bay. If the strikes were followed by "further military action . . . to ensure that the threat is fully removed and not restored" as the speech had promised, U.S. troops would likely have been the first fighting force wiped out by tactical nuclear weapons.

The fact of the already-operational Soviet missiles became public at a conference in Havana, Cuba, to mark the thirtieth anniversary of the crisis. That's where Soviet general Anatoly Gribkov, who had served as the army chief of operations during the missile crisis, revealed that nine nuclear-tipped Luna coastal defense missiles had been armed and ready to be launched against any U.S. invasion force.

Former secretary of defense Robert McNamara, who was also attending the meeting, was so shocked when he heard this that he had to hold on to a table to steady himself.

There was another exchange that took place at the conference in Havana on the thirtieth anniversary of the crisis, and while it carried none of the import of a nuclear miscalculation, it did open a mystery. At the conference, the existence of the "airstrike" speech was revealed, and Kennedy's former advisor and speechwriter Ted Sorensen asked the conference organizers who wrote it. Their answer was that they assumed he had.

Sorensen emphatically replied that he had not, for two reasons—one moral, one technical.

The moral argument was that Sorensen, who had registered as a conscientious objector during World War II, couldn't have formulated an argument in favor of something he so strongly opposed. Had he been required to do so, he surely wouldn't have forgotten the experience.

Sorensen's technical argument was that the draft didn't look like it had been typed on his secretary's typewriter, and he never put the type of classification stamps the airstrike speech bears on his documents.

But my research found that neither of these arguments fully holds up to closer scrutiny.

Many of the speeches in Sorensen's papers at the Kennedy Library are indeed marked classified, indicating that even if he didn't classify his own documents, others might have done so without his knowledge.

And, as we'll see later, much of the language in favor of the airstrike is written from a posture of revulsion at the idea of nuclear weapons.

For a moment, though, assuming Sorensen's recollection is accurate, then who did write the airstrike draft? Sorensen indicated it was most likely McGeorge Bundy, the president's national security advisor.

Bundy would certainly be the most likely candidate; at the time of the speech's writing, he was leading the "airstrike" group. Bundy was a talented and convincing writer as well and had thought and written extensively about nuclear matters. Along with Franklin Roosevelt's secretary of war, Henry Stimson, Bundy had written a famous 1947 article that appeared in *Harper's*. Titled "The Decision to Use the Atomic Bomb," the article is credited with America's national acceptance that dropping atomic bombs on Japan was justified and, ultimately, an act that may have saved a million American lives. A year later, he began working as a foreign policy speechwriter to presidential candidate Thomas Dewey.

But while Bundy is a natural candidate, there's no evidence in his papers that he wrote the speech, nor does he mention it in any of his reflections on that time.

It seems strange that somebody very close to this crisis sat down with a pen and a pad and tried to imagine what a president would say while staring Armageddon in the face, and then never mention it again.

Here is what we do know:

Minutes from the meeting on Friday, October 19, show that before the "hawk" and "dove" groups separated, Sorensen said that he thought he had absorbed enough to start on the draft of a speech for the president. So, at the moment Sorensen said he had what he needed to begin writing, the consensus was in favor of an airstrike, a development that Sorensen said was doing "neither our national security nor my ulcer any good." That would indicate that Sorensen had begun work on an airstrike speech.

Whatever speech Sorensen began, he later wrote in his memoir, "When I reflected on that task in my office, I found too many unanswered questions, and returned to the meeting with those questions, asking the quarantine backers why that plan was best, how it would get the missiles out, how it could prevent them from being finished and fired, and how could we avoid the blockade's indefinite extension. The answers helped clarify their thinking and mine, and enabled me to spend that night drafting in my office."

Sorensen finished the draft at 3:00 on Saturday morning, and later said the draft "went through more changes in the following forty-eight hours than any speech I wrote in my life" but did ultimately provide "a framework of basic policy around which an ExComm consensus could be formed and a presidential decision made."

There is no doubt that Sorensen wrote the blockade draft. Bundy himself acknowledged, "The draft Sorensen wrote that long Friday night marks in my own mind the point at which the president's advisers found a basic policy that he could be confidently expected to adopt. No such speech could be written for the airstrike. It was not a solution for which any of us could write words that John Kennedy would speak."

Is it possible that the draft Sorensen began, before returning to the meeting, was an airstrike draft, which was then expanded and completed by someone else? Or did Sorensen write a full airstrike draft and then later morph it into a blockade draft?

Sorensen writes that the airstrike speech "included a statement of America's intention to use nuclear weapons if necessary—a statement I would never have written, knowing JFK never would approve it."

However, the blockade speech and the airstrike speech offer nearly identical though veiled threats to use nuclear weapons. In the blockade speech, it appears as: "It shall be the policy of this Nation to regard any nuclear missile launched from Cuba against any nation in the Western Hemisphere as an attack by the Soviet Union on the United States, requiring a full retaliatory response on the Soviet Union."

In the airstrike speech, it reads that the United States will "regard any missile that might possibly remain and be launched from Cuba as an attack by the Soviet Union requiring a massive retaliatory response upon the Soviet Union."

The other nuclear language in the airstrike speech seems more likely to have come from someone morally *opposed* to nuclear weapons and fearful of their use. That is more likely to have been Sorensen than Bundy. "Nuclear weapons are so destructive, and ballistic missiles so swift, that a sudden shift in the nature of their threat can be deeply dangerous— especially when the trigger appears to be in the hands of [Fidel Castro] a violent and unstable revolutionary leader."

Additionally, there are several lines in the airstrike speech like "Our byword is: 'Negotiation yes, intimidation, no'" that sound, for lack of a better word, Sorensenian. Even the word *byword* is itself a clue. *Byword* makes its first appearance in Kennedy speeches during Kennedy's campaign for president in 1960, a time when Sorensen was working for him (but Bundy was not).

So how did the airstrike draft get written, and by whom?

Seeing the similarities in the two speeches indicates that if Sorensen didn't write the airstrike draft, then the blockade draft served as the source document, given the amount of overlapping language.

It's possible that material from one draft was simply repurposed into the other by someone else. After all, the justifications for the blockade are the exact same as the justifications for the airstrike, it's just that the action resulting from those justifications is different.

But, in this case, the timeline for that to have happened is very brief. If Sorensen didn't write the airstrike draft prior to or concurrent with the blockade draft, it had to have been written in the twenty-four-hour window between Saturday morning (when Sorensen first began sharing his blockade draft) and Sunday morning at 11:00 a.m., which was the point at which President Kennedy abandoned the idea of an airstrike.

And more likely, it had to be written in an even narrower window than that, because on Saturday afternoon, upon returning early from his campaign trip, Kennedy heard presentations on both options.

One of the few people who could have done that is Bundy, who likely would have seen Sorensen's first draft and was preparing to lead a presentation in favor of an airstrike later that afternoon; a presentation that had to begin with an outline of the president's speech announcing that course of action.

But if Bundy did take Sorensen's draft and begin modifying it, why make no mention of it?

It appears Bundy later regretted and tried to diminish his role as an airstrike advocate. Is he trying to sweep under the rug the fact that he wrote a quite convincing draft in favor of an airstrike?

There is a sizable clue in the draft of the speech itself—handwritten edits. Most of these are corrections of typographical errors. But a couple of them make changes of substance. For example, while the draft declares that the Soviet missile buildup is "in violation of Soviet assurances," the handwritten edits modify the text to say that the Soviet missile buildup is "in contradiction to all previous Soviet practice, even with members of the Warsaw Pact."

That certainly seems like a Bundy-ian sentiment given Bundy's expertise in both U.S. foreign policy and Soviet behavior, but did he write it?

In search of answers, I took these documents to Mark Songer, an expert in the field of forensic document examinations. After serving as a marine, Songer obtained a master's in forensic science and served as a special agent and forensic examiner with the Federal Bureau of Investigation. Over the years, he has analyzed handwriting on bank robbery notes, death threats to members of Congress, and suicide letters. Given that this speech might well have been humanity's suicide note, I asked him to evaluate the handwriting on it and compare it to handwriting that we know came from both Bundy and Sorensen.

Songer's conclusion, for which he signed a sworn affidavit, is that "examination and comparison of the questioned writings with the known Bundy writings revealed consistency in terms of letter-form, size and skill ability . . . these combinations of unique writing habits were observed on both questioned and known writings. Furthermore, the level of writing skill was found to be consistent with *Bundy's* known writings."

So we can say with a degree of confidence that Bundy at least edited the draft. But was he hand-editing his own draft or somebody else's?

In my experience, after having written something, I find it helps to print it and read it again (often aloud) to find not only the typos that escaped my weary eyes but the sentences that seemed serviceable on the page but are literally unspeakably long when delivered aloud. Thus, I have a lot of my own drafts in my files that are covered with my own handwritten edits.

Corrections of substance, however, are a different beast. A correction of substance is likely to come from someone other than the original author, and there are several of them here. For example, there is the added reference to the Soviet Union's behavior with its Warsaw Pact allies mentioned above, as well as a mention of "rumors" of offensive installations that is tweaked with the handwritten addition of the word *unconfirmed.*

So, we can say with some confidence that Bundy edited the draft, but can't say with confidence that he wrote it, leaving half of the mystery unsolved.

Until I came across a transcript in the National Security Archive. It was an interview conducted in March 1997 for the documentary series *The Cold War.* Sorensen was being interviewed by the historian Jeremy Isaacs's production crew, and was asked about the decision to impose a blockade instead of an airstrike. Sorensen answers the question by describing the general thinking around the two options, but then his story diverges from what he had said previously. In this telling, Sorensen is asked to write a note to Khrushchev that demanded he get rid of the missiles, which Sorensen can't bring himself to do for fear that anything perceived as an ultimatum would lead to wider conflict.

However, with both an airstrike and a blockade still on the table, Sorensen says,

> So I was asked to draft both speeches, both the speech for an airstrike, because the President would certainly announce it to the world and the nation about the time the planes took off, and the speech for the blockade. And I came back again and said, "Well, now, the blockade speech—how do we explain this, and what's the

blockade got to do with the missiles, and how's the blockade going to help?" And by getting answers to those questions, it not only strengthened my ability to write the speech: it strengthened the blockade camp, because we began to put together a much more coherent and, I might add, strong and logical approach.

This part of the interview was never aired. And so Sorensen's monumental (and only) admission that he had at least provided the initial draft of the airstrike speech disappeared into the show's archives.

But how could Sorensen have denied adamantly that he wrote this speech in 1992 and then admitted that he at least wrote some of it in 1997?

Robert Kennedy's observation about everybody's state of mind at the time may explain a lot about the confusion: "Each one of us was being asked to make a recommendation which would affect the future of all mankind, a recommendation which, if wrong and if accepted, could mean the destruction of the human race. That kind of pressure does strange things to a human being."

Could it have led someone to erase from memory or to deny that they had drafted what they later realized would have been a prelude to the end of the world? I think it's possible.

In October 2002, under admittedly less trying circumstances, I was asked to prepare a statement regarding the use of force against Iraq. At the time, it wasn't clear which way Senator Tom Daschle of South Dakota, my boss and the Senate majority leader, would vote. It depended on the wording of the resolution. So I wrote the draft as an argument against the use of force. When the resolution was changed to Senator Daschle's satisfaction, I was told he would be voting for it, and the draft should be modified to announce a vote in favor of the use of force. This was not a position I supported, and I struggled to make even the minor modifications the speech required to flip it from against the use of force to in favor of the use of force.

I mention the conundrum facing speechwriters who are asked to write in support of something they personally oppose, or vice versa, in chapter 4. In working on this chapter, I went back and looked at the version of the speech that supported the use of force. I know I wrote it, I remember where I was sitting, I remember struggling to figure out how to use the Track Changes function because I was trying to integrate edits from several places. I remember everything about having to write that speech, but I don't recognize a word of it. It's as if I simply blacked it out.

Did Sorensen forget what he had done because in the race to draft something, he had taken a few hours, cribbed largely from an existing draft that made a different argument, modified it, and, as that course of action was abandoned, promptly forgot about it?

Or was writing the speech something that was so terrifying, so anathema to his very being, that he simply erased from his memory the actual words he had written, while still being able to recall that he had been asked to write them? Barring another discovery, we can't know for sure.

But what we do know is that, today, as more nations pursue nuclear weapons, and dictators like North Korea's Kim Jong-un show a willingness to engage in nuclear brinksmanship, the debates Kennedy's advisors had, the outcomes they envisioned, the words they planned to speak, and the unknown words that would have filled those most consequential of parentheses do more than illuminate a harrowing path not taken—they shed light on a path we may again have to travel.

PART 5

The People Choose

Elections provide no shortage of undelivered speeches; for nearly every delivered victory or concession speech, there exists its undelivered opposite. When I asked for career advice from my first boss, Al Gore's chief speechwriter (and later producer on the television show *The West Wing*), Eli Attie, he responded: "Remember to write the second speech."

That's what had launched his career. In 1993, as senior aides assembled to craft New York mayor David Dinkins's Election Night victory remarks, Eli went into another room to contemplate what the other aides couldn't.

When that night's returns began to indicate that the Republican candidate, Rudy Giuliani, would be the one declaring victory, Eli offered up his draft.

Four years ago, we were joined by our highest ideals and our best hopes. And tonight even in this hard hour we are joined by that same commitment to strive and to struggle, to lift up those who have been left out, to ensure that the promise of New York is not the privilege of generations past but the birthright of generations to come.

The New York Times would later call Dinkins's remarks a "virtuoso lesson in loser's politesse."

In this section, we see two speeches that were never heard because of the choices the voters made. We have Illinois governor John Altgeld's farewell speech, which went undelivered because his pardon of the Haymarket prisoners set in motion a series of events that stoked anti-immigrant fervor and denied him reelection in 1896. His opponent then denied him the dignity of delivering a departing speech.

We also have Hillary Clinton's planned 2016 victory speech, a powerful statement from the person who would have been America's first female president. That chapter also includes a section on the history and ritual of concession, and why it is so powerful in our democracy.

THE FRIEND OF MAD DOGS.

Governor Altgeld of Illinois in freeing the Anarchists bitterly denounced Judge Gary and the jury that convicted them.

Governor Altgeld is depicted wielding the knife of his pardon power to release the hounds of socialism, anarchy, and murder. In the background is the monument to the police officers killed and injured in the Haymarket riot. (Courtesy of Chicago History Museum)

11

Illinois Governor John Peter Altgeld's
Farewell Address Following His Defeat in the
1896 Election, January 1897

The Value of a Soundbite

"In my judgment no epitaph can be written upon
the tomb of a public man that will so surely win
the contempt of the ages than to say of him that he
held office all of his life and never did anything for
humanity."

On the morning of June 26, 1893, Governor John Altgeld was one
of the first to arrive at the state capitol in Springfield, Illinois. He had
made a fateful decision. He summoned to his office Brand Whitlock,
the assistant secretary of state (and who would later become a reform-
minded mayor of Toledo, Ohio). Altgeld directed Whitlock to prepare
the pardons and to not share with anybody what he was doing.

With these actions, Altgeld was righting a grievous injustice. He was also setting in motion a series of events that would result in his defeat and in a trenchant farewell address going undelivered.

Seven years earlier, on May 4, 1886, crowds had gathered in Chicago's Haymarket Square for a rally in support of workers who were striking for an eight-hour workday. Though the rally was peaceful, tensions were high. Two striking workers had been killed by police the previous day. As police tried to disperse this crowd, a bomb went off. The blast and resulting gunfire killed seven police officers and four protesters.

The late 1800s were a time of upheaval and transition for America, and particularly for America's cities. The Industrial Revolution combined with an influx of immigrants had led to a wave of rapid urbanization. Nowhere was that felt more acutely than Chicago, a city whose population quadrupled—from a half million to two million—between 1880 and 1910. As a result, the wealthy and powerful had begun to feel increasingly threatened by working people, especially those of foreign birth, who were beginning to coalesce into a formidable labor movement and stand up for their rights.

The city's ruling elites saw the events surrounding the Haymarket Square rally as an opportunity to wipe out the city's labor movement, which did include a number of communists, anarchists, and other radicals. Eight men were quickly arrested, charged with murder, and branded as anarchists.

Despite the fact that none were ever connected to the bomb (several weren't even at the rally), they were tried and found guilty, largely on the proposition that their inflammatory antiestablishment rhetoric made them as guilty as any bomber. Four of the eight were hanged. A fifth committed suicide in his jail cell. The then governor, Richard Oglesby, who privately admitted the innocence of the men, reduced the sentences of the remaining three.

All were in jail when John Altgeld was elected governor in 1893.

Altgeld's journey made him an unlikely governor. He was born in what is today Germany, and when he was just a couple of months old, his family immigrated to the United States and began farming in Ohio. At age sixteen, he left home to join the Union army and served in the Civil War, where he contracted the malaria that would undermine his health for the rest of his life. Later, he became a schoolteacher and, in an early show of an interest in politics, was elected as a prosecuting attorney in Missouri.

In 1875, convinced he was ready for bigger things, he moved to Chicago. He opened a law office and lived above it. He plowed every penny he could save into real estate investing and was phenomenally successful, amassing a small fortune.

Still, he hadn't forgotten the poverty that marked his early life or his experience as a prosecutor in Missouri. He wrote a book in which he sought to "call attention briefly to the character of our penal machinery and if possible, lead others to examine it; feeling confident that, when once generally understood, improvements will be made therein which will benefit society and greatly lessen the sum of human misery."

In the book, he argued for an end to arrest quotas for police officers, and he pointed out the injustice of the system of fines that allowed the rich to pay their way out of problems while the poor were sent to jail. He then went further, proposing the entire criminal justice enterprise be reoriented toward rehabilitation.

The book didn't receive wide attention, but it led to two important friendships: George Schilling, one of the fathers of the labor movement in Chicago, and a young lawyer named Clarence Darrow.

With the freedom his wealth provided and his progressive political philosophy, Altgeld returned his attention to political office. In 1884, he made a failed bid for Congress, but made some waves by winning 45 percent of the votes as a Democrat running in a Republican district in a Republican year.

That year also marked a rise in labor activism, with the Federation of Organized Trades and Labor Unions (which would later become the American Federation of Labor) issuing a call to begin preparations to make 1886, two years later, a year of nationwide movement for the eight-hour day.

As part of that movement, marches and rallies were held in Chicago. On May 3, 1886, a picket of the McCormick Reaper Plant turned violent, with Chicago police attacking the picketing workers, killing at least two.

The outrage at this police brutality is what led to the call for a mass meeting in Haymarket Square on the evening of May 4. The meeting was somewhat of a disappointment before it even began, with only about 2,500 in attendance, compared to the 20,000 organizers had expected.

As the meeting wore on, rain threatened and the crowd dwindled further, to an estimated 200.

The final speaker, Methodist pastor and avowed anarchist Samuel Fielden, was concluding his remarks when those remaining were shocked to see a crowd of nearly equal size marching toward them—186 uniformed police officers.

Several police officers would later testify that Fielden screamed, "Here come the bloodhounds now, you do your duty and I'll do mine!" However, the more reliable testimony is that Fielden, as much in confusion as anything else, stated, "But we are peaceable."

At that moment, the police began wading into the assembled group, and somebody—never identified—heaved a dynamite bomb toward the police. The blast directly killed one police officer and set off a panic; the police began firing into the crowd and at fleeing protesters. When the gunfire stopped minutes later, seven police officers and four protesters were dead. More than sixty police officers and an uncounted number of protesters were injured. More than 250 shots had been fired.

While some members of the crowd were armed, and several nonpolice firearms were found at the scene afterward, there's no evidence that there was firing of weapons by civilians. It seemed that most of the police were killed or wounded by their own men.

Martial law was declared the next day, and the police rounded up hundreds of "known and suspected revolutionaries." Ultimately, eight men, including Fielden, were chosen to stand trial, although one of them, Albert Parsons, had fled and escaped arrest. (He would return of his own accord.) Tensions continued to run high, and newspapers called for swift justice.

Before he was hanged, Albert Parsons, the former Confederate soldier turned radical anarchist, summed up the trial in a letter to his wife: "The privileged class demands a victim, and we are offered a sacrifice to appease the hungry yells of an infuriated mob of millionaires who will be contented with nothing less than our lives. Monopoly triumphs! Labor in chains ascends the scaffold for having dared to cry out for liberty and right!"

Despite the events that consumed the city, the country, and the world; despite the outcry coming from many of his friends and associates; despite the fact that he had literally written the book on the miscarriages of justice that occurred with regularity in our penal system; and despite his belief that the chief of the Chicago police was "the man really responsible for the death of the police officers," Altgeld, then eyeing another run at political office, was silent.

Did he fear that speaking out would cost his real estate enterprise? After all, William P. Black, the Civil War hero and legal luminary who took on the job of defending the Haymarket prisoners, had seen his corporate retainers disappear. A conversation Altgeld had with his friend and labor leader George Schilling provided a window into his thinking: "I want to do something, not just make a speech . . . I want power, to get a hold of the handle that controls things. When I do, I will give it a twist."

Four months after the sentencing, Altgeld won a Cook County superior court judgeship. He would serve alongside the judge who had sentenced the men, Joseph E. Gary.

In 1892, declining outside contributions, Altgeld put $100,000 of his own fortune into the race and ran a progressive campaign for governor. The race exhausted Altgeld, and though he won in a close victory, it depleted him to the point that it wasn't clear if he'd be able to attend his inauguration in Springfield.

He did ultimately make it to Springfield and took the oath of office on Inauguration Day. Standing in the overheated Illinois House chamber, shivering despite wearing a full coat, Altgeld began his remarks, a progressive manifesto that proposed everything from greater care for the mentally ill, to infrastructure investments, to an estate tax, to an end to child labor. A couple of minutes in, Altgeld became too exhausted and, joking that the clerk has a "pleasant voice," asked him to take over reading the remarks.

A few days later, from his sickbed, Altgeld asked for the records from the Haymarket case.

Despite the hopes of his most fervent supporters, Altgeld began his governorship in a hands-off, almost desultory way. Convalescing for long periods of time, he let the legislature do as they wished, and they did work to eliminate sweatshops and child labor. But the Haymarket prisoners stayed very much on his mind.

His friend Clarence Darrow lobbied him for full pardons and expressed disappointment that a pardon wasn't Altgeld's first act as governor. Darrow later recounted Altgeld's reply: "If I conclude to pardon those men it will not meet with the approval that you expect . . . from that day I will be a dead man." Many of Altgeld's advisors suggested a politically safer middle course: a limited pardon on the grounds of mercy.

And yet, Altgeld believed that if the men were guilty, then they should remain in jail. And if they were innocent, "I will pardon them, by God, no matter what happens to my career."

As he reviewed the Haymarket case, Altgeld saw an unacceptable perversion of the law: "A violent incident fueled by inept police work; a series of flimsy murder charges that did not even pretend to be based upon direct evidence; a jury stacked with people proclaiming the guilt of the defendants; and a sham trial conducted with 'malicious ferocity.'"

And so Altgeld prepared a pardon message, eighteen thousand words long, outlining the flaws of the trial and the principles underlying his decision.

Slightly more than a month before he signed the pardons, Altgeld addressed the graduating seniors at the University of Illinois, and one begins to see his thinking emerge in that speech.

He spoke about the calls that anarchists were making to abolish government a "fatal mistake," pointing out that any new organization of the affairs of man would fall prey to human selfishness, but without the benefit of centuries of reform and institution-building that had, at least somewhat, tempered those impulses. Thus he argued for further reform, not revolution. "Let sunlight into dark places and the poisons collected there disappear," he told them. "So with the dark places in the government and civil affairs that are now festering with wrong; let the sunlight of eternal truth and justice shine on them and they will disappear.

"Wherever there is wrong; point it out to all the world, and you can trust the people to right it; wrongs thrive in secrecy and darkness."

That statement wasn't just a powerful line in a speech, it was a powerful and memorable summary of Altgeld's entire political philosophy.

While there's debate as to when the term *soundbite* entered our lexicon, most believe it was sometime in the 1970s. Television news producers would see a clip they wanted to use and demand that editors "take that bite." Of course, soundbites have been around a lot longer than has television. After all, what is Julius Caesar's statement in 46 B.C. in his letter to the Roman Senate, "Veni, vidi, vici" (I came, I saw, I conquered) if not a perfect (and perfectly alliterative) soundbite? Certainly, Caesar had more to say about the battle of Zela, but if all you read was the first line of the letter, you got the message.

And that's the point of a soundbite. To summarize a message in a way that is memorable, quotable, and one in which the bite gives you enough of a taste of the whole. There are some who argue that soundbites reflect everything that is wrong with our politics today.* After all, how can we engage deeply with issues if all we consume are nine seconds on the news,† or read 280 characters in a tweet?

Doesn't that make a soundbite the refined sugar of our political discourse—a rush of energy that is fattening without being filling? Yes and no. Often, when I teach speechwriting, I tell students to start their work on a speech by writing at the top of the page the perfect headline that you would want written by a reporter covering the speech. What I'm really asking them to do is to summarize what the speech is about. Once they do that, they're halfway to a soundbite, because now the task is to make that headline sticky.

For example, if you're Patrick Henry in 1775 preparing to speak against reconciliation with Britain, what is the headline you want? Probably something along the lines of: "Henry says that the choice facing Virginia is clear: fight for freedom or face a life of intolerable servitude."

From there, you're one step away from one of history's great soundbites: "I know not what course others may take; but as for me, give me liberty or give me death!"

And here is where I distinguish between "sound barks" and "soundbites." A sound bark is a snarky, clever statement. It can most often be found in its natural habitat: Twitter. It may be brief and pithy, but it doesn't introduce or explain an idea.

But a soundbite plays a valuable role. Bob Lehrman and Eric Schnure

---

* "There are some who believe" is a classic "straw man"—an argument in which the speaker rebuts a nameless idea, rather than an actual person or an actual quote.
† Nine seconds is not an exaggeration. A University of California study found that the length of a soundbite on broadcast news shrank from forty-three seconds in 1968 to nine seconds in 1992.

put it best, in a soundbite of their own: "If you can't make your point succinct and interesting, how can you be sure you have one?"

Altgeld had a point to make—about the need to serve justice and humanity above all. So, on June 26, he summoned Brand Whitlock to his office, as well as Whitlock's boss, Secretary of State Buck Hinrichsen. As he asked Whitlock to prepare to affix the state seal on the pardons, Hinrichsen questioned the move. Altgeld banged his fist on the desk and said, "It is right."

To complete the scene, there was another man in the room, a banker named E. S. Dreyer. Dreyer had served as the foreman on the grand jury that had approved the murder indictments against the accused anarchists. In the ensuing years, he was consumed by tremendous guilt for his role in this miscarriage of justice. He wanted to atone by being the one to personally deliver the pardon to the prisoners, so as soon as the papers were signed, Dreyer put them in his bag and ran for the train to get to Joliet, where the prisoners were held.

The next morning, as the news of the pardon began to break, Whitlock encountered Altgeld, and, by way of greeting, described how much he admired what the governor had done. Whitlock remembered Altgeld offering only a sad smile and saying, "It was merely doing right."

But the storm was fierce, and the reaction to the pardons was swift, loud, and unrelenting.

The New York Times wrote that "Governor Altgeld has done everything in his power . . . to encourage again the spirit of lawless resistance and of wanton assault upon the agents of authority . . . exactly in tone with the wildest Anarchist leaders."

The *Times* went on to say that Altgeld himself "would have developed into an out-and-out Anarchist if his lucky real estate speculations had not turned the course of his natural tendencies."

The *Chicago Tribune* wrote that the governor had not "a drop of true American blood in his veins. He does not reason like an American, does not feel like one, and consequently does not behave like one." The paper took to calling him "John Pardon Altgeld."

The Washington Post pointed out that this was expected behavior from a man who was "an alien himself."

Theodore Roosevelt, at a rally in Chicago, said Altgeld "condones and encourages the most infamous of murders."

One political cartoon at the time showed Altgeld cutting loose the tethers that held back a series of scary-looking dogs, one of which had already set upon a woman and her small children. The knife Altgeld held was labeled "Pardon" and the caption read: "The Friend of Mad Dogs."*

The three-year campaign that followed from the media, the city's elites, and his political opponents ultimately defeated Altgeld. In 1896, he lost his campaign for reelection.†

The *Chicago Tribune* gloried that Altgeld's defeat would mean an end to "his cynical misconduct, his criminal sympathies, his anarchistic tendencies."

The *New-York Tribune* wrote that John Riley Tanner's victory over "Altgeld the Anarchist" provided "cause for national rejoicing." Attacks like this continued for the remaining two months of Altgeld's term.

Even his last day in office offered no escape from bitterness. That morning, *The New York Times* warned that Altgeld "was prepared to make an exhibition of malignity not only toward the Republican Party, but toward the decent people of Illinois."

Every previous outgoing Illinois governor had been allowed to deliver a farewell message at his successor's inaugural, and Altgeld had prepared remarks, which he carried in his pocket. But the victor, John Riley Tanner, egged on by the *Chicago Tribune,* is believed to have declared, "Illinois has had enough of that anarchist." Altgeld was left sitting with his speech in his pocket.

The irony of this outcome becomes clear when one considers what Altgeld intended to say, most especially this line: "The presence of the defeated and retiring party is not necessary for the peaceful change of administration, yet in order to add the graces to republican form it is customary for the retiring party to be represented and participate in the ceremonies of inauguration." Here was Altgeld, prepared to celebrate the dignified transition of power at the exact moment that dignity was drained away.

---

* That cartoon appears at the beginning of this chapter.
† The Democratic nominee for president, William Jennings Bryan, had also lost, and by a greater margin in Illinois than Altgeld.

Journalist and author Harry Barnard's masterful biography of Altgeld states that the speech Altgeld had penned was "nothing but words of good will for his successor," and that was certainly true. The remarks extend Governor Tanner "the most cordial greeting and hearty good wishes. Loving Illinois as I do, I shall applaud his every act that tends to her advancement." However, a closer reading of his remarks reveals a steely warning about the dangers of pure partisanship, and the responsibility of those in power to govern in an open, honest, and ethical way.

He pointed out the ethical standard to which elected officials should hold themselves:

> It would be better to be Governor but for one day and follow the dictates of justice than hold office for fifty years by winking at wrong. In my judgment no epitaph can be written upon the tomb of a public man that will so surely win the contempt of the ages than to say of him that he held office all of his life and never did anything for humanity.

He issued a warning that "the selfish forces of greed are always ready to tear to pieces the noblest creations of patriotism."

And he included one more sentiment that resonates powerfully today as well. His words point out the stark difference between campaigning and governing, between inflaming public passions and making progress:

> To the members of that great political party to which I have the honor of belonging let me say that while we are relieved of the responsibility of administration our responsibility in another direction is increased, for in a republic it is the minority party which creates the sentiment and develops the principles which the government shall in the end carry out. Not being hampered or embarrassed by the detail of administration, the minority party can devote its best energies to the discussion of great principles, while the majority party, being obliged to conciliate conflicting interest and to compromise, is in that respect hampered.

In other words, it's the minority party's job to go back to the drawing board and develop and debate new ideas, and it's the majority party's job to sacrifice some of the ideals that made them the majority in order to govern. It is, in essence, a road map for how a democracy is *supposed* to work.

Altgeld returned to private life, lost his fortune when his bank was wiped out, and began to build it up again as a law partner of his old friend Clarence Darrow. In March 1902, he accepted an invitation to speak in Joliet. He complained of fatigue throughout the trip, but mustered one final stem-winder, concluding with an optimistic note, "Wrong may seem to triumph. Right may seem to be defeated. But the gravitation of eternal justice is upward toward the throne of God. Any political institution if it is to endure must be plumb with that line of justice."

As Altgeld left the stage, he collapsed. The cause was a cerebral hemorrhage. That evening he slipped into a coma. He died the next morning.

In eulogizing him, his friend, confidant, and law partner Clarence Darrow said: "He so loved justice and truth and liberty and righteousness that all the terrors that the earth could hold were less than the condemnation of his own conscience."

Altgeld's farewell address, like so many of his words, conveyed a message of morality, responsibility, decency, and the need for all those things to be manifest in our politics. Altgeld, himself an immigrant to America, believed that loving America meant holding it to its highest ideals, even if that required unpopular actions. It would have been an important message to be heard at the time it was meant to be given, the end of a dark chapter in our political life. Perhaps it can echo just a bit louder in our current one.

Dan Schwerin works with Hillary Clinton on her victory remarks on November 7, 2016. (© Barbara Kinney / Hillary for America)

12

Hillary Clinton's 2016 Victory Speech,

November 2016

Why We Venerate the

Ritual of Concession

"As hard as it might be to imagine,

your daughter will grow up and become

the president of the United States."

Aₛ Election Night 2016 approached, nobody on Hillary Clinton's campaign doubted that she would be giving a historic victory speech, the first woman elected president of the United States. But two schools of thought emerged within the campaign about what that speech should contain.

Jake Sullivan had worked with Secretary Clinton at the State Department. He began the campaign as a foreign policy advisor, but Hillary trusted him and liked him, and as the campaign rolled on, everyone recognized that he had effectively become the campaign's chief strategist, though his title had never changed.

Sullivan argued that there was no need to overthink the victory speech; the fact of the win was the real history-making moment, and the job of the speech was to evoke a feeling rather than drive a vision or set an agenda. Sullivan had another concern, which was that if Secretary Clinton's advisors went in attempting to accomplish several things it would trigger Hillary's impulse to try to do everything, and it would result in her adding a paragraph on this and a paragraph on that, until the whole of the resulting speech became less than the sum of its parts.

Secretary Clinton had run against Donald Trump, a candidate who left the previous rules and norms of campaigning by the wayside. Trump had refused to release his tax information, something all previous presidential candidates in modern times had done; he threatened, if he won, to jail his opponent; he publicly asked a foreign power to hack his opponent's emails; he attacked the family of a fallen U.S. soldier; and he indicated he might not accept the outcome of the election if the results didn't go his way (a threat on which he'd make good to violent and destructive effect four years later).

To Sullivan, there was one overriding imperative, and it was to take an election that had been negative and divisive and "basically left the entire country feeling terrible" and create a sense that we could put this chapter behind us and move forward. He wanted a speech that conveyed that whatever people had thought of Hillary before, they could see themselves in this victory and see in Hillary a president who would speak to their needs. No, we couldn't erase all the divisions in our country, but Sullivan believed Hillary would be a president who would heal them where possible and manage them where necessary, and do so much more confidently and capably than people who had watched the campaign might expect.

Communications Director Jen Palmieri felt somewhat differently. Palmieri had come to the Hillary campaign from her role as the White House communications director for President Barack Obama without taking a day off in between. Palmieri argued that Election Night was the moment at which Hillary would transition from candidate to president, and that moment would be a major statement not only for Hillary but for posterity. In Palmieri's view, Election Night wasn't just about two candidates, it was about decades of frustration coming to the fore, creating a moment of reckoning for the country. She felt Hillary had to speak to that.

Palmieri's thinking was influenced by another observation. As Palmieri traveled with the candidate through Western Pennsylvania and Appalachia and other places where support for Donald Trump and his protectionist, anti-immigrant appeal to working-class white voters ran high, she observed that "they couldn't even hear her voice." They just didn't think Hillary was talking to them. In other words, the Election Night speech had to be a moment in which Hillary demonstrated that "as divisive a figure as her opponents had made her, she's really good at digging in and governing and getting things done in a bipartisan way."

The various impulses and stresses were evident in Hillary's own description of her thinking:

> One challenge was how to balance the need to reach out to Trump voters and sound a note of reconciliation, while also giving my supporters the triumphant victory celebration they deserved. There was also history to consider. If everything went as hoped, I would be giving this speech as the first woman elected president. We had to find a way to mark the significance of the moment without letting it overwhelm everything else. Most of all, I wanted to reassure Americans about the strength of our democracy. The election had tested our faith in many ways. Trump had violated every norm in the book, including warning that he might not accept the results of the vote if it went against him. The Russians had interfered. So had the Director of the FBI, against long-standing Justice Department policy. And the news media had turned the whole thing into an absurd circus. A lot of Americans wondered what it all meant for our future. I wanted to answer those fears with a strong victory, a smooth transition, and an effective presidency that delivered real results . . . I would argue that despite our differences, a strong coalition had come together in defense of our core values.

On most presidential campaigns, the candidate's "closing argument" would get road tested and honed over the waning days of the campaign.

In fact, that's how most campaigns operate; from the final debate through Election Day, it's all about building an argument that reaches its apotheosis on Election Night.

But like so much of Hillary's seemingly snakebit campaign, unwelcome events intervened.

On the afternoon of October 28, with eleven days to go before the election, news broke that FBI director James Comey had sent a letter to Congress saying that the FBI had "learned of the existence of emails that appear to be pertinent to the investigation" into the private email server that Clinton had set up and used when she was secretary of state.

Clinton was en route from Cedar Rapids to Des Moines, Iowa, when the news hit. Upon arrival in Des Moines, she made a statement in which she expressed her confidence that any new emails wouldn't change the conclusion that there had been no wrongdoing. There's an old political saying: if you're explaining, you're losing. At a time when a campaign wants to be playing offense, the Clinton campaign was in frenetic motion, trying to limit the damage.

As campaign pollster Joel Benenson pointed out, "We had come out of the third debate strong. That Comey letter interrupted our momentum. Any day Hillary's emails were in the news was a bad day."

And so, as much of the campaign's high command was consumed with the Comey letter and its fallout, the task of writing the Election Night speech fell to chief speechwriter Dan Schwerin.

Schwerin had begun interning for Hillary Clinton in 2004 when Hillary was serving as a senator, and was hired on in 2006 to be the assistant to then chief of staff Tamara Luzzatto. For fun, he began writing up and emailing out the postgame reports of the Hill's Angels, the Clinton staff softball team. Hillary enjoyed the write-ups immensely, and Schwerin soon found himself in the press office, working with Communications Director Philippe Reines and speechwriter Jon Lovett.

When Clinton announced her first run for president, in 2007, Schwerin stayed in the Senate, handling the remaining official work, and writing short speeches and video scripts.

When Barack Obama became president and Hillary joined the administration as secretary of state, Hillary's confidante Lissa Muscatine headed to Foggy Bottom to become her director of speechwriting and

Schwerin received what he called his "proper speechwriting education" working for her.

When Secretary Clinton left the State Department, she tapped Schwerin to help her write her memoir of the State Department years, *Hard Choices*. And when she geared up for her second run for president, Schwerin was a natural choice to serve as her lead speechwriter.

Now Schwerin was working on the most important speech of his career, and he added his own goals and concerns to those that had been expressed by Sullivan and Palmieri. He wanted to make sure that nobody forgot that this was a victory, and he wanted to give Hillary's supporters a victory lap. At the same time, he wanted to try to resolve what was sure to be a fraught question: What and who exactly was it a victory for? How would Hillary speak to progressives, who "still have questions about her and are going to be listening for signs that she's not going to run away from her commitments, and that she's going to govern like a progressive"?

As the campaign began to right the ship after the Comey letter, the fear wasn't so much that Hillary would lose but rather that she would not get a lot of credit for winning. After all, Trump was an undisciplined, divisive candidate, and the Beltway consensus was sure to be that any other Democrat would have won bigger. Though it wasn't necessarily Hillary's first priority, her communications staff knew the press would want to know how Hillary intended to reach out to people who didn't vote for her.

Schwerin knew his job was to get those ten pounds of potatoes into a five-pound sack.

Roughly a week before the election, in keeping with speechwriterly superstition, Schwerin assigned his deputy Megan Rooney, who had previously served as a speechwriter for Michelle Obama in the White House and a writer for Hillary at the State Department, to begin drafting a concession, "not because I actually entertained the idea that we were going to lose, but because it felt like for karmic reasons we had to."

Earlier in the campaign, Schwerin had gotten into the habit of preparing three speeches after each primary: a victory speech, a defeat speech, and one for when the results were too close to call. For the Iowa caucuses, Schwerin had worked hard on a victory speech. But when the results indicated a vanishingly narrow victory, Hillary largely jettisoned her prepared remarks, spoke off the cuff for about six minutes, candidly admitted that she was "breathing a big sigh of relief," promised to "keep doing what I have done my entire life. I will keep standing up for you. I will keep fighting for you. I will always work to achieve the America that I believe in, where the promise of that dream that we hold out to our children and our grandchildren never fades, but inspires generations to come," and called it a night.

A week later in New Hampshire, defeat was so assured that no victory speech was prepared. From that point on, everyone internalized the lesson that they had been taught by Barack Obama in 2008: if the campaign is moving on to fight the next battle, you only really need one speech with a couple of minor modifications: you acknowledge the result at the top with "Tonight wasn't what we were hoping for" or "While it's still too early to tell" or "What a fantastic victory!" and then you move on to the message going forward.

This was the first time since Iowa, nine months earlier, that there would need to be two distinct speeches.

Part of the challenge for Schwerin, and for anyone who picked up a pen on Hillary's behalf, is that Clinton's rhetoric always seemed to be reaching for something that it couldn't quite find, an ongoing struggle laid all the barer by her husband's seemingly effortless affect in front of a microphone. In addition to turning to Schwerin, Hillary often reached out to people who had written for her in the past who could offer additional language that could perhaps come closer to that ineffable thing—a tighter argument, a more inspirational turn of phrase—something that would capture that rare and perfect alchemy between writer and speaker and text that, when delivered, doesn't have to beg for laughter or applause or tears but elicits it organically by first achieving, from the audience, the knowing nods of understanding.

Of course, this may have been an impossible task. While Clinton's words to the UN World Conference on Women in Beijing as First Lady in 1995, "Human rights are women's rights and women's rights are human rights," became a global rallying cry, the challenging—and hopefully changing—reality is that Americans have not historically seen women in positions of power in the most positive light. Unlikable, untrustworthy, ambitious, shrill, cold—a mountain of evidence suggests this is how we hear women's voices in general and especially when they seek untraditional roles.

Schwerin's approach to the process of speechwriting was very much in line with Hillary's analytical approach: assembling an argument, marshaling data and evidence, aligning the inputs from staff and advisors, and then deploying them in a text. What's more, he navigated the ceaseless speechwriting drama with humility and a good attitude, recognizing that even if he were the second coming of Cicero, Hillary and Bill would continue to solicit input from outside writers. So he tried, wherever possible, to reach out to this informal stable of writers in advance and integrate their words and suggestions.

On Sunday, November 6, Schwerin joined Secretary Clinton on the plane from Philadelphia to Cleveland to talk about the speech. There was a sense of relief among the traveling staff, because Director Comey had just come out that day with a second letter to Congress saying, in effect, never mind. Palmieri was one of the few not sharing that feeling, realizing that the exoneration served to once again put Secretary Clinton's emails in the news. The bleeding had stopped, but had the second Comey letter cauterized the wound, or reopened it? Either way, the finish line was in sight. Clinton could belatedly begin to focus on Election Day, now just two days away. By all accounts, she was feeling good.

Unlike the planes on which she had flown as secretary of state, the campaign's chartered Boeing 737 didn't have an office. Rather, Hillary operated out of a four-seat cluster near the front, usually flanked and faced by a revolving group that included her longtime personal aide and campaign vice chair Huma Abedin,* campaign chair John Podesta, Palmieri, Sullivan, and campaign manager Robby Mook.

When it came time to review speeches, Schwerin would usually crouch in the aisle, laptop balanced on one knee, taking edits as his hands simultaneously balanced and braced the computer, a position well known to traveling speechwriters.

On this flight, Schwerin took a seat. Hillary was eager to discuss her Election Night speech. As she mused aloud with Schwerin, she kept

---

* Abedin stopped traveling with the candidate for a period of time in early November, as the investigation of her estranged husband's online behavior revealed additional emails that gave new life to the Clinton email probe.

coming back to the idea of "reconciliation"—on several levels and between several different groups.

This, too, had to be integrated into the thinking about the speech. If reconciliation was to be a major theme going forward, what seeds could the victory speech plant? And what policies could the president-elect begin to outline that would, ideally, bring the country together?

While the campaign's attention turned to Election Night later than most, Schwerin had been imagining what Election Night might look like from the very outset. This was, after all, a historic campaign. And the words uttered at historic events are the ones that end up carved into monuments and memorials.

Another reality of political campaigns is that people who seek to influence the candidate often try to do so through the speechwriter. As Peggy Noonan writes in her memoir of the Reagan years, *What I Saw at the Revolution* (which also happens to be one of the best books on speechwriting), "Speechwriting naturally started rows because debates and arguments would go on for years but finally at some point policy had to be announced and articulated in speeches. By the very process of writing and declaring we were throwing down the gauntlet." Suggestions on how the candidate can "sound better" pour in from all corners: fellow staffers, fundraisers, supporters, policy advisors, job seekers, celebrities, inmates. Often, the suggested language comes through with a note saying, "If he/she would just say this, it would break through/solve all your problems."

When I was working for Senate Democratic leader Tom Daschle in 2001, we had a mantra: "Fundraisers are not focus groups." Meaning, the opinions and perspectives of your well-heeled and well-meaning supporters don't necessarily square with the wider electorate.

What's more, the opinions of friends, supporters, and, often, celebrities can get the candidate tangled up in all sorts of ways. In Hillary's case, one example of this was whether the candidate should refer to herself as "we" or "I." Earlier in her career, Hillary had struggled to use the singular personal pronoun, in part because she was temperamentally self-effacing. Also, in her earlier roles, she was frequently serving as a surrogate, speaking on behalf of an organization (or her husband). Therefore, "we" became her default. Early in the campaign, advisors had struggled to get her to say "I"—to sound like the leader she was.

She began to embrace the "I" only to have one influential commentator point out on television that Bernie Sanders's entire message was devoid of "I"—it was "We're going to pass Medicare for all and we're going to take on Wall Street." "We," in the view of the commentator, was the language of movements, and Hillary wasn't starting one.

When a candidate is doing well, language suggestions like that slow to a trickle, as anyone who would be making them is busy taking credit for the success. But when a candidate seems to be underperforming, the flow of unsolicited suggestions becomes a torrent.

This was certainly Schwerin's experience, and throughout the campaign, the "she should says" came at such a volume that he designated an email folder in which he deposited the unsolicited speech suggestions.

By the time he met with Hillary on the plane, Schwerin had completed a first draft and circulated it to the campaign high command, as well as longtime advisors Jim Kennedy and Don Baer.

Kennedy, in particular, had come up with many of Clinton's most memorable lines, including her 2008 concession in which she declared, "Although we weren't able to shatter that highest, hardest glass ceiling this time, thanks to you, it's got about 18 million cracks in it, and the light is shining through like never before, filling us all with the hope and the sure knowledge that the path will be a little easier next time."

The first draft of this Election Night speech made no mention of ceilings. Rather, the speech began with the claim that "Americans had put aside rancor and resentment and reached for what President Lincoln called 'the better angels of our nature.'" In an attempt to shoehorn in a campaign slogan that had never fully caught on, it read "after a long election that seemed at times like it could pull our nation apart, you proved once again that we truly are stronger together." In a line that did not make it through successive drafts, it also acknowledged and conflated Trump and Sanders by saying, "For all of his faults, Donald Trump did tap into something important. And so did Bernie Sanders."

In his comments on the draft, Kennedy pointed out that saying that Americans had put aside rancor and resentment sounded a little bit like she was blaming Americans for feeling rancor and resentment. Baer agreed that it didn't seem right to start by focusing on the negative.

Overall, as Baer would comment, the speech was solid but "begins to feel kind of everydayish."

Kennedy suggested some more hopeful, elevated language:

> Let us translate the sense of history and pride we feel in this moment into a sense of purpose and wonder about the possibilities for our future . . . and let us have a spirit of determination to seize this moment and never give up, never give in, as we seek that more perfect union of our provenance. We are here in this place, named for Senator Jacob Javits, a Republican, and a man who once said "you have an obligation to the society which protected you . . . which taught you, which supported you and nurtured you. You have an obligation to repay it." The debt of responsibility that falls on my shoulders tonight is great, but I will gladly repay it with every breath I take.

It felt to all involved like a solid draft, but one that was missing a moment of elevation, an unforgettable conclusion.

For Hillary, the emotional punch of her speeches typically came from the story of her mother's Dickensian life. The experience of Dorothy Rodham had been a touchstone for Hillary throughout the campaign; a mother who, at age eight, was put on a train with her three-year-old sister in tow, to live in California with harsh and unloving grandparents; and to be put to work as a housekeeper, cook, and nanny. But Hillary felt that the story had been told enough.

One of the challenges in writing for campaigns is that a cynical and jaded press, not to mention an exhausted and overscheduled speaker, often grow tired of using the same stories and quotes. Audiences, however, don't. Because while the press has to hear the candidate (and the candidate has to hear him- or herself) several times a day, audiences will only see them once or twice, and so a powerful story, even a repeated one, hits an audience with the same impact. As we discussed in chapter 1, Martin Luther King had given some version of his "I Have a Dream" speech dozens of times before delivering it on his largest stage, the 1963 March on Washington.

The challenge is to keep things fresh for the speaker and the press, without diminishing the emotional impact for the audience.

In the case of Robert Kennedy, it led to an inside joke. Throughout his 1968 campaign, Robert Kennedy launched into the conclusion of his stump speech with the words, "George Bernard Shaw once wrote, 'Some people see things as they are and say why? I dream things that never were and say, why not?'"

This became his standard peroration, followed by, "So I come here today to [wherever he was that day] to ask for your help. In the [number of] months before the convention in Chicago, I ask for your assistance."

And then using the rhetorical technique of anaphora, which means to repeat a word or phrase in the beginning of successive sentences, he would conclude with some version of the following:

> If you believe that the United States can do better. If you believe that we should change our course of action. If you believe that the United States stands for something here internally as well as elsewhere around the globe, I ask for your help and your assistance and your hand.
>
> And when we win in November and we begin a new period of time for the United States of America—I want the next generation of Americans to look back upon this period and say as they said of Plato: "Joy was in those days, but to live." Thank you very much.

The iconic quote from Shaw wasn't a quote but a paraphrase of a slightly different line. Either way, it reliably came just about a minute before the end of the speech. So, as *Life* magazine editor George Hunt related, "We quickly learned to use Shaw as a signal to head for the press bus."

It didn't take Kennedy long to realize that once he hit Shaw, reporters began filing out. And so, perhaps to alleviate his own boredom, and in a winking reference to the assembled journalists, one night, he launched into the conclusion of his speech with the words, "As George Bernard Shaw once said, run for the bus!"

That was one way to make a repeated story interesting.

Could something be done to refresh the story of Hillary's mother? To approach it from a new angle, a new perspective? Perhaps, Schwerin thought, the image of the little girl on the train could become a metaphor for a journey into the unknown.

As he wrestled with this approach, he remembered one email he had received, skimmed, and filed away. It had come through Lynn Rothschild, a donor, who wanted to connect Schwerin with Jorie Graham, a Pulitzer Prize–winning poet and professor of oratory and rhetoric at Harvard.

Graham had sent a series of emails. The first was about immigration, which Schwerin skimmed. The second he didn't even read. But the third caught his attention, because it began with the words: "Actually, if I really told you what I wished in my heart of hearts that she would say, it's this."

Graham had conjured up an image of an adult Hillary, walking down the narrow aisle of the westward-bound train. She comes upon her mother at the age of eight, a scared child holding the hand of her younger sister. In her imagining, Hillary takes her own mother in her arms and tells her, "I know this sounds impossible, but you are going to survive, you're going to thrive, you're going to have a daughter, and she's going to grow up to be president of this country."

In her note, Graham described the moment of inspiration, "I don't know why but I always see the prairie landscape going by those windows, the seats wooden with their metal frames. I see it as if it happened to me."

It was the emotional touchstone the speech needed. For campaign-watchers, it would also evoke what many thought was Hillary's finest moment during the campaign, when, in Las Vegas, a ten-year-old girl, speaking through tears, told Hillary that she feared her parents would be deported. In that moment, Hillary said, "Come here, babe," put an arm around the child's waist, and said, "I'm going to do everything I can so you don't have to be scared . . . I'll do the worrying, deal?"

Schwerin began modifying the idea to fit into the speech.

On Election Night, the Clinton campaign's high command was head-quartered at the Peninsula Hotel on New York City's Fifth Avenue, one block south of Trump Tower.

On the ninth floor of the hotel, offices were set up for the data and analytics team and for the lawyers. The Clintons occupied a suite directly across from the elevators. A buffet spread was set up in the hallway.

Schwerin and Rooney had an office one floor down.

At around 5:30 p.m., results were looking good. Turnout numbers in Florida, in particular, had the campaign's spirits buoyed. Schwerin and

Rooney, along with Sullivan, were summoned to come chat with Secretary Clinton. President Clinton was in the room, too.

Hillary first wanted to see a draft of the concession speech. She read it relatively quickly, set it aside, and said something to the effect of, "If it comes to it, we'll have to work on this, but it's more important we get the other one right if that's what happens."

The team turned to the victory speech. Bill Clinton wanted to add some language to the beginning about "*e pluribus unum*" and America not being an "us-versus-them country." Hillary wanted to add language about the American dream being big enough for everyone.

But mostly, her mind was on governing. She had been carting around transition briefing books and binders, and was thinking about how to move forward on all those policy proposals that got so little attention during the campaign but formed the foundation of an agenda for a more prosperous, inclusive America.

Schwerin and Rooney went back downstairs to continue working.

But at that moment, a note of concern was creeping into the high command. Numbers in Florida were starting to look worse than Clinton's team had hoped. The question was whether it was regional or national—after all, the campaign could still win without winning any Southern states. As more numbers came in, the outlook turned increasingly grim.

Around 8:00 p.m., campaign manager Robby Mook came to Palmieri with a disheartening report: "It isn't regional, we're a few points off everywhere; how should I talk to Hillary about it?"

The bad news continued as the Associated Press started calling states for Trump that Hillary's campaign thought they had an outside shot at winning: 10:25 p.m., Missouri; 10:36 p.m., Ohio; 10:50 p.m., Florida; 11:11 p.m., North Carolina. Just after midnight, Iowa.

Hillary's personal aide Huma Abedin had opened a line of communication with Trump advisor Kellyanne Conway a couple of days prior.

Shortly after 1:30 a.m., Huma dialed Conway's number. As Hillary later recalled in her memoir, Huma handed her phone to Hillary, Conway handed her phone to Trump. Hillary said, "You know, it's a really close race and it looks like you've won." Trump replied, "You were an incredible opponent, what an amazing campaign. Unbelievable."

The conversation barely lasted one minute.

Hillary then put in a call to President Obama. Her throat tightened as she said, "I'm sorry for letting you down."

At this point, most of the campaign's inner circle was in shock, moving in slow motion, speaking with flat affects, gazing off with thousand-yard stares. Campaign chairman John Podesta was dispatched to let the assembled crowd at the Javits Center know that there would be no speech that night.

Much as planning for a funeral rouses people from grief because there is a task at hand, the fact that Hillary would have to make a concession speech kicked people into motion again. Because the Javits Center was set to host an auto show the next day, a new venue had to be found. Schwerin and Rooney got to work revising Rooney's concession speech. In the harsh light of Trump's victory and the shock and grief of Hillary's supporters, the early draft felt too sanguine, too conciliatory. Hillary would have to acknowledge Trump's victory, but she could also challenge him to be a more inclusive president than he had been a candidate.

Despite the fact that every presidential campaign has one winner and at least one loser, prior to 1928, Americans had never *heard* a presidential concession speech. The act of concession was more often a private one, transmitted via telegram and then, later, by telephone. But in 1928, Democrat Al Smith, the first Catholic nominee of a major political party, sent Herbert Hoover a congratulatory message—and also delivered a radio address. Senator Adlai Stevenson, upon losing to Dwight Eisenhower in 1952, gave the first televised concession speech, one that is held up as a model for its decency and dignity. "That which unites us as American citizens is far greater than that which divides us as political parties. I urge you all to give to Gen. Eisenhower the support he will need to carry out the great task that lies before him. I pledge him mine. We vote as many. But we pray as one."

Since then, concession speeches have become a central tradition in our democracy, the moment at which we acknowledge how power is granted—and handed over. Because they are part of this democratic ritual, they have also become perhaps the most formulaic of all speeches. In 1996, *The New Yorker*'s Hendrik Hertzberg, who had previously served as a speechwriter for President Carter, outlined the standard concession speech thus:

1. a manful, rueful acknowledgment of the pain of defeat;
2. a message of congratulations to the victor . . . ;
3. a pledge, sometimes made over the shouted protests of the audience, to close ranks behind the people's choice;
4. thank-yous to wife, children, and supporters;
5. praise for the political system;
6. an assertion that what unites us as Americans is more important than what divides us;
7. a pledge to carry on the cause to which the campaign was allegedly devoted; and
8. a bit of concluding graciousness and/or ruefulness, preferably including a quotation, preferably from Lincoln

Ultimately, the job of the concession is (to adhere to Hertzberg's step 8), as Senator Stephen Douglas said upon his election loss to Abraham Lincoln, to remind people that "partisan feeling must yield to patriotism."

A powerful part of the ritual is the mortification of the loser. The concession is the moment at which the failing candidate, who over the course of the campaign has been celebrated, elevated, attacked, and mocked on a journey that has taken him or her to just the cusp of the position they sought most, becomes as relatable as they will ever be. They now have the experience of falling short of a goal and being laid low in front of others, an experience that is nearly universal.

In one memorable line, Adlai Stevenson described it as feeling like a little boy who had stubbed his toe in the dark: "He was too old to cry, but it hurt too much to laugh." Bob Dole, in 1996, observed that "tomorrow will be the first time in my life I don't have anything to do."

For the first time in months or even years, we see the candidate as a human being, a striver who has fallen short. And because those who voted for the winner have, in a direct way, done this to them, the losing candidate is sympathetic even to those who sought the outcome to begin with.

The concession speech also presents a moment for a candidate to remind the voters what they were fighting for in the first place, and cast it in the best possible light. And it provides fertile ground in which to plant the seeds of renewal, both personal and political.

Though it seems hardly believable in retrospect, Michael Dukakis's 1988 concession speech was interrupted by his supporters' chants of "Ninety-two! Ninety-two! Ninety-two!" in the hopes that Dukakis would run four years later. It was Hillary's "glass ceiling" line that helped crystallize (no pun intended) the hope that she would return to shatter it for good. In his concession at the end of the protracted 2000 presidential election, Al Gore voiced this idea directly, in quoting his father, also a former senator from Tennessee: "No matter how hard the loss, defeat may serve as well as victory to shake the soul and let the glory out."*

President Bill Clinton also had a role to play in the drama of Al Gore's concession; the fact that the election was ultimately decided not by the voters but a Supreme Court decision to stop the vote counting in Florida meant that calls for unity and civility, rather than a passing of the torch to his own vice president, would become the coda of that presidency. Early drafts of President Clinton's speech unearthed by journalist Philip Bump talk about "the critical challenge of healing the partisan breach, and restoring public confidence in our electoral system" with "a comprehensive, nationwide overhaul of the voting process, so that every American is guaranteed equal access to the ballot box, not just in principle, but in practice." Even that was a toned-down version of the stronger language Clinton speechwriter John Pollack had written: "The right to vote is the very foundation of our democracy. Our entire system rests on the premise that—come election day—every American speaks with an equal voice . . . There is no dispute over the fact that tens of thousands of Americans cast their ballots in Florida, only to discover that—for one reason or another—their vote didn't count." Ultimately, none of those words made it into Clinton's statement. Instead, Clinton chose not to mention the votes but rather the message he felt the voters were delivering: "The American people, however divided they were in this election, overwhelmingly want us to build on that vital center without rancor or personal attack." Two decades later, Paul Glastris, another member of

---

* Albert Gore Sr. later titled his memoir of the South and its politics *Let the Glory Out.*

Clinton's speechwriting team, shared with the writer Uri Friedman his belief that Clinton took "out anything that anyone could point to and say, 'Sore loser.'" Choosing not to focus presidential attention on the flaws in our election system was an understandable decision at the time, but a missed opportunity in retrospect.

The recognition that concessions can be beginnings as well as endings fueled one of the more bizarre occurrences of the 2008 campaign, when Barack Obama defeated Arizona senator John McCain. By the end of that campaign, McCain's running mate, Alaska governor Sarah Palin, was drawing larger, more enthusiastic crowds than her top-of-the-ticket running mate. She was also an immensely polarizing figure, tapping into many of the forces that would come to the fore with the election of Donald Trump.

On Election Night, as the McCain campaign gathered at the Biltmore Hotel in Scottsdale, Arizona, Palin wanted an opportunity to take the stage one last time, ostensibly to introduce her running mate, despite the fact that there was no plan to have her deliver remarks. She had already hand-edited a draft that had been prepared for her by a former George W. Bush speechwriter named Matthew Scully, and according to the book *Sarah from Alaska,* Palin told one of her aides she was determined to speak: "I've got the remarks, figure it out."

The McCain side of the campaign, which by that point was in open conflict with their running mate, felt it would be inappropriate and unprecedented, and had to forcefully tell Palin she wouldn't be speaking.*

For the McCain team, it wasn't so much a concern that Palin would give an incendiary speech that would disrupt the peaceful transition of power (Scully, a talented writer, was sometimes more aware of norms than was his client) but rather that it would distract from what was to be one of America's great heroes' last appearances on such a national stage. In that ritual, Palin had no role.

A draft of her undelivered concession indicates, however, that she may have wanted more than that one final turn in the national spotlight; she also wanted to be the phoenix that rose from the ashes of the McCain campaign. In addition to generous language about President-Elect Obama—

---

* It's not *quite* unprecedented—in 1992, Dan Quayle introduced George H. W. Bush, and in 2004, John Edwards introduced John Kerry.

"If he [Obama] governs America with the skill and grace we have often seen in him, and the greatness of which he is capable, we're gonna be just fine"—she also included the line, "It would be a happier night if elections were a test of valor and merit alone, but that is not for us to question now."

More self-serving was her closing sentiment: "America has made her choice. As for me, my convictions, my loyalties, and my hopes for this country remain the same. Now it is time for us to go our way, neither bitter nor vanquished, but instead confident in the knowledge that there will be another day . . . and we may gather once more . . . and find new strength . . . and rise to fight again."

If delivered, it would have been equal parts concession speech and declaration of candidacy; a grabbing of the mantle of leadership of the Republican Party. It would have demonstrated behavior that, while it seemed unprecedented at the time, was simply ahead of its time.

McCain alone delivered a concession speech that rivaled Stevenson's in its graciousness and eloquence.

> Senator Obama has achieved a great thing for himself and for his country. I applaud him for it, and offer my sincere sympathy that his beloved grandmother did not live to see this day—though our faith assures us she is at rest in the presence of her Creator and so very proud of the good man she helped raise.
>
> Senator Obama and I have had and argued our differences, and he has prevailed. No doubt many of those differences remain. These are difficult times for our country, and I pledge to him tonight to do all in my power to help him lead us through the many challenges we face.
>
> I urge all Americans who supported me to join me in not just congratulating him, but offering our next president our goodwill and earnest effort to find ways to come together, to find the necessary compromises, to bridge our differences and help restore our prosperity, defend our security in a dangerous world, and leave our children and grandchildren a stronger, better country than we inherited.

Later that evening, Palin and her family approached the stage at the hotel. Fearful that Palin would try to speak (and perhaps incite) the crowd that had hoped to drink in celebration and was now drinking in disappointment, McCain staffer Steve Schmidt ordered the AV team to unplug the lights and microphone.

There was some fear before the 2016 election that Trump would not participate in this civic ritual of concession; that he would, in the words of longtime political strategist Tad Devine, "light a match, put it to the fuse, and walk away on election night." In 2020, he indeed lit a fuse. But in 2016, that question turned out to be moot, because now the burden of concession fell upon Hillary.

The morning of November 9, wearing the purple she had intended to wear the night before as a way to symbolize red and blue coming together, Secretary Clinton thanked her family, her staff, her volunteers and contributors. She also apologized to them, making her the first presidential candidate to say "I'm sorry" in a concession speech: "This is not the outcome we wanted or we worked so hard for, and I'm sorry that we did not win this election for the values we share and the vision we hold for our country."

She talked about a nation "more deeply divided than we thought." She included language from the victory speech she had hoped to give: "We've spent a year and a half bringing together millions of people from every corner of our country to say with one voice that we believe that the American dream is big enough for everyone—for people of all races and religions, for men and women, for immigrants, for LGBT people, and people with disabilities. For everyone." But she concluded the thought with a charge and a warning, "So now, our responsibility as citizens is to keep doing our part to build that better, stronger, fairer America we seek."

Left unsaid was the glass ceiling reference that had worked its way into the victory speech several drafts in: "This is a victory for all Americans— men and women, boys and girls—because as our country has proven once again: When there are no ceilings, the sky's the limit."

Left unmade was her call that "we must not rest until every remaining ceiling is shattered, every standing barrier is broken, and every single American can live up to her or his God-given potential. That is the promise of America, and it will be my promise to you as the 45th President of the United States."

Left undescribed was her vision of "an America where women are respected and immigrants are welcomed . . . workers are paid fairly . . . where we believe in science."

Left unvoiced was her belief that "if you dig deep enough, through all the mud of politics, eventually you hit something hard and true. A foundation of fundamental values that unite us as Americans."

And left unspoken were the powerful words that would have concluded her victory speech:

This summer, a writer asked me: If I could go back in time and tell anyone in history about this milestone, who would it be?

And the answer was easy: my mother, Dorothy.

You may have heard me talk about her difficult childhood. She was abandoned by her parents when she was just 8 years old. They put her on a train to California, where she was mistreated by her grandparents and ended up out on her own, working as a housemaid. Yet she still found a way to offer me the boundless love and support she never received herself. She taught me the words of our Methodist faith: "Do all the good you can, for all the people you can, in all the ways you can, as long as ever you can."

I think about my mother every day. Sometimes, I think about her on that train. I wish I could walk down the aisle and find the little wooden seats where she sat, holding tight to her even-younger sister, alone, terrified. She doesn't yet know how much she will suffer. She doesn't yet know she will find the strength to escape that suffering—that is still a long way off. The whole future is still unknown as she stares out at the vast country moving past her. I dream of going up to her, and sitting down next to her, taking her in my arms and saying look at me, listen to me. You will survive. You will have a good family of your own, and three children. And as hard as it might be to imagine, your daughter will grow up and become the president of the United States.

I am as sure of this as anything I have ever known: America is the greatest country in the world. And, from tonight, going forward, together we will make America even greater than it has ever been—for each and every one of us.

PART 6

Events Intervene

It's not uncommon for a speech to go undelivered because of some unforeseen circumstance. In 1895, Samuel Clemens (Mark Twain) was scheduled to speak at the launching of the steamship *St. Paul* from a shipyard in Philadelphia. When the blocks were knocked away at the drydock, the ship refused to budge. By the time the ship could be successfully launched, Clemens had left for Europe (his draft speech, which he handed to a reporter, exists). More than a few college graduation speeches have gone undelivered on account of weather, or, more recently, event cancellations due to the coronavirus pandemic.

On April 21, 1999, my boss, Vice President Al Gore, was prepared to give a speech on Ellis Island celebrating the fiftieth anniversary of the North Atlantic Treaty Organization (NATO). The day before, as he was going through the final edits of that speech, we saw news out of Colorado. In the ensuing hours, we would learn that Eric Harris and Dylan Klebold had murdered twelve of their classmates and a teacher at Columbine High School, shocking the nation with what would be the first of many mass shootings to follow, an epidemic that rages unabated.

The speech Gore was to give became an appendage to the one he did give. His new opening: "I came here today to talk about an armed conflict an ocean away. But, I want to say a word about Jefferson County, Colorado. For there is a war here at home, too."

In 2001, the event that put plans—and life as we knew it—on hold was the terrorist attacks of September 11.

In those cases, the intervening events were national tragedies. But all sorts of unexpected events can get in the way of a planned speech.

In 2017, the intervening event was the hosts of the Academy Awards announcing the wrong film as that year's Best Picture, leaving director Barry Jenkins's speech undelivered. That speech not only tells a powerful story, it reminds us of why story is so powerful in the first place.

And sometimes the intervening event is the death of the speaker, as was the case for Pope Pius XI, Franklin Delano Roosevelt, Albert Einstein, and John F. Kennedy. In those cases, their unfinished words take on added poignancy, serving as their last words as well.

National Security Advisor Condoleezza Rice waits for President George W. Bush to arrive at the White House on Tuesday, September 11, 2001. (Courtesy of the US National Archives)

13

The Remarks Condoleezza Rice Had Intended to Give on the Bush Administration's Foreign Policy, September 11, 2001

The Process of Constructing a Speech

"Why put deadbolt locks on your doors
and stock up on cans of mace and then decide
to leave your windows open?"

Condoleezza Rice grew up in segregated Birmingham, Alabama, the daughter of academics who helped her become a high achiever and a polymath: by the age of three, she was learning French, music, and figure skating.

While she continued to play piano throughout her schooling, she realized that she would not make it as a concert pianist and became interested in international politics. She eventually earned a master's degree in political science and began a career in academia and foreign policy.

In 1991, she began serving as a Soviet affairs advisor on the national security staff of President George H. W. Bush. Upon leaving that role, she became the provost of Stanford University, where she had previously served as a professor. When George W. Bush began his run for president in 1999, she took a leave of absence from Stanford to serve as his foreign policy advisor. The younger Bush was less experienced in foreign policy than his father, and Rice became a tutor and a friend.

When George W. Bush was elected president, he named Rice as his national security advisor, making her the first woman to occupy that position. Rice immediately staked out a role that made her both more of a policy architect and more of a policy advocate than many of her predecessors. Indeed it was Rice, not Secretary of State Colin Powell, who became the Bush administration's first top foreign policy official to meet with Russian president Vladimir Putin, a departure from traditional protocol that hadn't occurred since Henry Kissinger served as national security advisor. Similarly, it was Rice, not Powell, who gave a major speech laying out the administration's foreign policy. And it was also Rice, not Powell, who, when invited to deliver the prestigious Rostov lecture at the Johns Hopkins School of Advanced International Studies, was determined to spearhead what she hoped would be the administration's signature foreign policy effort.

The invitation to speak was for the afternoon of September 11, 2001.

Dr. Rice's team saw her remarks as a chance to advance the administration's argument that the gravest threat to America's security was attack by long-range (intercontinental) ballistic missiles and that the answer was a need for a robust missile defense system.

Developing and deploying such a defense system had long been a goal for a small group of policy-makers who disagreed with the prevailing thinking on nuclear deterrence. Conventional wisdom (pun intended) held that the threat of massive retaliation was the only thing stopping a nuclear attack on America. The defenders of missile defense dismissed this thinking as, essentially, a "mutual suicide pact." In the words of President Reagan's secretary of defense Caspar Weinberger, building a missile defense system would mark "a radical rejection of benign acquiescence in mutual assured destruction."

As long as there have been missiles, there have been people thinking about missile defense. But the idea really entered the public conversation in 1983, when President Reagan called for the use of ground- and space-based systems to shield the country against a first-strike attack. The goal, he said, was to make "nuclear weapons impotent and obsolete."

Reagan called the plan the Strategic Defense Initiative. But the initiative was largely theoretical, dependent on yet-to-be-invented science fiction–sounding concepts like x-ray lasers powered by nuclear explosions. Senator Ted Kennedy derisively described these ideas as "reckless 'Star Wars' schemes." The nickname stuck.

Research and investment in missile defense did move forward, but because of the technical complexity of such a system (the analogy most often used was "hitting a bullet with a bullet"), support for long-range missile defense was more about ideological positioning than practical deployment.

And even if the cost and technical and political hurdles to building such a system were able to be overcome, there was a geopolitical hurdle as well. In 1972, the United States became a signatory to the Anti-Ballistic Missile (ABM) Treaty, which was explicitly designed to prevent countries from building missile defenses. The philosophy behind the treaty was that no defense would be perfect, so any missile defense would simply force adversaries to build up their missile *offenses,* leading to endless arms escalation. (Former Chinese Foreign Ministry spokesman Sun Yuxi put it lyrically when he said, "When you invent a new shield, you will invent new types of spear. It always goes on like that.")

And while the treaty became a foreign policy cornerstone, allowing for several follow-on agreements that reduced nuclear arsenals, many conservative policy-makers remained fearful that the ABM was becoming outdated, because it didn't account for ballistic missiles in the hands of rogue states or rogue actors.

One of those policy-makers was Donald Rumsfeld, who had served as secretary of defense under President Gerald Ford and returned to that role under President George W. Bush. In 1998, Rumsfeld chaired a commission to assess the ballistic missile threat to the United States, and though the report's findings were controversial, they stated that a rogue ballistic missile threat could emerge sooner than previously thought.

One month later, North Korea launched a missile that was intended to put a payload into orbit (a necessary precursor to an intercontinental ballistic missile), stoking those fears further.

When President Bush came into office in 2001, his foreign policy team was focused on the linked goals of missile defense and getting America out of the ABM treaty. In a speech to the National Defense University four months after becoming president, Bush laid out the arguments in favor of building a missile defense system (despite the still-unproven technology), as well as the need to "move beyond the constraints of the 30-year-old ABM Treaty."

Secretary of State Powell remained skeptical, preferring to bring allies along rather than act rashly and unilaterally in scrapping the treaty. Nor did he see much of a rush. Missile defense remained unproven, controversial, and costly, and people's views of it varied widely and wildly depending on the costs and trade-offs involved.

As foreign policy experts Ivo Daalder and James Lindsay pointed out that spring, "When Americans are asked if they support missile defense in the abstract, only one in three says 'no.' But when asked if they support it if it jeopardizes arms reductions with Russia, only one in three says 'yes.'"

Throughout 2001, with the administration requesting increased missile defense budgets and beginning to signal that it intended to pull out of the ABM Treaty, opportunities to discuss foreign policy became opportunities to advance the argument in favor of missile defense.

On September 9, 2001, Condoleezza Rice appeared on the NBC News program *Meet the Press* to argue that it "would not be . . . responsible of the President of the United States to not respond to that threat [of ballistic missiles]."

The guest who followed her was then senator Joe Biden, the powerful chairman of the Senate Foreign Relations Committee. Senator Biden proceeded to deconstruct Rice's argument, passionately arguing that missile defense "will not protect us from cruise missiles. It will not protect us from something being smuggled in. It will not protect us from an atom bomb in the rusty hull of a ship coming into a harbor. It will not protect us from anthrax . . . all of which the Defense Department says are much more likely threats than somebody sending an I.C.B.M. with a return address on it."

The next day, in a speech at the National Press Club, Biden pressed the point further, arguing that "missile defense has to be weighted carefully against all other spending and all other military priorities . . . in truth, our real security needs are much more earthbound and far less costly than missile defense."

(Biden's words seem especially prescient in retrospect; in the ten days that followed his appearance, America experienced both the attacks of September 11 as well as a series of deadly anthrax attacks on the offices of two Democratic senators and several news outlets.)

Meanwhile, both the economy and Bush's popularity were in decline. The Dow was down by nearly 10 percent since President Bush had taken office, unemployment was on the rise, and a poll that appeared on the front page of *The Washington Post* found that a majority of Americans no longer approved of the tax cut he had passed. His presidency was foundering, and even Republican senators were claiming that the Bush administration's foreign policy lacked a big picture.

Rice's team saw the speech she was slated to give two days after the *Meet the Press* appearance as a chance to lay out a clearer vision and an even more forceful argument in favor of missile defense, and against its detractors.

Here, too, she faced an uphill battle. Just a few months earlier, a poll by the Pew Research Center found that an overwhelming majority of Americans (77 percent to 10 percent) were more concerned about a terrorist bringing weapons into the United States than a missile attack from an unfriendly nation. On the question of what policy provides the best protection, another significant majority (53 percent to 34 percent) felt that the United States was best protected by treaties limiting the arms race as opposed to missile defense.

Holding the lead pen on the speech was John Gibson, a writer working for National Security Council who had previously served as the chief speechwriter for Secretary of Defense Bill Cohen. He had assembled a ten-page draft that he felt made the case for missile defense as well as possible. Now, as the morning of September 11 dawned, Gibson was going back and forth with Dr. Rice on final edits.

Rice was in her office at 8:46 a.m. when her assistant told her that a plane struck the World Trade Center. Like most Americans, Rice thought it was a horrible accident. She was in her regular 9:00 a.m. staff meeting when her assistant rushed in: a second plane had hit the other tower of the World Trade Center.

Even in the midst of world-changing events, speechwriters are often afflicted with a project-based myopia, trying to figure out if a speech will still happen and, if so, how much of it will need to be rewritten. Gibson remembers keeping his phone on throughout the afternoon, wondering if the speech would still be given and awaiting any additional edits from Dr. Rice, even as it became clear that the United States suffered the most devastating attack since the 1941 bombing of Pearl Harbor.

That speech was never given.

Two and a half years later, prior to Dr. Rice's testimony before a commission investigating the attacks, some of the contents of her speech appeared in a *Washington Post* story by Robin Wright.

Those words landed in a changed world, and they revealed just how far the administration's focus was from the threat that was materializing as they were being written. According to the excerpt leaked to the *Post*, Dr. Rice was to have conceded, "We need to worry about the suitcase bomb, the car bomb, and the vial of sarin released on the subway." However, she also planned to criticize those who downplayed the threat of long-range missiles, saying, "Why put deadbolt locks on your doors and stock up on cans of mace and then decide to leave your windows open?"

Dr. Rice's full draft remains classified as of this writing. But in searching for the speech, I was able to find, via a Freedom of Information Act request, the materials her team had assembled in preparing it. In some ways, those materials are as telling as the words themselves would have been.

In chapter 4, I wrote that I'm often asked if I could write speeches for *anyone.* And what the person asking the question usually means is whether I could write in favor of a person or policy that doesn't reflect my views or values. The truth is, speechwriters can be like lawyers in that they're able to make a sound argument regardless of the position being argued. (Unlike lawyers, however, nobody has a right to a good speech. The only right anyone has regarding a speech is the right to give it.) Speechwriting is as much a craft of argumentation as it is an art of poetry, and so there are tools and techniques that anyone can use to write a good speech for any speaker, in favor of any cause. The job of the speechwriter is to deploy those tools and techniques to best effect.

Looking through the materials Dr. Rice's team put together in developing the draft immediately makes sense, regardless of how one feels about missile defense.

First, there is the "throat clearing"—research to make the introductions and thank-yous a little more elevated and heartfelt. For example, knowing that Paul Nitze would be in the audience, the writing team wanted to find a vaguely remembered quote about Nitze from former secretary of state George Shultz. A researcher came back with: "Wise men come and wise men go, but decade after decade there is Paul Nitze."

Then there is the meat of the argument. In the case of this speech, that argument was going to be made largely through a speechwriting technique called *refutation*—an approach in which you line up arguments in order to knock them down. And a speech in favor of missile defense required quite a lot of it.

One of the key building blocks of the speech was an internal document titled *Misconceptions About Missile Defense,* which laid out the thirteen arguments Dr. Rice needed to refute. These included "the technology for missile defense simply does not work" and "missile defense costs too much money" and "deployment of missile defenses will split the U.S. from our allies who are opposed to this idea." The document selectively included findings from the same poll that found that 77 percent of Americans were more concerned about a terrorist threat than a missile attack, pointing out that 51 percent of Americans supported the Bush administration's missile defense proposal. It also included responses to the arguments that "the United States has exaggerated the . . . threat" and that missile defense "does not defend against other means of delivering a WMD payload to the U.S., such as a terrorist using a suitcase or car bomb."

The speech also intended to make use of another important element of persuasion: irrefutable advocates or unlikely allies. In this case, the research materials Rice's team compiled included an op-ed from Pulitzer Prize–winning columnist Thomas Friedman in which he pilloried the Bush arguments for missile defense: "The core problem with the Bush approach to missile defense. It is based on flimsy or dishonest arguments." However, in that piece, one paragraph is circled. "I am not theologically against missile defense, but it has to be judged by what it really is—a defense system that will always be, at best, a supplement to mutual assured destruction. . . . It is like wearing suspenders along with a belt."

Much like a movie publicist could read a review that said, "I left amazed that such a piece of trash could ever get made," and slap on the promotional poster "I left amazed," one could imagine a speechwriter taking that Friedman column and crafting the slightly more scrupulous line, "Even Tom Friedman, no great fan of our position, argues that a missile defense is 'like wearing suspenders with a belt.' Well, in a dangerous world, we can't risk getting caught with our pants down."

Another document in the speech file is a series of quotes from President Truman in which Truman speaks about the importance of leaders doing what is right, even if it may not be popular in the moment. That research document included these words from Truman:

Men make history and not the other way around. In periods where there is no leadership, society stands still. Progress occurs when courageous, skillful leaders seize the opportunity to change things for the better.

And:

How far would Moses have gone if he had taken a poll in Egypt? What would Jesus Christ have preached if he had taken a poll in the land of Israel? What would have happened to the Reformation if Martin Luther had taken a poll? It isn't polls or public opinion of the moment that counts. It's right and wrong and leadership.

If one of the goals of Dr. Rice's speech was to buttress President Bush's standing, a quote from President Truman would have served two goals. First, it would have put President Bush's actions and leadership in the context of other brave, decisive leaders. Second, it would have made the audience feel like a Democratic president was tacitly, across time and history, endorsing the actions of this Republican one.

Of course, Rice wanted to do this without contradicting herself, so the other items the speechwriters leaned on were previous articles and statements made by Dr. Rice herself.

Finally, the speech would have to deal with the issue of Senator Joe

Biden, one of the administration's most powerful and outspoken detractors. In this case, Rice's speechwriters leaned on a six-page document of specific rebuttals to Biden's arguments—including that missile defense becomes especially unaffordable in light of the tax cut that President Bush had signed into law earlier that year. So the rebuttal document included this line: "Like other major defense programs, such as those to develop new fighter aircraft or ships, missile defense will require significant funding. Even so, it will only represent a small fraction of the defense budget—about 2.5% in FY 2002."

The risk with refutation is that if you are working to refute arguments against you, you need to make those arguments appear minor or misguided. That can leave a speaker looking silly when one of those concerns you dismissed turns out to have been proven right.

In this case, Gibson's formulation—"We need to worry about the suitcase bomb, the car bomb, and the vial of sarin released in the subway . . . [but] why put deadbolt locks on your doors and stock up on cans of mace and then decide to leave your windows open"—became emblematic of an administration that was entirely focused on the wrong threat.

That topic came up again in 2005, when Condoleezza Rice was nominated to be secretary of state. Senator Jack Reed, the chairman of the Senate Armed Services Committee at the time, spoke against her nomination, leaning heavily on her focus on missile defense at the expense of attention to the other threats facing the United States.

She [Dr. Rice] also indicated many times that prior to 9/11 the policy of the Bush administration—and her advice by inference—was a strong focus on counter-terrorism. Yet I understand Dr. Rice was scheduled to deliver a speech on September 11 at Johns Hopkins in which she would indicate the cornerstone of the Bush foreign policy was missile defense. Having served in this body during that period of time, I can tell you the emphasis was on missile defense. It was not on counter-terrorism. It was not on the old-fashioned kind of boots on the ground, intelligence, striking brigades. It was a multibillion-dollar effort on developing a national missile system. I think her speech scheduled for that day was emblematic of what the focus was.

Six months after the attacks of September 11, Dr. Rice ultimately did deliver the Rostov Lecture. The remarks she made that day showed just how quickly and completely the world had changed. According to the *Washington Post* piece that broke the story about the original speech, administration officials said that the speech Rice ultimately delivered did not contain any of the original text. However, that wasn't quite accurate. Something from the original research did find its way into both drafts: the observation by George Shultz that "wise men come and wise men go, but decade after decade there is Paul Nitze."

Beyond that, nothing of the original draft survived. In the revamped speech, Rice spoke almost exclusively about the administration's anti-terrorism efforts. The only mention of missile defense was a reference to using "every tool at our disposal to meet this grave global threat." There was no need to fight a battle about the theoretical threat of missiles when America had been awakened to the clear and present threat of terrorism. Nor did Dr. Rice feel compelled to explain what could have been done differently or better leading up to the attacks. The world was changed, and navigating that changed world was her job. As she said that day, "An earthquake of the magnitude of 9/11 can shift the tectonic plates of international politics."

Director Barry Jenkins works with Alex Hibbert during the filming of Moonlight. *(Photo 12 / Alamy Stock Photo)*

14

Barry Jenkins's Best Picture Remarks for
Moonlight, February 2017

The Power of Story

"We are that boy."

William Safire, in his compendium of great speeches, *Lend Me Your Ears,* writes that for a speech to be great, it needs one thing wholly unrelated to composition or delivery; it needs "occasion." In his words:

> There comes a dramatic moment in the life of a person or a party or a nation that cries out for the uplift and release of a speech. Someone is called upon to articulate the hope, pride, or grief of all. The speaker becomes the cynosure, the brilliant object of guidance; he or she is all alone out there on the cusp, and the world stops to look and listen. That instant access to fame gives the edge to an inaugural address, or to a speech on some state occasion or award ceremony; the occasion, by being invested with solemnity or importance, boosts the speech itself.

In entertainment, there is no "occasion" more commanding than the Academy Awards, and as the 2017 Academy Awards approached, one of the films front and center in the conversation was *Moonlight,* a beautiful and nontraditional story about a boy named Chiron, coming of age in the projects of Liberty City, Miami, and his relationships with a drug-dealing father figure, a drug-addicted mother, his one true friend, Kevin, and a sexuality he doesn't quite know how to express.

It is not the type of story told often in film, and it was not the type of film that drew wide audiences, earning a modest $16 million in its first three months of release.

It did, however, receive critical acclaim and awards-show buzz. Jenkins maintained that he was shocked when *Moonlight* became a part of the awards conversation, and he saw the attention the film was receiving as an opportunity to send a message to all the people who don't often see their stories told in film.

At the Golden Globes, which took place the month before the Oscars, *Moonlight* was nominated in six categories and won for Best Motion Picture—Drama. In his time at the microphone, Jenkins urged those who had seen the film to "tell a friend" to go see it.

When the Academy Awards rolled around, *Moonlight* was nominated in eight categories, including Best Adapted Screenplay, Best Director, and Best Picture.

The Academy Awards were an opportunity for a much larger audience to hear about the film and for *Moonlight* to claim several historic firsts, potentially becoming the first film with an all-Black cast to win the Academy Award for Best Picture and the first film to explore LGBTQ themes to win Best Picture. Barry Jenkins also had the opportunity to become only the second Black person to direct a Best Picture–winning film.

That evening, at the Dolby Theatre in downtown Los Angeles, *Moonlight* continued to find success. In the first award to be presented that night, the film's costar Mahershala Ali won for Best Actor in a Supporting Role, becoming the first Muslim to win an Oscar.

Jenkins and playwright Tarell Alvin McCraney, who wrote the play on which the film was based, won the Oscar for Best Adapted Screenplay. Jenkins went through a rapid-fire series of thank-yous and again made a pitch that not only should the movie be seen but that people who aren't often reflected in film should feel seen by the film. "I tell my students . . . to be in love with the process, not the result. But I really wanted this result because a bajillion* people are watching and all you people out there who feel like there's no mirror for you, that your life is not reflected . . . we have your back."

McCraney picked up on the theme, saying, "This goes out to all those black and brown boys and girls and non–gender conforming who don't see themselves; we're trying to show them you and us . . . this is for you."

But there was something Jenkins hadn't shared, that he was holding back in case he won the award for directing, the next category up, or Best Picture, the final category of the night.

The Best Director award went to Damien Chazelle, who directed the year's other awards-show darling, the musical ode to Hollywood *La La Land.* Chazelle began his remarks by saying how honored he was to be in the company of directors like Jenkins.

Jenkins's last chance to share the story he wanted to share would come, if it did come, with the Best Picture award.

As the show reached its conclusion, it was time for Best Picture. *La La Land* was the heavy favorite to take home that award, having garnered as many overall nominations as any film in history. Until that point, the show had been running smoothly, though typically long. Flanking the stage were Brian Cullinan and Martha Ruiz, representatives from PricewaterhouseCoopers, the accounting firm responsible for tabulating the academy's votes and assembling the envelopes announcing the winners. Cullinan and Ruiz each had a complete set of envelopes with the names of the winners. Every time a presenter went onstage, one of them gave him or her the envelope for that category, while the other partner destroyed the backup to prevent confusion.

In the second-to-final award of the night, Ruiz handed Leonardo DiCaprio the envelope for the award he was about to present: Best Actress. But instead of destroying his corresponding envelope, Cullinan was busy taking and tweeting out a photo of the person who was announced as the winner: actress Emma Stone. At 9:03 p.m. Pacific time, Warren Beatty

---

* Not quite a bajillion, but more than thirty-two million people were watching.

and Faye Dunaway took the stage to present, celebrating the fiftieth anniversary of the film in which they starred, *Bonnie and Clyde*. Cullinan handed Beatty the wrong envelope, the backup envelope announcing Emma Stone as Best Actress.

Onstage, as a drumroll played in the background, Beatty opened the envelope and began, "And the Academy Award . . ." He then stopped and looked into the envelope again, as the audience laughed and Dunaway told him, "You're impossible." Beatty handed Dunaway the envelope, and she quickly read the title of the film printed there: *La La Land*.

The audience exploded as the cast and creators of *La La Land* took the stage.

At that point, Cullinan belatedly realized that he had handed Beatty the wrong envelope, and alerted the show's producers. By the time they could get to the stage, nearly a minute and a half had passed, in which time, the producers of *La La Land* had taken the microphone. Jordan Horowitz had given his complete acceptance speech ("There's a lot of love in this room, and let's use it to champion bold and creative and diverse work"), and Marc Platt was completing his ("Keep dreaming, because the dreams we dream today will provide the love, the compassion and the humanity that will narrate the stories of our lives tomorrow") when a production crew member arrived onstage to show the other producers the correct winner card. Fred Berger, also a producer of *La La Land*, had started talking, but stopped to look at the confusion behind him. As Beatty began to reapproach the microphone, almost in shock, Berger said, "We lost, by the way."

At this point, Jordan Horowitz took over, despite Beatty wanting to speak again. "You know what? . . . There's a mistake. *Moonlight*, you guys won Best Picture."

Now the *Moonlight* partisans in the room exploded in cheers as the rest of the audience buzzed in confusion and disbelief.

As Horowitz and Platt tried to get the team from *Moonlight* onto the stage, host Jimmy Kimmel attempted a couple of jokes: "I blame Steve Harvey for this"* and then, to Horowitz, "I would like to see you get an Oscar anyway. Why can't we just give out a whole bunch of 'em?"

---

* In 2015, Steve Harvey announced the wrong winner of the Miss Universe pageant.

Horowitz, in a display of remarkable composure, answered the jokes with earnestness, holding up the Best Picture Oscar and saying, "I'm going to be really proud to hand this to my friends from *Moonlight*."

Beatty took the microphone to explain what happened, and by that point, Jenkins was on the stage, and Beatty simply said, "This is *Moonlight*, the Best Picture."

Jenkins, now having ridden a two-minute emotional roller coaster from disappointment to elation, stepped to the microphone and said, "Even in my dreams, this could not be true. But to hell with dreams, I'm done with it, 'cause this is true. Oh my goodness."

Jenkins and Adele Romanski, his friend and the film's producer, each spoke again, but in the confusion, Romanski's message was blurred:

Thank you to the Acad—I don't know what to say. That was really . . . I'm not sure, I'm still not sure this is real. But thank you to the Academy. It is so humbling to be standing up here with hopefully still the *La La* crew? No, okay, they're gone. But it's very humbling to be up here. And I think, I hope even more than that, that it's inspiring to people, little black boys and brown girls and other folks watching at home, who feel marginalized and who take some inspiration from seeing this beautiful group of artists, helmed by this amazing talent, my friend Barry Jenkins, standing up here on this stage accepting this top honor.

In the immediate aftermath of the event, Jenkins tried to make sense of the emotions. "I'd never seen that happen before. It made a special feeling more special but not in the way I expected. The last 20 minutes of my life have been insane . . . beyond life changing."

Both onstage and afterward, Jenkins spent a lot of his time thanking the folks from *La La Land* for being so gracious.

But as the reality settled in, he grew increasingly frustrated. By the time he arrived at the after-parties, he was distraught. In his words, "something had changed. I wasn't sure what that thing was." It seemed that the conversation about the film wasn't about the film, it was about the flub. And so the narrative of the film got lost in the narrative of the event.

A year later, Jenkins agreed to give the keynote address at the South by Southwest Conference, and, for the first time, spoke about what he had intended to say had he given his Best Picture speech.

"Of the modes of persuasion," Aristotle wrote in book 1 of *The Rhetoric*, "there are three kinds. The first kind depends on the personal character of the speaker; the second on putting the audience into a certain frame of mind; the third on the proof, or apparent proof, provided by the words of the speech itself."

This is where we get, in the order Aristotle described them above, ethos, pathos, and logos.

Two thousand five hundred years later, we apply those elements in largely the same way.

Logos, of course, is logic or reason. It's the idea that the power of the argument alone can persuade. That doesn't necessarily mean simply putting forward numbers and statistics, it also means putting them in context. A famous example is John F. Kennedy's 1962 speech at Rice University in which he announced, "We choose to go to the Moon." Here is Kennedy, discussing the cost of this challenge:

> To be sure, all this costs us all a good deal of money. This year's space budget is three times what it was in January 1961, and it is greater than the space budget of the previous eight years combined. That budget now stands at five-billion, four hundred million dollars a year—a staggering sum, though somewhat less than we pay for cigarettes and cigars every year. Space expenditures will soon rise some more, from 40 cents per person per week to more than 50 cents a week for every man, woman and child in the United States, for we have given this program a high national priority—even though I realize that this is in some measure an act of faith and vision, for we do not now know what benefits await us.

Here, Kennedy is making a logical argument. We don't know what benefits we'll reap from getting to the moon, but I'm going to bet that they're more valuable than what we pay for cigarettes each year.

This is also a nice device to solve a problem facing many speakers: it's hard for listeners to assign scale to huge numbers. But people are very good at assigning comparisons, and those comparisons, which I call "social math," are good at getting audiences to see what's logical, and what is, to borrow a phrase from *Star Trek*'s Mr. Spock, "highly illogical."

Here's Microsoft founder and philanthropist Bill Gates giving a TED Talk in 2009 about the lack of investment in drugs to fight malaria: "Because the disease is only in the poorer countries, it doesn't get much investment. For example, there's more money put into baldness drugs than are put into malaria." As the audience began to laugh, Gates continued, "Now, baldness, it's a terrible thing. And rich men are afflicted. And so that's why that priority has been set. But malaria—even the million deaths a year caused by malaria greatly understate its impact. Over 200 million people at any one time are suffering from it."

That, too, is an appeal to logic. Even your author, who would stand to benefit from a baldness cure, wonders why that should be prioritized over the lives of millions.

Ethos is frequently misunderstood to mean "ethics." In Greek, however, *ethos* translates to "nature" or "character." In other words, what is the character of the speaker? Are they a trustworthy messenger? Connecting with the audience, and being seen as trustworthy, credible, and, yes, likable, is key.

In my first speechwriting internship, in Vice President Al Gore's office, I was put on "Howdahell Duty." This is a term coined by my speechwriting mentor Eric Schnure following a trip Al Gore made to Missoula, Montana. In advance of the trip, Eric called the local organizers to ask what was happening in town that Gore could reference. The answer was: "Nothing." The organizer continued, "We're a small town. All people ever talk about is the four-way intersection. Backs up traffic and drives people crazy. We call it 'Malfunction Junction.'"

Knowing Gore would inevitably be late, Eric scripted the line, "Sorry I'm late. The motorcade got stuck at Malfunction Junction." The crowd loved it. That one line sent a message to the audience: "This speaker knows something about us. He took the time to learn something about us." And perhaps, on a subconscious level, it leads them to think, *If he understands this problem we face, maybe we should listen to him when he discusses other problems we face.*

"Howdahell did he know that?" Eric was asked later. He observed that every speech should have a "howdahell," and indeed they should, because howdahells are a means of achieving the goal of ethos, character-izing the speaker as likable and trustworthy.

And so my job was to look at where Vice President Gore would be going next and find the Malfunction Junction, or the score of last Friday night's football game against the town rival, or the coffee shop that had the famous baked oatmeal that you just had to try. In other words, I was on Howdahell Duty.

The Kennedy moon speech, referenced above, has a wonderful how-dahell embedded in it, poking fun at Rice's football team.

But why, some say, the moon? Why choose this as our goal? And they may well ask why climb the highest mountain? Why, 35 years ago, fly the Atlantic? Why does Rice play Texas?*

Ethos is also why self-deprecating humor is such a powerful tool. If a speaker is willing to see themselves clearly, we can trust that they're also able to see the world clearly.

Pathos is emotion, the emotional state of the listener. And emotion is a powerful drug.

If you've spent any time moving in PR or advertising circles, you've likely heard some variation on the idea that humans are not thinking machines that feel but rather feeling machines that think. That insight, frequently misattributed, comes from neuroscientist Antonio Damasio, who used the formulation in describing his work on the role of emotions in cognition and decision-making.

When our analytic and emotional brains are in conflict, we tend to choose the emotional one, even if we wish and believe we didn't.

Another frequently misattributed quote is that "it is the mark of a truly educated person to be moved by statistics." George Bernard Shaw never said it; the British philosopher Bertrand Russell (sort of) did. But by this measure, most of us don't meet the "truly educated" threshold, because we aren't as moved as we should be by statistics, or logos, and we're inordinately moved by emotion, or pathos.

---

* Fun fact: that speech was given in September 1962. In October, Texas rolled into town, undefeated and ranked number one in the nation. Rice was winless and unranked. That day, Rice tied Texas 14–14, denying them a shot at the national championship.

There are wonderful studies that illustrate this point. In 2007, re-searchers at Carnegie Mellon University approached students in the library and asked them to take a short survey. They were paid five one-dollar bills for their time. But that survey was just pretext for the actual experiment, because inside the envelope, in addition to the five dollars, was one of two letters from Save the Children. One version of the letter included facts and statistics about food shortages in Africa. The second version had a picture of a little girl named Rokia and described her as a seven-year-old girl from Mali, who "is desperately poor and faces a threat of severe hunger or even starvation."

On the way out of the library, the students who took the survey were given the opportunity to donate some of those five dollars to Save the Children. On average, those who received the statistics letter gave $1.14. Those who got the Rokia letter gave more than twice as much: $2.38.

Interestingly, when survey participants were given both the story and the data, they gave $1.43. Somehow, the data *diminished* the desire to give. So the investigators repeated the test a different way. This time, all participants in the survey received the Rokia letter and photograph. The survey was what differed. Half the group was primed with an analytical question, a math problem. The second group was asked to write down one word they feel when they hear the word *baby*. The math group gave $1.26. The baby group gave $2.34.

Again, we're not thinking machines that feel, we're feeling machines that (occasionally) think. And if pathos is a powerful drug, the most ef-fective delivery mechanism is story. Our brains are hardwired for stories. Throughout human history, every culture and community has transmit-ted information and lessons through stories. As Chip and Dan Heath observe in *Made to Stick,* the power of a story is that "it provides simula-tion (knowledge about how to act) and inspiration (motivation to act)." What's more, when we're exposed to stories, we experience a rise in levels of the hormone oxytocin, which has the effect of helping forge trust and social bonds. As the Scottish philosopher Alasdair MacIntyre wrote, "Man is in his actions and practice essentially a storytelling animal."

Jenkins, a storyteller, understood intuitively the power that stories hold to connect us to one another. And he knew the story he wanted to tell, not just in his film but in his acceptance remarks. In fact, in the confusion around the awarding of the prize, he blurted out the first line of that story: "Even in my dreams, this could not be true."

That's because Jenkins's journey had been such an unlikely one. Jenkins, like the character Chiron, grew up in the Liberty City neighborhood of Miami. In making *Moonlight,* his journey came full circle to the same projects where he grew up. And as he was filming, he observed that one of the challenges in neighborhoods that are at best underserved and at worst ignored by leaders is that when the streetlights burn out, they aren't replaced. So there's not a lot of light at night. To make the film, they had to put up a lot of lights. And because of the lights, kids who didn't traditionally come out to play at night came out to play while they were shooting the movie.

Jenkins, who very much wanted to bring the community into the film, wanted to use his acceptance speech to joke that he got more than he bargained for, with kids running around, dressed "period inappropriately," interrupting shots, delaying shots, but fundamentally having a good time.

And Jenkins remembered one particular scene. In it, the main character, Chiron, has just been intimate with his friend Kevin, and Kevin is now dropping him off at home. It's the aftermath of a powerful moment of self-discovery. As Jenkins was directing the scene, he looked back at the "video village," the area where the monitors are set up so that the film crew can observe scenes as they're being filmed. And he sees that several kids from the community are sitting in the chairs normally reserved for the directors and producers, wearing their communications headsets. And at that moment, it hit Jenkins that these kids were watching the making of a film about them and their lives, and it was going to be directed by someone who grew up just like they had—and in that moment they were seeing in him the dream, as Jenkins put it, "I never allowed myself to have." In the short amount of time he would have had to speak, Jenkins wanted to distill from that small moment a larger message about what it can mean to see your own possibility.

Reflecting on that moment at South by Southwest a year after the Academy Awards, Jenkins said, "It floored me. And if I cried that night, it wasn't because we won Best Picture. I cried because I realized I'd denied myself that dream for so long, I didn't even recognize it when, through the help of my friends, I was able to give that dream to someone else."

And so, a portion of the speech he would have given, had not an accountant given the wrong envelope to Warren Beatty, was as follows:

Tarell [Alvin McCraney, cowriter] and I are Chiron. We are that boy. And when you watch "Moonlight," you don't assume a boy who grew up how and where we did would grow up and make a piece of art that wins an Academy Award—certainly don't think he would grow up to win Best Picture. I've said that a lot and what I've had to admit is that I placed those limitations on myself. I denied myself that dream. Not you, not anyone else—me. And so, to anyone watching this who sees themselves in us, let this be a symbol, a reflection that leads you to love yourself. Because doing so may be the difference between dreaming at all and somehow, through the Academy's grace, realizing dreams you never allowed yourself to have.

John F. Kennedy arrives in Dallas on November 22, 1963. (Photo by Cecil Stoughton / White House Photographs / John F. Kennedy Presidential Library and Museum)

One of the last known photographs of FDR, taken in 1945 by Nicholas Robbins for artist Elizabeth Shoumatoff's portrait painting session. (FDR Library Photograph Collection)

Albert Einstein in 1947 (Orren Jack Turner)

Pope Pius XI in 1930 (J. B. Malina)

15

Last Words: Pope Pius XI, JFK, FDR,
Einstein, and Their Unfinished Prophecies of
Peace, Various Years

We often search last words for deeper meaning, a message to the ages.

Although Thomas Jefferson's last words were to his servants in the early-morning hours of July 4, 1826, and went unrecorded, and his last recorded words were to his physician, "No doctor, nothing more," we instead focus on the fact that on the evening of July 3, Jefferson woke and asked with insistence, "Is it the Fourth?" It seems more appropriate that Jefferson's last words ask about the independence movement he helped set in motion fifty years earlier. That's because we want last words to be meaningful, lasting, and profound.

(If you asked Jefferson what he would have wanted his last words to be, he probably would have offered the letter he wrote to the mayor of Washington, D.C., to be read at the Fourth of July celebration he was too ill to attend. Meticulously composed in his own hand, it reads, "May [the Declaration of Independence] be to the world what I believe it will be, (to some parts sooner, to others later, but finally to all) the Signal of arousing men to burst the chains, under which Monkish ignorance and superstition had persuaded them to bind themselves, and to assume the blessings & security of self-government."

Of course, the reason we often take poetic license with last words is that people very rarely know what their last words will be, especially when death arrives unexpectedly. But regardless of whether the speaker knew that death was near or not, we ascribe to those words a weight that we might not otherwise.

Or maybe it's because we never got to hear those words delivered in life that we hear them more clearly in death.

Such was certainly the case with John F. Kennedy's fateful trip to Texas in November 1963.

In 1963, Kennedy was enormously popular. Having successfully navigated the Cuban missile crisis, he began the year with a 70 percent approval rating. In March, he held a 67 percent to 27 percent polling advantage over the leading Republican challenger, Arizona senator Barry Goldwater. Kennedy was also a cultural phenomenon; roughly half of all Americans had seen or heard a Kennedy *imitator*. But as the year went on, Kennedy's focus on civil rights began to take a toll. His popularity dipped overall, but nose-dived in the South. This made Texas all the more important politically. As *The New York Times* wrote in early November, "Even if Mr. Kennedy should write off most of the South, he is not writing off Texas's 25 votes." Kennedy was also working to reframe the conversation, telling the AFL-CIO convention in mid-November that jobs, more than civil rights, were the most important issue in the country.

One of the goals of that trip to Texas, one week following the AFL-CIO convention, was to shore up his support there. And when you look at the documents that were submitted to speechwriter Ted Sorensen and his team in order to prepare the speeches, they're familiar building blocks to anyone writing political speeches today: a political update memo from the Democratic National Committee, an article on the economic situation in Texas from the *Texas Business Review*, and "administration accomplishments" documents for Texas that included statistics on public works spending, small business aid, and oil and gas leasing progress. At the last minute, Sorensen also tossed in a collection of "Texas humor" Kennedy had requested.

The speech Kennedy was to give in Dallas was to an audience comprised of several different groups. It included members of the Dallas Citizens Council and the Dallas Assembly, two groups of local business and nonprofit leaders, with another contingent from the Graduate Research Center of the Southwest.

For speechwriters, audiences like this can pose a challenge: How do you address your remarks to all the groups while saying something meaningful to each? In politics, speeches always have at least two audiences: the audience inside the room and the audience outside the room as represented by the reporters and cameras gathered at the back. There are times when the audience inside the room is really a means to delivering a message to the audience outside the room. When Secretary of State George C. Marshall was invited to speak at Harvard upon receiving an honorary degree in June 1947, there wasn't an expectation that he would say much at all. But he saw fifteen thousand future leaders gathered in Harvard Yard as a perfect setting in which to deliver his thoughts on postwar reconstruction in Europe.

It was, indeed, a message that echoed far beyond its immediate audience, launching the plan that would come to bear Marshall's name and for which he would be awarded the Nobel Peace Prize. It wasn't a message for the graduates, whom Marshall didn't recognize or congratulate. They simply provided a convenient backdrop (or, more accurately, foreground) for his remarks. Usually, speakers will have some acknowledgment of the audience in the room even if the message is meant for outside the room, though my colleagues and I used to joke that every such speech should begin with the speaker saying, "Good afternoon, props."

In his prepared remarks, Kennedy gamely sought to find a unifying theme that would speak to each of these audiences, and he found it in the "link between leadership and learning." While the previous speeches Kennedy had given and those he planned to give on his Texas trip were generally workmanlike, including lists of accomplishments and solicitations of support, Kennedy decided to take a different approach with this speech and audience. For starters, it was intended to be almost entirely a speech about national security. That is why the most remembered and publicized piece of the speech is the conclusion. Kennedy planned on ending his speech with these words:

> We in this country, in this generation, are—by destiny rather than choice—the watchmen on the walls of world freedom. We ask, therefore, that we may be worthy of our power and responsibility, that we may exercise our strength with wisdom and restraint, and that we may achieve in our time and for all time the ancient vision of "peace on earth, good will toward men." That must always be

our goal, and the righteousness of our cause must always underlie our strength. For as was written long ago: "except the Lord keep the city, the watchman waketh but in vain."

Concluding with a reference to Psalm 127, and its sentiment that the most successful human ventures are in keeping with the will of God, may have been a political choice as much as a poetic one. Although Kennedy soft-pedaled his Catholicism in public, it wouldn't hurt to remind this largely Protestant Texas audience that he was a biblical Christian.

However, there was one domestic concern Sorensen, with Kennedy, wanted to address. Sorensen described it as "the fires of rage" that burned beneath the surface of America's peace and prosperity.

These fires of rage revealed themselves in an increasingly vocal right-wing effort to discredit and demonize Kennedy. One of the leaders of this effort was Edwin Walker, a former World War II general who helped foment riots at the University of Mississippi when the school attempted to integrate by admitting James Meredith in 1962. Walker also ran as a fringe candidate for governor of Texas. Using language similar to the attacks President Donald Trump and his supporters would wage on his political opponents a half century later, Walker declared that civil rights demonstrations in Washington and Texas were "pro-Kennedy, pro-Communist and pro-Socialist." In advance of Kennedy's arrival, Walker and his followers distributed leaflets accusing Kennedy of treason, of being "lax" on communism, and of "appointing anti-Christians to Federal office."

Kennedy sought to address this dangerous, angry, violence-inducing disassociation from reality in his address. He distinguished this kind of attitude from the constant complainers, the "dissident voices" who will always be "expressing opposition without alternatives, finding fault but never favor, perceiving gloom on every side and seeking influence without responsibility." Those voices, Kennedy was to say, "are inevitable."

While he accepted the inevitability of dissident voices, he was more concerned about those who *knowingly* promote and spread lies, in language that could easily apply to President Trump and his disingenuous claims of "fake news":

But today other voices are heard in the land—voices preaching doctrines wholly unrelated to reality, wholly unsuited to the sixties, doctrines which apparently assume that words will suffice without weapons, that vituperation is as good as victory and that peace is a sign of weakness. At a time when the national debt is steadily being reduced in terms of its burden on our economy, they see that debt as the greatest single threat to our security. At a time when we are steadily reducing the number of Federal employees serving every thousand citizens, they fear those supposed hordes of civil servants far more than the actual hordes of opposing armies.

In words that would later be reflected in the mistruths that led America to invade Iraq in 2003, his concern was the damage that misinformation, and a misinformed citizenry, cause:

Ignorance and misinformation can handicap the progress of a city or a company, but they can, if allowed to prevail in foreign policy, handicap this country's security. In a world of complex and continuing problems, in a world full of frustrations and irritations, America's leadership must be guided by the lights of learning and reason or else those who confuse rhetoric with reality and the plausible with the possible will gain the popular ascendancy with their seemingly swift and simple solutions to every world problem.

Kennedy's hope? "We cannot expect that everyone, to use the phrase of a decade ago, will 'talk sense to the American people.' But we can hope that fewer people will listen to nonsense."

Fewer people listening to and falling prey to nonsense. In his unspoken last speech, Kennedy left us with a warning against the type of angry, disassociated rhetoric that is causing such damage to, and within, democratic governments around the world today.

Sorensen would later write that Kennedy had a somewhat wry sense about death, joking often about his own mortality. But after Kennedy was killed, Sorensen reflected, "If fate somehow decreed that sooner or later some madman would succeed, better that it happened after JFK saved mankind in the Cuban missile crisis, paved the way for equal rights in this country, launched America's leadership in space, established the Peace Corps, and set a standard for leadership and eloquence that has inspired people all over the world."

While Kennedy couldn't have known he was nearing his end, in the course of researching this book, I've come across three additional speeches that three very different types of leaders were working on at the moment of their deaths.

Across nationality, language, and time, they are united by one thread—they focus on mankind's ability to live together, in peace. And what it will take to achieve that.

Pope Pius XI was born Achille Ratti in Northern Italy in 1857. He rose in the church to be Pope Benedict XV's emissary to Poland, and then to become archbishop of Milan. Upon the death of Benedict XV, he became a compromise choice to become pope, a role to which he ascended in 1922.

His journey would soon intersect with that of National Fascist Party leader Benito Mussolini, who was outspoken in his opposition to religion in general, and the Catholic church in particular. In the early 1900s, as a young man, Mussolini had written a pamphlet titled *God Does Not Exist* in which he declared, "The struggle against the religious absurdity is more than ever a necessity today. . . . To be still deluded would be cowardice." And yet, as historian David Kertzer observes in his Pulitzer Prize–winning history, *The Pope and Mussolini,* Pius XI formed an unlikely alliance with Mussolini, abetting his rise.

For Mussolini, embracing the church helped him outflank his country's socialists and communists, allowing him to gain the support of Italy's Popular Party, which had significant support among the clergy. On the strength of that support, he was able to become prime minister in 1922. For the pope, it allowed for the possibility of putting an end to the war between the Italian government and the Catholic church, perhaps even ending the separation of church and state and restoring the Catholic church's position of primacy in Italian life.

There were also elements of Mussolini's budding authoritarianism that appealed to the church at the time—namely, the ability of a totalitarian leader to enforce the church's views on personal conduct. This alliance was cemented in 1929 with an agreement called the Lateran Accords.

However, by the mid-1930s, Mussolini's cult of personality, his violent invasion of Ethiopia, and his embrace of Adolf Hitler in Germany—who had been repressing the Catholic church and threatening to expose its scandals—began to concern Pope Pius. When Hitler came to Italy in May 1938, the pope closed the Vatican museums so Hitler couldn't visit them. Later that summer, Mussolini, mimicking Hitler, announced a new series of anti-Semitic laws.

The pope, now in failing health, realized that his deal with Mussolini was a devil's bargain, and as the tenth anniversary of the Lateran Accords approached, he invited all the bishops of Italy to St. Peter's for a speech.

Mussolini was deeply, and rightly, concerned that the pope would denounce him and his alliance with Hitler. Months before, without letting his closest advisors know, Pius reached out to an American Jesuit, John LaFarge, who had written extensively on civil rights, to help him draft an encyclical against anti-Semitism and racism more broadly.

At the same time, the pope began composing a speech he wanted to give to the bishops, and with it a message for Mussolini.

But it became a race against the clock. The pope's health continued to decline, and his heart began failing. He was now struggling to survive until the tenth anniversary of his agreement with the Italian state so that he could deliver both the encyclical and the separate, but related, speech.

Meanwhile, his closest advisors had a sense of what he intended to do and were beseeching him to tone down his message or cancel the event entirely. The pope attempted to brush them off with humor and misdirection. Trying to underplay the seriousness of the words he intended to deliver, he told his advisors, "I shall make them laugh, as we shall speak of words public and private, spoken, written, and telephoned." But he would not share what he was about to say.

Still, word of the topics the pope intended to address began to leak out and incensed Mussolini, who railed that in the Vatican, they are always "against Italy, but not against the other nations that pursue similar and even more extreme policies, including on the racial question (like Hungary)!"

The pope was unmoved, and began putting his finishing touches on what his aide and confidant Domenico Tardini called an "extraordinarily important text." He had three hundred copies prepared for the bishops who would be gathering on February 11.

On February 10, one day before his address, the pope suffered a fatal heart attack.

On his desk at the time of his death was the draft encyclical and his handwritten notes from which he intended to deliver his speech.

Mussolini sent word to the Vatican secretary of state, Cardinal Pacelli, to destroy all three hundred copies of the speech. Cardinal Pacelli, a proponent of appeasement, ordered it done, even directing the printer to destroy all templates. Within weeks, Cardinal Pacelli was elevated to the papacy himself, taking the name Pius XII.

The new pope acted swiftly to heal any rift with Mussolini, to soften the church's stance toward Germany, and to erase any memory of his predecessor's call to conscience. And the encyclical on racism is lost to history.

But for weeks after the pope's death, the speech was rumored to have survived, with hints of its public protest continuing to percolate. A copy was in fact saved or salvaged, and on the twentieth anniversary of Pius XI's death in 1959, Pope John XXIII elected to deliver sections of the undelivered speech. The Vatican, however, declined to release some of the stronger portions of the speech, including the most severe denunciations of the fascists.

In 2006, Pope Benedict XVI authorized the Vatican Secret Archives to unseal the papers of Pius XI's papacy. In 2007, Pius XI's full undelivered final speech was reproduced for the first time in Italian historian Emma Fattorini's *Hitler, Mussolini, and the Vatican.*

When read in full, it's not quite as "devastating for fascism" as it was rumored to be. However, the late pope didn't pull any punches about how the Fascist state operates, twisting words and meanings to cast speakers in the worst possible light.

You know, dear and venerable brothers, how the words of the Popes are often construed. There are some, and not only in Italy, who take our allocutions and Our audiences, and alter them in a false sense, and so, starting even from a sound statement, have Us speak incredibly foolish and absurd things. There is a press capable of saying most anything that is opposed to Us and to Our concerns.

He then turned to a discussion of "observers and informers (you would do well to call them spies) who, of their own initiative or because charged to do so, listen to you in order to condemn you, after, it is understood, having understood nothing at all and if necessary just the opposite."

And in concluding, he exhorts his bishops to go out and preach the truth, and to preach peace.

Prophesy the perseverance of Italy in the faith preached by you and sealed by your blood; sacred bones, prophesy a complete and firm perseverance against the blows and threats that from near and far that threaten it and fight against it; prophesy, sacred bones, peace and prosperity, honor, above all, the honor of a people aware of its dignity and human and Christian responsibility; prophesy, dear and reverent bones, prophesy the arrival or the return of the true Faith to all the peoples all the nations, all the races, all joined together and all of the same blood in the common link of the great human family; prophesy, apostoli bones, order tranquility, peace, peace, peace for all the world that instead seems seized by a homicidal and suicidal folly of weapons; peace demands that we implore the God of peace and hope to attain it. So be it!

Though he doesn't mention Nazism or Fascism, it is clear what the pope is attacking. And paired with an encyclical on race and racism, it would have been a powerful message of peace and brotherhood.

Had those words been spoken in 1939, when there was "still space for maneuver and before Europe descended into the abyss," Emma Fattorini argues, both the church and the world would look much different.

Had the church made "a break with Nazism rather than a slow and agonizing suffocation," perhaps the world would have awakened earlier to its moral call.

On December 8, 1941, when President Franklin Delano Roosevelt entered the U.S. House of Representatives to address a joint session of Congress, the first paragraph of his speech read, "Yesterday, December 7, 1941, a date which will live in world history, the United States of America was simultaneously and deliberately attacked by naval and air forces of the Empire of Japan."

The president crossed out the words *world history* and *simultaneously* and added others to arrive at one of the most iconic statements in American history: "Yesterday, December 7, 1941—a date which will live in infamy—the United States of America was suddenly and deliberately attacked by the naval and air forces of the Empire of Japan."

Now, three and a half years after the surprise Japanese attack on Pearl Harbor, FDR, his health failing, was preparing to deliver another address, and he was looking past the Second World War to peace.

By April 1945, US forces had reached the Elbe River, sixty miles from the Nazi headquarters in Berlin. In the Pacific, the bloody battle between U.S. and Japanese forces for Okinawa was under way. Two months earlier, Roosevelt had met with British prime minister Winston Churchill and the secretary general of the Soviet Union, Joseph Stalin, in Yalta to discuss what a postwar Europe would look like.

Roosevelt planned to deliver a radio address that would be simulcast to 350 Democratic Party dinners (called Jefferson Day Dinners in honor of Thomas Jefferson, founder of the Democratic-Republican Party in the early 1790s) and carried by the major radio networks.

It was to be part of a program that included addresses by Vice President Harry Truman and Secretary of the Navy James Forrestal. The Associated Press announcement of the program noted that "the Chief Executive's schedule would not allow him to attend the principal dinner in Washington."

In truth, the president was convalescing in Warm Springs, Georgia, having arrived on March 30. He was described at the time as looking "very tired" and being uncharacteristically silent and aloof during the Easter church service the next day. The last known photograph of Roosevelt shows him looking wan and sallow, with large dark circles under his eyes.

He did, however, find the energy to work on the speech he was to give on the radio. He was shuffling between three separate drafts. One was prepared by the Democratic National Committee. A second draft was prepared by one of Roosevelt's speechwriters, the playwright Robert E. Sherwood, who originated the phrase "arsenal of democracy" and would later go on to write a Pulitzer Prize–winning biography of Roosevelt.* A third draft came from Jonathan Daniels, Roosevelt's press secretary at the time.

Dueling drafts are not uncommon in the world of political speeches. Some elected officials like to see multiple drafts from multiple writers, cherry-picking their favorite parts of each. And most writers recognize that to hold the pen is to hold the power, and work to make their draft the foundation of the final speech. In his memo transmitting the drafts to the president, Daniels's attempts to stick a dagger in Sherwood's draft while denigrating the DNC's submission will be recognizable to anyone who has worked in political speechwriting. "As I told you on the phone, I'm a little hesitant about presenting my own draft, but I felt that Bob [Sherwood]'s was a little diffuse. . . . Merely for the files on this speech I am also enclosing copy of the draft prepared by someone at the Democratic National Committee. I am sure it is not suitable."

Ironically, it's the DNC version combined with the Sherwood version (and almost none of the Daniels draft) that formed the final version.

In the early afternoon of the twelfth, Roosevelt was sitting for a portrait when his head drooped forward. He told his cousin Daisy Suckley, "I have a terrific pain in the back of my head." Those were his final words.

Jefferson Day Dinners across the country were canceled.

America did not hear Vice President Truman call Roosevelt "one of the greatest living statesmen in the world." Nor did Democrats hear his warning that "his [FDR's] achievements have caused a few Democrats to assume that with such leadership, party organization becomes unimportant."

Truman intended to speak about the "grave responsibility" America had to "win the peace."

---

* Robert E. Sherwood, *Roosevelt and Hopkins: An Intimate History* (New York: Harper and Brothers, 1948).

Peace was on Roosevelt's mind as well.

He intended to say:

Today we have learned in the agony of war that great power in-
volves great responsibility.* Today we can no more escape the
consequences of German and Japanese aggression than could we
avoid the consequences of the attacks by the Barbary Corsairs† a
century and a half before.

We, as Americans, do not choose to deny our responsibility.

Nor do we intend to abandon our determination that, within
the lives of our children and our children's children, there will not
be a third world war.

We seek peace—enduring peace. More than an end to war,
we want an end to the beginning of all wars—yes an end to the
brutal, inhuman, and thoroughly impractical method of settling
the differences between governments.

And how to do this? FDR leaned on the example of Jefferson, a scientist. "If civilization is to survive, we must cultivate the science of human
relationships—the ability of all peoples, of all kinds, to live together and
work together, in the same world, at peace."

Peace, and how to achieve it, also appears in Albert Einstein's undelivered final words. In 1955, Einstein had accepted an invitation to give a
national address on the seventh anniversary of Israel's independence. The
speech was to be given on April 27 and would be heard by as many as
sixty million listeners.‡

The year 1955 was to be a big year for Einstein. It marked the fiftieth

---

* Most people think this statement originated with Uncle Ben from *Spider-Man.* It has
actually appeared in various forms, from the French National Convention in 1793 to
Winston Churchill saying it early in his career, in 1906.

† An interesting historical reference here, only because it's not clear how many Americans,
even at the time, would understand the reference to, and historical parallel with, the Barbary
pirates.

‡ Einstein joked, when told of the potential size of his audience, "So, I shall now have a
chance to become world famous."

anniversary of his relativity theory, and though plans were under way to celebrate that achievement, Einstein declined to participate because he felt that very few of the scientists who wanted to celebrate him had taken him seriously at the time.

Einstein handwrote his forty-six-page "General Theory of Relativity" in his home in Berlin, and the document fundamentally altered our understanding of the universe. Later, Einstein gifted the document to the Hebrew University of Jerusalem, and it was fitting because just as he had a complicated relationship with his theory and its late-arriving adherents, he had a similarly complicated relationship with his Judaism, the State of Israel, and how the two intersected and interacted.

Einstein didn't believe in a personal God, tied up in the fates of man. To him, faith was a recognition that there was mystery and beauty in the universe and that the experience of this mystery was religion. "To sense that behind anything that can be experienced there is something that our minds cannot grasp, whose beauty and sublimity reaches us only indirectly: this is religiousness. In this sense, and in this sense only, I am a devoutly religious man."

At the same time, he did feel a sense of connection to his Judaism, and to Israel. In 1921, Einstein toured the United States with Zionist leader and future Israeli president Chaim Weizmann to raise money for the World Zionist Organization. (Weizmann, like Einstein, was a scientist by training, and his discoveries had helped produce ever-more powerful explosives during World War I, just as Einstein's discoveries would in World War II.) In 1923, Einstein delivered the first lecture at Hebrew University. And after Weizmann's death in 1952, Einstein was even offered Israel's presidency, which he declined, saying, "I know a little about nature, but hardly anything about human beings."

In his written statement formally turning down the offer, he shared that "my relationship to the Jewish people has become my strongest human bond, ever since I became fully aware of our precarious situation among the nations of the world."

He also felt connected to Judaism's humanism, writing in 1938, "The bond that has united the Jews for thousands of years and that unites them today is, above all, the democratic ideal of social justice coupled with the ideal of mutual aid and tolerance among all men."

As Walter Isaacson notes in his biography of Einstein, Einstein saw the creation of Israel as not only a political act but "one of the important moral achievements to emerge from the Second World War."

Though Einstein was an avowed Zionist, he was clear-eyed about the challenges of coexistence. Earlier, he had warned Weizmann that a failure of Jews to find a way to live at peace with Arabs would demonstrate that "we have learned absolutely nothing during our 2,000 years of suffering."

In February 1955, Israel's ambassador to the United States, Abba Eban, appeared on the CBS program *Face the Nation* to argue that the rearming of Arab states was putting Israel's existence at risk: "British planes and tanks to Jordan; American arms to Iraq; Soviet bombers, fighters, tanks and submarines to Egypt; and no arms for Israel . . . What kind of policy is this?"

Eban's words received a mild rebuke from the Eisenhower administration, but caught the attention of Einstein, who wrote to the Israeli consulate in New York, suggesting that Eban and he meet to discuss how Einstein might be able to help.

When Eban and his deputy Reuven Dafni arrived at Einstein's home in Princeton, New Jersey, Einstein got right to the point, volunteering to record a talk and taking out a pen and an old-fashioned inkwell to begin writing.

His remarks began by explaining to the world why Israel exists in the first place. A draft of the speech reads, "The establishment of the State of Israel was internationally approved and recognized largely for the purpose of rescuing the remnant of the Jewish people from unspeakable horrors of persecution and oppression. Another purpose was to provide conditions in which the spiritual and cultural life of Hebrew society could find free expression. Thus the establishment of Israel is an event which actively engages the conscience of this generation."

The draft also called attention to the hostility of Israel's neighbors and the world's indifference to it.*

---

* For the purposes of this chapter, I will refer to the speech that was released by the Jewish Telegraphic Agency as *Eban's draft*—although it certainly contained input, ideas, and language from Einstein. I'll refer to the translation of Einstein's own writing as *Einstein's draft*.

It is therefore, a bitter paradox to find that a state which was destined to be a shelter for a martyred people is itself threatened by grave dangers to its own security. The universal conscience cannot be indifferent to such a peril. One of the important moral achievements to emerge from the Second World War should be preserved from this unnatural danger.

The pressure of Arab hostility and the counter-pressure of Israel's defence have created a constant tension. It is anomalous that world opinion should not actively seek to bring an end to the Arab hostility which is the root cause of the tension. One of the fundamental causes of this crisis is the policy of the Great Powers, which finds expression in one-sided military pacts and arms agreements. The basic premise of this policy is the desire to prepare the Middle East for its role in the event of a world struggle between East and West.

This, however, is not a correct or enlightened starting point for a regional policy in the Middle East. The destructive capacity of modern weapons makes such a conflict utterly unthinkable. It is wrong to embark on a global security policy which creates local imbalances and to do this in the name of a prospect of war which should be ruled out as inconceivable.

What is not clear is whether Einstein signed off on this text. Certainly, he agreed with these arguments, but the language reflects a lot of what Eban had been saying for years.

After some time writing and discussing, Eban realized that Einstein would need some more time to compose his thoughts, and he and Dafni made plans to return another day, while Dafni prepared for the nationwide address.

When Eban arrived for the next meeting less than a week later, Einstein had already been hospitalized.

While at the hospital, Einstein continued to work on a slightly different draft from the one he had structured with Eban. Instead of beginning with an explanation and defense of Israel, Einstein's newer draft began with a description of why he was making these remarks. He did so in typically self-deprecating fashion, describing his intellectual capacity as "feeble" and recognizing that his remarks would explicitly not serve any single agenda.

> I speak to you today not as an American citizen and not as a Jew, but as a human being who seeks with the greatest seriousness to look at things objectively. What I seek to accomplish is simply to serve with my feeble capacity truth and justice at the risk of pleasing no one.

He then sought to broaden the aperture, from the conflict between Israelis and Arabs to the topic of conflict in general, noting how it provided a microcosm of the larger issues that roil the world, and that he wanted to discuss. If Eban wanted the speech to be about Israel, Einstein wanted the focus shifted a few degrees, on the need to get "Israel right" as a model for getting larger conflicts right.

> At issue is the conflict between Israel and Egypt. You may consider this a small and insignificant problem and may feel that there are more serious things to worry about. But this is not true. In matters concerning truth and justice there can be no distinction between big problems and small; for the general principles which determine the conduct of men are indivisible. Whoever is careless with the truth in small matters cannot be trusted in important affairs.
>
> This indivisibility applies not only to moral but also to political problems; for little problems cannot be properly appreciated unless they are understood in their interdependence with big problems. And the big problem in our time is the division of mankind into two hostile camps: the Communist World and the so-called Free World. Since the significance of the terms Free and Communist is in this context hardly clear to me, I prefer to speak of a power conflict between East and West, although, the world being round, it is not even clear what precisely is meant by the terms East and West. In essence, the conflict that exists today is no more than an old-style struggle for power, once again presented to mankind in semireligious trappings.

Whereas Eban's draft only glancingly references atomic weapons ("The destructive capacity of modern weapons makes such a conflict utterly unthinkable"), Einstein wanted to put a stronger focus on it, talking in both lyrical ("a ghostly character") and absolute ("mankind is doomed") terms about what a conflict with atomic weapons would mean for mankind:

> The difference is that, this time, the development of atomic power has imbued the struggle with a ghostly character; for both parties know and admit that, should the quarrel deteriorate into actual war, mankind is doomed. Despite this knowledge, statesmen in responsible positions on both sides continue to employ the well-known technique of seeking to intimidate and demoralize the opponent by marshaling superior military strength. They do so even though such a policy entails the risk of war and doom. Not one statesman in a position of responsibility has dared to pursue the only course that holds out any promise of peace, the course of supranational security, since for a statesman to follow such a course would be tantamount to political suicide. Political passions, once they have been fanned into flames, exact their victims.

Einstein stopped writing at this point. He wouldn't leave the hospital, nor would he accept surgery to prolong his life, saying, "It is tasteless to prolong life artificially. I have done my share; it is time to go. I will do it elegantly." On April 18, 1955, his aorta ruptured, killing him. Einstein was seventy-six years old.

Two weeks after Einstein's death, the Israeli consulate in New York made Einstein's speech public. The description of the writing process, as told by the Jewish Telegraphic Agency, is revealing. "Prof. Einstein prepared his notes in consultation with Israel Ambassador Abba Eban who visited him at his home in Princeton two weeks before his final illness. With the exception of a single missing page, they were *expanded into literary form* [italics mine] by Israel Consul Reuven Dafni, who participated in the conference between Dr. Einstein and Mr. Eban. This partial text, as edited by Dr. Einstein and released by the Consulate, reads . . ."

While the sanitized, more politicized version certainly makes Israel's arguments, I prefer Einstein's notes for how they make humanity's: "Political passions, once they have been fanned into flames, exact their victims."

Four of the best-known leaders of the twentieth century all prepared to make appeals to peace in different forms at the end of their lives. In the 2,500 years of documented speeches, as in literature, there are really only a handful of themes, repeated over and over: good and evil, war and peace, love and hate, courage and cowardice, achievement and destruction. Societies change, technology changes, but these human themes remain timeless—and so will the need for humans to listen to and rally behind or against those who speak them aloud. Speeches remain our most human way to educate, inform, inspire, incite, and move people to action. In the end, words delivered—and those undelivered—are the real first draft of history, of actions taken or avoided, of paths traveled or not traveled, of leaders chosen or forsaken. They prove that the past is prologue, and for every generation, the work of peace, of understanding, of compassion is theirs to make real over and over again. After all, as Thomas Hobbes wrote, "understanding being nothing else, but conception caused by speech."

Appendix

Selected Undelivered Speech Texts

Wamsutta James Remarks, to Have Been Delivered at Plymouth, Massachusetts, September 1970

I speak to you as a man—a Wampanoag Man. I am a proud man, proud of my ancestry, my accomplishments won by a strict parental direction ("You must succeed—your face is a different color in this small Cape Cod community!"). I am a product of poverty and discrimination from these two social and economic diseases. I, and my brothers and sisters, have painfully overcome, and to some extent we have earned the respect of our community. We are Indians first—but we are termed "good citizens." Sometimes we are arrogant but only because society has pressured us to be so.

It is with mixed emotion that I stand here to share my thoughts. This is a time of celebration for you—celebrating an anniversary of a beginning for the white man in America. A time of looking back, of reflection. It is with a heavy heart that I look back upon what happened to my People.

Even before the Pilgrims landed it was common practice for explorers to capture Indians, take them to Europe and sell them as slaves for 220 shillings apiece. The Pilgrims had hardly explored the shores of Cape Cod for four days before they had robbed the graves of my ancestors and stolen their corn and beans. Mourt's Relation describes a searching party of sixteen men. Mourt goes on to say that this party took as much of the Indians' winter provisions as they were able to carry.

Massasoit, the great Sachem of the Wampanoag, knew these facts, yet he and his People welcomed and befriended the settlers of the Plymouth Plantation. Perhaps he did this because his Tribe had been depleted by an epidemic. Or his knowledge of the harsh oncoming winter was the reason for his peaceful acceptance of these acts. This action by Massasoit was perhaps our biggest mistake. We, the Wampanoag, welcomed you, the white man, with open arms, little knowing that it was the beginning of the end; that before 50 years were to pass, the Wampanoag would no longer be a free people.

What happened in those short 50 years? What has happened in the last 300 years?

History gives us facts and there were atrocities; there were broken promises—and most of these centered around land ownership. Among ourselves we understood that there were boundaries, but never before had we had to deal with fences and stone walls. But the white man had a need to prove his worth by the amount of land that he owned. Only ten years later, when the Puritans came, they treated the Wampanoag with even less kindness in converting the souls of the so-called "savages." Although the Puritans were harsh to members of their own society, the Indian was pressed between stone slabs and hanged as quickly as any other "witch."

And so down through the years there is record after record of Indian lands taken and, in token, reservations set up for him upon which to live. The Indian, having been stripped of his power, could only stand by and watch while the white man took his land and used it for his personal gain. This the Indian could not understand; for to him, land was survival, to farm, to hunt, to be enjoyed. It was not to be abused. We see incident after incident, where the white man sought to tame the "savage" and convert him to the Christian ways of life. The early Pilgrim settlers led the Indian to believe that if he did not behave, they would dig up the ground and unleash the great epidemic again.

The white man used the Indian's nautical skills and abilities. They let him be only a seaman—but never a captain. Time and time again, in the white man's society, we Indians have been termed "low man on the totem pole."

Has the Wampanoag really disappeared? There is still an aura of mystery. We know there was an epidemic that took many Indian lives—some Wampanoags moved west and joined the Cherokee and Cheyenne. They were forced to move. Some even went north to Canada! Many Wampanoag put aside their Indian heritage and accepted the white man's way for their own survival. There are some Wampanoag who do not wish it known they are Indian for social or economic reasons.

What happened to those Wampanoags who chose to remain and live among the early settlers? What kind of existence did they live as "civilized" people? True, living was not as complex as life today, but they dealt with the confusion and the change. Honesty, trust, concern, pride, and politics wove themselves in and out of their [the Wampanoags'] daily living. Hence, he was termed crafty, cunning, rapacious, and dirty.

History wants us to believe that the Indian was a savage, illiterate, uncivilized animal. A history that was written by an organized, disciplined people, to expose us as an unorganized and undisciplined entity. Two distinctly different cultures met. One thought they must control life; the other believed life was to be enjoyed, because nature decreed it. Let us remember, the Indian is and was just as human as the white man. The Indian feels pain, gets hurt, and becomes defensive, has dreams, bears tragedy and failure, suffers from loneliness, needs to cry as well as laugh. He, too, is often misunderstood.

The white man in the presence of the Indian is still mystified by his uncanny ability to make him feel uncomfortable. This may be the image the white man has created of the Indian; his "savageness" has boomeranged and isn't a mystery; it is fear; fear of the Indian's temperament!

High on a hill, overlooking the famed Plymouth Rock, stands the statue of our great Sachem, Massasoit. Massasoit has stood there many years in silence. We the descendants of this great Sachem have been a silent people. The necessity of making a living in this materialistic society of the white man caused us to be silent. Today, I and many of my people are choosing to face the truth. We ARE Indians!

Although time has drained our culture, and our language is almost extinct, we the Wampanoags still walk the lands of Massachusetts. We may be fragmented, we may be confused. Many years have passed since we have been a people together. Our lands were invaded. We fought as hard to keep our land as you the whites did to take our land away from us. We were conquered, we became the American prisoners of war in many cases, and wards of the United States Government, until only recently.

Our spirit refuses to die. Yesterday we walked the woodland paths and sandy trails. Today we must walk the macadam highways and roads. We are uniting. We're standing not in our wigwams but in your concrete tent. We stand tall and proud, and before too many moons pass we'll right the wrongs we have allowed to happen to us.

We forfeited our country. Our lands have fallen into the hands of the aggressor. We have allowed the white man to keep us on our knees. What has happened cannot be changed, but today we must work towards a more humane America, a more Indian America, where men and nature once again are important; where the Indian values of honor, truth, and brotherhood prevail.

You the white man are celebrating an anniversary. We the Wampanoags will help you celebrate in the concept of a beginning. It was the beginning of a new life for the Pilgrims. Now, 350 years later it is a beginning of a new determination for the original American: the American Indian.

There are some factors concerning the Wampanoags and other Indians across this vast nation. We now have 350 years of experience living amongst the white man. We can now speak his language. We can now think as a white man thinks. We can now compete with him for the top jobs. We're being heard; we are now being listened to. The important point is that along with these necessities of everyday living, we still have the spirit, we still have the unique culture, we still have the will and, most important of all, the determination to remain as Indians. We are determined, and our presence here this evening is living testimony that this is only the beginning of the American Indian, particularly the Wampanoag, to regain the position in this country that is rightfully ours.

Boston Mayor Kevin White's Remarks on Busing, to Have Been Delivered as Part of His State of the City Speech, December 1974

. . . The fourth challenge to our city, busing, is the most critical.

We are a city in trouble, a people divided and a community confused, angry, and afraid.

Our common objectives today must be to maintain the safety of our children and the sanity of our city.

And to these ends I have taken and will take the following ~~eight~~ four* steps:

One . . . I am announcing today that we have hired competent out-side legal counsel to represent the Boston school committee.

[Professor Philip Kurland] Is a nationally respected constitutional lawyer who has agreed to appeal Judge Garrity's desegregation ruling to the supreme court, and to request a stay of execution pending the out-come of the court's definitive judgement.

Two . . . I have directed the city's corporation counsel to make funds available to support the legal efforts by the home and school association to be heard before the court.

The association has already retained independent counsel, and will now have the financial support needed to pursue their legal argument. I have authorized $100,000 funding their efforts to ensure that court-imposed remedies be limited to areas where intentional constitutional violations occurred. That argument, coupled with considerations for health and safety, may offer a compelling case to exclude East Boston, Charlestown, and the North End from inclusion in phase II.

Three . . . as part of our expanding legal initiative, I have retained special outside counsel to represent the mayor and this city in court.

Our new attorney is both experienced and knowledgeable. He will be entrusted to coordinate all our legal efforts, and will serve as my personal representative in the courtroom.

---

* In the original text, *eight* is replaced with *four*—indicating that the mayor hoped to distill the eight steps down to four. However, the draft still contains eight steps. In translating this to text, I've shown some of the hand-edited deletions in ~~strikethrough~~ and additions in [brackets].

Four . . . ~~I will ask [I am asking]~~ the judge ~~to~~ [should] appoint immediately a court master to monitor the facts, inform the court, and ~~establish a biracial citizens committee to~~ oversee community participation in all phases of planning and execution.

And five . . . ~~I am calling upon~~ the judge ~~to~~ [should] name a representative citizens committee to propose remedies and make a plan work. It should begin immediately to solve the most severe and obvious failures of the first phase, and only then discuss modifications and suggest changes for phase II.

We are already half-way toward the final day of criticism and judgement on the second phase. But the court has yet to develop any real mechanism for community input. The state board made an arrogant mistake when it failed to change the South Boston district upon the recommendations of its own hearing officer (two years ago) who conducted.

For the judge to fail now to reach out for broad-based citizen involvement, would be a serious mistake that could fatally flaw ~~all his plans~~ [any of his efforts]

Six . . . I have secured a firm commitment from Governor Dukakis that the state will assume the cost of the process of implementation of any desegregation plan.

Seven . . . I ~~will request~~ [have asked] ~~that~~ the governor [to direct] the National Guard to immediately begin a special training program in preparedness ~~for~~ [in the event] mobilization [becomes necessary]

The Boston police will not bear the burden for public safety alone. Severe safety problems still exist with the first phase, and we will be unable to provide sufficient numbers or adequate coverage for any extension of the areas involved as now proposed in phase II.

And eight . . . ~~I have asked Judge Garrity to order the permanent closing of South Boston High School, and, at my direction, the public facilities department has located more than 1,000 spaces, available as an immediate alternative location, in the downtown area.~~

From the bitter experiences of these past four months, it is clear that violence and frustration are not the result of any single act or group. They are rather, the products of our collective failure. Our failure as a people to deal with issues and face problems together—to make the plan with which we must live, reflect both our wishes and our needs.

~~For my part, I have made errors of judgement, in my efforts to lead and carry out my responsibilities as I saw them.~~

~~But~~ For all of us who share a love for this city . . . which represents not only a heritage, but also a source of fulfillment and happiness . . . there are certain fundamental truths. Truths that we all must face as a new year and a new school term begin.

- The truth that this city is no different from any other.
- That bigotry and racial intolerance are wrong.
- The truth that equal education in school and equal opportunity in life are inalienable rights.
- The truth that the law must be obeyed unless and until it is changed by legal means.

But there are other truths . . . truths too rarely acknowledged . . . too frequently forgotten:

- The sometime unspoken truth that phase I—the state plan—is in part seriously flawed, unworkable, and unfair.
- The truth that some children in this city are being denied any education because of tension in the schools.
- ~~The truth that phase 1 is failing because people are excluded from the process of planning, politicians are evasive, and the judge remains rigid and insensitive to community concerns.~~
- And the truth that ~~many~~ [some] community leaders, both white and black, are more concerned about headlines than heartaches . . . ~~blaming everyone but themselves~~.

(Pause)

If we remember nothing else during these tragic days for Boston, it should be that . . . what matters most are the children of this city. And it is for them that I ask for your understanding, your patience, your help, and yes, your prayers for this new year.

Thank you

John F. Kennedy's Remarks Announcing Airstrikes on Cuba, to Have Been Delivered in October 1962

My fellow Americans:

With a heavy heart, and in necessary fulfillment of my oath of office, I have ordered—and the United States Air Force has now carried out—military operations, with conventional weapons only, to remove a major nuclear weapons build-up from the soil of Cuba. This action has been taken under Article 51 of the Charter of the United Nations and in fulfillment of the requirements of the national safety. Further military action has been authorized to ensure that this threat is fully removed and not restored.

~~Let me first tell you what has been going on. What it is that we have had to attack. In sum~~* There have been [unconfirmed] rumors of offensive installations in Cuba for some weeks, but it is only within the last week that we have had unmistakable and certain evidence of the character and magnitude of the Communist offensive deployment. What this evidence established beyond doubt is that in a rapid, secret and frequently denied military operation, the Communists were attempting to establish a series of offensive nuclear missile bases on the communist island of Cuba. Three of these missile sites contained launchers, 4 to a site, to be loaded with Medium Range Ballistic Missiles, two for each launcher, for a total of 24. Each of these 24 missiles would be capable of carrying a 3000 pound nuclear warhead of about 2 megatons in yield—or 100 times as destructive as the bomb which destroyed Hiroshima—for a distance of more than 1000 nautical miles. Twelve other launch pads under construction were designed for intermediate range ballistic missiles—capable of travelling more than twice as far and causing several times as much destruction—and thus capable of devastating most of the United States mainland, most of Latin America and most of Canada. In addition, large numbers of medium range jet bombers capable of carrying nuclear weapons were being uncrated on Cuba, while appropriate air bases were being prepared.

---

* To demonstrate what's in the original draft, I've ~~struck through~~ handwritten deletions and [bracketed] handwritten additions.

The presence in Cuba of these large, long-range and clearly offensive weapons of sudden destruction constituted a threat to the peace and security of this Hemisphere—in naked and deliberate defiance of the Rio pact of 1947, the traditions of this nation and Hemisphere, the Joint Resolution of the 87th Congress and my own warnings to the communists on September 4 and 13. This action also contradicted the repeated assurances of Soviet and Cuban spokesmen, both publicly and privately delivered, that the arms build-up in Cuba would retain its original defensive character. The size of this undertaking makes clear that it had been planned some months ago. Yet only last month, after I had clearly stated that ground-to-ground missiles would be regarded as an offensive threat, the Soviet Government stated that "the armaments and military equipment sent to Cuba are designed exclusively for defensive purposes . . . there is no need for the Soviet Union to shift its weapons for the repulsion of aggression, for a retaliatory blow (that is, its strategic or offensive weapons) to any other country, for instance Cuba . . . the Soviet Union has so powerful rockets to carry these nuclear warheads that there is no need to search for sites for them beyond the boundaries of the Soviet Union." And only last Thursday, as this offensive build-up went on, Soviet Foreign Minister Gromyko told me in my office that, "as to Soviet assistance to Cuba, he was instructed to make it clear, as the Soviet Government had already done, that such assistance pursued solely the purpose of contributing to the defense capabilities of Cuba . . . Training by Soviet specialists of Cuban nationals in handling defensive armaments was by no means offensive. If it were otherwise, the Soviet Government would have never become involved rendering such assistance."

The United States of America need not and cannot tolerate defiance, deception and offensive threats on the part of any nation, large or small. Nuclear weapons are so destructive, and ballistic missiles are so swift, that a sudden shift in the nature of their threat can be deeply dangerous— especially when the trigger appears to be in the hands of a violent and unstable revolutionary leader. For many years, both the Soviet Union and the United States have deployed such weapons around the world with great care, never upsetting the precarious status quo which balanced off the use of those weapons in the absence of some vital challenge. These deployments are not comparable. Our own weapon systems, such as Polaris and Minuteman, have always emphasized invulnerability because they are intended to be retaliatory not offensive, and because our history—unlike that of the Soviets since World War II—demonstrates that we have no desire to dominate or conquer other nations or impose our system upon them. Nevertheless American citizens have become adjusted to living daily on the bull's eye of Soviet missiles located inside the USSR or in submarines.

But this sudden and extraordinary build-up of communist missiles in an area well-known to have a special and historical relationship to the United States, in ~~violation~~ [contradiction to all previous Soviet practice, even with members of the Warsaw Pact, in (indecipherable)], of Soviet assurances, and in defiance of American and hemispheric policy, was a provocative and unjustified change in the status quo which could not be accepted by this country, if our courage and our commitments are ever to be believed in the future.

If the 1930's taught us any lesson at all, it was that aggressive conduct, if allowed to grow unchecked and unchallenged, will ultimately lead to war. This nation is opposed to war—but it is true to its word.

The discovery of this desperate and enormously dangerous move has required, in the last week, a most searching study of the courses of action open to us. The world can be sure that our choice of rapid, sure and minimum ~~fire~~ force was made only after all other alternatives had been most searchingly surveyed. Every other course of action involved risks of delay and of obfuscation which were wholly unacceptable—and with no prospect of real progress in removing ~~their~~ this intolerable [communist] nuclear intrusion into the Americans.[sic] The size, speed, and secrecy of the deployment, the bare-faced falsehoods surrounding it, and the newly revealed character of the conspirators involved made plain that no appeal, no warning, no offer would shift them from their course. Prolonged delay would have meant enormously increased danger, and immediate warning would have greatly enlarged the loss of life on all sides. It became my duty to act.

(Follows a description of first reports of action.)

The tragedy here—self-evidently—is in the loss of innocent lives on all sides. For the United States Government I hereby accept responsibility for this action and pledge that all appropriate efforts will be made, on request, to assist the families of these innocent victims. Neither Cubans nor Russians, as individuals, can be held accountable for the extraordinary and irresponsible conspiracy which has required this action. This was Communist militarism in action—neither more nor less.

We are, of course, reporting our actions at once to the Organization of American States and the United Nations. We shall ask the first for support and the second for understanding. We believe that the world will be relieved that a new threat of nuclear terror has been kept out of the Americas; and that the documentary evidence we shall be able to present will make the necessity of our action clear to all who care for freedom.

The nuclear age is one of great danger, inevitably. Perhaps the most dangerous of all its aspects is the hazard that the will and determination of this nation may be overtaken by that force that aims so openly and so ruthlessly at world domination. If we had allowed the present plot to succeed, that danger would have been multiplied.

As it is, we remain, as we have been right along, steadfastly determined to do our best to limit the world's dangers and lower its tensions. We are prepared ourselves to consider with the Soviet Union and with all Governments how sudden and clandestine threats of the sort may be prevented, for all of us. We remain steadfast to all our other commitments—and in particular I should publicly emphasize that we are more determined than ever to defend the freedom of West Berlin. And I remind you that no one has ever tried, either openly or covertly, to make West Berlin a military base—much less a nuclear threat.

Now what of the future?

First, I ask that the American people remain calm and self-confident and go about their business. There will be no major war; the strength and determination of your defenses are answer against that.

Second, the military blockade of Cuba will continue until other effective assurances can be obtained against any repetition of this conspiracy.

Such a blockade can clearly be authorized both by the requirements of US self-defense and by the Organ of Consultation of the Organization of American States, acting under Articles 6 and 8 of the Rio Treaty and this year's Punta del Este Resolution. All ships bound for Cuba, from whatever nation or port, will be halted and searched—and those containing cargoes of weapons or refusing to halt be dealt with appropriately under the rules of international law. Such a blockade may be extended, if needed, to other types of cargo and carrier.

Third, I have directed our military forces to continue and increase their close surveillance of Cuba, as contemplated in the OAS Communique of October 6; to take further military action, if necessary, against offensive capabilities, and finally, to regard any missile that might possibly remain and be launched from Cuba as an attack by the Soviet Union requiring a massive retaliatory response upon the Soviet Union.

Fourth, as a military precaution, I have reinforced our base at Guantanamo, evacuated the dependents of our personnel there and ordered additional military units to stand by on an alert basis.

Fifth, I am asking Soviet Chairman Khrushchev to meet with me at the earliest opportunity with respect to the prevention of any further conspiracies which may strain the relations between our two countries. We do not wish to war with the Soviet Union—we are a peaceful people who desire to live in peace with all other peoples. I am prepared to discuss with the Soviet Chairman how both of us might remove existing tensions instead of creating new ones. Our attitude on this was only recently shown in our acquiescence in the Iranian Government's announcement that it would not permit the establishment of foreign missile bases upon its territory—and in our efforts to halt the testing and spread of nuclear weapons, and to end the arms race and all overseas bases in a fair and effective treaty. But we could not negotiate with a gun at our heads—a gun that imperiled innocent Cubans as well as Americans. Our byword is: "Negotiation yes, Intimidation no".

Finally, I have directed the United States Information Agency to use all available resources in making clear our position to the unhappy people of Cuba. We have no quarrel with the Cuban people, only sympathy and hope. They did not consent to the building of this intolerable threat. Their lives and land are being used as pawns by those who deny them freedom. We have no wish to war on them, or impose any system upon them. Our objective, on the contrary, to give them back the dream of their revolution—the dream which Fidel Castro repudiated when he sold them out to the communists who may now sell him out in turn. Our objective in the world is peace and freedom—including the peace and freedom of the Cuban people.

John P. Altgeld's Retiring Address as Governor of Illinois, to Have Been Delivered on January 11, 1897

This occasion does not invite extended remarks from me. The world has decreed that an actor who has played his part shall simply make his bow and retire from the stage. Men turn their faces toward the rising sun and so it should be, for while the past may admonish it is the future that inspires.

But we may pause long enough to note character of this occasion and the lesson it teaches. It took the world thousands of years to reach a point where such a scene as this was possible. Mankind struggled through weary and bloody centuries before anything like government was evolved and then there followed dark ages before it became possible to take the reins of government out of the hands of one political party and place them in the hands of a hostile party without blood shed. The scene which we witness here today shows the triumph of republican government and teaches us that the journey of man, when viewed from headland to headland, has been onward and upward; that passion is retiring and reason is mounting the throne, and we may congratulate ourselves upon the fact that in this great advancement America has set the example for the nations.

The presence of the defeated and retiring party is not necessary for the peaceful change of administration, yet in order to add the graces to republican form it is customary for the retiring party to be represented and participate in the ceremonies of inauguration, and to-day the great party which I have the honor to represent, not only assists in these ceremonies, but it expresses the hope that the new administration will direct the destinies of this mighty State along the paths of honor and of glory. While politically divided we are all Illinoisans and the greatness and the grandeur of this State rise above all considerations of persons or of party. Her past thrills, her present awes and her future dazzles the intellect of man.

To the distinguished gentleman who is to stand at her head I extend the most cordial greeting and hearty good wishes. Loving Illinois as I do I shall applaud his every act that tends to her advancement. I have given her four of my best years and have brought all my offerings to her altar. Had it been necessary to do so I should have considered life itself but a small sacrifice in her interest and I retire from her service and from the high office to which her people elected me without any trace of bitterness or disappointment. I have tried to further the best interests of my country, and while I erred in many cases they were errors of judgment and I go forth with a peaceful conscience. I have endeavored to carry out those principles that form the basis of free government and I have acted on the conviction that it would be better to be Governor but for one day and follow the dictates of justice than to hold office for fifty years by winking at wrong. In my judgment no epitaph can be written upon the tomb of a public man that will so surely win the contempt of the ages than to say of him that he held office all his life and never did anything for humanity. We believe that the institutions of the State are in excellent condition. Some of my friends feel that we have been cleaning house; that we have been putting things in order. Permit me to say that if any of the measures which we have inaugurated should prove beneficial to the country the people will be in no wise indebted to me, for when a public man gives to his country the very best services in his power he has done no more than he agreed to do and has done no more than the public had a right to expect. I do not endorse the charge that republics are ungrateful. I believe that in the end there is a disposition to give every man his meed. In fact, many men have been loaded by republics with honors which were far beyond their deserts. We turn the affairs of the State over to our successors.

I would remind my distinguished successor that there is no such thing as repose in the universe; that the centripetal and centrifugal laws are constantly at work; that nothing stands still; that nothing is ever perfect; that there is a perpetual development and a constant disintegration, and that the institutions of this State must go on developing, reaching a higher and a higher plane successively, or they must retrograde, and I will further say to him that rarely does the hand of fate open the gate to a more alluring pathway of glory than is open to him now. Illinois is already the guiding star of the American constellation. Her people have outstripped all other peoples of the earth and they will surely shape the destiny of this republic. Their institutions of every kind and character should be the models for the earth and the flame of intelligence burning on her prairies and by the inland sea must brighten the sky for all people, and there could not possibly be a greater achievement than to assist in directing the thought and shaping the institutions of such a people.

But I warn my distinguished friend and successor that the task is not a light one. It is beset with the greatest difficulties and will require wisdom, courage and intense determination and persistence. The selfish forces of greed are always ready to tear to pieces the noblest creations of patriotism. Hence it has been well said that the tablets of immortality are harder than flint and that only persevering genius can engrave a name or an act there.

To the members of that great political party to which I have the honor of belonging let me say that while we are relieved of the responsibility of administration our responsibility in another direction is increased, for in a republic it is the minority party which creates the sentiment and develops the principles which the government shall in the end carry out. Not being hampered or embarrassed by the detail of administration, the minority party can devote its best energies to the discussion of great principles, while the majority party, being obliged to conciliate conflicting interests and to compromise, is in that respect hampered and generally spends its force in endeavoring to carry out a policy already determined upon by the country and is not able to deal in an independent manner with new questions which are from time to time evolved. It is the minority party that has made progress possible not only in this country but in Europe. In England it was the minority party that repeatedly forced the government to adopt new and great reforms. The immortal orators of England spoke for the minority. In our country the great forensic efforts which helped to move the nation forward were made by men who stood in the ranks of the minority. In fact, every great reform in our country had to first confront a hostile majority. In a sense the mission of the minority is of a higher order than that of the majority. True, it does not deal in spoils, it has no fleshpots to distribute, but it is its high mission to discover the eternal essence of things and to point out the way of justice.

We go out of power with nothing to regret. Conscious of having struggled for a great cause we smile at the frowns of fate and go forth with renewed hope and a firmer purpose. We need not inquire what were the reasons for our defeat. We know there were some conditions for which we were not responsible, and on account of these conditions the currents began to run against us nearly three years ago and they ran with such irresistible force two years ago that they covered the State like a deluge, submerging everything. In the last campaign the same currents were still running with the same force, other hostile forces were added which in themselves seem irresistible. Our party was obliged to reform as it were in the face of the enemy. It eliminated many elements of weakness, elements which for years had tended to neutralize the party and make it impotent, so that it stood for no definite or great principle and was incapable of making an aggressive fight. After eliminating these elements of weakness the party made one of the grandest campaigns ever witnessed.

But all this belongs to the past. No American has a right to stand with his face toward that which is gone. Government is the constant meeting of new conditions. It is not the things of yesterday but the things of to-morrow that must engage our attention. The principles we hold are the only ones upon which free government can endure. Let us renew our devotion to them and kindle anew our enthusiasm. Let us not follow the example of those who try to use the names of Jefferson and Jackson to hide the most undemocratic principles and even the most destructive practices. In so far as the new administration, federal and State, shall adhere to the great doctrines of human right and shall adhere to those great principles that lie at the very basis of republican institutions let us give them our hearty commendation and support, but let us be watchful and whenever it shall seem to us that the welfare and prosperity of our great country are being endangered let us raise the alarm and let us all the time feel an abiding confidence that right will in the end prevail.

Hillary Clinton's Election Night Remarks, to Have Been Delivered on November 8, 2016

My fellow Americans: today, you sent a message to the whole world: our values endure, our democracy stands strong, and our motto remains "e pluribus unum"—out of many, one.

We will not be defined only by our differences. We will not be an "us versus them" country. The American dream is big enough for everyone.

Through a long, hard campaign, we were challenged to choose be-tween two very different visions for America: how we grow together, how we live together, and how we face a world full of peril and promise together.

Fundamentally, this election challenged us to decide what it means to be an American in the 21st century.

And by reaching for unity, decency, and what President Lincoln called "the better angels of our nature"—we met that challenge.

Today, with your children on your shoulders . . . neighbors at your side . . . friends old and new, standing as one . . . you renewed our democracy. And because of the honor you have given me, you changed its face forever.

I've met women who were born before women had the right to vote. They've been waiting a hundred years for tonight. I've met little boys and girls who didn't understand why a woman has never been president before.

Now they know—and the world knows—that in America, every boy and every girl can grow up to be whatever they dream—even President of the United States.

This is a victory for all Americans—men and women, boys and girls—because as our country has proven once again: When there are no ceilings, the sky's the limit.

Now we must not rest until every remaining ceiling is shattered, every standing barrier is broken, and every single American can live up to her or his God-given potential. That is the promise of America, and it will be my promise to you as the 45th President of the United States.

My friends, I am humbled and grateful to stand with you on this historic night.

To Bill, Chelsea, Marc, Charlotte, Aidan and our entire family, my love for you means more than I can ever express.

To Tim Kaine and Anne Holton . . . thank you for being our partners on this incredible journey. I can't wait to start this next chapter side-by-side.

To Barack and Michelle Obama . . . you've turned hope into change and called us to higher ground. You rescued our economy, kept us safe, and restored our leadership in the world. Our country owes you an enormous debt of gratitude, and so do I.

To Bernie Sanders and his millions of supporters who joined our campaign . . . I can't wait to turn the platform we wrote together into real progress for America.

And to Donald Trump—it's no secret that he and I don't see the world the same way, and in this campaign we weren't shy about airing our differences. But he fought relentlessly right up until the finish, and we wish him and his family well.

I am grateful beyond words to the men and women at Headquarters in Brooklyn and across our country who poured their hearts into this campaign. To all the volunteers, community leaders, activists, and union organizers who knocked on doors, talked to neighbors, posted on Facebook, ate way too much cold pizza and drank way too much warm beer . . . thank you.

Most of all, I'm grateful to the American people who voted in this election. Many of us are rejoicing in the outcome. Some of us are not. It's never easy to be on the losing side of an election. Believe me, I know that first-hand.

But whether you supported us or not, by participating, you showed your faith in our democracy. We debate and argue, and sometimes it gets heated, but in the end, we all love our country. Now we owe it to America and each other to strive for common ground and common purpose.

We have so much to build on. Eight years ago, we were in the throes of the worst financial crisis since the Great Depression. Today, we've had 73 straight months of job growth. Poverty is going down and incomes are finally going up.

Now we face a different kind of challenge—one in its own way just as serious and urgent.

From Americans of every political persuasion, we've heard cynicism— and real anger—at a political system and an economy that seem only to work for those at the top. Eight years after the crisis, too many powerful interests still protect their own profits and privileges at the expense of everyone else.

We've also heard the frustration of so many in our country who feel devalued and disrespected—like there isn't a place for them in America.

When I launched my campaign on a sun-drenched day a year-and-a-half ago, on an island dedicated to Franklin Delano Roosevelt, I knew that our challenges demanded bold, persistent action.

But it wasn't until I traveled to every corner of our country, listening and talking with hard-working Americans about the problems that keep them up at night, that I felt the full force of people's concerns.

I also felt the full force of their incredible determination, resilience and hope.

I met parents working two or three jobs for years who still can't afford college for their kids . . . and students burdened by debt who struggle to imagine a future they can call their own . . . but also young people starting businesses and families, working in every way they can to make the world a better place.

I met young black men and women who are too often made to feel like their lives are disposable. I saw them open America's eyes to the reality of systemic racism and turn injustice into activism.

I met police officers who put their lives on the line to keep us safe. And veterans who've sacrificed so much to keep us free. We as a nation have not always kept faith with those who serve—yet their patriotism burns as bright as ever.

I met people who work long hours caring tenderly for children and the elderly, but still don't get the respect or the wages they deserve. They're organizing and marching and reminding us all that no one who works full time in America should live in poverty.

I met laid-off coal miners in West Virginia and steelworkers in Ohio who see a changing world and don't want to be left behind. Our country can never abandon the men and women who toiled and bled to keep our factories running and our lights shining generation after generation. They are ready to be part of a new future and we can't build it without them.

My heart broke for Latino families who have been made to feel like strangers in their own land. I'll never forget the little girl in Nevada who started to cry as she told me how scared she was that her parents would be taken away from her.

But my heart soared when I met DREAMers who contribute so much to our country—and when I saw so many immigrants working to become citizens so they can vote and shape the future of the nation they love.

My soul has been touched by the mothers who lost children and started a movement for peace and justice . . .

And by the open hearts and deep faith of people all over our country. Like the pastor in South Carolina who shared his bible with me, open to 1st Corinthians.

Love never fails, it tells us. In the end, that is one of the greatest lessons of this campaign.

If you dig deep enough, through all the mud of politics, eventually you hit something hard and true. A foundation of fundamental values that unite us as Americans.

You proved that today.

In a country divided by race and religion, class and culture, and often paralyzing partisanship, a broad coalition of Americans embraced a shared vision of a hopeful, inclusive, big-hearted America.

An America where women are respected and immigrants are welcomed . . . where veterans are honored, parents are supported, and workers are paid fairly.

An America where we believe in science . . . where we look beyond people's disabilities and see their possibilities . . . where marriage is a right and discrimination is wrong, no matter who you are, what you look like, where you come from or who you love.

An America where everyone counts and everyone has a place. A place <u>and</u> a purpose. Because we all have a role to play in our great American story.

And yes, that absolutely includes everyone who voted for other candidates or who didn't vote at all.

Scripture tells us, "To everything, there is a season." We have come through a time of division. Now is a time for unity. Now is a time, as it says in Isaiah, for all of us to become repairers of the breach.

It's going to take all of us doing our part—as neighbors, citizens, one country, together. I still believe "It Takes a Village." None of us can raise a family, build a business, heal a community or lift a country by ourselves.

We refuse to see America as a zero-sum game. Some people getting ahead doesn't have to mean others falling behind. Economic and social justice are about addition, not subtraction. We can <u>all</u> rise together.

I think that starts with listening to each other . . . and hearing each other. There's been so much misunderstanding and suspicion. We all need to do a better job of putting ourselves in each other's shoes—especially if our views seem miles apart. No matter how deep our differences, there's always more common ground between us than we think.

There will be missteps—I've made my share—but I promise you this:

I will always strive to be a President for <u>all</u> Americans. Not just for the people who supported me in this election. For everyone.

I will be a Commander-in-Chief who respects and honors our men and women in uniform, and stands by our allies and friends. And I will do everything I can to keep our country safe and strong.

I will work my heart out to make life better for you and your family.

And I invite leaders in Congress and across the country [to] join me. If they do, I'll be ready to work with them anytime, anyplace.

I know it will be tempting to jump right back into the fray, to try to score points by tearing each other down. But Americans have had enough. They're ready for us to do our jobs.

The transition we launch tonight cannot just be from one Administration to another, while the rest of Washington remains stuck in business as usual. It must be a transition to a new ethic of patriotism and pragmatic progressivism that always puts the interests of the nation first.

My friends, because of you, I close this campaign with a deeper faith than ever that our country's best days are still ahead of us.

Forty-seven years ago, when I was an idealistic college student, I said to my classmates that our goal should be to make what appears to be impossible, possible.

Well, I'm older now. I'm a mother and a grandmother. But I still believe with all my heart that we can make the impossible, possible. Look at what we're celebrating tonight.

This summer, a writer asked me: If I could go back in time and tell anyone in history about this milestone, who would it be?

And the answer was easy: my mother, Dorothy.

You may have heard me talk about her difficult childhood. She was abandoned by her parents when she was just 8 years old. They put her on a train to California, where she was mistreated by her grandparents and ended up out on her own, working as a housemaid. Yet she still found a way to offer me the boundless love and support she never received herself. She taught me the words of our Methodist faith: "Do all the good you can, for all the people you can, in all the ways you can, as long as ever you can."

I think about my mother every day. Sometimes, I think about her on that train. I wish I could walk down the aisle and find the little wooden seats where she sat, holding tight to her even-younger sister, alone, terrified.

She doesn't yet know how much she will suffer. She doesn't yet know she will find the strength to escape that suffering—that is still a long way off. The whole future is still unknown as she stares out at the vast country moving past her. I dream of going up to her, and sitting down next to her, taking her in my arms and saying look at me, listen to me. You will survive. You will have a good family of your own, and three children. And as hard as it might be to imagine, your daughter will grow up and become the president of the United States.

I am as sure of this as anything I have ever known: America is the greatest country in the world. And, from tonight, going forward, together we will make America even greater than it has ever been—for each and every one of us.

Thank you. God bless you. And may God bless America.

John F. Kennedy's Remarks at the Dallas Trade Mart, to Have Been Delivered on November 22, 1963

I am honored to have this invitation to address the annual meeting of the Dallas Citizens Council, joined by the members of the Dallas Assembly—and pleased to have this opportunity to salute the Graduate Research Center of the Southwest.

It is fitting that these two symbols of Dallas progress are united in the sponsorship of this meeting. For they represent the best qualities, I am told, of leadership and learning in this city—and leadership and learning are indispensable to each other. The advancement of learning depends on community leadership for financial and political support and the products of that learning, in turn, are essential to the leadership's hopes for continued progress and prosperity. It is not a coincidence that those communities possessing the best in research and graduate facilities—from MIT to Cal Tech—tend to attract the new and growing industries. I congratulate those of you here in Dallas who have recognized these basic facts through the creation of the unique and forward-looking Graduate Research Center.

This link between leadership and learning is not only essential at the community level. It is even more indispensable in world affairs. Ignorance and misinformation can handicap the progress of a city or a company, but they can, if allowed to prevail in foreign policy, handicap this country's security. In a world of complex and continuing problems, in a world full of frustrations and irritations, America's leadership must be guided by the lights of learning and reason or else those who confuse rhetoric with reality and the plausible with the possible will gain the popular ascendancy with their seemingly swift and simple solutions to every world problem.

There will always be dissident voices heard in the land, expressing opposition without alternatives, finding fault but never favor, perceiving gloom on every side and seeking influence without responsibility. Those voices are inevitable.

But today other voices are heard in the land—voices preaching doctrines wholly unrelated to reality, wholly unsuited to the sixties, doctrines which apparently assume that words will suffice without weapons, that vituperation is as good as victory and that peace is a sign of weakness. At a time when the national debt is steadily being reduced in terms of its burden on our economy, they see that debt as the greatest single threat to our security. At a time when we are steadily reducing the number of Federal employees serving every thousand citizens, they fear those supposed hordes of civil servants far more than the actual hordes of opposing armies.

We cannot expect that everyone, to use the phrase of a decade ago, will "talk sense to the American people." But we can hope that fewer people will listen to nonsense. And the notion that this Nation is headed for defeat through deficit, or that strength is but a matter of slogans, is nothing but just plain nonsense.

I want to discuss with you today the status of our strength and our security because this question clearly calls for the most responsible qualities of leadership and the most enlightened products of scholarship. For this Nation's strength and security are not easily or cheaply obtained, nor are they quickly and simply explained. There are many kinds of strength and no one kind will suffice. Overwhelming nuclear strength cannot stop a guerrilla war. Formal pacts of alliance cannot stop internal subversion. Displays of material wealth cannot stop the disillusion of diplomats subjected to discrimination.

Above all, words alone are not enough. The United States is a peaceful nation. And where our strength and determination are clear, our words need merely to convey conviction, not belligerence. If we are strong, our strength will speak for itself. If we are weak, words will be of no help.

I realize that this Nation often tends to identify turning-points in world affairs with the major addresses which preceded them. But it was not the Monroe Doctrine that kept all Europe away from this hemisphere—it was the strength of the British fleet and the width of the Atlantic Ocean. It was not General Marshall's speech at Harvard which kept communism out of Western Europe—it was the strength and stability made possible by our military and economic assistance.

In this administration also it has been necessary at times to issue specific warnings—warnings that we could not stand by and watch the Communists conquer Laos by force, or intervene in the Congo, or swallow West Berlin, or maintain offensive missiles on Cuba. But while our goals were at least temporarily obtained in these and other instances, our successful defense of freedom was due not to the words we used, but to the strength we stood ready to use on behalf of the principles we stand ready to defend.

This strength is composed of many different elements, ranging from the most massive deterrents to the most subtle influences. And all types of strength are needed—no one kind could do the job alone. Let us take a moment, therefore, to review this Nation's progress in each major area of strength.

First, as Secretary McNamara made clear in his address last Monday, the strategic nuclear power of the United States has been so greatly modernized and expanded in the last 1,000 days, by the rapid production and deployment of the most modern missile systems, that any and all potential aggressors are clearly confronted now with the impossibility of strategic victory—and the certainty of total destruction—if by reckless attack they should ever force upon us the necessity of a strategic reply.

In less than 3 years, we have increased by 50 percent the number of Polaris submarines scheduled to be in force by the next fiscal year, increased by more than 70 percent our total Polaris purchase program, increased by more than 75 percent our Minuteman purchase program, increased by 50 percent the portion of our strategic bombers on 15-minute alert, and increased by 100 percent the total number of nuclear weapons available in our strategic alert forces. Our security is further enhanced by the steps we have taken regarding these weapons to improve the speed and certainty of their response, their readiness at all times to respond, their ability to survive an attack, and their ability to be carefully controlled and directed through secure command operations.

But the lessons of the last decade have taught us that freedom cannot be defended by strategic nuclear power alone. We have, therefore, in the last 3 years accelerated the development and deployment of tactical nuclear weapons, and increased by 60 percent the tactical nuclear forces deployed in Western Europe.

Nor can Europe or any other continent rely on nuclear forces alone, whether they are strategic or tactical. We have radically improved the readiness of our conventional forces—increased by 45 percent the number of combat ready Army divisions, increased by 100 percent the procurement of modern Army weapons and equipment, increased by 100 percent our ship construction, conversion, and modernization program, increased by 100 percent our procurement of tactical aircraft, increased by 30 percent the number of tactical air squadrons, and increased the strength of the Marines. As last month's "Operation Big Lift"—which originated here in Texas—showed so clearly, this Nation is prepared as never before to move substantial numbers of men in surprisingly little time to advanced positions anywhere in the world. We have increased by 175 percent the procurement of airlift aircraft, and we have already achieved a 75 percent increase in our existing strategic airlift capability. Finally, moving beyond the traditional roles of our military forces, we have achieved an increase of nearly 600 percent in our special forces— those forces that are prepared to work with our allies and friends against the guerrillas, saboteurs, insurgents and assassins who threaten freedom in a less direct but equally dangerous manner.

But American military might should not and need not stand alone against the ambitions of international communism. Our security and strength, in the last analysis, directly depend on the security and strength of others, and that is why our military and economic assistance plays such a key role in enabling those who live on the periphery of the Communist world to maintain their independence of choice. Our assistance to these nations can be painful, risky and costly, as is true in Southeast Asia today. But we dare not weary of the task. For our assistance makes possible the stationing of 3–5 million allied troops along the Communist frontier at one-tenth the cost of maintaining a comparable number of American soldiers. A successful Communist breakthrough in these areas, necessitating direct United States intervention, would cost us several times as much as our entire foreign aid program, and might cost us heavily in American lives as well.

About 70 percent of our military assistance goes to nine key countries located on or near the borders of the Communist bloc—nine countries confronted directly or indirectly with the threat of Communist aggression—Viet-Nam, Free China, Korea, India, Pakistan, Thailand, Greece, Turkey, and Iran. No one of these countries possesses on its own the resources to maintain the forces which our own Chiefs of Staff think needed in the common interest. Reducing our efforts to train, equip, and assist their armies can only encourage Communist penetration and require in time the increased overseas deployment of American combat forces. And reducing the economic help needed to bolster these nations that undertake to help defend freedom can have the same disastrous result. In short, the $50 billion we spend each year on our own defense could well be ineffective without the $4 billion required for military and economic assistance.

Our foreign aid program is not growing in size, it is, on the contrary, smaller now than in previous years. It has had its weaknesses, but we have undertaken to correct them. And the proper way of treating weaknesses is to replace them with strength, not to increase those weaknesses by emasculating essential programs. Dollar for dollar, in or out of government, there is no better form of investment in our national security than our much-abused foreign aid program. We cannot afford to lose it. We can afford to maintain it. We can surely afford, for example, to do as much for our 19 needy neighbors of Latin America as the Communist bloc is sending to the island of Cuba alone.

I have spoken of strength largely in terms of the deterrence and resistance of aggression and attack. But, in today's world, freedom can be lost without a shot being fired, by ballots as well as bullets. The success of our leadership is dependent upon respect for our mission in the world as well as our missiles—on a clearer recognition of the virtues of freedom as well as the evils of tyranny.

That is why our Information Agency has doubled the shortwave broadcasting power of the Voice of America and increased the number of broadcasting hours by 30 percent, increased Spanish language broadcasting to Cuba and Latin America from 1 to 9 hours a day, increased seven-fold to more than 3–5 million copies the number of American books being translated and published for Latin American readers, and taken a host of other steps to carry our message of truth and freedom to all the far corners of the earth.

And that is also why we have regained the initiative in the exploration of outer space, making an annual effort greater than the combined total of all space activities undertaken during the fifties, launching more than 130 vehicles into earth orbit, putting into actual operation valuable weather and communications satellites, and making it clear to all that the United States of America has no intention of finishing second in space.

This effort is expensive—but it pays its own way, for freedom and for America. For there is no longer any fear in the free world that a Communist lead in space will become a permanent assertion of supremacy and the basis of military superiority. There is no longer any doubt about the strength and skill of American science, American industry, American education, and the American free enterprise system. In short, our national space effort represents a great gain in, and a great resource of, our national strength—and both Texas and Texans are contributing greatly to this strength.

Finally, it should be clear by now that a nation can be no stronger abroad than she is at home. Only an America which practices what it preaches about equal rights and social justice will be respected by those whose choice affects our future. Only an America which has fully educated its citizens is fully capable of tackling the complex problems and perceiving the hidden dangers of the world in which we live. And only an America which is growing and prospering economically can sustain the worldwide defenses of freedom, while demonstrating to all concerned the opportunities of our system and society.

It is clear, therefore, that we are strengthening our security as well as our economy by our recent record increases in national income and output—by surging ahead of most of Western Europe in the rate of business expansion and the margin of corporate profits, by maintaining a more stable level of prices than almost any of our overseas competitors, and by cutting personal and corporate income taxes by some $11 billion, as I have proposed, to assure this Nation of the longest and strongest expansion in our peacetime economic history.

This Nation's total output—which 3 years ago was at the $500 billion mark—will soon pass $600 billion, for a record rise of over $100 billion in 3 years. For the first time in history we have 70 million men and women at work. For the first time in history average factory earnings have exceeded $100 a week. For the first time in history corporation profits after taxes—which have risen 43 percent in less than 3 years—have an annual level of $27.4 billion.

My friends and fellow citizens: I cite these facts and figures to make it clear that America today is stronger than ever before. Our adversaries have not abandoned their ambitions, our dangers have not diminished, our vigilance cannot be relaxed. But now we have the military, the scientific, and the economic strength to do whatever must be done for the preservation and promotion of freedom.

That strength will never be used in pursuit of aggressive ambitions—it will always be used in pursuit of peace. It will never be used to promote provocations—it will always be used to promote the peaceful settlement of disputes.

We in this country, in this generation, are—by destiny rather than choice—the watchmen on the walls of world freedom. We ask, therefore, that we may be worthy of our power and responsibility, that we may exercise our strength with wisdom and restraint, and that we may achieve in our time and for all time the ancient vision of "peace on earth, good will toward men." That must always be our goal, and the righteousness of our cause must always underlie our strength. For as was written long ago: "except the Lord keep the city, the watchman waketh but in vain."

Acknowledgments

Friends and colleagues have been hearing me talk about this idea for a book for more than a decade, and so many of them made it possible for me to finally write it.

Chief among them is Sarah Muller, a researcher extraordinaire who tackled unending and unreasonable queries with creativity and energy and an unflinchingly good spirit. This book simply would not have been possible without her.

Rafe Sagalyn and Jennifer Joel formed a dream team of literary agents. I still don't know who was the good cop and who was the bad cop, and Rafe would be the first to tell me that means I'm using the wrong analogy. I'll be forever grateful for Rafe's encouragement and prodding over lunches at CF Folks early on in this process, and Rafe and Jenn's support throughout.

I'm also convinced that the proposal itself would not have been nearly as attractive in content if it weren't so attractive in design, and I owe that to Brooks King.

There were times in this process where I couldn't look at what I'd written for another minute. If Sarah Murphy was similarly afflicted, she certainly didn't show it—patiently reading draft after draft and chapter after chapter, returning each with comments that helped me clarify and sharpen my arguments. I'm grateful for Sarah's work, and that of Noah Eaker, Zachary Wagman, and the entire team at Flatiron Books.

I told Jofie Ferrari-Adler at Simon & Schuster that his early enthusiasm for this project would make him the first editor to be acknowledged in a book that he didn't edit and published by a publisher he didn't work for. Promise kept.

Jake Petzold helped me assemble an early dossier of undelivered speeches, and Michael Hill, a friend and a historian's historian, helped me sharpen my approach to this book.

Michael Greenbaum and his team of amazing, fast, accurate transcriptionists at Hired Hand allowed me to turn garbled recordings of interviews into (hopefully less garbled) prose.

Someone once told me that the true cost of a book isn't the cover price, it's the hours you're asking someone to spend with your words. If that's the case, my dear friends and colleagues Eric Schnure and Ken Baer paid a steep price indeed, and I'm forever grateful for their willingness to read chapters and field random calls. Angela Ferrante read early versions of this manuscript and provided important guidance on the audiobook.

I'm deeply indebted to the entire gang at West Wing Writers, who covered for me when I finally, finally, took a leave to get this book written. I couldn't ask for better friends or partners than Ben Yarrow, Jonas Kieffer, Vinca LaFleur, Jeff Shesol, and, in particular, Paul Orzulak. I have worked with Paul in one form or another for over twenty years. (For our anniversary, I gave Paul a catalytic converter, because that particular car part contains platinum and it was our platinum anniversary, and because we've both handled a lot of hot air.) Paul's enthusiasm for this project and his willingness to read drafts of the manuscript went above and beyond the call of either partnership or friendship.

I'm so lucky that in my work the line between client and friend is constantly blurring, and so I won't name them all for fear of outing them as clients; I'd like to thank the many friends who have allowed me to help them tell their stories. You know who you are.

I'm also grateful to Tom Hill, David Ko, Jonathan Lerner, and Alex Michael, who all provided constant encouragement for this project.

Early in the writing process, I realized that each chapter could have been a book unto itself, and each required an education. So many distinguished authors, historians, and educators fielded and then humored my cold calls and emails. Of course, any errors of fact and interpretation fall on me alone.

For the chapter on the March on Washington, State Representative (and author) Drew Hansen spoke to me so long ago he probably doesn't even remember it. Brenda Jones, communications director to former congressman John Lewis, provided guidance and perspective, and Courtland Cox was willing to sift through fifty years of memories to offer his perspective.

For Wamsutta James's speech, I'm deeply grateful for the time and partnership provided by his son Moonanum James, who passed away in 2020; Paul Grant-Costa, the executive editor of the Yale Indian Papers Project; and Mahtowin Munro, the colcader of the United American Indians of New England.

For the chapter on Emma Goldman and Helen Keller, I'm grateful to Helen Selsdon at the American Foundation for the Blind. For the chapter on Richard Nixon, I borrowed heavily from both the words and the wisdom of my occasional lunch companion Lee Huebner.

For the chapter on Mayor Kevin White, Marta Crilly at the City of Boston archives was a tremendous guide. I was also lucky to have found and connected with two stars of the story, Ira Jackson and Robert Schwartz.

For King Edward's non-abdication speech, I'm grateful to a series of researchers in the UK who helped me navigate various archives as my remote eyes and ears and arms and legs: Eleanor Doughty, Hywel Maslyn, and Peter Day. Of particular help was Amy Boylan at the Balliol College library. I'm deeply indebted to my friend and neighbor (or is it neighbour) Charles Kenny, who is, if not an actual prince, a prince of a guy.

The chapter on Abe Beame and New York City's bankruptcy was the project that started this book, and it began with an article by Sam Roberts of *The New York Times,* who also pointed me in the right direction to track down the original speech. Ira Millstein and Sally Sasso shared stories and helped me track down source material, and Dick Ravitch was generous with his recollections. I was lucky to have the opportunity to interview two of the key players before they passed away: Felix Rohatyn and Sid Frigand. John O'Connell at the Ford Library helped me tell the coda to the story. And Jeannie Sherman at the Connecticut State Library helped me find the fun details about Ella Grasso's speech that night.

For Eisenhower's apology for the failure of the D-day invasion, I am grateful for the guidance and encouragement of author Jerome O'Connor, and the thinking being done on the subject of apology by Joy Clarkson.

For Hirohito's undelivered apology for World War II, Eiichi Ito, the head of the Japanese reading room at the Library of Congress, helped me track down the speech in the original Japanese, while Cameron Penwell, also at the Library of Congress, was invaluable in helping find supplemental reading on the Hirohito speech. Louisa Rubinfien went above and beyond, serving as both translator and teacher on imperial history, language, and thinking. Her translation of Hirohito's undelivered speech was reviewed by Jordan Sand.

For the chapter on the Cuban missile crisis, I'm deeply grateful to Stacey Chandler and Hailey Philbin at the John F. Kennedy Presidential Library and Museum. Patrick Cirenza was generous in sharing his thinking on the mystery of the speech's authorship, and Adam Frankel shared his experiences working with Ted Sorensen. I'm also grateful to a veritable who's who of that era's history for sharing their thoughts with me: Kai Bird, Marty Sherwin, Graham Allison, and Bob Dallek.

For the chapter on John Altgeld, Robert D. Sampson's writing and guidance were indispensable.

For Hillary Clinton's undelivered victory speech, I'm grateful to Dan Schwerin, Megan Rooney, Jim Kennedy, Joel Benenson, Jake Sullivan, Jen Palmieri, and Alex Hornbrook for taking the time to talk with me about their recollections. Sara Al-Maashouq was indispensable in helping me research the history of concession speeches.

For the chapter on the speech Condoleezza Rice was to have given on September 11, Malisa Culpepper and Alison Wheelock helped me navigate the George W. Bush Presidential Library and Museum collections and the process of submitting a FOIA request.

For Barry Jenkins, it was great to get the behind-the-scenes story of what happened from Jon Macks.

There were several other people who spoke to me about speeches that didn't make it into this book: Nina Totenberg, Linda Greenhouse (you can guess what kind of speech I was looking for there), Joe Fitzgerald, John McConnell, Matthew Scully, Brian Reich, and Bill Quandt. The conversations were an education unto themselves. Hannah Shipley was invaluable in helping me keep all the various pieces organized.

The fact that I can even describe myself as a speechwriter is something I owe to a series of bosses and mentors: Ron Klain, who hired me for my first speechwriting job with Al Gore; Tom Daschle, who showed me that the writer-speaker relationship could be a real partnership; and James Carville, who taught me that a desk is a perfectly fine place to write assuming there's not a ballpark, horse track, or Cajun restaurant available.

I'm thankful for my daughters, Ada and Sophia, to whom I've dedicated the book. And Deb Swacker, who gamely watched me engage in stare-downs with boxes of research material and listened to me talk about writing this book for years.

Finally, I'm grateful to my parents.

As in everything, Mom, thank you for telling me this was perfect.

Dad, thank you for telling me it wasn't. I miss you.

Bibliography

Introduction

"Bush and Gore in Tight Race; Florida Will Prove Decisive." *New York Times*, November 8, 2000. https://www.nytimes.com/2000/11/08/politics/bush -and-gore-in-tight-race-florida-will-prove-decisive.html.

Clines, Francis X. "The 1993 Elections: Dinkins; Mayor Is Gracious in Defeat as He Calls for New Yorkers to 'Move Forward.'" *New York Times*, November 4, 1993. https://www.nytimes.com/1993/11/04/nyregion/1993 -elections-dinkins-mayor-gracious-defeat-he-calls-for-new-yorkers-move .html.

Friedman, Thomas L. "Foreign Affairs; MAD Isn't Crazy." *New York Times*, July 24, 2001. https://www.nytimes.com/2001/07/24/opinion/foreign -affairs-mad-isn-t-crazy.html.

John F. Kennedy Presidential Library and Museum. "'For John F. Kennedy's Inauguration' by Robert Frost (Undeliv. Inaugural Poem)." Accessed August 13, 2019. https://www.jfklibrary.org/learn/about-jfk/life-of-john-f-kennedy /fast-facts-john-f-kennedy/for-john-f-kennedys-inauguration-by-robert -frost-undelivered-poem.

National Security Council—Media Communications and Speechwriting. George W. Bush Library, Dallas, Texas.

"The 1993 Elections: Excerpts of Speeches, in Victory and Defeat." *New York Times,* November 3, 1993. https://www.nytimes.com/1993/11/03/nyregion /the-1993-elections-deciding-excerpts-of-speeches-in-victory-and-defeat .html.

Popova, Maria. "On Art and Government: The Poem Robert Frost Didn't Read at JFK's Inauguration." *Brain Pickings.* Accessed August 13, 2019. https://www.brainpickings.org/2013/01/22/robert-frost-dedication-jfk -inauguration/.

Quandt, William B. *Camp David: Peacemaking and Politics.* Washington, D.C.: Brookings Institution Press, 1986.

Quandt, William B. Interview by Jeff Nussbaum. June 21, 2019.

Sacks, Mike. *And Here's the Kicker: Conversations with 21 Top Humor Writers on Their Craft.* Cincinnati: Writer's Digest Books, 2009.

Schlesinger, Arthur M. *A Thousand Days: John F. Kennedy in the White House.* Boston: Mariner Books, 2002.

Thompson, Nicholas. *The Hawk and the Dove: Paul Nitze, George Kennan, and the History of the Cold War.* New York: Henry Holt, 2009.

Wright, Robin. "Top Focus Before 9/11 Wasn't on Terrorism." *Washington Post,* April 1, 2004. https://www.washingtonpost.com/archive/politics/2004 /04/01/top-focus-before-911-wasnt-on-terrorism/a8def448-9549-4fde -913d-b69a2dd2bf25/.

1: John Lewis on the March on Washington, August 1963

"August 1963, D.C. Braces for March on Washington." *Washington Post.* Accessed August 9, 2019. https://www.washingtonpost.com /local/august-1963-dc-braces-for-march-on-washington/2013/08/21 /f0b6b81e-09e8-11e3-b87c-476db8ac34cd_gallery.html?utm_term= .226f03dc1453.

"Barney Frank Remarks at 2012 Democratic National Convention." You-Tube video, 8:54. Posted by "DNCConvention2012," September 7, 2012. https://www.youtube.com/watch?v=xYcwkg-7eMU.

Cox, Courtland. Interview by Jeff Nussbaum. January 12, 2021.

Digital SNCC Gateway. "John Lewis." SNCC Staff. Accessed August 9, 2019. https://snccdigital.org/people/john-lewis/.

Ghosts of DC. "1963 March on Washington Plans Included Alcohol Ban." Last updated August 28, 2013. https://ghostsofdc.org/2013/08/28/1963 -march-washington-plans-included-alcohol-ban/.

Hansen, Drew D. *The Dream: Martin Luther King, Jr., and the Speech That Inspired a Nation.* New York: Ecco, 2005.

Johnson, Angus. "John Lewis was the youngest speaker . . ." Thread Reader. Last updated July 18, 2020. https://threadreaderapp.com/thread /1284472208006545408.html.

Jones, Clarence B., and Stuart Connelly. *Behind the Dream: The Making of the Speech That Transformed a Nation.* New York: St. Martin's Press, 2011.

Kenworthy, E. W. "200,000 March for Civil Rights in Orderly Washington Rally; President Sees Gain for Negro." *New York Times,* August 29, 1963. https://timesmachine.nytimes.com/timesmachine/1963/08/29/89957615 .pdf.

King—SNCC staff biographies, 1964. Box 1, Folder 13. Mary E. King papers, 1962–1999. Wisconsin Historical Society, Madison, WI. http://content .wisconsinhistory.org/cdm/ref/collection/p15932coll2/id/24299.

Kohut, Andrew. "From the Archives: JFK's America." Pew Research Center. July 5, 2019. https://www.pewresearch.org/fact-tank/2019/07/05/jfks-america/.

Lawson, Mary Sterner. "Slater King (1927–1969)." New Georgia Encyclopedia. Last updated June 3, 2019. https://www.georgiaencyclopedia.org /articles/history-archaeology/slater-king-1927-1969.

Lewis, John, and Michael D'Orso. *Walking in the Wind: A Memoir of the Movement.* Orlando: Harvest Books, 1999.

MacGregor, Morris J. *Steadfast in the Faith: The Life of Patrick Cardinal O'Boyle.* Washington, D.C.: Catholic University of America Press, 2006.

National Archives. "What Was the March on Washington." Heroes & Villains. Accessed August 9, 2019. http://www.nationalarchives.gov.uk/education /heroesvillains/g6/cs3/.

NealJConway.com. "Cardinal O'Boyle and the 1963 March On Washington." Last updated July 23, 2013. http://www.nealjconway.com/catholic/oboyle /oboylemarch.html.

"'Normalcy-Never Again': Draft, Circa 1963 August." Writings by Martin Luther King, Jr., circa 1947–1968, Morehouse College Martin Luther King, Jr., Collection: Series 2: Writings by Martin Luther King, Jr. Robert W. Woodruff Library. Atlanta, GA.

"Note to Self: Congressman John Lewis." YouTube video, 6:29. Posted by "CBS This Morning," July 6, 2017. https://www.youtube.com/watch?v =BlD2qsfiBrg.

SNCC. "Original Draft of SNCC's March on Washington Speech, Delivered by SNCC's Chairman John Lewis." SNCC Legacy Project. Accessed September 15, 2020. https://snccdigital.org/inside-sncc/policy-statements /march-washington-speech/.

Steinberg, Dan. "When the March on Washington Canceled Two Senators Games." *Washington Post,* September 3, 2013. https://www.washingtonpost

.com/news/dc-sports-bog/wp/2013/09/03/when-the-march-on-washington
-canceled-two-senators-games/?utm_term=.6cc3c909b400.

"Thursday, August 16 Draft of Julian Castro's Convention Keynote remarks."
August 16, 2012. Jeff Nussbaum Personal Collection.

"Transcript: Ann Romney's Convention Speech." NPR, August 28, 2012. https://
www.npr.org/2012/08/28/160216442/transcript-ann-romneys-convention
-speech.

"Transcript: Gov. Chris Christie's Convention Speech." NPR, August 28, 2012.
https://www.npr.org/2012/08/28/160213518/transcript-gov-chris-christies
-convention-speech.

"Transcript: Julian Castro's DNC Keynote Address." NPR, September 4, 2012.
https://www.npr.org/2012/09/04/160574895/transcript-julian-castros-dnc
-keynote-address.

Winters, Michael Sean. "Blast from the Past: Cardinal Patrick O'Boyle."
National Catholic Reporter, August 2, 2010. https://www.ncronline.org/blogs
/distinctly-catholic/blast-past-cardinal-patrick-oboyle.

Zeleny, Jeff. "New Democratic Voice Challenges Republican Vision." *New
York Times,* September 5, 2012. https://www.nytimes.com/2012/09/05/us
/politics/julian-castro-addresses-democrats-at-convention.html.

2: Wamsutta Frank James on the 350th Anniversary of the Pilgrims Landing at Plymouth Rock, September 1970

Belcher, Edward R. "Notes on Cole's Hill." Pilgrim Hall Museum. Accessed
August 1, 2019. http://www.pilgrimhallmuseum.org/pdf/Notes_Coles_Hill
.pdf.

Blake, Andrew. "Indian Charges Censorship, Spurns Orator's Role." *Boston
Globe,* September 24, 1970.

Browne, Patrick. "Cole's Hill Sarcophagus and Pilgrim Remains." Historical
Digression. Last modified September 30, 2013. https://historicaldigression
.com/2013/09/30/coles-hill-sarcophagus-and-pilgrim-remains/.

Carr, Robert, and Andrew Blake. "Stage Plymouth Protest: Indians Take Over
Mayflower II." *Boston Globe,* November 27, 1970.

"Chatham Indian Skipped Pilgrim Event, Chief Claims Speech Censored."
Cape Cod Standard-Times, September 17, 1970.

"Indian Speaker Says State Muzzled Him." *Cape Cod Standard-Times,* September
25, 1970.

"The Indian Who Wouldn't Be Muzzled." *Massachusetts Teacher,* December
1970.

James, Moonanum. Interview by Jeff Nussbaum. June 4, 2019.

Kovach, Bill. "In a Time of Change, Plymouth, Mass. Looks Back 350 Years." *New York Times,* September 14, 1970.

Massaro, John J. "Doing the 'Pilgrim Bit' in Jet Style." *Hartford Courant,* August 30, 1970.

NavSource Online. "USS Independence (CVA-62) (*later* CV-62)." Last updated March 11, 2018. https://www.navsource.org/archives/02/62co.htm.

"Plummer M. Shearin Dies." *Washington Post,* January 2, 1998. https://www .washingtonpost.com/archive/local/1998/01/02/plummer-m-shearin-dies /ce597459-4640-4ef7-8eb8-b61a42ede36a/.

"Sargent Apologizes for Censored Speech." *Cape Codder,* October 22, 1970, 5.

"350th Anniversary: A Year-Long Event." *Boston Globe,* September 19, 1970.

United States Navy. "USS Independence (CV 62)." Last modified June 15, 2009. https://www.navy.mil/navydata/ships/carriers/histories/cv62-independence /cv62-independence.html.

"Wife Writes State: James' Boycott Backed." *Cape Cod Standard-Times,* September 25, 1970.

3: Emma Goldman at Her Sentencing, October 1893, and Helen Keller at the Suffrage Parade, March 1913

Ackerman, Ken. "Emma Goldman—Speaking Out for Free Bread, Going to Jail. PART I." Viral History. Last updated March 25, 2011. https:// kennethackerman.com/emma-goldman-speaking-out-for-free-bread-going -to-jail-part-i/.

American Foundation for the Blind. "Letter from Helen Keller to the Editor of the New York Call in Opposition of Emma Goldman's Arrest for Teaching Effective Birth Control Methods." Helen Keller Archive, Individuals, General Correspondence, Gabrielsen-Grummon. https:// www.afb.org/HelenKellerArchive?a=d&d=A-HK01-03-B056-F11- 004&e=-------en-20--1--txt--emma+goldman------3-7-6-5-3------- Keller%2C+Helen-------0-1.

"Anarchy's Den." *New York World,* July 28, 1892. Berkeley Library University of California. http://www.lib.berkeley.edu/goldman/pdfs/AnarchysDen -NewYorkWorld1892.pdf.

Berkeley Library University of California. "Emma Goldman and Free Speech." Emma Goldman Papers. http://www.lib.berkeley.edu/goldman /MeetEmmaGoldman/emmagoldmanandfreespeech.html.

Blatty, David. "From Darkness into Light: Helen Keller & Alexander Graham Bell." Biography, June 18, 2019. https://www.biography.com/news /alexander-graham-bell-and-helen-keller.

Brown, James. "Anarchism and American Traditions: Emma Goldman's Emerson and Thoreau." Annual Meeting of the American Studies Association. Internal paper presentation, Grand Hyatt, San Antonio, TX, November 26, 2014. http://citation.allacademic.com/meta/p412702_index.html.

Emerson, Ralph Waldo. "'Table Talk': 18 December 1864 (1864–1866)." *The Later Lectures of Ralph Waldo Emerson: 1843–1871,* edited by Ronald A. Bosco and Joel Myerson. Athens: University of Georgia Press, 10.

"Emma Goldman on Trial." *New York Times,* October 5, 1893. https://timesmachine.nytimes.com/timesmachine/1893/10/05/109730675.pdf.

"5,000 Women in Biggest of Suffrage Pageants." *Baltimore Sun*, March 4, 1913. ProQuest.

Goldman, Emma. *Living My Life.* New York: Dover Publications, 1970.

"Helen Keller Speaks Out." YouTube video, 3:08. Posted by "Helen Keller Channel," April 11, 2011. https://www.youtube.com/watch?v=8ch_H8pt9M8.

Huyssen, David. "We Won't Get out of the Second Gilded Age the Way We Got out of the First." *Vox,* April 1, 2019. https://www.vox.com/first-person/2019/4/1/18286084/gilded-age-income-inequality-robber-baron.

Keller, Helen. "How I Became a Socialist." *New York Call,* November 3, 1912. Marxists Internet Archive. https://www.marxists.org/reference/archive/keller-helen/works/1910s/12_11_03.htm.

Keller, Helen. "Why Men Need Women Suffrage." *New York Call,* October 17, 1913. Helen Keller Reference Archive. Marxists Internet Archive. https://www.marxists.org/reference/archive/keller-helen/works/1910s/13_10_17.htm.

"The Law's Limit." *New York World,* October 17, 1893. Berkeley Library, University of California. http://www.lib.berkeley.edu/goldman/pdfs/TheLawsLimit_NewYorkWorld_October17–1893.pdf.

Library of Congress. "Marching for the Vote: Remembering the Woman Suffrage Parade of 1913." American Women: Topical Essays. Accessed September 15, 2020. https://guides.loc.gov/american-women-essays/marching-for-the-vote.

Lumsden, Linda J. "Beauty and the Beasts: Significance of Press Coverage of the 1913 National Suffrage Parade." *JM&C Quarterly* 77, no. 3 (Autumn 2000).

McElroy, Wendy. *The Debates of Liberty: An Overview of Individualist Anarchism, 1881–1908.* Lanham, MD: Lexington Books, 2003.

Miller, Madeline. "From Circe to Clinton, Why Powerful Women Are Cast as Witches." *Guardian,* April 7, 2018. https://www.theguardian.com/books/2018/apr/07/cursed-from-circe-to-clinton-why-women-are-cast-as-witches.

Nielsen, Kim E. "The Grown Up Helen Keller." *Alabama Heritage* (Spring 2009).

Ohio History Central. "Panic of 1893." Accessed August 15, 2019. http://www.ohiohistorycentral.org/w/Panic_of_1893.

"Police Idly Watched Abuse of Women; Shocking Insults to Suffrage Paraders Testified To at Washington Inquiry." *New York Times,* March 7, 1913. https://timesmachine.nytimes.com/timesmachine/1913/03/07/100390575.html.

Safire, William. *Lend Me Your Ears: Great Speeches in History,* updated and expanded edition. New York: W. W. Norton, 2004.

"Suffrage Invasion Is On in Earnest; In Special Trains Women Hurry to Take Part in Washington Pageant." *New York Times,* March 2, 1913. https://timesmachine.nytimes.com/timesmachine/1913/03/02/100609767.html?pageNumber=15.

4: President Richard Nixon's Refusal to Resign, August 1974

American Rhetoric. "Richard M. Nixon *Checkers.*" Last updated December 12, 2018. https://www.americanrhetoric.com/speeches/richardnixoncheckers.html.

Engel, Matthew. "Proud Wife Turns 'Axis of Evil' Speech into a Resignation Letter." *Guardian,* February 26, 2002. https://www.theguardian.com/world/2002/feb/27/usa.matthewengel.

Feran, Tom. "Eisenhower and Nixon." *Cleveland.com,* February 19, 2013. https://www.cleveland.com/books/2013/02/eisenhower_and_nixon_two_terms.html.

Harrop, Froma. "Richard Nixon's 'Checkers Speech': When Blue-Collar Whites Turned Republican." *Seattle Times,* September 22, 2012. http://old.seattletimes.com/html/opinion/2019226561_harropcolumnbluecollarwhitesxml.html?syndication=rss.

Huebner, Lee. "The Checkers Speech After 60 Years." *Atlantic,* September 22, 2012. https://www.theatlantic.com/politics/archive/2012/09/the-checkers-speech-after-60-years/262172/.

Mattson, Kevin. *Just Plain Dick: Richard Nixon's Checkers Speech and the "Rocking, Socking" Election of 1952,* reprint edition. New York: Bloomsbury, 2013.

"Nixon Says He Won't Resign." *Washington Post,* August 7, 1974. ProQuest.

PBS. "President Nixon's Resignation Speech, August 8, 1974." Presidential Links. Accessed September 15, 2020. https://www.pbs.org/newshour/spc/character/links/nixon_speech.html.

Price, Ray. Option B, August 5, 1974, Speech. Box 118, Folder Option B—Resignation, Draft 8/4/74 (See also Statement 8/5 and Resignation

8/8). President's Personal Files (White House Special Files: Staff Member and Office Files), Richard Nixon Presidential Library and Museum, Yorba Linda, CA.

Price, Raymond. *With Nixon.* New York: Viking Adult, 1977.

Rueb, Emily S. "Philippe Petit's Walk Between the Towers, Aug. 7, 1964." *New York Times,* August 7, 2014. https://cityroom.blogs.nytimes.com/2014/08/07/philippe-petits-walk-between-the-towers-aug-7-1974/.

Simon, Richard, and Ricardo Alonso-Zaldivar. "Senate Approves Arming Pilots." *Los Angeles Times,* September 6, 2002. https://www.latimes.com/archives/la-xpm-2002-sep-06-na-pilots6-story.html.

"Top 10 Performing Politicians." *Time.* Accessed December 3, 2020. http://content.time.com/time/specials/packages/article/0,28804,1850902_1850905_1850907,00.html.

Watergate.info. "The Speech That Might Have Been: Nixon Refuses to Resign." Last updated December 22, 1996. https://watergate.info/1996/12/22/nixon-refuses-to-resign-speech.html.

Woestendiek, John. "The Dog Who Rescued Richard Nixon." *Baltimore Sun,* September 22, 2002. https://www.baltimoresun.com/entertainment/arts/bal-pets092202-story.html.

5: Mayor Kevin White on School Busing, December 1974

Botwright, Ken O. "S. Boston High Opening; Leaders Optimistic, Wary." *Boston Globe,* January 8, 1975.

Clendinen, Dudley. "Boston City Schools, Once Beacons, Losing Students and Pride." *New York Times,* September 20, 1981. https://www.nytimes.com/1981/09/20/us/boston-city-schools-once-beacons-losing-students-and-pride.html.

Coleman, James S. *Equality of Educational Opportunity.* Washington, D.C.: U.S. Department of Health, Education, and Welfare, Office of Education, 1966. https://files.eric.ed.gov/fulltext/ED012275.pdf.

Delmont, Matthew. "The Lasting Legacy of the Busing Crisis." *Atlantic,* March 29, 2016. https://www.theatlantic.com/politics/archive/2016/03/the-boston-busing-crisis-was-never-intended-to-work/474264/.

Eggers, William D., and John O'Leary. *If We Can Put a Man on the Moon: Getting Big Things Done in Government.* Boston: Harvard Business Review Press, 2009.

"Eyes on the Prize: The Keys to the Kingdom (1974–1980)." *Facing History and Ourselves* video, 57:46. Accessed August 14, 2019. https://www.blackstonian.org/2016/01/video-eyes-on-the-prize-boston-episode/.

Formisano, Ronald P. *Boston Against Busing: Race, Class, and Ethnicity in the 1960s and 1970s.* Chapel Hill: University of North Carolina Press, 2012.

Gellerman, Bruce. "'It Was Like a War Zone': Busing in Boston." WBUR, September 5, 2014. https://www.wbur.org/news/2014/09/05/boston-busing-anniversary.

Glovsky, Sarah. Interview by Jeff Nussbaum. June 19, 2019.

History Place. "Letter to George Meade." Abraham Lincoln. Accessed August 14, 2019, http://www.historyplace.com/lincoln/lett-6.htm.

Hornburger, Jane M. "Deep Are the Roots: Busing in Boston." *Journal of Negro Education* 45, no. 3 (1976): 237.

Husted, Ron. "Reported Crimes in Boston Up 25% over Last Year." *Boston Globe,* December 27, 1974.

Irons, Meghan E., Shelley Murphy, and Jenna Russell. "History Rolled In on a Yellow School Bus." *Boston Globe,* September 6, 2014. https://www.bostonglobe.com/metro/2014/09/06/boston-busing-crisis-years-later/DS35nsuqp0yh8f1q9aRQUL/story.html.

Jackson, Ira. Interview by Jeff Nussbaum. June 6, 2019.

Jordan, Robert. "Police Stay 'for Duration,' White Says." *Boston Globe,* September 17, 1974.

Jordan, Robert. "Question 7, Hub School Reform Fails." *Boston Globe,* November 6, 1974.

Jordan, Robert. "White Pledges to Fight for Education, Safety: Highlights of State of the City address." *Boston Globe,* January 7, 1975.

Kifner, John. "Boston Prepares for More Busing." *New York Times,* September 7, 1975. https://www.nytimes.com/1975/09/07/archives/boston-prepares-for-more-busing.html.

Kifner, John. "Judge Names Boston Mayor Co-Defendant in School Busing Case." *New York Times,* September 28, 1974.

Kifner, John. "South Boston Crowd Attacks Black as Tension Rises." *New York Times,* October 8, 1974. https://www.nytimes.com/1974/10/08/archives/south-boston-crowd-attacks-black-as-tensions-rise-south-boston.html.

Lukas, J. Anthony. *Common Ground: A Turbulent Decade in the Lives of Three American Families.* New York: Vintage Books, 1986.

Lupo, Alan. *Liberty's Chosen Home: The Politics of Violence in Boston.* Boston: Beacon Press, 1988.

McCain, John. "Address by Senator John McCain to the United States Naval Academy Class of 1993." Speech, U.S. Naval Academy, Annapolis, MD, May 26, 1993. https://www.usna63.org/tradition/history/grad-speech.html.

McCullough, David. *Truman.* New York: Simon & Schuster, 1992.

Murphy, Cullen. "Outtakes: The Rise of Provisional History." *Atlantic,* July 1, 2000. https://www.theatlantic.com/magazine/archive/2000/07/outtakes/378267/.

Murphy, Shelley. "Bulger Linked to '70s Antibusing Attacks." *boston.com,* April 22, 2001. http://archive.boston.com/news/local/massachusetts/articles/2001/04/22/bulger_linked_to_70s_antibusing_attacks/.

Northeastern University. "Letter to Residents from the Boston Home and School Association." Digital Repository Service. Created September 11, 1974. Accessed August 14, 2019. https://repository.library.northeastern.edu/downloads/neu:rx915n128?datastream_id=content.

Oakes, Bob, and Kathleen McNerney. "New Book Offers Glimpse into 'Whitey' Bulger's Early Years." WBUR, February 19, 2013. https://www.wbur.org/news/2013/02/19/whitey-bulger-book.

Overbea, Luix. "After 14 Years, Busing in Boston Rolls to a Stop." *Christian Science Monitor,* December 30, 1988. https://www.csmonitor.com/1988/1230/avisa.html.

Perlstein, Rick. *The Invisible Bridge: The Fall of Nixon and the Rise of Reagan.* New York: Simon & Schuster, 2014.

"READ: Sen. John McCain's Farewell Statement." CNN, August 27, 2018. https://www.cnn.com/2018/08/27/politics/john-mccain-farewell-statement/index.html.

Ross, Elizabeth. "The Legacy of Forced Busing in Boston." *Christian Science Monitor,* September 26, 1994. https://www.csmonitor.com/1994/0926/26091.html.

Salter, Mark. Interview by Jeff Nussbaum. November 24, 2020.

Salter, Mark. *The Luckiest Man: Life with John McCain.* New York: Simon & Schuster, 2020.

Schonberg, Harold C. "South Boston Schools Shut in Clashes over Stabbing." *New York Times,* December 12, 1974. https://www.nytimes.com/1974/12/12/archives/south-boston-schools-shut-in-clashes-over-stabbing-south-boston.html.

Schwartz, Robert. Interview by Jeff Nussbaum. June 12, 2019.

"Text of the State of the City Address." *Boston Herald American,* January 7, 1975.

Today in Civil Rights History. "President Clinton on Affirmative Action: 'Mend It, Don't End It.'" Accessed August 14, 2019. http://todayinclh.com/?event=affirmative-action-mend-it-dont-end-it.

White, Kevin. "Busing in Boston—A Beleaguered Mayor Speaks Out." Interview by *U.S. News & World Report,* full transcript released to the press on March 30, 1975.

6: Edward VIII's Refusal to Abdicate the Throne, December 1936

Bates, Stephen. "Monarch's Unheard Public Appeal to Hang On to Throne." *Guardian,* January 30, 2003. https://www.theguardian.com/uk/2003/jan/30/artsandhumanities.monarchy.

BBC. "King Edward VIII Microphone." A History of the World. Accessed August 19, 2019. http://www.bbc.co.uk/ahistoryoftheworld/objects/wm1Q2Ad7Q6Ozr-NfeLCWAg.

BBC. "Reith Diaries Dec 1936." History of the BBC. Accessed August 19, 2019. http://downloads.bbc.co.uk/historyofthebbc/Reith_diaries_Dec_1936_edit.pdf.

Beaken, Robert. *Cosmo Lang: Archbishop in War and Crisis.* London: I. B. Tauris, 2012.

Bloch, Michael. *The Reign and Abdication of King Edward VIII.* London: Transworld Publishers, 1991.

Bowcott, Owen, and Stephen Bates. "Car Dealer Was Wallis Simpson's Secret Lover." *Guardian,* January 30, 2003. https://www.theguardian.com/uk/2003/jan/30/freedomofinformation.monarchy3.

Cadbury, Deborah. *Princes at War: The Bitter Battle Inside Britain's Royal Family in the Darkest Days of WWII.* London: Bloomsbury, 2015.

Cannadine, David. "Churchill and the British Monarchy." *Transactions of the Royal Historical Society* 11 (2001): 249–272.

Casciani, Dominic. "King's Abdication Appeal Blocked." BBC News, January 30, 2003. http://news.bbc.co.uk/2/hi/uk_news/2707489.stm.

Channon, Henry. *Chips: The Diaries of Sir Henry Channon,* edited by Robert Rhodes James. London: Weidenfeld & Nicolson, 1967.

Davidson, J. C. C. *Memoirs of a Conservative: J. C. C. Davidson's Memoirs and Papers 1910–1937,* edited by Robert Rhodes James. London: Weidenfeld & Nicolson, 1969.

Davies, Caroline, Neil Tweedie, and Peter Day. "Edward VIII's Unspoken Abdication Speech." *Telegraph,* January 31, 2003. https://www.telegraph.co.uk/news/uknews/1420505/Edward-VIIIs-unspoken-abdication-speech.html.

Halle, Kay. *The Irrepressible Churchill.* Cleveland: World Publishing, 1966.

Harris, Carolyn. "Royalty and the Atlantic World 4: The Duke and Duchess of Windsor's Arrival in the Bahamas in 1940." *Carolyn Harris,* April 2, 2013. http://www.royalhistorian.com/royalty-and-the-atlantic-world-4-the-duke-and-duchess-of-windsors-arrival-in-the-bahamas-in-1940/.

History Place. "Edward VIII Abdicates the Throne." Great Speeches Collection. Accessed August 19, 2019. http://www.historyplace.com/speeches/edward.htm.

Jenkins, Roy. *Churchill: A Biography*, Cover Torn edition. London: Pan Books, 2002.

Katz, Brigit. "Newly Released Documents Reveal Churchill's Efforts to Suppress Details of Nazi Plot." *Smithsonian Magazine*, July 21, 2017. https://www.smithsonianmag.com/smart-news/newly-released -documents-reveal-churchills-efforts-suppress-details-nazi-plot-180964131 /#4HvsUtrfMdoeioVs.99.

Langworth, Richard M. "How Churchill Saw Others: Stanley Baldwin." *International Churchill Society*, winter 1998/1999. https://winstonchurchill.org /publications/finest-hour/finest-hour-101/how-churchill-saw-others-stanley -baldwin/.

Ott, Tim. "Why Edward VIII Abdicated the Throne to Marry Wallis Simpson." Biography, June 13, 2019. https://www.biography.com/news/edward-viii -abdicate-throne-wallis-simpson.

Pearson, John. *The Private Lives of Winston Churchill*. London: Bloomsbury Reader, 2013.

Phillips, Adrian. *The King Who Had to Go: Edward VIII, Mrs Simpson and the Hidden Politics of the Abdication Crisis*. London: Biteback Publishing, 2017.

Roberts, Andrew. *Churchill: Walking with Destiny*, 5th printing edition. New York: Viking Press, 2018.

Rose, Kenneth. *King George V*. London: Weidenfeld & Nicolson, 1983.

Smith, Frederick Winston Furneaux. *The Life of Viscount Monckton Brenchley*. London: Weidenfeld & Nicolson, 1969.

Tingle, Rory. "When Edward VIII Went to See Hitler: Never-Before-Seen Photos Emerge for Sale of Duke of Windsor's Infamous Trip to Nazi Germany in 1937." *Daily Mail*, October 8, 2018. https://www.dailymail.co.uk /news/article-6251937/Never-seen-photos-Edward-VIII-visiting-Mercedes -Benz-factory.html.

Vickers, Hugo. *Behind Closed Doors: The Tragic, Untold Story of Wallis Simpson*. London: Hutchinson, 2011.

Young, G. M. *Stanley Baldwin*. London: Rupert Hart-Davis, 1952.

Ziegler, Philip. *King Edward VIII*, international edition. New York: Harper-Collins, 2012.

7: New York City Mayor Abe Beame Declares Bankruptcy, October 1975

Address to the National Press Club. October 29, 1975. Box 18. President's Speeches and Statements. Gerald R. Ford Presidential Library, Ann Arbor, MI.

Al Smith Dinner, New York, October 16, 1975. Box 753. Office of the Governor: Ella Grasso. Connecticut State Library State Archives, Hartford, CT.

Auletta, Ken. "The Fixer." *New Yorker,* February 4, 2007. http://www.newyorker.com/magazine/2007/02/12/the-fixer.

Auletta, Ken. *The Streets Were Paved with Gold: The Decline of New York, an American Tragedy.* New York: Vintage Books, 1980.

Blau, Reuven. "Ford to City: Drop Dead: President's Snub Inspired, Not Discouraged, Ex-Gov. Hugh Carey." *New York Daily News,* August 8, 2011. https://www.nydailynews.com/news/politics/ford-city-drop-dead-president-snub-inspired-not-discouraged-ex-gov-hugh-carey-article-1.947295.

Churchill, Winston. "We Shall Fight on the Beaches." Speech, London, June 4, 1940. International Churchill Society. https://winstonchurchill.org/resources/speeches/1940-the-finest-hour/we-shall-fight-on-the-beaches/.

Frigand, Sid. Interview by Jeff Nussbaum. February 6, 2008.

Harrigan, Peter. "Balk by UFT pushing city to default." *Staten Island Advance,* October 17, 1975. https://www.silive.com/news/2014/07/advance_historic_page_from_oct_4.html.

Hess, David. "Mo Udall, Quick-Witted Congressman, Forced to Retire." *Baltimore Sun,* April 20, 1991. https://www.baltimoresun.com/news/bs-xpm-1991-04-20-1991110026-story.html.

Hillstrom, Thomas. "Teachers Agree to Aid NYC." *Wilmington Morning Star,* October 17, 1975. https://news.google.com/newspapers?nid=1454&dat=19751017&id=SLgsAAAAI BAJ&sjid=4AkEAAAAIBAJ&pg=4466,3757952&hl=en.

Kennedy, John F. "Special Message to the Congress on Urgent National Needs." Speech excerpt, Washington, D.C., May 25, 1961. NASA. https://www.nasa.gov/vision/space/features/jfk_speech_text.html.

Kilpatrick, Carroll. "LBJ Tells Nation He Won't Run, Restricts Raids on N. Vietnam: Johnson Declares He Won't Seek or Accept Nomination." *Washington Post,* April 1, 1968. A1.

Lankevich, George J. *New York City: A Short History.* New York: New York University Press, 1998.

Lerner, Mitchell. "Vietnam and the 1964 Election: A Defense of Lyndon Johnson." In *The United States and the Vietnam War: Leadership and Diplomacy in the Vietnam War,* edited by Walter L. Hixson. New York: Garland Publishing, 2000. 1–16.

Phillips-Fein, Kim. "Lessons from the Great Default Crisis of 1975." *Nation,* October 16, 2013. https://www.thenation.com/article/lessons-great-default-crisis-1975/.

Ravitch, Dick. Interview by Jeff Nussbaum. October 20, 2015.

Ravitch, Richard. *So Much to Do: A Full Life of Business, Politics, and Confronting Fiscal Crisis.* New York: PublicAffairs, 2014.

Reagan, Ronald. "Address to the Nation on the Iran Arms and Contra Aid Controversy." Speech, Washington, D.C., November 13, 1986. Ronald Reagan Presidential Library and Museum. https://www.reaganlibrary.gov /archives/speech/address-nation-iran-arms-and-contra-aid-controversy -november-13-1986.

Rhodes, Ben. "Inside the White House During the Syrian 'Red Line' Crisis." *The Atlantic,* June 3, 2018. https://www.theatlantic.com/international /archive/2018/06/inside-the-white-house-during-the-syrian-red-line-crisis /561887/.

Robert Hartmann Papers. Gerald R. Ford Presidential Library, Ann Arbor, MI.

Roberts, Sam. "Infamous 'Drop Dead' Was Never Said by Ford." *New York Times,* December 28, 2006. https://www.nytimes.com/2006/12/28/nyregion /28veto.html.

Roberts, Sam. "When New York Teetered on the Brink of Bankruptcy." *New York Times,* July 25, 2013. http://cityroom.blogs.nytimes.com/2013/07/25 /when-new-york-teetered-on-the-brink-of-bankruptcy/.

Rohatyn, Felix. "Voice of New York." *New York* magazine, April 11, 1988.

Rothman, Lily. "The Story Behind George H. W. Bush's Famous 'Read My Lips, No New Taxes' Promise." *Time,* December 1, 2018. https://time.com /3649511/george-hw-bush-quote-read-my-lips/.

Serviss, Lew, and Azi Paybarah. "'One Day—It's Like a Miracle—It Will Disappear': What Trump Has Said About the Pandemic and Masks." *Hartford Courant,* October 2, 2020. https://www.courant.com/coronavirus/ct -nw-nyt-trump-quotes-covid-19-20201002-4gdxkic4gra7pccvqap2llp54a -story.html.

Smothers, Ronald. "New M.A.C. Bonds Sell at Premium." *New York Times,* August 19, 1975. https://www.nytimes.com/1975/08/19/archives/new-mac -bonds-sell-at-premium-underwriter-calls-trading-a-qualified.html.

Starting Blocks. "LeBron James: 'Not 2, Not 3, Not 4, Not 5, Not 6, Not 7' Titles . . . None?: Video." Cleveland.com, January 12, 2019. https://www .cleveland.com/ohio-sports-blog/2011/06/lebron_james_not_2_not_3_not _4.html.

"Statement of Sherman in 1884 Is Recalled." *New York Times,* September 24, 1974. https://www.nytimes.com/1974/09/24/archives/statement-of -sherman-in-1884-is-recalled.html.

United Federation of Teachers. "50 Years." Accessed August 8, 2019. http:// www.uft.org/files/attachments/uft-50-years-book.pdf.

Week Staff. "Generals in the White House." *Week,* January 1, 2007. https:// theweek.com/articles/528787/generals-white-house.

Weisman, Steven R. "Teachers Reject 150-Million Loan City Needs Today."
    New York Times, October 17, 1975. https://timesmachine.nytimes.com
    /timesmachine/1975/10/17/83178387.html?pageNumber=1.

**8: Dwight Eisenhower's Apology for the Failure of the D-Day Invasion,
June 1944**

American Rhetoric. "Ronald Reagan Iran Contra Address to the Nation."
    Last modified July 17, 2018. https://www.americanrhetoric.com/speeches
    /ronaldreaganirancontraspeech.htm.
Butcher Diary, June 28–July 14, 1944 (1)(2). 1944. Box 168. Principal File.
    Dwight D. Eisenhower Pre-Presidential Papers. Eisenhower Presidential Li-
    brary and Museum.
Butcher, Harry C. *My Three Years with Eisenhower: The Personal Diary of Captain
    Harry C. Butcher, USNR, Naval Aide to General Eisenhower, 1942 to 1945.*
    New York: Simon & Schuster, 1946.
Carville, James, and Paul Begala. *Buck Up, Suck Up . . . And Come Back When
    You Foul Up: 12 Winning Secrets from the War Room.* New York: Simon &
    Schuster, 2003.
"CBS Reports (1964): D-Day Plus 20 Years—Eisenhower Returns to Nor-
    mandy." CBS News, June 5, 2019. https://www.cbsnews.com/video/cbs
    -reports-1964-d-day-plus-20-years-eisenhower-returns-to-normandy/.
Clarkson, Joy. "Mea Culpa: The Rhetoric of Apology and Confession." *Joy
    Clarkson* (blog), November 13, 2017. Accessed August 8, 2019. https://
    joyclarkson.com/home/2017/11/13/mea-culpa-the-rhetoric-of-apology-and
    -confession.
"D-Day 75: How Close Did D-Day Come to Failure?" BBC. Accessed August
    8, 2019. http://www.bbc.co.uk/guides/zgtttfr.
D-day statement to soldiers, sailors, and airmen of the Allied Expeditionary
    Force. June 1944. Collection DDE-EPRE. Eisenhower, Dwight D: Papers.
    Pre-Presidential, 1916–1952. Dwight D. Eisenhower Library; National Ar-
    chives and Records Administration.
Eisenhower, Dwight D. *Crusade in Europe,* reprint edition. Baltimore: Johns
    Hopkins University Press, 1997.
Eisenhower, Dwight D. In Case of Failure Message. June 5, 1944. Box 168,
    Butcher Diary, June 28–July 14, 1944 (2), Principal File, Eisenhower's Pre-
    Presidential Papers. Dwight D. Eisenhower Presidential Library.
Elsbach, Kimberly D. "Review of *Accounts, Excuses, and Apologies: A Theory of
    Image Restoration Strategies,* by William L. Benoit." *Administrative Science
    Quarterly* 42, no. 3 (September 1997): 584–586.

Hanania, Richard. "Does Apologizing Work? An Empirical Test of the Conventional Wisdom." *SSRN* (September 1, 2015). https://papers.ssrn.com /sol3/papers.cfm?abstract_id=2654465.

Hand, Roger. "'Okay, We'll Go.'–An Analysis of Eisenhower's Decisions Launching Overlord." *Army History,* no. 44 (Spring 1997): 23. https://www .jstor.org/stable/26304382.

Margaret Thatcher Foundation. "Remarks by President Bush ('This Will Not Stand, This Aggression Against Kuwait')." Accessed August 8, 2019. https:// www.margaretthatcher.org/document/110704.

Memmott, Mark. "It's True: 'Mistakes Were Made' Is the King of Non-Apologies." NPR, May 14, 2013. https://www.npr.org/sections/thetwo-way/2013/05/14 /183924858/its-true-mistakes-were-made-is-the-king-of-non-apologies.

Miller, Merle. *Ike the Soldier: As They Knew Him.* New York: G. P. Putnam's Sons, 1987.

Rives, Tim. "'OK, We'll Go.' Just What Did Ike Say When He Launched the D-Day Invasion 70 Years Ago?" *Prologue.* (Spring 2014). https://www .archives.gov/files/publications/prologue/2014/spring/d-day.pdf.

Rives, Tim. "General Dwight D. Eisenhower's D-Day Radio Address to the Allied Nations (June 6, 1944)." Library of Congress. Accessed August 8, 2019. http://www.loc.gov/static/programs/national-recording-preservation -board/documents/EisenhowerDDayRadioAddress.pdf.

Safire, William. "On Language: Invasion of the Verbs." *New York Times,* October 6, 1985. https://www.nytimes.com/1985/10/06/magazine/on-language -invasion-of-the-verbs.html.

Simon, Scott. "The Speech Eisenhower Never Gave on the Normandy Invasion." NPR, June 8, 2013. https://www.npr.org/2013/06/08/189535104 /the-speech-eisenhower-never-gave-on-the-normandy-invasion.

"Text: President Bush Addresses the Nation." *Washington Post,* September 20, 2001. https://www.washingtonpost.com/wp-srv/nation/specials/attacked /transcripts/bushaddress_092001.html.

9: Emperor Hirohito Apologizes for World War II, 1948

Atomic Heritage Foundation. "Potsdam Declaration." Accessed September 15, 2020. https://www.atomicheritage.org/key-documents/potsdam -declaration.

Bix, Herbert P. *Hirohito and the Making of Modern Japan.* New York: HarperCollins, 2000.

Boehm, Mike. "Lennox Tierney Dies at 101; Advocate for Asian Art in Southland." *Los Angeles Times,* June 26, 2015. https://www.latimes.com/local /obituaries/la-me-lennox-tierney-20150626-story.html.

"Cache of Rare 'Waka' Poems Written by Hirohito Emerge." *Asahi Shimbun,* January 2, 2019. http://www.asahi.com/ajw/articles/AJ201901020035 .html.

Carter, Dan T. *The Politics of Rage: George Wallace, the Origins of the New Conservatism, and the Transformation of American Politics.* Baton Rouge: Louisiana State University Press, 1995.

Columbia University. "The Potsdam Declaration (July 26, 1945)." Asia for Educators. Accessed August 7, 2019. http://afe.easia.columbia.edu/ps/japan /potsdam.pdf.

Dower, John W. *Embracing Defeat: Japan in the Wake of World War II.* New York: W. W. Norton, 2000.

"Emperor Showa Wanted to Express 'Deep Regret' in Speech, Documents Reveal." NHK World-Japan, January 22, 2020. https://www3.nhk.or.jp /nhkworld/en/news/backstories/817/.

Fisher, Max. "The Emperor's Speech: 67 Years Ago, Hirohito Transformed Japan Forever." *Atlantic,* August 15, 2012. https://www.theatlantic.com /international/archive/2012/08/the-emperors-speech-67-years-ago-hirohito -transformed-japan-forever/261166/.

Haney López, Ian. *Dog Whistle Politics.* Oxford: Oxford University Press, 2014.

Hastings, Max. "Ask MHQ: How Hirohito Escaped the Hangman's Noose." HistoryNet, August 10, 2010. https://www.historynet.com/ask-mhq -hirohito.htm.

"Hirohito's 'Jewel Voice Broadcast.'" *Air Force Magazine,* August 2012. Archive.org. https://web.archive.org/web/20130910212019/http://www .airforcemag.com/MagazineArchive/Pages/2012/August%202012 /0812keeper.aspx.

Kodera, Atsushi. "Pictures of World War II Imperial Shelter Released to Public for First Time in 50 years." *Japan Times,* August 1, 2015. https:// www.japantimes.co.jp/news/2015/08/01/national/history/pictures -world-war-ii-imperial-shelter-released-public-first-time-50-years/#.XB -otVxKiUk.

Kyodo. "Emperor Hirohito 'Too Weak' to Stop Japan Entering Second World War, Declassified Documents Show." *South China Morning Post,* July 20, 2017. https://www.scmp.com/news/asia/east-asia/article/2103390 /powerless-hirohito-opposed-japanese-involvement-second-world-war.

Kyodo. "The Coup Against the Emperor's Broadcast That Never Was." *Japan Times,* August 6, 2015. https://www.japantimes.co.jp/news/2015/08/06 /national/history/coup-emperors-broadcast-never/#.XQkCIIhKiUk.

LaPlante, Matthew D. "MacArthur Aide: U.S. Must Learn from Errors." *Salt Lake Tribune,* December 7, 2006. https://archive.sltrib.com/article.php?id =4794305&itype=NGPSID.

Large, Stephen. *Emperor Hirohito and Showa Japan: A Political Biography.* New York: Routledge, 1992.

Luntz, Frank I. *Words That Work: It's Not What You Say, It's What People Hear.* New York: Hyperion, 2008.

Morin, Richard. "Behind the Numbers Confessions of a Pollster." *Washington Post,* October 16, 1988. https://www.washingtonpost.com /archive/opinions/1988/10/16/behind-the-numbers-confessions-of -a-pollster/3523c065-11b5-42ba-9986-c317bdecf2dd/?utm_term= .3638818efa2e.

National Diet Library, Japan. "Incoming Classified Message From: CINCAF-PAC Adv Tokyo, Japan To: War Department." Accessed August 7, 2019. https://www.ndl.go.jp/constitution/e/shiryo/03/064/064_002l.html.

National Diet Library, Japan. "Press Release, Gen. MacArthur Sees Liberalism in Imperial Rescript." Accessed August 7, 2019. https://www.ndl.go.jp /constitution/e/shiryo/03/057/057_001l.html.

Rinjiro, Sodei. *Dear General MacArthur: Letters from the Japanese During the American Occupation.* Lanham, MD: Rowman & Littlefield, 2006.

Safire, William. *Safire's Political Dictionary.* Oxford: Oxford University Press, 2008.

Sebestyen, Victor. "How the Emperor Became Human (and MacArthur Became Divine)." *Longreads,* November 2015. https://longreads.com /2015/11/11/how-the-emperor-became-human-and-macarthur-became -divine/.

Sunstein, Cass R. "In Politics, Apologies Are for Losers." *New York Times,* July 27, 2019. https://www.nytimes.com/2019/07/27/opinion/sunday/when -should-a-politician-apologize.html.

United States Department of State. "The Nuremberg Trial and the Tokyo War Crimes Trials (1945–1948)." Milestones: 1945–1952. Accessed August 7, 2019. https://history.state.gov/milestones/1945-1952 /nuremberg.

Vincent, Lynn, and Sara Vladic. *Indianapolis: The True Story of the Worst Sea Disaster in U.S. Naval History and the Fifty-Year Fight to Exonerate an Innocent Man.* New York: Simon & Schuster, 2018.

「朕(ちん)ノ不徳(ふとく)ナル、深(ふか)ク天下(てんか)ニ愧(は)ヅ」の衝撃大論争「昭和天皇国民への謝罪詔書草稿」四つの謎 / 加藤恭子;高橋紘;秦郁彦【他】; *Bungei shunju,* August 2003, 166–180.

「詔書草稿」をこう読んだ-熟読玩味した十一人の目に映じたこの文書の意義; *Bungei shunju,* August 2003, 182–189.

10: President Kennedy on the Military Operation That Destroyed the Nuclear Weapons Buildup in Cuba, October 1962

American Rhetoric. "Cuban Missile Crisis Address to the Nation Delivered 22 October 1962." John F. Kennedy. Accessed August 16, 2019. https://americanrhetoric.com/speeches/jfkcubanmissilecrisis.html.

Bernstein, Adam. "Charles Bartlett, Pulitzer-Winning Journalist and Kennedy Loyalist, Dies at 95." *Washington Post,* February 18, 2017. https://www.washingtonpost.com/national/charles-bartlett-pulitzer-winning-journalist-and-kennedy-loyalist-dies-at-95/2017/02/18/0c9d22d0-f553-11e6-b9c9-e83fce42fb61_story.html?utm_term=.7373a5c9ba2f.

Bird, Kai. *The Color of Truth: McGeorge Bundy and William Bundy: Brothers in Arms.* New York: Simon & Schuster, 1998.

Bundy, McGeorge. *Danger and Survival: Choices About the Bomb in the First Fifty Years.* New York: Random House, 1988.

Chang, Laurence, and Peter Kornbluh, ed. *The Cuban Missile Crisis, 1962: A National Security Archive Documents Reader.* New York: The New Press, 1998.

Chicago History Today. "Kennedy's Cold (10-19-1962)." Last updated October 19, 2016. https://chicagohistorytoday.wordpress.com/2016/10/19/kennedys-cold-10-19-1962/.

Clinton, William J. "Remarks at a Ceremony Presenting the Presidential Medal of Freedom to Former President Jimmy Carter and Rosalynn Carter in Atlanta." Remarks, Atlanta, GA, August 9, 1999. Govinfo. https://www.govinfo.gov/content/pkg/PPP-1999-book2/pdf/PPP-1999-book2-doc-pg1421.pdf.

"50th Anniversary of the Missile Gap Controversy." Transcript of forum, Boston, MA, September 26, 2011. John F. Kennedy Presidential Library and Museum. https://www.jfklibrary.org/events-and-awards/forums/past-forums/transcripts/50th-anniversary-of-the-missile-gap-controversy.

"JFK in Cleveland, Ohio (October 19, 1962)." YouTube video, 7:35. Posted by "David Von Pein's JFK Channel," March 1, 2015. https://www.youtube.com/watch?v=7XkAIUMuhZc.

John F. Kennedy Presidential Library and Museum. "Congressional Campaign Trip: Cleveland, Ohio, Arrival, Rally, Motorcade, Departure." White House Photographs. Created October 19, 1962. Accessed August 16, 2019. https://www.jfklibrary.org/asset-viewer/archives/JFKWHP/1962/Month%2010/Day%2019/JFKWHP-1962-10-19-B.

John F. Kennedy Presidential Library and Museum. "President's Speech Air Attack." 6–4–2: Cuba: Cuban Crisis, 1962: Kennedy-Khrushchev Letters, etc. Accessed August 16, 2019. https://www.jfklibrary.org/asset-viewer/archives/RFKAG/217/RFKAG-217-001.

John F. Kennedy Presidential Library and Museum. "Remarks at Cook County Democratic Party Dinner, Chicago, Illinois, 19 October 1962."

Papers of John F. Kennedy, Presidential Papers. President's Office Files. https://www.jfklibrary.org/asset-viewer/archives/JFKPOF/041/JFKPOF -041-017.

Kennedy, John F. "Remarks of Senator John F. Kennedy at Citizens for Kennedy Rally, Waldorf Astoria." Remarks, New York, September 14, 1960. John F. Kennedy Presidential Library and Museum. https://www .jfklibrary.org/archives/other-resources/john-f-kennedy-speeches/citizens -for-kennedy-rally-nyc-19600914.

Kennedy, Robert F. *Thirteen Days: A Memoir of the Cuban Missile Crisis.* New York: W. W. Norton, 1999.

Lindsay, James M. "TWE Remembers: Secret Soviet Tactical Nuclear Weapons in Cuba (Cuban Missile Crisis; a Coda)." Council on Foreign Relations, October 29, 2012. https://www.cfr.org/blog/twe-remembers-secret-soviet -tactical-nuclear-weapons-cuba-cuban-missile-crisis-coda.

May, Ernest R., and Philip D. Zelikow. *The Kennedy Tapes: Inside the White House During the Cuban Missile Crisis,* concise edition. New York: W. W. Norton, 2002.

Papers of Robert F. Kennedy. Attorney General Papers. Attorney General's Confidential File. 6–4–2: Cuba: Cuban Crisis, 1962: Kennedy-Khrushchev Letters, Etc.

Songer, Mark. "Affidavit of Mark Songer." Affidavit. Denver, CO. September 3, 2019. Robson Forensic.

Sorensen, Ted. *Counselor: A Life at the Edge of History,* reprint edition. New York: Harper Perennial, 2009.

Sorensen, Ted. Interview by Jeremy Isaacs Productions. *Cold War*, CNN, March 1997. https://nsarchive2.gwu.edu/coldwar/interviews/episode-10 /sorensen2.html.

Stimson, Henry. "Stimson on the Bomb." Atomic Heritage Foundation. Accessed August 16, 2019. https://www.atomicheritage.org/key-documents /stimson-bomb.

Tamayo, Juan O. "Secret Nukes: The Untold Story of the Cuban Missile Crisis." *Miami Herald,* October 13, 2012. https://www.miamiherald.com/latest -news/article1943643.html.

11: Illinois Governor John Peter Altgeld's Farewell Address Following His Defeat in the 1896 Election, January 1897

Adelman, William J. "The Haymarket Affair." Illinois Labor History Society. Accessed August 15, 2019. http://www.illinoislaborhistory.org/the-haymarket-affair.

"Altgeld and the Anarchists." *New York Times,* June 28, 1893. https:// timesmachine.nytimes.com/timesmachine/1893/06/28/109703245.pdf.

Altgeld, John P. *Live Questions.* Chicago: Geo S. Bowen & Sons, 1899. https://archive.org/details/livequestions00altg/page/4.

Altgeld, John P. *Our Penal Machinery and Its Victims.* Chicago: A. C. McClurg, 1886. https://archive.org/details/ourpenalmachiner00altguoft/page/n5,n8.

Altgeld, John Peter. *The Mind and Spirit of John Peter Altgeld: Selected Writings and Addresses,* edited by Henry M. Christman. Champaign: University of Illinois Press, 1960.

Avrich, Paul. *The Haymarket Tragedy.* Princeton, NJ: Princeton University Press, 1984.

Barnard, Harry. *Eagle Forgotten: The Life of John Peter Altgeld.* New York: Duell, Sloan and Pearce, 1938.

"Bomb Thrown into a Crowd of Policemen." *Chicago Tribune,* May 5, 1886. ProQuest.

Chicago Historical Society Haymarket Affair Digital Collection. "Illinois vs. August Spies et al. Trial Transcript No. 1. Testimony of Louis Haas (Second Appearance), 1886 July 27." Accessed August 15, 2019. http://www.chicagohistoryresources.org/hadc/transcript/volumek/251-300/K258-284.htm.

De Grazia, Edward. "The Haymarket Bomb." *Law and Literature* 18, no. 3 (2006): 283–322. Accessed September 25, 2020. doi:10.1525/lal.2006.18.3.283.

Famous Trials by Professor Douglas O. Linder. "The Pardon of the Haymarket Prisoners (June 26, 1893)." Accessed August 15, 2019. https://famous-trials.com/haymarket/1182-pardon.

George Mason University. "Haymarket Martyr Albert Parsons's Last Words to His Wife." History Matters: The U.S. Survey Course on the Web. Accessed August 15, 2019. http://historymatters.gmu.edu/d/46/.

"Give Me Liberty or Give Me Death!" Colonial Williamsburg, March 3, 2020. https://www.colonialwilliamsburg.org/learn/deep-dives/give-me-liberty-or-give-me-death/.

Lehrman, Robert A., and Eric Schnure. *The Political Speechwriter's Companion: A Guide for Writers and Speakers,* 2nd edition. Thousand Oaks, CA: CQ Press, 2020.

McNamara, Robert. "How a Bomb Tossed in 1886 Impacted the American Labor Movement." ThoughtCo., January 18, 2019. https://www.thoughtco.com/1886-haymarket-square-riot-chicago-1773901.

Safire, William. "On Language: Sound Bite, Define Yourself!" *New York Times,* November 13, 1988. https://www.nytimes.com/1988/11/13/magazine/on-language-sound-bite-define-yourself.html.

Sampson, Robert D. "Governor John Peter Altgeld Pardons the Haymarket Prisoners." Illinois Labor History Society. Accessed August 15, 2019. http://

www.illinoislaborhistory.org/labor-history-articles/governor-john-peter
-altgeld-pardons-the-haymarket-prisoners.

"Schilling, George A. (1850–1938)." Abraham Lincoln Presidential Library
and Museum. Accessed August 15, 2019. http://alplm.libraryhost.com/?p
=creators/creator&id=63.

University of Minnesota Law Library. "In Memoriam John Peter Altgeld."
Clarence Darrow Digital Collection. Accessed August 15, 2019. http://
moses.law.umn.edu/darrow/documents/In_Memoriam_Altgeld.pdf.

Zorn, Eric. "Altgeld's Legacy Shows True Impact of 'Tough Decision.'" *Chicago
Tribune,* March 6, 1999. https://www.chicagotribune.com/news/ct-xpm
-1999-03-16-9903160060-story.html.

12: Hillary Clinton's 2016 Victory Speech, November 2016

Benenson, Joel. Interviewed by Jeff Nussbaum. September 1, 2019.

Bump, Philip. "How Bill Clinton's Statement on Al Gore's 2000 Presidential
Concession Evolved." *Atlantic,* March 14, 2014. https://www.theatlantic
.com/politics/archive/2014/03/how-bill-clintons-statement-al-gores-2000
-presidential-concession-evolved/359196/.

Bush, Daniel. "How Trump Could Rewrite Concession Speech History."
PBS NewsHour, October 31, 2016. https://www.pbs.org/newshour/politics
/trump-rewrite-concession-speech-history.

Cauterucci, Christina. "Hillary Clinton Is the First Presidential Candidate to
Say 'I'm Sorry' in Concession Speech." *Slate,* November 15, 2016. https://
slate.com/human-interest/2016/11/hillary-clinton-is-the-first-presidential
-candidate-to-say-im-sorry-in-concession-speech.html.

Clinton, Hillary. "Hillary Clinton's Concession Speech (Full Text)." Speech,
New York City, November 9, 2016. CNN. https://www.cnn.com/2016/11
/09/politics/hillary-clinton-concession-speech/index.html.

Clinton, Hillary. *What Happened.* New York: Simon & Schuster, 2017.

Clinton, William J. "Remarks on the Resolution of the 2000 Presidential Election and an Exchange with Reporters in North Aylesbury, United Kingdom."
Speech, North Aylesbury, United Kingdom, December 14, 2000. U.S. Government Publishing Office. https://www.govinfo.gov/content/pkg/PPP
-2000-book3/pdf/PPP-2000-book3-doc-pg2696-2.pdf.

Conroy, Scott. *Sarah from Alaska: The Sudden Rise and Brutal Education of a
New Conservative Superstar.* New York: PublicAffairs, 2009.

Easton, Lauren. "Calling the Presidential Race State by State." Associated
Press, November 9, 2016. https://blog.ap.org/behind-the-news/calling-the
-presidential-race-state-by-state.

"FOIA 2006–0221-F-2000 Presidential Election Vote Count in Florida." Clinton Digital Library. Accessed December 4, 2020. https://clinton .presidentiallibraries.us/items/show/14500.

Friedman, Uri. "The Damage Will Last." *Atlantic,* November 27, 2020. https://www.theatlantic.com/ideas/archive/2020/11/trumps-refusal-to -concede-wasnt-some-sideshow/617215/.

Hertzberg, Hendrik. "Concession Stand." *New Yorker,* November 3, 1996. https://www.newyorker.com/magazine/1996/11/11/concession -stand.

"Hillary Clinton Declares 'Women's Rights Are Human Rights.'" PBS, September 8, 1995. https://www.pbs.org/weta/washingtonweek/web-video/hillary -clinton-declares-womens-rights-are-human-rights.

"Hillary Clinton Statement on Emails Investigation." C-SPAN, October 28, 2016. https://www.c-span.org/video/?417629–2/hillary-clinton-calls-release -information-email-investigation.

Hunt, George P. "Editors' Note." *Life,* June 21, 1968.

Kennedy, Robert F. "Remarks at the University of Kansas, March 18, 1968." Kennedy Family. John F. Kennedy Presidential Library and Museum. Accessed August 6, 2019. https://www.jfklibrary.org/learn/about-jfk/the -kennedy-family/robert-f-kennedy/robert-f-kennedy-speeches/remarks-at -the-university-of-kansas-march-18-1968.

McGregor, Jena. "Remembering a Speech from 'the Most Beautiful Loser' After Trump Won't Commit to Accepting Results." *Washington Post,* October 20, 2016. https://www.washingtonpost.com/news/on-leadership/wp/2016 /10/20/remembering-a-speech-from-the-most-beautiful-loser-after-trump -wont-commit-to-accepting-results/.

Noonan, Peggy. *What I Saw at the Revolution: A Political Life in the Reagan Era.* New York: Random House, 1990.

P2016. "Travels of Hillary Clinton." Accessed August 8, 2019. http://www .p2016.org/clinton/clintoncal1016.html.

Palmieri, Jen. Interview by Jeff Nussbaum. January 13, 2019.

Revesz, Rachel. "Hillary Clinton Hugs Sobbing Girl Worried That Her Parents Are to Be Deported." *Independent,* February 18, 2016. https://www .independent.co.uk/news/world/americas/us-elections/hillary-clinton-hugs -sobbing-girl-worried-that-her-parents-are-to-be-deported-a6881611.html.

Schwerin, Dan. Interview by Jeff Nussbaum. January 11, 2017.

Scully, Matthew. Interview by Jeff Nussbaum. August 31, 2020.

Silver, Nate. "The Comey Letter Probably Cost Clinton the Election." *FiveThirtyEight,* May 3, 2017. https://fivethirtyeight.com/features/the-comey-letter -probably-cost-clinton-the-election/.

Smith, Ben. "Why Palin Didn't Get a Concession Speech." *Politico,* April 26, 2009. https://www.politico.com/blogs/ben-smith/2009/04/why-palin-didnt -get-a-concession-speech-017822.

Snow, Katie, and Kelly Hagan. "Sarah Palin's Never-Heard Victory, Concession Speeches." ABC News, November 4, 2009. https://abcnews.go.com/GMA /Politics/sarah-palin-speeches-heard/story?id=8988514.

Stein, Jeff. "Hillary Clinton: I'm Breathing a 'Big Sigh of Relief' After Iowa Caucus." *Vox,* February 2, 2016. https://www.vox.com/2016/2/2/10892714 /hillary-clinton-iowa-reaction.

Sullivan, Jake. Interview by Jeff Nussbaum. January 16, 2019.

"Text of Gore's Concession Speech." *New York Times,* December 13, 2000. https://www.nytimes.com/2000/12/13/politics/text-of-goreacutes -concession-speech.html.

Updike, John. "Hub Fans Bid Kid Adieu." *New Yorker,* October 22, 1960. https://www.newyorker.com/magazine/1960/10/22/hub-fans-bid-kid-adieu.

Walshe, Shushannah, and Scott Conroy. "Sarah Palin's Lost Speeches." *Daily Beast,* July 14, 2017. https://www.thedailybeast.com/sarah-palins-lost -speeches.

Part 6: Events Intervene

Twain, Mark. "An Undelivered Speech." Undelivered speech, Philadelphia, PA, March 25, 1895. *Project Gutenberg's Mark Twain's Speeches.* https://www .gutenberg.org/files/3188/3188-h/3188-h.htm.

13: The Remarks Condoleezza Rice Had Intended to Give on the Bush Administration's Foreign Policy, September 11, 2001

Balz, Dan. "Poll Finds Public Wary on Tax Cut." *Washington Post,* September 11, 2001.

Boese, Wade. "U.S. Withdraws from ABM Treaty, Response Muted." *Arms Control Today,* July/August 2002. https://www.armscontrol.org/act/2002-07 /news/us-withdraws-abm-treaty-global-response-muted.

Bush, George W. "President Bush Speech on Missile Defense." Speech given at the White House, Washington, D.C., May 1, 2001. https://fas.org/nuke /control/abmt/news/010501bush.html.

Commission to Assess the Ballistic Missile Threat to the United States. *Executive Summary of the Report of the Commission to Assess the Ballistic Missile Threat to the United States.* by Hon. Donald H. Rumsfeld, Dr. Barry M. Blechman, Gen. Lee Butler, USAF (Ret.), Dr. Richard L. Garwin, Dr. William R. Graham, Dr. William Schneider, Jr., Gen. Larry D. Welch, USAF

(Ret.), Dr. Paul D. Wolfowitz, and Hon. R. James Woolsey. Washington, D.C.: Printing and Production Graphics, 1998. https://fas.org/irp/threat/bm-threat.htm.

Daalder, Ivo H., and James M. Lindsay. "Unilateral Withdrawal from the ABM Treaty Is a Bad Idea." Brookings, April 30, 2001. https://www.brookings.edu/opinions/unilateral-withdrawal-from-the-abm-treaty-is-a-bad-idea/.

"Dow Jones Industrial Average." U.S. Securities and Exchange Commission. Accessed May 25, 2020. https://www.sec.gov/Archives/edgar/data/357298/000035729801500016/dowjones.html.

"Floor Statement on the Nomination of Condoleezza Rice to Be Secretary of State." Sen. Jack Reed, January 25, 2005. https://www.congress.gov/109/crec/2005/01/25/CREC-2005-01-25-senate.pdf.

Gertanzang, James. "Weinberger Sees End of 'Mutual Suicide Pact.'" Los Angeles Times, October 10, 1985. https://www.latimes.com/archives/la-xpm-1985–10–10-mn-15630-story.html.

Glass, Andrew. "President Reagan Calls for Launching 'Star Wars' Initiative, March 23, 1983." Politico, March 23, 2017. https://www.politico.com/story/2017/03/president-reagan-calls-for-launching-star-wars-initiative-march-23-1983-236259.

Lehrman, Robert A., and Eric Schnure. The Political Speechwriter's Companion: A Guide for Writers and Speakers, 2nd edition. Thousand Oaks, CA: CQ Press, 2020.

Meet the Press, September 9, 2001. NBCUniversal. 2001. https://video-alexanderstreet-com.ezproxy.cul.columbia.edu/watch/meet-the-press-september-9–2001 (subscription required).

"Modest Support for Missile Defense, No Panic on China." Pew Research Center, June 11, 2001. https://www.people-press.org/2001/06/11/modest-support-for-missile-defense-no-panic-on-china/.

Mufson, Steven. "Sen. Biden Attacks Missile Defense Plan as Costly, Risky." Washington Post, September 11, 2001.

National Security Council—Media Communications and Speechwriting. George W. Bush Library, Dallas, TX.

Perlez, Jane. "Rice on Front Line in Foreign Policy Role." New York Times, August 19, 2001. https://www.nytimes.com/2001/08/19/world/rice-on-front-line-in-foreign-policy-role.html.

Progressive Management. Hitting a Bullet with a Bullet: A History of Ballistic Missile Defense (BMD)—Nike, Sprint and Spartan, Strategic Defense Initiative (SDI) Star Wars. 2016.

Reagan, Ronald. "Address to the Nation on Defense and National Security." Speech given at the White House, Washington, D.C., March 23, 1983. https://www.reaganlibrary.gov/research/speeches/32383d.

Rice, Condoleezza. "Remarks by National Security Advisor Condoleezza Rice on Terrorism and Foreign Policy." Lecture given at the Paul H. Nitze School of Advanced International Studies, Washington, D.C., April 29, 2002. https://georgewbush-whitehouse.archives.gov/news/releases/2002/04/20020429-9.html.

"'Star Wars': How the Term Arose." *New York Times,* September 25, 1985. https://www.nytimes.com/1985/09/25/world/star-wars-how-the-term-arose.html.

Twin, Alexandra. "Bears vs. Bulls on Wall St." CNN Money, September 10, 2001. https://money.cnn.com/2001/09/10/markets/markets_newyork/.

"US Ballistic Missile Defense Timeline: 1945–Today." Union of Concerned Scientists, March 29, 2019. https://www.ucsusa.org/resources/us-missile-defense-timeline.

Wright, Robin. "Top Focus Before 9/11 Wasn't on Terrorism." *Washington Post,* April 1, 2004. https://www.washingtonpost.com/archive/politics/2004/04/01/top-focus-before-911-wasnt-on-terrorism/a8def448-9549-4fde-913d-b69a2dd2bf25/.

14: Barry Jenkins's Best Picture Remarks for *Moonlight,* February 2017

Academy Awards Acceptance Speech Database. "Year: 2016 (89th) Academy Awards, Category: Best Picture: Moonlight." Accessed August 9, 2019. http://aaspeechesdb.oscars.org/results.aspx?AC=NEXT_RECORD&XC=/results.aspx&B U=http%3A%2F%2Faaspeechesdb.oscars.org%2F&TN=aatrans&SN=AUTO24937&SE =767&RN=14&M-R=0&TR=0&TX=1000&ES=0&CS=0&XP=&RF=WebReportList&E F=&DF=WebReportOscars&RL=0&EL=0&DL=0&NP=255&ID=&M-F=oscarsmsg.ini& MQ=&TI=0&DT=&ST=0&IR=0&NR=0&N-B=0&SV=0&SS =0&BG=&FG=&QS=&OEX=ISO-8859–1&OEH=utf-8.

Box Office Mojo. "Moonlight 2016." Accessed August 9, 2019. https://www.boxofficemojo.com/movies/?page=weekend&id=moonlight2016.htm.

Carroll, Rory, and Andrew Pulver. "Moonlight Wins Best Picture Oscar, After Warren Beatty Gives Gong to La La Land." *Guardian,* February 27, 2017. https://www.theguardian.com/film/2017/feb/27/moonlight-wins-best-picture-oscars-academy-award-2017.

Feinberg, Scott. "Oscars Primer: What You Need to Know Before Tonight's Ceremony." *Hollywood Reporter,* February 26, 2017. https://www.hollywoodreporter.com/race/oscars-primer-what-you-need-know-before-tonights-ceremony-980175.

Heath, Chip, and Dan Heath. *Made to Stick: Why Some Ideas Survive and Others Die.* New York: Random House, 2007.

Kennedy, John F. "John F. Kennedy Moon Speech—Rice Stadium." Speech, Houston, TX, September 12, 1962. NASA. https://er.jsc.nasa.gov/seh/ricetalk.htm.

Lehrman, Robert A., and Eric Schnure. *The Political Speechwriter's Companion: A Guide for Writers and Speakers,* 2nd edition. Thousand Oaks, CA: CQ Press, 2020.

McHenry, Jackson. "Here's What Barry Jenkins Would Have Said at the Oscars, If Given the Chance." *Vulture,* March 12, 2018. https://www.vulture.com/2018/03/barry-jenkins-reads-his-moonlight-oscars-acceptance-speech.html.

N'Duka, Amanda. "'Moonlight' Writers Dedicate Oscar Win to the Underrepresented." *Deadline,* February 26, 2017. https://deadline.com/2017/02/moonlight-best-adapted-screenplay-oscar-2017-1202004715/.

Rose, Lacey. "Race, Barriers and Battling Nerves: A Candid Conversation with Oscar's Only 4 African-American Directing Nominees in 90 Years." *Hollywood Reporter,* February 23, 2018. https://www.hollywoodreporter.com/features/race-barriers-battling-nerves-a-candid-conversation-oscars-4-african-american-directing-nominees-90–1087644?utm_source=Sailthru&utm_medium=email&utm_campaign=THR%20Breakin g%20News_2018-02-23%2007:15:00_lhuff&utm_term=hollywoodreporter_breakingnews.

Safire, William. *Lend Me Your Ears: Great Speeches in History,* 2nd edition. New York: W. W. Norton, 2004.

Schmerling, Robert H. "Is Aspirin a Wonder Drug?" *Harvard Health Publishing,* December 22, 2016. https://www.health.harvard.edu/blog/aspirin-wonder-drug-2016122210916.

Stix, Gary. "Fact or Fiction?: Oxytocin Is the 'Love Hormone.'" *Scientific American,* September 8, 2014. https://www.scientificamerican.com/article/fact-or-fiction-oxytocin-is-the-love-hormone/.

Strause, Jackie. "Oscars: 'La La Land' Director Damien Chazelle Becomes Youngest Best Director Winner." *Hollywood Reporter,* February 26, 2017. https://www.hollywoodreporter.com/news/damien-chazelles-best-director-oscars-2017-win-makes-him-youngest-winner-980243.

THR Staff. "Golden Globes: 'Moonlight' Wins Best Motion Picture, Drama." *Hollywood Reporter,* January 1, 2017. https://www.hollywoodreporter.com/news/moonlight-wins-best-motion-picture-drama-golden-globes-2017-960354.

THR Staff. "Oscars 2017: The Order That the Awards Will Be Announced." *Hollywood Reporter,* February 26, 2017. https://www.hollywoodreporter.com/news/oscars-2017-guide-order-awards-presented-980082.

Twain, Mark. *Project Gutenberg's Mark Twain's Speeches.* Project Gutenberg. 2006. https://www.gutenberg.org/files/3188/3188-h/3188-h.htm.

Yan, Holly. "Mahershala Ali Becomes First Muslim Actor to Win an Oscar." CNN, February 27, 2017. https://www.cnn.com/2017/02/27/entertainment /mahershala-ali-first-muslim-oscar-winner-trnd/index.html.

Yee, Lawrence, Stuart Oldham, and Jacob Bryant. "New Photos Show PWC Accountant Tweeting, Mixing Envelopes Backstage at Oscars (EXCLU-SIVE)." *Variety*, March 1, 2017. https://variety.com/2017/film/news/oscar -best-picture-gaffe-brian-cullinan-envelope-1201999283/.

15: Last Words: Pope Pius XI, JFK, FDR, and Einstein, and Their Unfinished Prophecies of Peace, Various Years

Alvarez, David. *Washington Post*, May 31, 2013. https://www.washingtonpost .com/opinions/2013/05/31/224e4830-9c5f-11e2-9bda-edd1a7fb557d _story.html?_=ddid-8-1563203160&noredirect=on&utm_term= .a94c332748a7.

Berger, Paul. "What Was Albert Einstein's True Relationship to Judaism—and Zionism?" *Forward*, November 22, 2015. https://forward.com/news /325189/what-was-einsteins-relationship-to-judaism-and-zionism/.

"Draft Speech of Vice-President Harry S. Truman for Jefferson Day Dinner, Washington, D.C." April 1945. Container 289. Harry S. Truman Papers as U.S. Senator and Vice President, 1935–1945. Harry S. Truman Library, Independence, MO.

Eban, Abba. *Personal Witness: Israel Through My Eyes.* New York: G. P. Putnam's Sons, 1992.

Einstein, Albert. "A Final Undelivered Message to the World, April 1955." In *Einstein on Politics: His Private Thoughts and Public Stands on Nationalism, Zionism, War, Peace, and the Bomb,* edited by David E. Rowe and Robert Schulman. Princeton, NJ: Princeton University Press, 2013. 506–507.

"Einstein Cremated; Bequeathed His Brain to Medical Research." Jewish Telegraphic Agency, April 21, 1955. http://pdfs.jta.org/1955/1955-04-20 _076.pdf?_ga=2.233642523.409623967.1565642018-563851594 .1562694758.

Faber, Harold. "Lost Copy of 'Day of Infamy' Speech Found." *New York Times*, April 2, 1984. https://timesmachine.nytimes.com/timesmachine/1984/04 /02/093684.html.

Fattorini, Emma. *Hitler, Mussolini, and the Vatican: Pope Pius XI and the Speech That Was Never Made.* Cambridge: Polity Press, 2011.

George C. Marshall Foundation. "The Marshall Plan Speech." Accessed August 12, 2019. https://www.marshallfoundation.org/marshall/the-marshall -plan/marshall-plan-speech/.

Glass, Andrew. "Jefferson and Adams Die Hours Apart, July 4, 1826." *Politico,* July 3, 2016. https://www.politico.com/story/2016/07/two-founding-fathers-die-hours-apart-july-4-1826-224943.

"Jefferson Dinners to Hear Roosevelt." *New York Times,* April 6, 1945. https://timesmachine.nytimes.com/timesmachine/1945/04/06/88211743.html?pageNumber=18.

John F. Kennedy. "Remarks Prepared for Delivery at the Trade Mart in Dallas, TX, November 22, 1963 [Undelivered]." Speech, Dallas, TX, November 22, 1963. John F. Kennedy Presidential Library and Museum. https://www.jfklibrary.org/archives/other-resources/john-f-kennedy-speeches/dallas-tx-trade-mart-undelivered-19631122.

Kohut, Andrew. "From the Archives: JFK's America." Pew Research Center, July 5, 2019. https://www.pewresearch.org/fact-tank/2019/07/05/jfks-america/.

Loftus, Joseph A. "Johnson Promised Place on a '64 Kennedy Ticket." *New York Times,* November 1, 1963. https://timesmachine.nytimes.com/timesmachine/1963/11/01/89969513.html?pageNumber=1.

Markel, Howard. "Franklin D. Roosevelt's Painfully Eloquent Final Words." PBS, April 12, 2018. https://www.pbs.org/newshour/health/the-quiet-final-hours-of-franklin-d-roosevelt.

Mussolini, Benito. *God Does Not Exist,* translated by George Seldes. Lausanne, Switzerland: 1904. https://archive.org/details/GodDoesNotExist.

Onion, Rebecca. "The 'Wanted for Treason' Flyer Distributed in Dallas Before JFK's Visit." *Slate,* November 15, 2013. https://slate.com/human-interest/2013/11/jfk-assassination-flyer-distributed-in-dallas-by-edwin-walker-s-group-before-his-visit.html.

Pace, Eric. "Gen. Edwin Walker, 83, Is Dead." *New York Times,* November 2, 1993. https://timesmachine.nytimes.com/timesmachine/1993/11/02/481393.html?pageNumber=34.

Pomfret, John D. "Kennedy Calls Jobs Vital, Outranking Civil Rights." *New York Times,* November 16, 1963. https://timesmachine.nytimes.com/timesmachine/1963/11/16/89973625.html.

Rabinowitz, Gavin. "Einstein's Theory of Relativity on Display for First Time." Phys.org, March 7, 2010. https://phys.org/news/2010-03-einstein-theory-relativity.html.

Rogers, William Warren, Jr. "The Death of a President, April 12, 1945: An Account from Warm Springs." *Georgia Historical Quarterly* 75, no. 1 (Spring 1991): 109.

Schneider, Gregory S. "Jefferson's Powerful Last Public Letter Reminds Us What Independence Day Is All About." *Washington Post,* July 3, 2017.

https://www.washingtonpost.com/news/retropolis/wp/2017/07/03
/jeffersons-last-public-letter-reminds-us-what-independence-day-is-all
-about/?utm_term=.3aaba89a7fc9.

Smith, Peter. "Undelivered Speech Reflects Kennedy's Strong Catholic Ties."
Pittsburgh Post-Gazette, November 21, 2013. https://www.post-gazette.com
/news/nation/2013/11/22/Undelivered-speech-reflects-Kennedy-s-strong
-Catholic-ties/stories/201311220137.

Sorensen, Ted. *Counselor: A Life at the Edge of History*, reprint edition. New
York: Harper Perennial, 2009.

Thomas Jefferson Foundation. "Jefferson's Last Words." Thomas Jefferson
Encyclopedia. Accessed August 12, 2019. https://www.monticello.org/site
/research-and-collections/jeffersons-last-words.

Notes

Introduction

4 **"I've been in politics for a long time"**: "Bush and Gore in Tight Race; Florida Will Prove Decisive," *New York Times,* November 8, 2000, https:// www.nytimes.com/2000/11/08/politics/bush-and-gore-in-tight-race-florida -will-prove-decisive.html.

10 **Sadat and the Egyptian delegation:** William B. Quandt, *Camp David: Peacemaking and Politics* (Washington, D.C.: Brookings Institution Press, 1986), 238.

10 **Carter told Sadat:** Ibid., 239.

11 **tossed into one box:** William B. Quandt, interview by Jeff Nussbaum, June 21, 2019.

12 **"In that case we have no choice":** Nicholas Thompson, *The Hawk and the Dove: Paul Nitze, George Kennan, and the History of the Cold War* (New York: Henry Holt, 2009), 108–109.

1: John Lewis on the March on Washington, August 1963

18 **arrested more than thirty times:** King—SNCC staff biographies, 1964, Box 1, Folder 13, Mary E. King papers, 1962–1999, Wisconsin Historical

Society, Madison, Wisconsin, http://content.wisconsinhistory.org/cdm/ref
/collection/p15932coll2/id/24299.

18 **arrested forty-five times:** "Note to Self: Congressman John Lewis," You-
Tube video, 6:29, posted by "CBS This Morning," July 6, 2017, https://www
.youtube.com/watch?v=BlD2qsfiBrg.

18 **"felt defiance in every direction":** "John Lewis," SNCC Staff, Digital SNCC
Gateway, accessed August 9, 2019, https://snccdigital.org/people/john-lewis/.

18 **Courtland Cox:** Courtland Cox, interview by Jeff Nussbaum, January
12, 2021.

18 **SNCC members didn't want a march *in* Washington:** John Lewis and
Michael D'Orso, *Walking in the Wind: A Memoir of the Movement* (Orlando:
Harvest Books, 1999), 213.

18 **"I didn't want to be part of a parade":** Ibid., 234.

19 **Forman advocated for the mention:** Mary Sterner Lawson, "Slater King
(1927–1969)," New Georgia Encyclopedia, last updated June 3, 2019, https://
www.georgiaencyclopedia.org/articles/history-archaeology/slater-king-1927
-1969.

19 **"Tom came up with the notion":** Lewis and D'Orso, *Walking in the Wind,* 216.

20 **69 percent had heard about the march:** Andrew Kohut, "From the Archives: JFK's America," Pew Research Center, July 5, 2019, https://www
.pewresearch.org/fact-tank/2019/07/05/jfks-america/.

20 **Senators did not play:** Dan Steinberg, "When the March on Washington Canceled Two Senators Games," *Washington Post,* September 3, 2013,
https://www.washingtonpost.com/news/dc-sports-bog/wp/2013/09/03
/when-the-march-on-washington-canceled-two-senators-games/?utm_term
=.6cc3c909b400.

20 **"That's the most protection":** Ibid.

20 **Four thousand army troops:** "What Was the March on Washington?,"
Heroes & Villains, National Archives, accessed August 9, 2019, http://www
.nationalarchives.gov.uk/education/heroesvillains/g6/cs3/.

20 **350 firefighters:** "August 1963, D.C. Braces for March on Washington,"
Washington Post, accessed August 9, 2019, https://www.washingtonpost.com
/local/august-1963-dc-braces-for-march-on-washington/2013/08/21/f0b6b81e
-09e8-11e3-b87c-476db8ac34cd_gallery.html?utm_term=.226f03dc1453.

20 **a ban on liquor sales:** "1963 March on Washington Included Alcohol
Ban," Ghosts of DC, last updated August 28, 2013, https://ghostsofdc.org
/2013/08/28/1963-march-washington-plans-included-alcohol-ban/.

21 **"What are you doing that for?":** Drew D. Hansen, *The Dream: Martin Luther
King, Jr., and the Speech That Inspired a Nation* (New York: Ecco, 2005), 142.

21 **he worked to desegregate:** Michael Sean Winters, "Blast from the Past: Cardinal Patrick O'Boyle," *National Catholic Reporter,* August 2, 2010, https://www.ncronline.org/blogs/distinctly-catholic/blast-past-cardinal-patrick-oboyle.

21 **He developed programs to aid Black people:** Morris J. MacGregor, *Steadfast in the Faith: The Life of Patrick Cardinal O'Boyle* (Washington, D.C.: Catholic University of America Press, 2006), 219.

21 **encouraged parishioners to attend:** Clarence B. Jones and Stuart Connelly, *Behind the Dream: The Making of the Speech That Transformed a Nation* (New York: St. Martin's Press, 2011), 53.

21 **"Catholic Church's most prominent representative":** Hansen, *The Dream,* 143.

23 **"Here is the problem":** "Barney Frank Remarks at 2012 Democratic National Convention," YouTube video, 8:54, posted by "DNCConvention2012," September 7, 2012, https://www.youtube.com/watch?v=xYcwkg-7eMU.

24 **"Tonight, I want to talk":** "Transcript: Ann Romney's Convention Speech," NPR, August 28, 2012, https://www.npr.org/2012/08/28/160216442/transcript-ann-romneys-convention-speech.

24 **"The greatest lesson Mom ever taught me":** "Transcript: Gov. Chris Christie's Convention Speech," NPR, August 28, 2012, https://www.npr.org/2012/08/28/160213518/transcript-gov-chris-christies-convention-speech.

25 **"The more I thought":** Lewis and D'Orso, *Walking in the Wind,* 220.

25 **"Both the Democrats and the Republicans":** "Original Draft of SNCC's March on Washington Speech, Delivered by SNCC's Chairman John Lewis," SNCC Legacy Project, SNCC, accessed September 15, 2020, https://snccdigital.org/inside-sncc/policy-statements/march-washington-speech/.

25 **"the boy from Troy":** "Note to Self: Congressman John Lewis," YouTube video.

26 ***Demand Promissory Note***: Jones and Connelly, *Behind the Dream,* 75.

26 **"yes, black men as well as white men":** "'Normalcy-Never Again': Draft, circa 1963 August," Writings by Martin Luther King, Jr., circa 1947–1968, Morehouse College Martin Luther King, Jr., Collection: Series 2: Writings by Martin Luther King, Jr., Robert W. Woodruff Library, Atlanta, GA.

27 **King decided to cut it:** Hansen, *The Dream,* 87.

27 **King's advisor Clarence Jones recalled:** Jones and Connelly, *Behind the Dream,* 54.

29 **historian Angus Johnston notes:** Angus Johnston, "John Lewis Was the Youngest Speaker . . . ," Thread Reader, last updated July 18, 2020, https://threadreaderapp.com/thread/1284472208006545408.html.

33 "America didn't become the land": "Thursday, August 16 Draft of Julian Castro's Convention Keynote Remarks," August 16, 2012, Jeff Nussbaum Personal Collection.

34 "America didn't become the land": "Transcript: Julian Castro's DNC Keynote Address," NPR, September 4, 2012, https://www.npr.org/2012/09/04/160574895/transcript-julian-castros-dnc-keynote-address.

35 "The applause in the arena": Jeff Zeleny, "New Democratic Voice Challenges Republican Vision," *New York Times,* September 5, 2012, https://www.nytimes.com/2012/09/05/us/politics/julian-castro-addresses-democrats-at-convention.html.

35 "close enough, it felt": Lewis and D'Orso, *Walking in the Wind,* 224.

36 the "harshest" of the speeches: E. W. Kenworthy, "200,000 March for Civil Rights in Orderly Washington Rally; President Sees Gain for Negro," *New York Times,* August 29, 1963, https://timesmachine.nytimes.com/timesmachine/1963/08/29/89957615.pdf.

36 The only injuries that day: "August 1963, D.C. Braces for March on Washington."

36 "I think it was the right thing": "John Lewis Marches On," *Moyers & Company,* season 2, episode 34.

37 "First I find my landing strip": Hansen, *The Dream,* 97.

2: Wamsutta Frank James on the 350th Anniversary of the Pilgrims Landing at Plymouth Rock, September 1970

39 Cole's Hill: Edward R. Belcher, "Notes on Cole's Hill," Pilgrim Hall Museum, accessed August 1, 2019, http://www.pilgrimhallmuseum.org/pdf/Notes_Coles_Hill.pdf.

39 you'll find a sarcophagus: Patrick Browne, "Cole's Hill Sarcophagus and Pilgrim Remains," Historical Digression, last modified September 30, 2013, https://historicaldigression.com/2013/09/30/coles-hill-sarcophagus-and-pilgrim-remains/.

41 On September 11, 1970: Moonanum James, interview by Jeff Nussbaum, June 4, 2019; "USS Independence (CV 62)," United States Navy, last modified June 15, 2009, https://www.navy.mil/navydata/ships/carriers/histories/cv62-independence/cv62-independence.html.

41 The captain, Gerald O'Rourke: NavSource Online, "USS Independence (CVA-62) (*later* CV-62)"; "Plummer M. Shearin Dies," *Washington Post,* January 2, 1998, https://www.washingtonpost.com/archive/local/1998/01/02/plummer-m-shearin-dies/ce597459-4640-4ef7-8eb8-b61a42ede36a/.

41 **"We're not a militant group"**: "The Indian Who Wouldn't Be Muzzled," *Massachusetts Teacher,* December 1970, 5.

41 **fifteen months of events:** John J. Massaro, "Doing the 'Pilgrim Bit' in Jet Style," *Hartford Courant,* August 30, 1970, 3F.

41 **parades, tours, speeches:** "350th Anniversary: A Year-Long Event," *Boston Globe,* September 9, 1970, A2.

46 **"consolidate his thoughts":** "Chatham Indian Skipped Pilgrim Event, Chief Claims Speech Censored," *Cape Cod Standard-Times,* September 17, 1970.

46 **"You can't go around":** "Indian Speaker Says State Muzzled Him," *Cape Cod Standard-Times,* September 25, 1970.

46 **"Why is my son":** Andrew Blake, "Indian Charges Censorship, Spurns Orator's Role," *Boston Globe,* September 24, 1970, 3.

46 **James had joined a plane flight:** Massaro, "Pilgrim Bit," 3F.

46 **James looked at his original draft:** Blake, "Indian Charges Censorship," 3.

46 **to deliver such a speech:** "Indian Who Wouldn't Be Muzzled," 5.

47 **"Chief Massasoit who met the Pilgrims":** Bill Kovach, "In a Time of Change, Plymouth, Mass. Looks Back 350 Years," *New York Times,* September 14, 1970.

47 **There, on the front page:** Ed Jenner, *Boston Globe,* September 13, 1970, 1.

47 **"went on the warpath":** "Wife Writes State: James' Boycott Backed," *Cape Cod Standard-Times,* September 25, 1970.

47 **Mrs. James received a conciliatory letter:** "Sargent Apologizes for Censored Speech," *Cape Codder,* October 22, 1970, 5.

48 **When asked to leave:** Robert Carr and Andrew Blake, "Stage Plymouth Protest: Indians Take Over Mayflower II," *Boston Globe,* November 27, 1970, 1.

3: Emma Goldman at Her Sentencing, October 1893, and Helen Keller at the Suffrage Parade, March 1913

55 **"The existing system":** Wendy McElroy, *The Debates of Liberty: An Overview of Individualist Anarchism, 1881–1908* (Lanham, MD: Lexington Books, 2003), 33.

55 **"I am his wife":** "Anarchy's Den," *New York World,* July 28, 1892, Berkeley Library, University of California, http://www.lib.berkeley.edu/goldman/pdfs /AnarchysDen-NewYorkWorld1892.pdf.

55 **"The bullets did not kill":** Ken Ackerman, "Emma Goldman—Speaking Out for Free Bread, Going to Jail. Part I," Viral History, last updated March 25, 2011, https://kennethackerman.com/emma-goldman-speaking-out-for -free-bread-going-to-jail-part-i/.

55 **"It isn't the man"**: David Huyssen, "We Won't Get out of the Second Gilded Age the Way We Got out of the First," *Vox,* April 1, 2019, https://www.vox.com/first-person/2019/4/1/18286084/gilded-age-income-inequality-robber-baron.

55 **so-called Panic of 1893**: "Panic of 1893," Ohio History Central, accessed August 15, 2019, http://www.ohiohistorycentral.org/w/Panic_of_1893.

55 **the notes she had prepared**: Emma Goldman, *Living My Life* (New York: Dover Publications, 1970), 120.

57 **"but when she began"**: "Emma Goldman on Trial," *New York Times,* October 5, 1893, https://timesmachine.nytimes.com/timesmachine/1893/10/05/109730675.pdf.

57 **"Most of you left Russia"**: Ackerman, "Emma Goldman."

57 **"preparations for a forcible rescue"**: Goldman, *Living My Life,* 131.

57 **The police had put known radicals**: Ibid., 131–132.

58 **"In view of the fact"**: "The Law's Limit," *New York World,* October 17, 1893, Berkeley Library, University of California, http://www.lib.berkeley.edu/goldman/pdfs/TheLawsLimit_NewYorkWorld_October17-1893.pdf.

58 **in a final act of defiance**: Ibid.

58 **she bade the journalists goodbye**: Goldman, *Living My Life,* 132.

61 **the opposing counsel had argued**: Ibid., 129–130.

62 **"You always remain"**: "Emma Goldman and Free Speech," Emma Goldman Papers, Berkeley Library, University of California, http://www.lib.berkeley.edu/goldman/MeetEmmaGoldman/emmagoldmanandfreespeech.html.

62 **In 1886, when Keller was six**: David Blatty, "From Darkness into Light: Helen Keller & Alexander Graham Bell," Biography, June 18, 2019, https://www.biography.com/news/alexander-graham-bell-and-helen-keller.

63 **disabilities as civil rights issues**: Kim E. Nielsen, "The Grown Up Helen Keller," *Alabama Heritage* (Spring 2009): 24.

63 **"How I Became a Socialist"**: Helen Keller, "How I Became a Socialist," *New York Call,* November 3, 1912, Marxists Internet Archive, https://www.marxists.org/reference/archive/keller-helen/works/1910s/12_11_03.htm.

63 **"to bring before the country"**: "Suffrage Invasion Is On in Earnest; in Special Trains Women Hurry to Take Part in Washington Pageant," *New York Times,* March 2, 1913, https://timesmachine.nytimes.com/timesmachine/1913/03/02/100609767.html?pageNumber=15.

63 **The rally began with a parade**: Linda J. Lumsden, "Beauty and the Beasts: Significance of Press Coverage of the 1913 National Suffrage Parade," *JM&C Quarterly* 77, no. 3 (Autumn 2000): 595.

64 "There would be nothing like this": "Police Idly Watched Abuse of Women; Shocking Insults to Suffrage Paraders Testified to at Washington Inquiry," *New York Times,* March 7, 1913, https://timesmachine.nytimes.com /timesmachine/1913/03/07/100390575.html.

64 A resolution was adopted: "5,000 Women in Biggest of Suffrage Pageants," *Baltimore Sun,* March 4, 1913, ProQuest.

66 "speak normally": "Helen Keller Speaks Out," YouTube video, 3:08, posted by "Helen Keller Channel," April 11, 2011, https://www.youtube.com /watch?v=8ch_H8pt9M8.

66 "the riot forced even anti-suffrage": Lumsden, "Beauty and the Beasts," 593.

66 Keller continued to put forward: Nielsen, "The Grown Up Helen Keller," 24.

66 "She has consecrated her life": "Letter from Helen Keller to the Editor of the New York Call in Opposition of Emma Goldman's Arrest for Teaching Effective Birth Control Methods," Gabrielsen-Grummon, Individuals, General Correspondence, Helen Keller Archive, American Foundation for the Blind, created April 6, 1916, accessed September 15, 2020, https://www.afb.org/ HelenKellerArchive?a=d&d=A-HK01-03-B056-F11-004&e=-------en-20--1 --txt--emma+goldman------3-7-6-5-3-------Keller%2C+Helen-------0-1.

67 "When women vote": Helen Keller, "Why Men Need Women Suffrage," *New York Call,* October 17, 1913, Helen Keller Reference Archive, Marxists Internet Archive, https://www.marxists.org/reference/archive/keller-helen /works/1910s/13_10_17.htm.

67 William Safire cites the saying: William Safire, *Lend Me Your Ears: Great Speeches in History,* updated and expanded edition (New York: W. W. Norton, 2004), 35.

68 three hundred marchers: "Marching for the Vote: Remembering the Woman Suffrage Parade of 1913," American Women: Topical Essays, Library of Congress, accessed September 15, 2020, https://guides.loc.gov/american -women-essays/marching-for-the-vote.

68 Joan of Arc: Madeline Miller, "From Circe to Clinton, Why Powerful Women Are Cast as Witches," *Guardian,* April 7, 2018, https://www .theguardian.com/books/2018/apr/07/cursed-from-circe-to-clinton-why -women-are-cast-as-witches.

68 Cleopatra or Anne Boleyn: Ibid.

68 "Speech is power": Ralph Waldo Emerson, "'Table Talk': 18 December 1864 (1864–1866)," *The Later Lectures of Ralph Waldo Emerson: 1843–1871,* ed. Ronald A. Bosco and Joel Myerson (Athens: University of Georgia Press, 10), 363.

68 devotee of Emerson's writing: James Brown, "Anarchism and American Traditions: Emma Goldman's Emerson and Thoreau," Annual Meeting of the

American Studies Association (internal paper presentation, San Antonio, TX, November 26, 2014), http://citation.allacademic.com/meta/p412702_index .html.

4: President Richard Nixon's Refusal to Resign, August 1974

72 **What Price didn't know:** Email conversation with former Nixon speechwriter Lee Huebner, January 10, 2020.

72 **"and on this most final":** Raymond Price, *With Nixon* (New York: Viking Adult, 1977), 328.

73 **Frum's wife:** Matthew Engel, "Proud Wife Turns 'Axis of Evil' Speech into a Resignation Letter," *Guardian,* February 26, 2002, https://www.theguardian .com/world/2002/feb/27/usa.matthewengel.

74 **"When we came out of the war":** "Richard M. Nixon *Checkers,*" American Rhetoric, last updated December 12, 2018, https://www.americanrhetoric .com/speeches/richardnixoncheckers.html.

76 **"a sort of comic":** John Woestendiek, "The Dog Who Rescued Richard Nixon," *Baltimore Sun,* September 22, 2002, https://www.baltimoresun.com /entertainment/arts/bal-pets092202-story.html.

76 **"a glimpse of a low-rent future":** Tom Feran, "Eisenhower and Nixon," *Cleveland.com,* February 19, 2013, https://www.cleveland.com/books/2013 /02/eisenhower_and_nixon_two_terms.html.

76 **he played a piano concerto:** "Top 10 Performing Politicians," *Time,* accessed December 3, 2020, http://content.time.com/time/specials/packages /article/0,28804,1850902_1850905_1850907,00.html.

77 **"a new conservative populism in America":** Froma Harrop, "Richard Nixon's 'Checkers Speech': When Blue-Collar Whites Turned Republican," *Seattle Times,* September 22, 2012, http://old.seattletimes.com/html/opinion /2019226561_harropcolumnbluecollarwhitesxml.html?syndication=rss.

77 **"The Fifties were not the Eisenhower years":** Kevin Mattson, *Just Plain Dick: Richard Nixon's Checkers Speech and the "Rocking, Socking" Election of 1952,* reprint edition (New York: Bloomsbury USA, 2013), front matter.

77 **This worried Price:** Price, *With Nixon,* 330.

78 **along with eighty-six of his colleagues:** Richard Simon and Ricardo Alonso-Zaldivar, "Senate Approves Arming Pilots," *Los Angeles Times,* September 6, 2002, https://www.latimes.com/archives/la-xpm-2002-sep-06-na-pilots6 -story.html.

79 **"Option B":** Price, *With Nixon,* 330.

79 "I thought the break in": Option B, August 5, 1974, Speech by Raymond Price, Box 118, Folder Option B—Resignation, Draft 8/4/74 (See also Statement 8/5 and Resignation 8/8), President's Personal Files (White House Special Files: Staff Member and Office Files), Richard Nixon Presidential Library and Museum, Yorba Linda, CA, 8–9.

79 "We have heard much": Ibid., 11.

80 "There is a time to fight": Ibid., 18.

81 "Good Evening": "The Speech That Might Have Been: Nixon Refuses to Resign," Watergate.info, last updated December 22, 1996, https://watergate.info/1996/12/22/nixon-refuses-to-resign-speech.html.

84 Petit was finalizing his preparations: Emily S. Rueb, "Philippe Petit's Walk Between the Towers, Aug. 7, 1964," *New York Times,* August 7, 2014, https://cityroom.blogs.nytimes.com/2014/08/07/philippe-petits-walk-between-the-towers-aug-7-1974/.

85 NIXON SAYS HE WON'T RESIGN: "Nixon Says He Won't Resign," *Washington Post,* August 7, 1974, ProQuest.

85 "the interest of the nation": "President Nixon's Resignation Speech, August 8, 1974," Presidential Links, PBS, accessed September 15, 2020, https://www.pbs.org/newshour/spc/character/links/nixon_speech.html.

85 "A first draft is attached": Price, *With Nixon,* 339–340.

5: Mayor Kevin White on School Busing, December 1974

87 mayor Kevin White pulled up: Robert Jordan, "Police Stay 'for Duration,' White Says," *Boston Globe,* September 17, 1974, 33.

88 a fire was set: Bob Oakes and Kathleen McNerney, "New Book Offers Glimpse into 'Whitey' Bulger's Early Years," WBUR, February 19, 2013, https://www.wbur.org/news/2013/02/19/whitey-bulger-book.

88 a Molotov cocktail had been thrown: Shelley Murphy, "Bulger Linked to '70s Antibusing Attacks," Boston.com, April 22, 2001, http://archive.boston.com/news/local/massachusetts/articles/2001/04/22/bulger_linked_to_70s_antibusing_attacks/.

88 Whitey Bulger, an organized crime boss: Ibid.

88 the Coleman Report: James S. Coleman, *Equality of Educational Opportunity* (Washington, D.C.: U.S. Department of Health, Education, and Welfare, Office of Education, 1966), https://files.eric.ed.gov/fulltext/ED012275.pdf, 21–22.

89 Ford, whose disagreement: John Kifner, "Boston Prepares for More Busing," *New York Times,* September 7, 1975, https://www.nytimes.com/1975/09/07/archives/boston-prepares-for-more-busing.html.

89 "That stupid son of a bitch": William D. Eggers and John O'Leary, *If We Can Put a Man on the Moon: Getting Big Things Done in Government* (Boston: Harvard Business Review Press, 2009), 84.

89 five white, mostly Irish, members: Robert Schwartz, interview by Jeff Nussbaum, June 12, 2019.

90 "the city and state had consistently denied": Jane M. Hornburger, "Deep Are the Roots: Busing in Boston," *Journal of Negro Education* 45, no. 3 (1976): 237.

90 Garrity issued his decision: J. Anthony Lukas, *Common Ground: A Turbulent Decade in the Lives of Three American Families* (New York: Vintage Books, 1986), 238.

90 eighty schools and eighteen thousand students: Bruce Gellerman, "'It Was Like a War Zone': Busing in Boston," WBUR, September 5, 2014, https://www.wbur.org/news/2014/09/05/boston-busing-anniversary.

90 "exact his pound of flesh": Ira Jackson, interview by Jeff Nussbaum, June 6, 2019.

90 colorful analogy of Dr. William Reid: Ronald P. Formisano, *Boston Against Busing: Race, Class, and Ethnicity in the 1960s and 1970s* (Chapel Hill: University of North Carolina Press, 2012), 70.

91 Garrity refused to comment: Lukas, *Common Ground,* 240; Eggers and O'Leary, *If We Can Put a Man on the Moon,* 83.

91 "heavily Irish and Italian": Kevin White, "Busing in Boston—A Beleaguered Mayor Speaks Out," interview by *U.S. News & World Report,* full transcript released to the press on March 30, 1975.

91 "an isolated, mile-square neighborhood": Kifner, "Boston Prepares."

92 Helicopters buzzed overhead: Meghan E. Irons, Shelley Murphy, and Jenna Russell, "History Rolled In on a Yellow School Bus," *Boston Globe,* September 6, 2014, https://www.bostonglobe.com/metro/2014/09/06/boston-busing-crisis-years-later/DS35nsuqp0yh8f1q9aRQUL/story.html; "Eyes on the Prize: The Keys to the Kingdom (1974–1980)," *Facing History and Ourselves* video, 57:46, accessed August 14, 2019, https://www.blackstonian.org/2016/01/video-eyes-on-the-prize-boston-episode/.

92 The headmaster, William Reid: Irons, Murphy, and Russell, "History Rolled In."

92 Ira Jackson was on-site: Ira Jackson, interview by Jeff Nussbaum, June 6, 2019.

93 The crowd cursed: Gellerman, "'It Was Like a War Zone."

93 BOSTON SCHOOLS DESEGREGATED: Ibid.

93 **fewer than four hundred students:** Ibid.

93 **Rumors about guns:** Alan Lupo, *Liberty's Chosen Home: The Politics of Violence in Boston* (Boston: Beacon Press, 1988), 243.

94 **"Tomorrow's test":** Ibid., 247.

94 **twenty-two people had been arrested:** Ibid., 276.

94 **then on December 11:** Harold C. Schonberg, "South Boston Schools Shut in Clashes over Stabbing," *New York Times,* December 12, 1974, https://www .nytimes.com/1974/12/12/archives/south-boston-schools-shut-in-clashes-over -stabbing-south-boston.html.

95 **"Suddenly, the young driver":** Ibid.

95 **decoy buses were sent:** Ibid.

95 **last through Christmas:** Ken O. Botwright, "S. Boston High Opening; Leaders Optimistic, Wary," *Boston Globe,* January 8, 1975, 1.

95 **dealing with a court order:** "Eyes on the Prize."

95 **"eighty percent of the people":** White, interview.

95 **named White himself:** John Kifner, "Judge Names Boston Mayor Co-Defendant in School Busing Case," *New York Times,* September 28, 1974.

96 **Though White admitted:** Lupo, *Liberty's Chosen Home,* 178.

96 **"I didn't think":** Jordan, "Police Stay 'for Duration.'"

96 **they had chosen:** Robert Jordan, "Question 7, Hub School Reform Fails," *Boston Globe,* November 6, 1974.

96 **Cullen Murphy:** Cullen Murphy, "Outtakes: The Rise of Provisional History," *Atlantic,* July 1, 2000, https://www.theatlantic.com/magazine/archive /2000/07/outtakes/378267/.

96 **Lincoln wrote:** "Letter to George Meade," Abraham Lincoln, History Place, accessed August 14, 2019, http://www.historyplace.com/lincoln/lett-6 .htm; Murphy, "Outtakes."

97 **Historian David McCullough writes:** David McCullough, *Truman* (New York: Simon & Schuster, 1992), 576.

97 **crime in Boston had spiked:** Ron Husted, "Reported Crimes in Boston Up 25% over Last Year," *Boston Globe,* December 27, 1974, 3.

97 **"suburban liberals":** Rick Perlstein, *The Invisible Bridge: The Fall of Nixon and the Rise of Reagan* (New York: Simon & Schuster, 2014), 290.

97 **fund the Home and School Association:** "Letter to Residents from the Boston Home and School Association," Digital Repository Service, Northeastern University, created September 11, 1974, accessed August 14, 2019, https://repository .library.northeastern.edu/downloads/neu:rx915n128?datastream_id=content.

98 **director Leon Panetta:** Matthew Delmont, "The Lasting Legacy of the Busing Crisis," *Atlantic,* March 29, 2016, https://www.theatlantic.com/politics/archive/2016/03/the-boston-busing-crisis-was-never-intended-to-work/474264/.

100 **Mayor White stepped:** Robert Jordan, "White Pledges to Fight for Education, Safety: Highlights of Sate of the City Address," *Boston Globe,* January 7, 1975.

100 **"take whatever action necessary":** "Text of the State of the City Address," *Boston Herald American,* January 7, 1975, 25.

101 **"I don't like to make threats":** Lupo, *Liberty's Chosen Home,* 227.

101 **"We had no credible role":** Jackson, interview.

102 **"The last thing we wanted":** Ibid.

102 **"Mend it":** "President Clinton on Affirmative Action: 'Mend It, Don't End It,'" Today in Civil Rights History, accessed August 14, 2019, http://todayinclh.com/?event=affirmative-action-mend-it-dont-end-it.

102 **"take whatever action is necessary":** Jordan, "White Pledges."

103 **Ray Flynn, the anti-busing councilman:** Luix Overbea, "After 14 Years, Busing in Boston Rolls to a Stop," *Christian Science Monitor,* December 30, 1988, https://www.csmonitor.com/1988/1230/avisa.html.

103 **White flight to suburban and parochial schools:** Dudley Clendinen, "Boston City Schools, Once Beacons, Losing Students and Pride," *New York Times,* September 20, 1981, https://www.nytimes.com/1981/09/20/us/boston-city-schools-once-beacons-losing-students-and-pride.html.

103 **60 percent of the students:** Elizabeth Ross, "The Legacy of Forced Busing in Boston," *Christian Science Monitor,* September 26, 1994, https://www.csmonitor.com/1994/0926/26091.html.

103 **headmaster of South Boston High School:** Clendinen, "Boston City Schools."

103 **"My parents would not have believed this":** Sarah Glovsky, interview by Jeff Nussbaum, June 19, 2019.

6: Edward VIII's Refusal to Abdicate the Throne, December 1936

108 **"a miracle":** Rory Tingle, "When Edward VIII Went to See Hitler: Never-Before-Seen Photos Emerge for Sale of Duke of Windsor's Infamous Trip to Nazi Germany in 1937," *Daily Mail,* October 8, 2018, https://www.dailymail.co.uk/news/article-6251937/Never-seen-photos-Edward-VIII-visiting-Mercedes-Benz-factory.html.

108 **"tender seedling":** Ibid.

108 **führer's residence:** Brigit Katz, "Newly Released Documents Reveal Churchill's Efforts to Suppress Details of Nazi Plot," *Smithsonian Magazine,*

July 21, 2017, https://www.smithsonianmag.com/smart-news/newly-released -documents-reveal-churchills-efforts-suppress-details-nazi-plot-180964131 /#4HvsUtrfMdoeioVs.99.

108 **Thelma Furness:** Philip Ziegler, *King Edward VIII,* international edition (New York: HarperCollins, 2012), 223; Henry Channon, *Chips: The Diaries of Sir Henry Channon,* ed. Robert Rhodes James (London: Weidenfeld & Nicolson, 1967), 50.

108 **Edward became obsessed:** Tim Ott, "Why Edward VIII Abdicated the Throne to Marry Wallis Simpson," Biography, June 13, 2019, https://www .biography.com/news/edward-viii-abdicate-throne-wallis-simpson.

108 **Edward would later write:** Ibid.

109 **Edward and his brothers signed:** Michael Bloch, *The Reign and Abdication of King Edward VIII* (London: Transworld Publishers, 1991), 232.

109 **Shortly after 9:30 p.m.:** "Reith Diaries Dec 1936," History of the BBC, accessed August 19, 2019, http://downloads.bbc.co.uk/historyofthebbc/Reith _diaries_Dec_1936_edit.pdf.

109 **Technicians had set up:** "King Edward VIII Microphone," A History of the World, BBC, accessed August 19, 2019, http://www.bbc.co.uk /ahistoryoftheworld/objects/wm1Q2Ad7Q6Ozr-NfeLCWAg.

110 **A half hour before:** "Reith Diaries Dec 1936."

111 **"During these hard days":** "Edward VIII Abdicates the Throne," Great Speeches Collection, History Place, accessed August 19, 2019, http://www .historyplace.com/speeches/edward.htm.

111 **Upon delivering:** Frederick Winston Furneaux Smith, *The Life of Viscount Monckton Brenchley* (London: Weidenfeld & Nicolson, 1969), 152.

112 **unfit to become king:** Adrian Phillips, *The King Who Had to Go: Edward VIII, Mrs Simpson and the Hidden Politics of the Abdication Crisis* (London: Biteback Publishing, 2017), 6.

112 **Alan "Tommy" Lascelles:** Ibid., 13.

112 **"an abnormal being":** Robert Beaken, *Cosmo Lang: Archbishop in War and Crisis* (London: I. B. Tauris, 2012), 92.

112 **"After I am dead":** Ziegler, *King Edward VIII,* 199.

112 **"I pray to God":** Kenneth Rose, *King George V* (London: Weidenfeld & Nicolson, 1983), 392.

112 **he advocated sending:** Deborah Cadbury, *Princes at War: The Bitter Battle Inside Britain's Royal Family in the Darkest Days of WWII* (London: Bloomsbury, 2015), 14.

113 **Throughout 1936:** Ziegler, *King Edward VIII,* 230–231.

113 **Reports of the meeting:** Ibid., 232–233.

113 **Simpson's divorce case:** Ibid., 294.

114 **Baldwin had hoped:** Bloch, *The Reign and Abdication of King Edward VIII,* 141–142.

114 **Some historians claim:** Andrew Roberts, *Churchill: Walking with Destiny,* 5th printing edition (New York: Viking Press, 2018), 74.

114 **Churchill's role in the morganatic marriage:** Bloch, *The Reign and Abdication of King Edward VIII,* 197.

114 **Churchill's relationship with Baldwin:** Kay Halle, *The Irrepressible Churchill* (Cleveland: World Publishing, 1966), 181.

114 **Churchill did serve:** Ibid., 131–134; Richard M. Langworth, "How Churchill Saw Others: Stanley Baldwin," International Churchill Society, winter 1998/1999, https://winstonchurchill.org/publications/finest-hour /finest-hour-101/how-churchill-saw-others-stanley-baldwin/.

115 **For Baldwin, rumors of Churchill's role:** Bloch, *The Reign and Abdication of King Edward VIII,* 141–142.

115 **A Church of England bishop named Alfred Blunt:** Hugo Vickers, *Behind Closed Doors: The Tragic, Untold Story of Wallis Simpson* (London: Hutchinson, 2011), 300.

115 **Blunt had barely heard of Simpson:** Ziegler, *King Edward VIII,* 308.

117 **"I want you to do":** Mark Salter, *The Luckiest Man: Life with John McCain* (New York: Simon & Schuster, 2020), 1.

117 **"I would have greatly":** John McCain, "Address by Senator John McCain to the United States Naval Academy Class of 1993" (speech, U.S. Naval Academy, Annapolis, MD, May 26, 1993), https://www.usna63.org/tradition /history/grad-speech.html.

117 **Salter felt free:** Mark Salter, interview by Jeff Nussbaum, November 24, 2020.

118 **McCain's farewell:** "READ: Sen. John McCain's farewell statement," CNN, August 27, 2018, https://www.cnn.com/2018/08/27/politics/john -mccain-farewell-statement/index.html.

118 **"frantically keen":** Ziegler, *King Edward VIII,* 316.

118 **"a plausible and blatant attempt":** Ibid.

118 **"No word about abdication":** Caroline Davies, Neil Tweedie, and Peter Day, "Edward VIII's Unspoken Abdication Speech," *Telegraph,* January 31, 2003, https://www.telegraph.co.uk/news/uknews/1420505/Edward-VIIIs -unspoken-abdication-speech.html.

119 **"The sovereign can make no public statement":** Dominic Casciani, "King's Abdication Appeal Blocked," BBC News, January 30, 2003, http:// news.bbc.co.uk/2/hi/uk_news/2707489.stm.

119 **"my first blunder"**: G. M. Young, *Stanley Baldwin* (London: Rupert Hart-Davis, 1952), 242.

119 **"parliamentary and literary life"**: David Cannadine, "Churchill and the British Monarchy," *Transactions of the Royal Historical Society* 11 (2001): 253.

119 **Clementine, joked:** John Pearson, *The Private Lives of Winston Churchill* (London: Bloomsbury Reader, 2013), 365.

120 **"King's Party"**: Bloch, *The Reign and Abdication of King Edward VIII*.

120 **"great danger"**: Ibid., 196.

120 **four months of silence:** Ibid.

120 **"many little tricks"**: Churchill archives, 2/264/16.

120 **"completely on the rampage"**: J. C. C. Davidson, *Memoirs of a Conservative: J. C. C. Davidson's Memoirs and Papers 1910–1937*, ed. Robert Rhodes James (London: Weidenfeld & Nicolson, 1969), 414–415.

120 **"Your majesty need not"**: Churchill archives, 2/264/16–26.

121 **Churchill rose to ask a question:** Jenkins, *Churchill*, 502.

121 **"formula which we had all helped"**: Churchill archives, 2/265/102–103, box 161.

121 **a reference the king wanted:** Ziegler, *King Edward VIII*, 330.

122 **"By ancient custom"**: The fullest possible text has been complied by reports and images available through the BBC and the *Guardian*; Stephen Bates, "Monarch's Unheard Public Appeal to Hang On to Throne," *Guardian*, January 30, 2003, https://www.theguardian.com/uk/2003/jan/30/artsandhumanities.monarchy; Davies, Tweedie, and Day, "Edward VIII's Unspoken Abdication Speech."

123 **"Mrs. Simpson has had no wish"**: Balliol College Historic Collections, Department of Monckton Trustees 14 f52–54.

124 **an additional affair:** Owen Bowcott and Stephen Bates, "Car Dealer Was Wallis Simpson's Secret Lover," *Guardian*, January 30, 2003, https://www.theguardian.com/uk/2003/jan/30/freedomofinformation.monarchy3.

124 **"appeal for your utmost influence"**: Carolyn Harris, "Royalty and the Atlantic World 4: The Duke and Duchess of Windsor's Arrival in the Bahamas in 1940," *Carolyn Harris*, April 2, 2013, http://www.royalhistorian.com/royalty-and-the-atlantic-world-4-the-duke-and-duchess-of-windsors-arrival-in-the-bahamas-in-1940/.

124 **"Duke believes"**: Katz, "Newly Released Documents."

124 **Roy Jenkins notes:** Jenkins, *Churchill*, 503.

7: New York City Mayor Abe Beame Declares Bankruptcy, October 1975

128 **Municipal Assistance Corporation (MAC):** George J. Lankevich, *New York City: A Short History* (New York: New York University Press, 1998), 216.

128 **The first round of MAC bonds:** Ronald Smothers, "New M.A.C. Bonds Sell at Premium," *New York Times,* August 19, 1975, https://www.nytimes.com/1975/08/19/archives/new-mac-bonds-sell-at-premium-underwriter-calls-trading-a-qualified.html.

128 **"Abe Beame is an accountant":** Ed Koch, "Voice of New York," *New York,* April 11, 1988, 80.

129 **Teachers' Retirement System wouldn't invest:** "50 Years," United Federation of Teachers, accessed August 8, 2019, http://www.uft.org/files/attachments/uft-50-years-book.pdf.

130 **Ravitch would later write:** Richard Ravitch, *So Much to Do: A Full Life of Business, Politics, and Confronting Fiscal Crisis* (New York: PublicAffairs, 2014), 91.

130 **Sid Frigand, the mayor's press secretary:** Sid Frigand, interview by Jeff Nussbaum, February 6, 2008.

130 *New Yorker* **would later describe:** Ken Auletta, "The Fixer," *New Yorker,* February 4, 2007, http://www.newyorker.com/magazine/2007/02/12/the-fixer.

131 **Contingency Planning Committee:** Ken Auletta, *The Streets Were Paved with Gold: The Decline of New York, an American Tragedy* (New York: Vintage Books, 1980), 240.

131 **Frigand began:** Ibid.

132 **Shanker wouldn't budge:** Ravitch, *So Much to Do,* 91.

132 **BALK BY UFT:** Peter Harrigan, "Balk by UFT pushing city to default," *Staten Island Advance,* October 17, 1975, https://www.silive.com/news/2014/07/advance_historic_page_from_oct_4.html.

132 **TEACHERS REJECT 150-MILLION LOAN:** Steven R. Weisman, "Teachers Reject 150-Million Loan City Needs Today," *New York Times,* October 17, 1975, https://timesmachine.nytimes.com/timesmachine/1975/10/17/83178387.html?pageNumber=1.

132 **United Press International reported:** Thomas Hillstrom, "Teachers Agree to Aid NYC," *Wilmington Morning Star,* October 17, 1975, https://news.google.com/newspapers?nid=1454&dat=19751017&id=SLgsAAAAIBAJ&sjid=4AkEAAAAIBAJ&pg=4466,3757952&hl=en.

132 **By some estimates:** Sam Roberts, "When New York Teetered on the Brink of Bankruptcy," *New York Times,* July 25, 2013, http://cityroom.blogs.nytimes.com/2013/07/25/when-new-york-teetered-on-the-brink-of-bankruptcy/.

132 **Ford began hearing from leaders:** Kim Phillips-Fein, "Lessons from the Great Default Crisis of 1975," *Nation,* October 16, 2013, https://www.thenation.com/article/lessons-great-default-crisis-1975/.

132 **"This is not a natural disaster":** Ibid.

133 **Shanker later called it blackmail:** United Federation of Teachers, "50 Years."

133 **"What I cannot understand":** Address to the National Press Club, October 29, 1975, Box 18, President's Speeches and Statements, Gerald R. Ford Presidential Library, Ann Arbor, MI.

133 **"I can tell you":** Ibid.

135 **harsher than many of his advisors intended:** Sam Roberts, "Infamous 'Drop Dead' Was Never Said by Ford," *New York Times,* December 28, 2006, https://www.nytimes.com/2006/12/28/nyregion/28veto.html.

135 **Nelson Rockefeller:** Ibid.

135 **"I am fundamentally opposed":** Second Draft, October 24, 1975, Box 178, Folder 10/29/75—New York City Speech (1), Robert Hartmann Papers, Gerald R. Ford Presidential Library, Ann Arbor, MI; Memorandum for the President from L. William Seidman, October 27, 1975, Box 178, Folder 10/29/75—New York City Speech (3), Robert Hartmann Papers, Gerald R. Ford Presidential Library, Ann Arbor, MI.

135 **In several of the earlier drafts:** Fifth Draft, October 26, 1975, Box 178, Folder 10/29/75—New York City Speech (3), Robert Hartmann Papers, Gerald R. Ford Presidential Library, Ann Arbor, MI.

135 **handwritten changes:** Sixth Draft, October 28, 1975, Box 178, Folder 10/29/75—New York City Speech (3), Robert Hartmann Papers, Gerald R. Ford Presidential Library, Ann Arbor, MI.

136 FORD TO CITY: Reuven Blau, "Ford to City: Drop Dead: President's Snub Inspired, Not Discouraged, Ex-Gov. Hugh Carey," *New York Daily News,* August 8, 2011, https://www.nydailynews.com/news/politics/ford-city-drop-dead-president-snub-inspired-not-discouraged-ex-gov-hugh-carey-article-1.947295.

136 **"I would account myself a fool":** Week Staff, "Generals in the White House," *Week,* January 1, 2007, https://theweek.com/articles/528787/generals-white-house.

136 **"I will not accept if nominated":** "Statement of Sherman in 1884 Is Recalled," *New York Times,* September 24, 1974, https://www.nytimes.com/1974/09/24/archives/statement-of-sherman-in-1884-is-recalled.html.

136 **"I shall not seek":** Carroll Kilpatrick, "LBJ Tells Nation He Won't Run, Restricts Raids on N. Vietnam: Johnson Declares He Won't Seek or Accept Nomination," *Washington Post,* April 1, 1968, A1.

136 **"If nominated, I will run"**: David Hess, "Mo Udall, Quick-Witted Congressman, Forced to Retire," *Baltimore Sun,* April 20, 1991, https://www .baltimoresun.com/news/bs-xpm-1991-04-20-1991110026-story.html.

136 **"We are not about to send"**: Mitchell Lerner, "Vietnam and the 1964 Election: A Defense of Lyndon Johnson," in *The United States and the Vietnam War: Leadership and Diplomacy in the Vietnam War,* ed. Walter L. Hixson (New York: Garland Publishing, 2000), 11.

137 **"Read my lips"**: Lily Rothman, "The Story Behind George H. W. Bush's Famous 'Read My Lips, No New Taxes' Promise," *Time,* December 1, 2018, https://time.com/3649511/george-hw-bush-quote-read-my-lips/.

137 **"We did not"**: Ronald Reagan, "Address to the Nation on the Iran Arms and Contra Aid Controversy" (speech, Washington, D.C., November 13, 1986), Ronald Reagan Presidential Library and Museum, https://www .reaganlibrary.gov/archives/speech/address-nation-iran-arms-and-contra-aid -controversy-november-13-1986.

137 **"a red line for us"**: Ben Rhodes, "Inside the White House During the Syrian 'Red Line' Crisis," *Atlantic,* June 3, 2018, https://www.theatlantic.com /international/archive/2018/06/inside-the-white-house-during-the-syrian-red -line-crisis/561887/.

137 **"one day—like a miracle"**: Lew Serviss and Azi Paybarah, "'One Day— It's Like a Miracle—It Will Disappear': What Trump Has Said About the Pandemic and Masks," *Hartford Courant,* October 2, 2020, https://www.courant .com/coronavirus/ct-nw-nyt-trump-quotes-covid-19-20201002-4gdxkic4gra 7pccvqap2llp54a-story.html.

137 **"Not one, not two"**: Starting Blocks, "LeBron James: 'Not 2, Not 3, Not 4, Not 5, Not 6, Not 7' Titles . . . None?: Video," *Cleveland.com,* January 12, 2019, https://www.cleveland.com/ohio-sports-blog/2011/06/lebron_james _not_2_not_3_not_4.html.

138 **"This nation should commit itself"**: John F. Kennedy, "Special Message to the Congress on Urgent National Needs" (speech excerpt, Washington, D.C., May 25, 1961), NASA, https://www.nasa.gov/vision/space/features/jfk _speech_text.html.

138 **Winston Churchill declared:** Winston Churchill, "We Shall Fight on the Beaches" (speech, London, June 4, 1940), International Churchill Society, https://winstonchurchill.org/resources/speeches/1940-the-finest-hour/we -shall-fight-on-the-beaches/.

138 **these changes allowed Ford to backtrack:** Dick Ravitch, interview by Jeff Nussbaum, October 20, 2015. After a version of this chapter was published by *The New Yorker* in October 2015, I had a conversation with Dick

Ravitch, who wanted to clarify several points. This insight is one of those clarifications.

139 **bankruptcy negotiating tactic:** Phillips-Fein, "Lessons."

8: President Dwight Eisenhower's Apology for the Failure of the D-Day Invasion, June 1944

143 **"a tense and coiled spring":** Dwight D. Eisenhower, *Crusade in Europe*, reprint edition (Baltimore: Johns Hopkins University Press, 1997), 249.

144 **"isolated original attacking forces":** Ibid., 250.

144 **The rain had not stopped:** Roger Hand, "'Okay, We'll Go.'–An Analysis of Eisenhower's Decisions Launching Overlord," *Army History*, no. 44 (Spring 1997): 23, https://www.jstor.org/stable/26304382.

144 **A delay beyond the sixth:** Merle Miller, *Ike the Soldier: As They Knew Him* (New York: G. P. Putnam's Sons, 1987), 600.

144 **"The question":** Tim Rives, "'OK, We'll Go.' Just What Did Ike Say When He Launched the D-Day Invasion 70 Years Ago?," *Prologue*, spring 2014, https://www.archives.gov/files/publications/prologue/2014/spring/d-day.pdf, 38.

144 **In planning the assault:** Ibid.

145 **Monty, usually cautious:** Miller, *Ike the Soldier*, 613.

145 **5,400 craft:** Hand, "Okay, We'll Go," 23.

145 **"I don't like it":** Scott Simon, "The Speech Eisenhower Never Gave on the Normandy Invasion," NPR, June 8, 2013, https://www.npr.org/2013/06/08/189535104/the-speech-eisenhower-never-gave-on-the-normandy-invasion.

146 **Captain Harry Butcher:** Harry C. Butcher, *My Three Years with Eisenhower: The Personal Diary of Captain Harry C. Butcher, USNR, Naval Aide to General Eisenhower, 1942 to 1945* (New York: Simon & Schuster, 1946), 558.

146 **"I hope to God I'm right":** Simon, "The Speech Eisenhower Never Gave."

147 **he would tear up the draft:** Miller, *Ike the Soldier*, 616.

147 **"order of the day":** Timothy Rives, "General Dwight D. Eisenhower's D-Day Radio Address to the Allied Nations (June 6, 1944)," Library of Congress, accessed August 8, 2019, http://www.loc.gov/static/programs/national-recording-preservation-board/documents/EisenhowerDDayRadioAddress.pdf.

147 **was to be broadcast:** D-day statement to soldiers, sailors, and airmen of the Allied Expeditionary Force, June 1944, Collection DDE-EPRE, Eisenhower, Dwight D: Papers, Pre-Presidential, 1916–1952, Dwight D. Eisenhower Library, National Archives and Records Administration.

147 **He had begun composing:** Ibid.

148 **"free men of the world":** Ibid.

148 **"I am a verb":** William Safire, "On Language: Invasion of the Verbs," *New York Times,* October 6, 1985, https://www.nytimes.com/1985/10/06 /magazine/on-language-invasion-of-the-verbs.html.

148 **"a passive-evasive way":** Mark Memmott, "It's True: 'Mistakes Were Made' Is the King of Non-Apologies," NPR, May 14, 2013, https://www.npr .org/sections/thetwo-way/2013/05/14/183924858/its-true-mistakes-were -made-is-the-king-of-non-apologies.

149 **George H. W. Bush famously said:** "Remarks by President Bush ('This Will Not Stand, This Aggression Against Kuwait')," Margaret Thatcher Foundation, accessed August 8, 2019, https://www.margaretthatcher.org/document /110704.

149 **"Tonight, we are a country":** "Text: President Bush Addresses the Nation," *Washington Post,* September 20, 2001, https://www.washingtonpost.com/wp -srv/nation/specials/attacked/transcripts/bushaddress_092001.html.

150 **Eisenhower said in the interview:** "CBS Reports (1964): D-Day Plus 20 Years—Eisenhower Returns to Normandy," CBS News, June 5, 2019, https:// www.cbsnews.com/video/cbs-reports-1964-d-day-plus-20-years-eisenhower -returns-to-normandy/.

150 **diary of Captain Harry Butcher:** BUTCHER DIARY, June 28–July 14, 1944 (1)(2), 1944, Box 168, Principal File, Dwight D. Eisenhower Pre-Presidential Papers, Eisenhower Presidential Library and Museum.

151 **Gary Sheffield argued:** "D-Day 75: How Close Did D-Day Come to Failure?," BBC, accessed August 8, 2019, http://www.bbc.co.uk/guides/zgtttfr.

9: Emperor Hirohito Apologizes for World War II, 1948

154 **Hirohito had become emperor:** Stephen Large, *Emperor Hirohito and Showa Japan: A Political Biography* (New York: Routledge, 1992), from the introduction.

155 **prevailing opinion:** Kyodo, "Emperor Hirohito 'Too Weak' to Stop Japan Entering Second World War, Declassified Documents Show," *South China Morning Post,* July 20, 2017, https://www.scmp.com/news/asia/east-asia /article/2103390/powerless-hirohito-opposed-japanese-involvement-second -world-war.

155 **Hirohito had been advised:** Atsushi Kodera, "Pictures of World War II Imperial Shelter Released to Public for First Time in 50 Years," *Japan Times,* August 1, 2015, https://www.japantimes.co.jp/news/2015/08/01/national

/history/pictures-world-war-ii-imperial-shelter-released-public-first-time-50
-years/#.XB-otVxKiUk.

155 **They requested his presence:** Lynn Vincent and Sara Vladic, *Indianapolis: The True Story of the Worst Sea Disaster in U.S. Naval History and the Fifty-Year Fight to Exonerate an Innocent Man* (New York: Simon & Schuster, 2018), 308.

155 **with the Potsdam Declaration:** "The Potsdam Declaration (July 26, 1945)," Asia for Educators, Columbia University, accessed August 7, 2019, http://afe.easia.columbia.edu/ps/japan/potsdam.pdf.

156 **"There must be eliminated":** "Potsdam Declaration," Atomic Heritage Foundation, accessed September 15, 2020, https://www.atomicheritage.org /key-documents/potsdam-declaration.

156 **"Continuing the war":** Vincent and Vladic, *Indianapolis*, 308.

156 **"emergency diets":** Max Fisher, "The Emperor's Speech: 67 Years Ago, Hirohito Transformed Japan Forever," *Atlantic*, August 15, 2012, https:// www.theatlantic.com/international/archive/2012/08/the-emperors-speech -67-years-ago-hirohito-transformed-japan-forever/261166/; John W. Dower, *Embracing Defeat: Japan in the Wake of World War II* (New York: W. W. Norton, 2000), 91.

156 **Hirohito's advisors:** Vincent and Vladic, *Indianapolis*, 315.

157 **In a historic first:** Ibid.

157 **last-minute coup attempt:** Kyodo, "The Coup Against the Emperor's Broadcast That Never Was," *Japan Times*, August 6, 2015, https://www .japantimes.co.jp/news/2015/08/06/national/history/coup-emperors -broadcast-never/#.XQkCIIhKiUk.

157 **The emperor of Japan spoke:** Fisher, "The Emperor's Speech."

157 *surrender* **and** *defeat***:** "Hirohito's 'Jewel Voice Broadcast,'" *Air Force Magazine*, August 2012, Archive.org, https://web.archive.org/web /20130910212019/http://www.airforcemag.com/MagazineArchive/Pages /2012/August%202012/0812keeper.aspx.

157 **second reading:** Herbert P. Bix, *Hirohito and the Making of Modern Japan* (New York: HarperCollins, 2000) 527.

157 **Between March and April 1946:** Dower, *Embracing Defeat*, 326.

158 **American brigadier general Elliott Thorpe:** Ibid., 327.

158 **"Destroy him":** "Incoming Classified Message From: CINCAFPAC Adv Tokyo, Japan To: War Department," National Diet Library, Japan, accessed August 7, 2019, https://www.ndl.go.jp/constitution/e/shiryo/03/064/064 _002l.html; Sodei Rinjiro, *Dear General MacArthur: Letters from the Japanese During the American Occupation* (Lanham, MD: Rowman & Littlefield, 2006), 66.

158 **war criminal:** Bix, *Hirohito*, 544.

158 **among America's allies:** Victor Sebestyen, "How the Emperor Became Human (and MacArthur Became Divine)," *Longreads*, November 2015, https://longreads.com/2015/11/11/how-the-emperor-became-human-and-macarthur-became-divine/.

158 **a quarter to a half:** Dower, *Embracing Defeat*, 327.

158 **In February 1946:** Sebestyen, "How the Emperor Became Human (and MacArthur Became Divine)."

158 **Letters received by General MacArthur:** Rinjiro, *Dear General MacArthur*, 71.

159 **"undertakes a leading part":** "Press Release, Gen. MacArthur Sees Liberalism in Imperial Rescript," National Diet Library, Japan, accessed August 7, 2019, https://www.ndl.go.jp/constitution/e/shiryo/03/057/057_001l.html.

159 **"revitalized and refocused":** Dower, *Embracing Defeat*, 334.

160 **"crimes against peace":** "The Nuremberg Trial and the Tokyo War Crimes Trials (1945–1948)," Milestones: 1945–1952, United States Department of State, accessed August 7, 2019, https://history.state.gov/milestones/1945-1952/nuremberg.

163 **In the summer of 1948:** Dower, *Embracing Defeat*, 329.

163 **the emperor delivered a secret message:** Ibid.

165 **George Wallace, who, after losing:** Dan T. Carter, *The Politics of Rage: George Wallace, the Origins of the New Conservatism, and the Transformation of American Politics* (Baton Rouge: Louisiana State University Press, 1995), 96.

165 **According to Haney López:** Ian Haney López, *Dog Whistle Politics* (Oxford: Oxford University Press, 2014), 16.

166 **In *Safire's Political Dictionary*:** William Safire, *Safire's Political Dictionary* (Oxford: Oxford University Press, 2008), 190.

166 **"subtle changes":** Ibid., 190.

166 ***pretty* in one poll:** Richard Morin, "Behind the Numbers Confessions of a Pollster," *Washington Post*, October 16, 1988, https://www.washingtonpost.com/archive/opinions/1988/10/16/behind-the-numbers-confessions-of-a-pollster/3523c065-11b5-42ba-9986-c317bdecf2dd/?utm_term=.3638818efa2e.

166 **Frank Luntz:** Frank I. Luntz, *Words That Work: It's Not What You Say, It's What People Hear* (New York: Hyperion, 2008), 46.

166 **"It's not what you say":** Ibid., xi.

167 **Professor William Benoit:** Kimberly D. Elsbach, "Review of *Accounts, Excuses, and Apologies: A Theory of Image Restoration Strategies,* by William L. Benoit," *Administrative Science Quarterly* 42, no. 3 (September 1997): 584–586.

167 **"Accepting full blame"**: Joy Clarkson, "Mea Culpa: The Rhetoric of Apology and Confession," *Joy Clarkson* (blog), November 13, 2017, accessed August 8, 2019, https://joyclarkson.com/home/2017/11/13/mea-culpa-the -rhetoric-of-apology-and-confession.

167 **Ronald Reagan's statement:** "Ronald Reagan Iran Contra Address to the Nation," American Rhetoric, last modified July 17, 2018, https://www .americanrhetoric.com/speeches/ronaldreaganirancontraspeech.htm.

168 **"A few months ago"**: Ibid.

168 **Recent studies have shown:** Richard Hanania, "Does Apologizing Work? An Empirical Test of the Conventional Wisdom," *SSRN* (September 1, 2015), https://papers.ssrn.com/sol3/papers.cfm?abstract_id=2654465.

168 **professor Cass Sunstein:** Cass R. Sunstein, "In Politics, Apologies Are for Losers," *New York Times,* July 27, 2019, https://www.nytimes.com/2019/07 /27/opinion/sunday/when-should-a-politician-apologize.html.

168 **Lennox Tierney:** Mike Boehm, "Lennox Tierney Dies at 101; Advocate for Asian Art in Southland," *Los Angeles Times,* June 26, 2015, https://www .latimes.com/local/obituaries/la-me-lennox-tierney-20150626-story.html.

168 **"MacArthur refused to admit"**: Matthew D. LaPlante, "MacArthur Aide: U.S. Must Learn from Errors," *Salt Lake Tribune,* December 7, 2006, https:// archive.sltrib.com/article.php?id=4794305&itype=NGPSID.

169 *Bungei shunju*: 「朕(ちん)ノ不徳(ふとく)ナル、深(ふか)ク天下(てんか)ニ愧(は)ヅ」の衝撃大論争「昭和天皇国民への謝罪詔書草稿」四つの謎 / 加藤恭子;高橋紘;秦郁彦【他】; *Bungei shunju*, August 2003, 166–180. 「詔書草稿」をこう読んだ-熟読玩味した十一人の目に映じたこの文書の意義; *Bungei shunju*, August 2003, 182–189.

169 **"I really want to include remorse"**: "Emperor Showa Wanted to Express 'Deep Regret' in Speech, Documents Reveal," NHK World-Japan, January 22, 2020, https://www3.nhk.or.jp/nhkworld/en/news/backstories/817/.

170 **"Awakened from sleep"**: "Cache of Rare 'Waka' Poems Written by Hirohito Emerge," *Asahi Shimbun,* January 2, 2019, http://www.asahi.com/ajw /articles/AJ201901020035.html.

10: President Kennedy on the Military Operation That Destroyed the Nuclear Weapons Buildup in Cuba, October 1962

173 **Kennedy's public schedule:** "Congressional Campaign Trip: Cleveland, Ohio, Arrival, Rally, Motorcade, Departure," White House Photographs, John F. Kennedy Presidential Library and Museum, created October 19, 1962,

accessed August 16, 2019, https://www.jfklibrary.org/asset-viewer/archives
/JFKWHP/1962/Month%2010/Day%2019/JFKWHP-1962-10-19-B.

173 **"fellow Democrats":** "JFK in Cleveland, Ohio (October 19, 1962)," You-
Tube video, 7:35, posted by "David Von Pein's JFK Channel," March 1, 2015,
https://www.youtube.com/watch?v=7XkAIUMuhZc.

173 **"It has been said":** "Remarks at Cook County Democratic Party Dinner, Chicago, Illinois, 19 October 1962," Papers of John F. Kennedy, Presidential Papers, President's Office Files, John F. Kennedy Presidential Library
and Museum, https://www.jfklibrary.org/asset-viewer/archives/JFKPOF/041
/JFKPOF-041-017.

174 **"the satellite missile race":** "50th Anniversary of the Missile Gap Controversy" (transcript of forum, Boston, MA, September 26, 2011), John F.
Kennedy Presidential Library and Museum, https://www.jfklibrary.org/events
-and-awards/forums/past-forums/transcripts/50th-anniversary-of-the-missile
-gap-controversy.

174 **They had recommended:** McGeorge Bundy, *Danger and Survival: Choices
About the Bomb in the First Fifty Years* (New York: Random House, 1988), 232.

174 **consensus of Kennedy's advisors:** Ernest R. May and Philip D. Zelikow,
The Kennedy Tapes: Inside the White House During the Cuban Missile Crisis,
concise edition (New York: W. W. Norton, 2002), 113.

175 **LeMay summarized it thus:** Ibid., 117.

175 **McGeorge Bundy came to visit:** Laurence Chang and Peter Kornbluh,
eds., *The Cuban Missile Crisis, 1962: A National Security Archive Documents
Reader* (New York: The New Press, 1998), 135.

175 **"straw boss":** Bundy, *Danger and Survival,* 400.

175 **The Color of Truth:** Kai Bird, *The Color of Truth: McGeorge Bundy and
William Bundy: Brothers in Arms* (New York: Simon & Schuster, 1998), 234.

175 **"did some strange flip-flops":** Ibid., 233.

175 **"didn't like it":** Ibid., 232.

176 **"I now know how Tojo felt":** Bundy, *Danger and Survival,* 398.

176 **as Kennedy concluded his remarks:** "Kennedy's Cold (10–19–
1962)," Chicago History Today, last updated October 19, 2016, https://
chicagohistorytoday.wordpress.com/2016/10/19/kennedys-cold-10-19-1962/.

176 **Bundy described his morning meeting:** Chang and Kornbluh, *The Cuban
Missile Crisis,* 134.

177 **Charles Bartlett:** Adam Bernstein, "Charles Bartlett, Pulitzer-Winning
Journalist and Kennedy Loyalist, Dies at 95," *Washington Post,* February 18,
2017, https://www.washingtonpost.com/national/charles-bartlett-pulitzer

-winning-journalist-and-kennedy-loyalist-dies-at-95/2017/02/18/0c9d22d0
-f553-11e6-b9c9-e83fce42fb61_story.html?utm_term=.7373a5c9ba2f.

177 *Thirteen Days*: Robert F. Kennedy, *Thirteen Days: A Memoir of the Cuban Missile Crisis* (New York: W. W. Norton, 1999), 36.

177 **President Jimmy Carter:** William J. Clinton, "Remarks at a Ceremony Presenting the Presidential Medal of Freedom to Former President Jimmy Carter and Rosalynn Carter in Atlanta" (remarks, Atlanta, GA, August 9, 1999), Govinfo, https://www.govinfo.gov/content/pkg/PPP-1999-book2/pdf/PPP-1999-book2-doc-pg1421.pdf.

179 **followed by "further military action":** James M. Lindsay, "TWE Remembers: Secret Soviet Tactical Nuclear Weapons in Cuba (Cuban Missile Crisis; a Coda)," Council on Foreign Relations, October 29, 2012, https://www.cfr.org/blog/twe-remembers-secret-soviet-tactical-nuclear-weapons-cuba-cuban-missile-crisis-coda.

179 **Soviet general Anatoly Gribkov:** Juan O. Tamayo, "Secret Nukes: The Untold Story of the Cuban Missile Crisis," *Miami Herald,* October 13, 2012, https://www.miamiherald.com/latest-news/article1943643.html.

179 **Robert McNamara, who was also attending:** Ibid.

180 **"The Decision to Use the Atomic Bomb":** Henry Stimson, "Stimson on the Bomb," Atomic Heritage Foundation, accessed August 16, 2019, https://www.atomicheritage.org/key-documents/stimson-bomb.

181 **"national security nor my ulcer":** Ted Sorensen, *Counselor: A Life at the Edge of History,* reprint edition (New York: Harper Perennial, 2009), 293.

181 **"When I reflected":** Ibid.

181 **"went through more changes":** Ibid.

181 **"The draft Sorensen wrote":** Bundy, *Danger and Survival,* 401.

182 **"It shall be the policy":** "Cuban Missile Crisis Address to the Nation Delivered 22 October 1962," American Rhetoric, John F. Kennedy, accessed August 16, 2019, https://americanrhetoric.com/speeches/jfkcubanmissilecrisis.html.

182 **"regard any missile":** "President's Speech Air Attack," 6–4–2: Cuba: Cuban Crisis, 1962: Kennedy-Khrushchev Letters, etc., John F. Kennedy Presidential Library and Museum, accessed August 16, 2019, https://www.jfklibrary.org/asset-viewer/archives/RFKAG/217/RFKAG-217-001.

182 **"Nuclear weapons are so destructive":** Ibid.

182 *Byword* **makes its first appearance:** John F. Kennedy, "Remarks of Senator John F. Kennedy at Citizens for Kennedy Rally, Waldorf Astoria" (remarks, New York City, September 14, 1960), John F. Kennedy Presidential Library and

Museum, https://www.jfklibrary.org/archives/other-resources/john-f-kennedy
-speeches/citizens-for-kennedy-rally-nyc-19600914.

182 **Kennedy abandoned the idea:** Bird, *The Color of Truth,* 234.

183 **Mark Songer:** Mark Songer, "Affidavit of Mark Songer" (affidavit, Denver, CO, September 3, 2019), Robson Forensic.

184 **"So I was asked":** Ted Sorensen, interview by Jeremy Isaacs Productions,
Cold War, CNN, March 1997, https://nsarchive2.gwu.edu/coldwar/interviews
/episode-10/sorensen2.html.

185 **"Each one of us":** Kennedy, *Thirteen Days,* 35.

Part 5: The People Choose

189 **Four years ago:** "The 1993 Elections: Excerpts of Speeches, in Victory
and Defeat," *New York Times,* November 3, 1993, https://www.nytimes.com
/1993/11/03/nyregion/the-1993-elections-deciding-excerpts-of-speeches-in
-victory-and-defeat.html.

190 **"virtuoso lesson":** Francis X. Clines, "The 1993 Elections: Dinkins;
Mayor Is Gracious in Defeat as He Calls for New Yorkers to 'Move Forward,'"
New York Times, November 4, 1993, https://www.nytimes.com/1993/11/04
/nyregion/1993-elections-dinkins-mayor-gracious-defeat-he-calls-for-new
-yorkers-move.html.

11: Illinois Governor John Peter Altgeld's Farewell Address Following His Defeat in the 1896 Election, January 1897

193 **June 26, 1893:** Robert D. Sampson, "Governor John Peter Altgeld Pardons the Haymarket Prisoners," Illinois Labor History Society, accessed August
15, 2019, http://www.illinoislaborhistory.org/labor-history-articles/governor
-john-peter-altgeld-pardons-the-haymarket-prisoners.

194 **Chicago's Haymarket Square:** Paul Avrich, *The Haymarket Tragedy*
(Princeton, NJ: Princeton University Press, 1984), 189.

194 **Chicago, a city:** John Peter Altgeld, *The Mind and Spirit of John Peter
Altgeld: Selected Writings and Addresses,* ed. Henry M. Christman (Champaign:
University of Illinois Press, 1960), 1.

195 **"call attention briefly":** John P. Altgeld, *Our Penal Machinery and
Its Victims* (Chicago: A. C. McClurg, 1886), https://archive.org/details
/ourpenalmachiner00altguoft/page/n5,n8.

195 **fathers of the labor movement:** "Schilling, George A. (1850–1938)," Abraham Lincoln Presidential Library and Museum, accessed August 15, 2019, http://alplm.libraryhost.com/?p=creators/creator&id=63.

195 **Altgeld returned his attention:** Altgeld, *The Mind and Spirit*, 5.

195 **Federation of Organized Trades and Labor Unions:** William J. Adelman, "The Haymarket Affair," Illinois Labor History Society, accessed August 15, 2019, http://www.illinoislaborhistory.org/the-haymarket-affair.

195 **May 3, 1886:** Avrich, *The Haymarket Tragedy*, 189.

195 **mass meeting:** Robert McNamara, "How a Bomb Tossed in 1886 Impacted the American Labor Movement," ThoughtCo., January 18, 2019, https://www.thoughtco.com/1886-haymarket-square-riot-chicago-1773901.

196 **anarchist Samuel Fielden:** Harry Barnard, *Eagle Forgotten: The Life of John Peter Altgeld* (New York: Duell, Sloan and Pearce, 1938), 104; Sampson, "Governor John Peter Altgeld."

196 **"Here come the bloodhounds":** "Illinois vs. August Spies et al. trial transcript no. 1. Testimony of Louis Haas (second appearance), 1886 July 27," Chicago Historical Society Haymarket Affair Digital Collection, accessed August 15, 2019, http://www.chicagohistoryresources.org/hadc/transcript/volumek/251-300/K258-284.htm.

196 **dynamite bomb:** "Bomb Thrown into a Crowd of Policemen," *Chicago Tribune*, May 5, 1886, ProQuest.

196 **no evidence that there was firing:** Barnard, *Eagle Forgotten*, 106.

196 **"known and suspected revolutionaries":** Avrich, *The Haymarket Tragedy*, 221.

196 **"The privileged class":** "Haymarket Martyr Albert Parsons's Last Words to His Wife," History Matters: The U.S. Survey Course on the Web, George Mason University, accessed August 15, 2019, http://historymatters.gmu.edu/d/46/.

196 **"the man really responsible":** Edward De Grazia, "The Haymarket Bomb," *Law and Literature* 18, no. 3 (2006): 310, accessed September 25, 2020, doi:10.1525/lal.2006.18.3.283.

197 **"I want to do something":** Barnard, *Eagle Forgotten*, 118; Sampson, "Governor John Peter Altgeld."

197 **Altgeld began his remarks:** Altgeld, *The Mind and Spirit*, 49–62.

197 **Altgeld became too exhausted:** Barnard, *Eagle Forgotten*, 168.

197 **Altgeld asked for the records:** Ibid., 185; Sampson, "Governor John Peter Altgeld."

197 **Darrow later recounted:** Sampson, "Governor John Peter Altgeld."

198 **"I will pardon them"**: Altgeld, *The Mind and Spirit,* 10.

198 **"A violent incident"**: Eric Zorn, "Altgeld's Legacy Shows True Impact of 'Tough Decision,'" *Chicago Tribune,* March 6, 1999, https://www.chicagotribune.com/news/ct-xpm-1999-03-16-9903160060-story.html.

198 **pardon message**: John P. Altgeld, *Live Questions* (Chicago: Geo S. Bowen & Sons, 1899), 328, https://archive.org/details/livequestions00altg/page/4.

198 **"Wherever there is wrong"**: Ibid., 334.

198 **the term *soundbite***: William Safire, "On Language: Sound Bite, Define Yourself!," *New York Times,* November 13, 1988, https://www.nytimes.com/1988/11/13/magazine/on-language-sound-bite-define-yourself.html.

199 **"I know not what"**: "Give Me Liberty or Give Me Death!," *Colonial Williamsburg,* March 3, 2020, https://www.colonialwilliamsburg.org/learn/deep-dives/give-me-liberty-or-give-me-death/.

200 **"If you can't make"**: Robert A. Lehrman and Eric Schnure, *The Political Speechwriter's Companion: A Guide for Writers and Speakers,* 2nd edition (Thousand Oaks, CA: CQ Press, 2020), 18.

200 **So, on June 26:** Barnard, *Eagle Forgotten,* 214; Sampson, "Governor John Peter Altgeld."

200 **Whitlock remembered:** Barnard, *Eagle Forgotten,* 215; Sampson, "Governor John Peter Altgeld."

200 **"Altgeld has done"**: "Altgeld and the Anarchists," *New York Times,* June 28, 1893, https://timesmachine.nytimes.com/timesmachine/1893/06/28/109703245.pdf.

200 **The *Chicago Tribune* wrote:** Barnard, *Eagle Forgotten,* 393.

200 **The *Washington Post* pointed out:** Sampson, "Governor John Peter Altgeld."

201 **One political cartoon:** "The Pardon of the Haymarket Prisoners (June 26, 1893)," *Famous Trials by Professor Douglas O. Linder,* accessed August 15, 2019, https://famous-trials.com/haymarket/1182-pardon.

201 **The *Chicago Tribune* gloried:** Barnard, *Eagle Forgotten,* 393.

201 **The *New-York Tribune* wrote:** Ibid., 395.

201 **John Riley Tanner:** Ibid., 397.

201 **"The presence of the defeated"**: Altgeld, *The Mind and Spirit,* 376.

203 **"Wrong may seem to triumph"**: Barnard, *Eagle Forgotten,* 435

203 **"He so loved justice"**: "In Memoriam John Peter Altgeld," Clarence Darrow Digital Collection, University of Minnesota Law Library, accessed August 15, 2019, http://moses.law.umn.edu/darrow/documents/In_Memoriam_Altgeld.pdf.

12: Hillary Clinton's 2016 Victory Speech, November 2016

205 **Jake Sullivan had worked:** Jake Sullivan, interview by Jeff Nussbaum, January 16, 2019.

206 **Palmieri felt somewhat differently:** Jen Palmieri, interview by Jeff Nussbaum, January 13, 2019.

207 **Hillary's own description:** Hillary Clinton, *What Happened* (New York: Simon & Schuster, 2017), 381.

208 **afternoon of October 28:** Nate Silver, "The Comey Letter Probably Cost Clinton the Election," *FiveThirtyEight,* May 3, 2017, https://fivethirtyeight .com/features/the-comey-letter-probably-cost-clinton-the-election/.

208 **Clinton was en route:** "Travels of Hillary Clinton," P2016, accessed August 8, 2019, http://www.p2016.org/clinton/clintoncal1016.html.

208 **Upon arrival:** "Hillary Clinton Statement on Emails Investigation," C-SPAN, October 28, 2016, https://www.c-span.org/video/?417629-2/hillary -clinton-calls-release-information-email-investigation.

208 **pollster Joel Benenson:** Joel Benenson, interview by Jeff Nussbaum, September 1, 2019.

208 **Schwerin had begun interning:** Dan Schwerin, interview by Jeff Nussbaum, January 11, 2017.

210 **"breathing a big sigh":** Jeff Stein, "Hillary Clinton: I'm Breathing a 'Big Sigh of Relief' After Iowa Caucus," *Vox,* February 2, 2016, https://www.vox .com/2016/2/2/10892714/hillary-clinton-iowa-reaction.

210 **Clinton's words to the UN:** "Hillary Clinton Declares 'Women's Rights Are Human Rights,'" PBS, September 8, 1995, https://www.pbs.org/weta /washingtonweek/web-video/hillary-clinton-declares-womens-rights-are -human-rights.

210 **Unlikable, untrustworthy:** William Cheng, "The Long, Sexist History of 'Shrill' Women," *Time,* March 23, 2016, https://time.com/4268325/history -calling-women-shrill/.

212 **Peggy Noonan writes:** Peggy Noonan, *What I Saw at the Revolution: A Political Life in the Reagan Era* (New York: Random House, 1990), 77–78.

215 **"George Bernard Shaw once wrote":** Robert F. Kennedy, "Remarks at the University of Kansas, March 18, 1968," Kennedy Family, John F. Kennedy Presidential Library and Museum, accessed August 6, 2019, https://www .jfklibrary.org/learn/about-jfk/the-kennedy-family/robert-f-kennedy/robert-f -kennedy-speeches/remarks-at-the-university-of-kansas-march-18-1968.

215 **"George Bernard Shaw once said":** George P. Hunt, "Editors' Note," *Life,* June 21, 1968, 3.

216 **in Las Vegas:** Rachel Revesz, "Hillary Clinton Hugs Sobbing Girl Worried That Her Parents Are to Be Deported," *Independent,* February 18, 2016, https://www.independent.co.uk/news/world/americas/us-elections/hillary-clinton-hugs -sobbing-girl-worried-that-her-parents-are-to-be-deported-a6881611.html.

217 **Associated Press started calling:** Lauren Easton, "Calling the Presidential Race State by State," Associated Press, November 9, 2016, https://blog.ap.org /behind-the-news/calling-the-presidential-race-state-by-state.

217 **Shortly after 1:30 a.m.:** Clinton, *What Happened,* 385.

218 **Hillary then put in a call:** Ibid., 387.

218 **Senator Adlai Stevenson, upon losing:** Jena McGregor, "Remembering a Speech from 'the Most Beautiful Loser' After Trump Won't Commit to Accepting Results," *Washington Post,* October 20, 2016, https://www.washingtonpost .com/news/on-leadership/wp/2016/10/20/remembering-a-speech-from-the -most-beautiful-loser-after-trump-wont-commit-to-accepting-results/.

218 *New Yorker*'s **Hendrik Hertzberg:** Hendrik Hertzberg, "Concession Stand," *New Yorker,* November 3, 1996, https://www.newyorker.com /magazine/1996/11/11/concession-stand.

219 **"partisan feeling must yield":** McGregor, "Remembering a Speech."

220 **"No matter how hard the loss":** "Text of Gore's Concession Speech," *New York Times,* December 13, 2000, https://www.nytimes.com/2000/12/13 /politics/text-of-goreacutes-concession-speech.html.

220 **Early drafts of President Clinton's speech:** Philip Bump, "How Bill Clinton's Statement on Al Gore's 2000 Presidential Concession Evolved," *Atlantic,* March 14, 2014, https://www.theatlantic.com/politics/archive/2014/03/how -bill-clintons-statement-al-gores-2000-presidential-concession-evolved/359196/.

220 **toned-down version:** "FOIA 2006–0221-F-2000 Presidential Election Vote Count in Florida," Clinton Digital Library, accessed December 4, 2020, 3, https://clinton.presidentiallibraries.us/items/show/14500.

220 **"The American people, however divided":** William J. Clinton, "Remarks on the Resolution of the 2000 Presidential Election and an Exchange with Reporters in North Aylesbury, United Kingdom" (speech, North Aylesbury, United Kingdom, December 14, 2000), U.S. Government Publishing Office, 2696, https://www.govinfo.gov/content/pkg/PPP-2000-book3/pdf/PPP-2000 -book3-doc-pg2696-2.pdf.

220 **Paul Glastris:** Uri Friedman, "The Damage Will Last," *Atlantic,* November 27, 2020, https://www.theatlantic.com/ideas/archive/2020/11/trumps -refusal-to-concede-wasnt-some-sideshow/617215/.

221 **speechwriter named Matthew Scully:** Matthew Scully, interview by Jeff Nussbaum, August 31, 2020.

221 *Sarah from Alaska*: Scott Conroy, *Sarah from Alaska: The Sudden Rise and Brutal Education of a New Conservative Superstar* (New York: PublicAffairs, 2009), 11.

221 For the McCain team: Ben Smith, "Why Palin Didn't Get a Concession Speech," *Politico,* April 26, 2009, https://www.politico.com/blogs/ben-smith /2009/04/why-palin-didnt-get-a-concession-speech-017822.

221 she may have wanted more: Kate Snow and Kelly Hagan, "Sarah Palin's Never-Heard Victory, Concession Speeches," ABC News, November 4, 2009, https:// abcnews.go.com/GMA/Politics/sarah-palin-speeches-heard/story?id=8988514.

222 "America has made her choice": Shushannah Walshe and Scott Conroy, "Sarah Palin's Lost Speeches," *Daily Beast,* July 14, 2017, https://www .thedailybeast.com/sarah-palins-lost-speeches.

223 staffer Steve Schmidt: Snow and Hagan, "Sarah Palin's Never-Heard Victory."

223 political strategist Tad Devine: Daniel Bush, "How Trump Could Rewrite Concession Speech History," *PBS NewsHour,* October 31, 2016, https:// www.pbs.org/newshour/politics/trump-rewrite-concession-speech-history.

223 Secretary Clinton thanked: Christina Cauterucci, "Hillary Clinton Is the First Presidential Candidate to Say 'I'm Sorry' in Concession Speech," *Slate,* November 15, 2016, https://slate.com/human-interest/2016/11/hillary-clinton -is-the-first-presidential-candidate-to-say-im-sorry-in-concession-speech.html.

223 "more deeply divided": Hillary Clinton, "Hillary Clinton's Concession Speech (Full Text)" (speech, New York City, November 9, 2016), CNN, https://www.cnn.com/2016/11/09/politics/hillary-clinton-concession-speech /index.html.

Part 6: Events Intervene

227 In 1895, Samuel Clemens: Mark Twain, "An Undelivered Speech" (undelivered speech, Philadelphia, PA, March 25, 1895), *Project Gutenberg's Mark Twain's Speeches,* https://www.gutenberg.org/files/3188/3188-h/3188 -h.htm.

13: The Remarks Condoleezza Rice Had Intended to Give on the Bush Administration's Foreign Policy, September 11, 2001

232 his national security advisor: Jane Perlez, "Rice on Front Line in Foreign Policy Role," *New York Times,* August 19, 2001, https://www.nytimes.com /2001/08/19/world/rice-on-front-line-in-foreign-policy-role.html.

232 **Caspar Weinberger:** James Gertanzang, "Weinberger Sees End of 'Mutual Suicide Pact,'" *Los Angeles Times,* October 10, 1985, https://www.latimes.com/archives/la-xpm-1985-10-10-mn-15630-story.html.

233 **in 1983, when President Reagan:** Andrew Glass, "President Reagan Calls for Launching 'Star Wars' Initiative, March 23, 1983," *Politico,* March 23, 2017, https://www.politico.com/story/2017/03/president-reagan-calls-for-launching-star-wars-initiative-march-23-1983-236259.

233 **"nuclear weapons impotent":** Ronald Reagan, "Address to the Nation on Defense and National Security" (speech, White House, Washington, D.C., March 23, 1983), https://www.reaganlibrary.gov/research/speeches/32383d.

233 **"reckless 'Star Wars' schemes":** "'Star Wars': How the Term Arose," *New York Times,* September 25, 1985, https://www.nytimes.com/1985/09/25/world/star-wars-how-the-term-arose.html.

233 **"hitting a bullet with a bullet":** Progressive Management, *Hitting a Bullet with a Bullet: A History of Ballistic Missile Defense (BMD)—Nike, Sprint and Spartan, Strategic Defense Initiative (SDI) Star Wars* (Progressive Management, 2016), introduction.

233 **Anti-Ballistic Missile (ABM) Treaty:** Wade Boese, "U.S. Withdraws from ABM Treaty, Response Muted," *Arms Control Today,* July/August 2002, https://www.armscontrol.org/act/2002-07/news/us-withdraws-abm-treaty-global-response-muted.

233 **"When you invent a new shield":** *Meet the Press,* September 9, 2001, NBC-Universal, 2001, https://video-alexanderstreet-com.ezproxy.cul.columbia.edu/watch/meet-the-press-september-9-2001 (subscription required).

233 **In 1998, Rumsfeld chaired:** Commission to Assess the Ballistic Missile Threat to the United States, *Executive Summary of the Report of the Commission to Assess the Ballistic Missile Threat to the United States,* by Hon. Donald H. Rumsfeld, Dr. Barry M. Blechman, Gen. Lee Butler, USAF (Ret.), Dr. Richard L. Garwin, Dr. William R. Graham, Dr. William Schneider, Jr., Gen. Larry D. Welch, USAF (Ret.), Dr. Paul D. Wolfowitz, Hon. R. James Woolsey (Washington, D.C.: Printing and Production Graphics, 1998), https://fas.org/irp/threat/bm-threat.htm.

233 **One month later, North Korea:** "US Ballistic Missile Defense Timeline: 1945–Today," Union of Concerned Scientists, March 29, 2019, https://www.ucsusa.org/resources/us-missile-defense-timeline.

234 **speech to the National Defense University:** George W. Bush, "President Bush Speech on Missile Defense" (speech, White House, Washington, D.C., May 1, 2001), https://fas.org/nuke/control/abmt/news/010501bush.html.

234 **Powell remained skeptical:** Perlez, "Rice on Front Line."

234 **"When Americans are asked"**: Ivo H. Daalder and James M. Lindsay, "Unilateral Withdrawal from the ABM Treaty Is a Bad Idea," Brookings, April 30, 2001, https://www.brookings.edu/opinions/unilateral-withdrawal-from-the-abm-treaty-is-a-bad-idea/.

234 **On September 9, 2001**: *Meet the Press,* September 9, 2001.

234 **"missile defense has to be weighted"**: Steven Mufson, "Sen. Biden Attacks Missile Defense Plan as Costly, Risky," *Washington Post,* September 11, 2001, A4.

235 **The Dow was down**: "Dow Jones Industrial Average," U.S. Securities and Exchange Commission, accessed May 25, 2020, https://www.sec.gov/Archives/edgar/data/357298/000035729801500016/dowjones.html; Alexandra Twin, "Bears vs. Bulls on Wall St.," CNN Money, September 10, 2001, https://money.cnn.com/2001/09/10/markets/markets_newyork/.

235 **a poll that appeared**: Dan Balz, "Poll Finds Public Wary on Tax Cut," *Washington Post,* September 11, 2001, A1.

235 **a poll by the Pew Research Center**: "Modest Support for Missile Defense, No Panic on China," Pew Research Center, June 11, 2001, https://www.people-press.org/2001/06/11/modest-support-for-missile-defense-no-panic-on-china/.

236 **Dr. Rice was to have conceded**: Robin Wright, "Top Focus Before 9/11 Wasn't on Terrorism," *Washington Post,* April 1, 2004, https://www.washingtonpost.com/archive/politics/2004/04/01/top-focus-before-911-wasnt-on-terrorism/a8def448-9549-4fde-913d-b69a2dd2bf25/.

237 **same poll that found**: "Modest Support for Missile Defense, No Panic on China."

237 **the research materials**: "MAD Isn't Crazy," 2001, Folder, 09/11/2001, Rice—Nitze School (Cancelled) [2], National Security Council—Media Communications and Speechwriting, George W. Bush Library, Dallas, TX.

239 **six-page document**: "Misconceptions About Missile Defense," 2001, Rice—Nitze School (Cancelled) [2], National Security Council—Media Communications and Speechwriting, George W. Bush Library, Dallas, TX.

239 **Senator Jack Reed**: "Floor Statement on the Nomination of Condoleezza Rice to Be Secretary of State," Sen. Jack Reed, January 25, 2005, https://www.reed.senate.gov/news/speeches/floor-statement-on-the-nomination-of-condoleezza-rice-to-be-secretary-of-state.

240 **did not contain**: Wright, "Top Focus Before 9/11 Wasn't on Terrorism."

240 **original research**: Rice, "Remarks by National Security Advisor Condoleezza Rice on Terrorism and Foreign Policy."

240 **the revamped speech**: Ibid.

240 **"An earthquake"**: Ibid.

14: Barry Jenkins's Best Picture Remarks for *Moonlight,* February 2017

243 **William Safire, in his compendium:** William Safire, *Lend Me Your Ears: Great Speeches in History,* 2nd edition (New York: W. W. Norton, 2004), 32.

244 **$16 million:** "Moonlight 2016," Box Office Mojo, accessed August 9, 2019, https://www.boxofficemojo.com/movies/?page=weekend&id =moonlight2016.htm.

244 **Jenkins maintained:** Lacey Rose, "Race, Barriers and Battling Nerves: A Candid Conversation with Oscar's Only 4 African-American Directing Nominees in 90 Years," *Hollywood Reporter,* February 23, 2018, https:// www.hollywoodreporter.com/features/race-barriers-battling-nerves-a -candid-conversation-oscars-4-african-american-directing-nominees-90- 1087644?utm_source=Sailthru&utm_medium=email&utm_campaign =THR%20Breaking%20News_2018-02-23%2007:15:00_lhuff&utm_term =hollywoodreporter_breakingnews.

244 ***Moonlight* was nominated in six:** THR Staff, "Golden Globes: 'Moonlight' Wins Best Motion Picture, Drama," *Hollywood Reporter,* January 1, 2017, https://www.hollywoodreporter.com/news/moonlight-wins-best -motion-picture-drama-golden-globes-2017-960354.

244 **Mahershala Ali won:** Holly Yan, "Mahershala Ali Becomes First Muslim Actor to Win an Oscar," CNN, February 27, 2017, https://www.cnn.com /2017/02/27/entertainment/mahershala-ali-first-muslim-oscar-winner-trnd /index.html.

245 **"I tell my students":** Amanda N'Duka, "'Moonlight' Writers Dedicate Oscar Win to the Underrepresented," *Deadline,* February 26, 2017, https://deadline.com/2017/02/moonlight-best-adapted-screenplay-oscar -2017-1202004715/.

245 **"This goes out":** Ibid.

245 **the final category:** THR Staff, "Oscars 2017: The Order That the Awards Will Be Announced," *Hollywood Reporter,* February 26, 2017, https://www .hollywoodreporter.com/news/oscars-2017-guide-order-awards-presented -980082.

245 **The Best Director award:** Jackie Strause, "Oscars: 'La La Land' Director Damien Chazelle Becomes Youngest Best Director Winner," *Hollywood Reporter,* February 26, 2017, https://www.hollywoodreporter.com/news /damien-chazelles-best-director-oscars-2017-win-makes-him-youngest-winner -980243.

245 ***La La Land* was the heavy favorite:** Scott Feinberg, "Oscars Primer: What You Need to Know Before Tonight's Ceremony," *Hollywood Reporter,*

February 26, 2017, https://www.hollywoodreporter.com/race/oscars-primer
-what-you-need-know-before-tonights-ceremony-980175.

245 **Cullinan was busy:** Lawrence Yee, Stuart Oldham, and Jacob Bryant,
"New Photos Show PWC Accountant Tweeting, Mixing Envelopes Backstage
at Oscars (EXCLUSIVE)," *Variety,* March 1, 2017, https://variety.com/2017
/film/news/oscar-best-picture-gaffe-brian-cullinan-envelope-1201999283/.

246 **"And the Academy Award":** "Year: 2016 (89th) Academy Awards, Category:
Best Picture: Moonlight," Academy Awards Acceptance Speech Database, accessed August 9, 2019, http://aaspeechesdb.oscars.org/results.aspx?AC=NEXT
_RECORD&XC=/results.aspx&BU=http%3A%2F%2Faaspeechesdb.oscars
.org%2F&TN=aatrans&SN=AUTO24937&SE=767&RN=14&MR=0&TR
=0&TX=1000&ES=0&CS=0&XP=&RF=WebReportList&EF=&DF
=WebReportOscars&RL=0&EL=0&DL=0&NP=255&ID=&MF=oscarsmsg
.ini&MQ=&TI=0&DT=&ST=0&IR=0&NR=0&NB=0&SV=0&SS=0&BG
=&FG=&QS=&OEX=ISO-8859–1&OEH=utf-8.

246 **"There's a lot of love":** Ibid.

247 **"I'm going to be really proud":** Ibid.

247 **"This is *Moonlight*":** Ibid.

247 **"Even in my dreams":** Ibid.

247 **"Thank you to the Acad":** Ibid.

247 **"I'd never seen":** Rory Carroll and Andrew Pulver, "Moonlight Wins
Best Picture Oscar, After Warren Beatty Gives Gong to La La Land," *Guardian,* February 27, 2017, https://www.theguardian.com/film/2017/feb/27
/moonlight-wins-best-picture-oscars-academy-award-2017.

247 **"something had changed":** Rose, "Race, Barriers and Battling Nerves."

248 **"To be sure":** John F. Kennedy, "John F. Kennedy Moon Speech—Rice
Stadium" (speech, Houston, TX, September, 12, 1962), NASA, https://er.jsc
.nasa.gov/seh/ricetalk.htm.

249 **"Sorry I'm late":** Robert A. Lehrman and Eric Schnure, *The Political
Speechwriter's Companion: A Guide for Writers and Speakers,* 2nd edition (Thousand Oaks, CA: CQ Press, 2020), 214–215.

250 **"But why, some say, the moon?":** Kennedy, "John F. Kennedy Moon Speech."

251 **Chip and Dan Heath observe:** Chip Heath and Dan Heath, *Made to
Stick: Why Some Ideas Survive and Others Die* (New York: Random House,
2007), 206.

251 **when we're exposed:** Gary Stix, "Fact or Fiction?: Oxytocin Is the
'Love Hormone,'" *Scientific American,* September 8, 2014, https://www
.scientificamerican.com/article/fact-or-fiction-oxytocin-is-the-love-hormone/.

253 "**Tarell [Alvin McCraney, cowriter]**": Jackson McHenry, "Here's What Barry Jenkins Would Have Said at the Oscars, If Given the Chance," *Vulture*, March 12, 2018, https://www.vulture.com/2018/03/barry-jenkins-reads-his -moonlight-oscars-acceptance-speech.html.

15: Last Words: Pope Pius XI, JFK, FDR, and Einstein, and Their Unfinished Prophecies of Peace, Various Years

255 "**No doctor, nothing more**": "Jefferson's Last Words," Thomas Jefferson Encyclopedia, Thomas Jefferson Foundation, accessed August 12, 2019, https://www.monticello.org/site/research-and-collections/jeffersons-last -words.

255 **the letter he wrote:** Gregory S. Schneider, "Jefferson's Powerful Last Public Letter Reminds Us What Independence Day Is All About," *Washington Post*, July 3, 2017, https://www.washingtonpost.com/news/retropolis/wp/2017/07 /03/jeffersons-last-public-letter-reminds-us-what-independence-day-is-all -about/?utm_term=.3aaba89a7fc9.

255 "**May [the Declaration of Independence]**": Andrew Glass, "Jefferson and Adams Die Hours Apart, July 4, 1826," *Politico*, July 3, 2016, https:// www.politico.com/story/2016/07/two-founding-fathers-die-hours-apart-july -4-1826-224943.

256 **In 1963, Kennedy:** Andrew Kohut, "From the Archives: JFK's America," Pew Research Center, July 5, 2019, https://www.pewresearch.org/fact-tank /2019/07/05/jfks-america/.

256 "**Even if Mr. Kennedy**": Joseph A. Loftus, "Johnson Promised Place on a '64 Kennedy Ticket," *New York Times*, November 1, 1963, https:// timesmachine.nytimes.com/timesmachine/1963/11/01/89969513.html ?pageNumber=1.

256 **Kennedy was also working:** John D. Pomfret, "Kennedy Calls Jobs Vital, Outranking Civil Rights," *New York Times*, November 16, 1963, https:// timesmachine.nytimes.com/timesmachine/1963/11/16/89973625.html.

256 "**Texas humor**": Ted Sorensen, *Counselor: A Life at the Edge of History*, reprint edition (New York: Harper Perennial, 2009), 360.

257 **Secretary of State George C. Marshall:** "The Marshall Plan Speech," George C. Marshall Foundation, accessed August 12, 2019, https://www .marshallfoundation.org/marshall/the-marshall-plan/marshall-plan-speech/.

257 **for his remarks:** Ibid.

257 "**We in this country**": John F. Kennedy, "Remarks Prepared for Delivery at the Trade Mart in Dallas, TX, November 22, 1963 [Undelivered]" (speech,

Dallas, TX, November 22, 1963), John F. Kennedy Presidential Library and Museum, https://www.jfklibrary.org/archives/other-resources/john-f-kennedy -speeches/dallas-tx-trade-mart-undelivered-19631122.

258 **Psalm 127:** Peter Smith, "Undelivered Speech Reflects Kennedy's Strong Catholic Ties," *Pittsburgh Post-Gazette,* November 21, 2013, https://www.post -gazette.com/news/nation/2013/11/22/Undelivered-speech-reflects-Kennedy -s-strong-Catholic-ties/stories/201311220137.

258 **"the fires of rage":** Sorensen, *Counselor,* 375.

258 **Edwin Walker:** Eric Pace, "Gen. Edwin Walker, 83, Is Dead," *New York Times,* November 2, 1993, https://timesmachine.nytimes.com/timesmachine /1993/11/02/481393.html?pageNumber=34.

258 **Walker declared:** Rebecca Onion, "The 'Wanted for Treason' Flyer Distributed in Dallas Before JFK's Visit," *Slate,* November 15, 2013, https://slate .com/human-interest/2013/11/jfk-assassination-flyer-distributed-in-dallas-by -edwin-walker-s-group-before-his-visit.html.

258 **"dissident voices":** Kennedy, "Remarks Prepared for Delivery."

259 **"But today other voices":** Ibid.

260 **"If fate somehow decreed":** Sorensen, *Counselor,* 377.

260 ***God Does Not Exist*:** Benito Mussolini, *God Does Not Exist,* trans. George Seldes (Lausanne, Switzerland: 1904), 2, https://archive.org/details /GodDoesNotExist.

261 **draft an encyclical:** David Alvarez, *Washington Post,* May 31, 2013, https://www.washingtonpost.com/opinions/2013/05/31/224e4830-9c5f -11e2-9bda-edd1a7fb557d_story.html?_=ddid-8-1563203160&noredirect =on&utm_term=.a94c332748a7.

261 **"I shall make them laugh":** Emma Fattorini, *Hitler, Mussolini, and the Vatican: Pope Pius XI and the Speech That Was Never Made* (Cambridge: Polity Press, 2011), 182.

261 **"against Italy":** Ibid., 184.

262 **In 2006, Pope Benedict XVI:** Roseanne T. Sullivan, "Who Knows? The Truth About Pope Pius XI and His Much-Maligned Successor," *Dappled Things,* accessed December 4, 2020, https://dappledthings.org/12098/who -knows-the-truth-about-pope-pius-xi-and-his-much-maligned-successor/

262 **"devastating for fascism":** Fattorini, *Hitler, Mussolini, and the Vatican,* 197.

262 **"You know, dear":** Ibid., 213.

264 **"Yesterday, December 7, 1941":** Harold Faber, "Lost Copy of 'Day of Infamy' Speech Found," *New York Times,* April 2, 1984, https://timesmachine .nytimes.com/timesmachine/1984/04/02/093684.html.

264 **Associated Press announcement:** "Jefferson Dinners to Hear Roosevelt," *New York Times,* April 6, 1945, https://timesmachine.nytimes.com/timesmachine/1945/04/06/88211743.html?pageNumber=18.

264 **the president was convalescing:** William Warren Rogers Jr., "The Death of a President, April 12, 1945: An Account from Warm Springs," *Georgia Historical Quarterly* 75, no. 1 (Spring 1991): 109.

265 **"I have a terrific pain":** Howard Markel, "Franklin D. Roosevelt's Painfully Eloquent Final Words," PBS, April 12, 2018, https://www.pbs.org/newshour/health/the-quiet-final-hours-of-franklin-d-roosevelt.

265 **"one of the greatest":** "Draft Speech of Vice-President Harry S. Truman for Jefferson Day Dinner, Washington, D.C.," April 1945, Container 289, Harry S. Truman Papers as U.S. Senator and Vice President, 1935–1945, Harry S. Truman Library, Independence, MO.

265 **Truman intended to speak:** Ibid.

267 **Later, Einstein gifted:** Gavin Rabinowitz, "Einstein's Theory of Relativity on Display for First Time," Phys.org, March 7, 2010, https://phys.org/news/2010-03-einstein-theory-relativity.html.

267 **"To sense that":** Paul Berger, "What Was Albert Einstein's True Relationship to Judaism—and Zionism?," *Forward,* November 22, 2015, https://forward.com/news/325189/what-was-einsteins-relationship-to-judaism-and-zionism/.

267 **"my relationship to the Jewish people":** Ibid.

268 **he had warned Weizmann:** Ibid.

268 **Eban's words:** Abba Eban, *Personal Witness: Israel Through My Eyes* (New York: G. P. Putnam's Sons, 1992), 242.

270 **"I speak to you today":** Albert Einstein, "A Final Undelivered Message to the World, April 1955," in *Einstein on Politics: His Private Thoughts and Public Stands on Nationalism, Zionism, War, Peace, and the Bomb,* ed. David E. Rowe and Robert Schulman (Princeton, NJ: Princeton University Press, 2013), 506–507.

271 **On April 18, 1955:** "Einstein Cremated; Bequeathed His Brain to Medical Research," *Jewish Telegraphic Agency Daily News Bulletin,* April 21, 1955, http://pdfs.jta.org/1955/1955-04-20_076.pdf?_ga=2.233642523.409623967.1565642018-563851594.1562694758.